Beat Suter, René Bauer, Mela Kocher (eds.)
Narrative Mechanics

Beat Suter (PhD), born in 1962, works as lecturer and researcher in game design at the Zurich University of the Arts (ZHdK) and manages GameLab and Game Archive. He has a PhD in literary studies.

René Bauer, born in 1972, studied German philology and literary studies, biology and computer linguistics at the University of Zurich. He works as lecturer, researcher, and head of master education in game design at the Zurich University of the Arts (ZHdK).

Mela Kocher (PhD), born in 1972. After publishing her dissertation in 2007 on aesthetics and narratology in video games, she spent two years on a post-doc project at the University of California, San Diego. Today she works as senior researcher in game design at the Zurich University of the Arts (ZHdK).

Beat Suter, René Bauer, Mela Kocher (eds.)

Narrative Mechanics

Strategies and Meanings in Games and Real Life

[transcript]

This book has been supported by the Zurich University of the Arts, its GameLab and its subject area Game Design. Open Access has been funded by its Media and Information Centre.

Z ‾ hdk ‾‾

Bibliographic information published by the Deutsche Nationalbibliothek
The Deutsche Nationalbibliothek lists this publication in the Deutsche National-bibliografie; detailed bibliographic data are available in the Internet at http://dnb.d-nb.de

First published in 2021 by transcript Verlag, Bielefeld
© **Beat Suter, René Bauer, Mela Kocher (eds.)**

Cover layout: Maria Arndt, Bielefeld
Cover illustration: uvmap_wald © Max Moswitzer
Layout: Beat Suter
English editing: Katja Klier, London

Print-ISBN 978-3-8376-5345-8
PDF-ISBN 978-3-8394-5345-2
https://doi.org/10.14361/9783839453452

Contents

Introduction

Beat Suter, René Bauer and Mela Kocher

Stories are what the world is about. Somehow everyone can relate to stories. They are engaging, they are filled with references and bits of information and little gaps and secrets that inspire interpretation, imagination, feedback and follow-ups. And we don't just tell, we 'play' stories on a daily basis. Engaging with narratives is a familiar part of our everyday lives. Theater, music, dance and sports have prepared us for more complex forms of playing analog and digital games and taught us that narrative is not just something that we find in books and letters, but can appear anywhere in life – in political charades and propaganda, in enactments, or in complex digital role playing and strategy games. Increasingly, we have to deal with fake narratives, which means we have to sharpen our minds to separate fiction from fact, truth from lies, while involved in news games and political games and work-life games day by day. Against this background, it is not a coincidence that video games emerge as a central focus for both practical experimentation and analytical research.

Narrative and interactivity are no longer incompatible. We have become much more experienced in dealing with them in the digital sphere. In fact, they are very closely interwoven, both in games and social media as well as in real life. This is a good reason for taking a closer look at how narrative mechanics in the context of digital and analog action and behavior patterns work, and how they influence us. Games especially are a playground where we can experiment and find new ways of dealing with challenges.

If narrative is understood as a mode, it can take many forms. As Roland Barthes puts it at the beginning of his analysis of narrative: "There are countless forms of narrative in the world. First of all, there is a prodigious variety of genres, each of which branches out into a variety of media, as if all substances could be relied upon to accommodate man's stories. Among the vehicles of narrative are articulated language, whether oral or written, pictures, still or moving, gestures, and an ordered mixture of all those substances [...]." (Barthes 1975: 237) In this essay, Barthes attempts to get to the bottom of narrative structures while analyzing meaning and functions. It was an attempt to broaden the horizon of what may constitute a narrative. With the advent of the new media, however, further aspects had to be considered. Further up the timeline, after the millennium, many game studies scholars consistently argued for the separation of narrative and non-narrative digital media, works, products or artifacts. "Gaming is seen [...] as configurative practice, and the gaming situation as a combination of ends, means, rules, equipment, and manipulative action." (Eskelinen 2001) Eskelinen goes as far as to say that: "[...] stories are just uninteresting ornaments of gift-wrappings to games, and laying any emphasis on studying these kinds of marketing tools is just a waste of time and energy." (ibid) But Marie-Laure Ryan brought the separated lines back together when she introduced the qualitative concept of narrative as one of two modalities. She proposed making a distinction between "being narrative" and "possessing narrativity". (Ryan 2004: 9) In her view, a work does not have to be narrative, but it can have a certain narrativity that is awakened in the viewer or listener or user (cf. Punday 2017), for example in a dance, a piece of music, an image – or as we may add, a game. Today, games also belong to Barthes' vehicles of narrative, since they are almost always able to develop a sense of narrativity in the player. Many of them may not be narratives per se in a traditional way, but they have and evoke some narrativity before, during and after play. Consequently, what Eskelinen debunks as marketing tools may be better understood as narrative mechanics and strategies that support the players' immersion in the game and are intertwined with gameplay mechanics and other important elements of game development. And of course, if we observe such narrative mechanics and strategies in a wider sense in real-life situations, it is obvious that they are often used as marketing tools and for manipulation and propaganda purposes in politics, economics, sports, etc.

Narrative mechanics are thus a certain kind of game mechanics that serve as motivational design for a game (or a situation in life). They influence the story through player actions that create events. Like classic game mechanics, they have rules, provide options and decisions, and help create the "Magic Circle" in which a game is played. With narrative mechanics, the player's actions have consequences for gameplay and narrative. Narrative mechanics can even become so powerful that they act as a container for a game like *The Last of Us* (2013), and are instrumental in finding a cure against the infection that ravages the world.

Video games represent "grands récits", grand narratives: they convey values and emotions, they are meaningful, globally coded or related to specific cultural areas. They are established narratives, which, like memes and other digital metaphors and aesthetic propositions, are subject to certain sets of rules. In this sense, we understand them as a specific kind of (game) mechanics. This leads us to the following questions: What conclusions can be drawn from interactive narratives for the rules of society? How detached from other real-world circles of meaning are the "Magic Circles" of games and other symbolic orders such as political speeches and actions, urban architecture, religions or gender issues?

CONTEXT

Over decades of debate, narratological and ludic positions have developed in game studies, with fixed assignations of meaning: on the one hand, the game as narrative, and on the other hand, the game as a set of rules. In several conferences, we examined narratives as game mechanics, and game mechanics as narratives, and thus their correlations and mutual interdependence: Which strategies and aesthetic practices has interactive storytelling developed over the last 15 years? In which ways have literary, philosophical and architectural paradigms established themselves in the "grands récits" of various computer game genres – from historical adventure games to today's art games and open-world games? In turn, how have new technologies (VR, interfaces, gadgets like the Apple Watch, or social media software) created new types of narrative experience? And in what regard have they created the "Magic Circle" of games and, for example, produced new types of (post-)literature? Have the innovations in the video game industry affected the great tales of reality?

This book is a follow-up to the publication *Games and Rules* which focused on game mechanics as motivational design and tried to contribute to the clarification of terms and concepts related to game mechanics, rule systems and motivation design on a fundamental level, since the professional discourse is still characterized by controversy.

Although game studies scholars generally agree that the mechanics of a game organize the rule-based changes of game states due to interactions, the specific understanding and definitions of game mechanics diverge for the most part. Concepts of game mechanics are either associated with a reception-oriented gameplay or lean towards formalistic models of object-oriented software. While narratologists understand a game primarily as a storytelling vehicle, from a ludological perspective, narrative structures are usually regarded as a (subordinate) part of game mechanics. An understanding of rule systems, needs, challenges, modes of reward and punishment, and thus the motivational design of interactive content such as digital games, is also linked to the various descriptions and aesthetics of game mechanics. In this way, rewards and punishments can unfold in the narrative system as elements of cut-scenes (narrative set pieces) or through dialogues with game characters, while at the level of game progress, they can also be accompanied by points deductions or allowances. Narrative tools today are increasingly mixed and do not interrupt the gameplay as much, as scripted sequences, ambient actions and evolving locations are used much more often. Beyond these micro-level functionalities, game mechanics and motivational design also have social and cultural relevance in that they address the functioning of systems itself.

UNRAVELING THE COMMON THREAD

In order to break down the complexity and variety of concepts and approaches, the present volume with its 22 essays by 18 authors is divided into four parts, each being driven by a specific set of questions. The narrative/story spanning these book sections and their themes starts out with the key question: "What are narrative mechanics, their rules, their magic circle, their motivational structures?" (first section: "Playing with Narratives"). This leads into the question of "How do these narrative mechanics work in different game genres?" (second section: "Expanding the Narrative"), followed by a wider perspective: "Where do narrative mechanics go beyond the realm of games? How are they present in politics and culture? (third section: "Games, Politics and Society"). Echoes of these debates can be found in the case studies, which in turn address the question: "Where can we find traces and applied techniques of narrative mechanics in games, media and politics? And how exactly are they implemented?"

Laying the groundwork, the section "Playing with Narratives" contains basic texts on narrative mechanics. René Bauer and Beat Suter's essay "Narrative Mechanics" outlines a theory of various narrative mechanics and their motivational strategies from text to film, to games and political narratives, based on different types of rules and connections.

Beat Suter then delves deeper into this typology in "Narrative Patterns in Video Games". Narrative structures already become visible in the context (advertising, visuals, etc.) of a game and continue into the game itself, where specific forms of narrative are applied, from mere backstory to the classic journey of the hero, fragmented quests and multilinear interactive narrative mechanics.

In "Teaching Narrative Design", Teun Dubbelman puts the spotlight on the (also social) mechanics behind the development of narrative design. His understanding is based on the fact that narrative emerges from a cognitive process of "meaning making" – thus suggesting that the text consistently presents a tool for the design of the narrative, enabling the "interplay between mechanics and the other narrative devices".

Chris Polus' text "The Narrative Role of Sound in Games" shows how sounds or sound effects are always co-narrators, whether as "motivational sounds", "hygiene sounds" or "nice-to-have sounds". Sounds tell tales about the size of the rooms, the type of rooms, the materials and the interactions. In doing so, they also open up spaces of the imaginary.

The second section, "Expanding the Narrative", focuses in on the question of the form and function of narrative mechanics by further exploring the intertextual system of games in a variety of game and text genres. The article "*Mukokuseki* and the Narrative Mechanics in Japanese Games" by Hiloko Kato and René Bauer shows how much games are a product of the interplay between various cultural narratives. *Mukokuseki* is a Japanese cultural technique that fragments cultural strands such as text, image, sound and mechanics and reassembles them in a new way, transcending the boundaries of cultural and national specifics. The result is not only the "typically Japanese" game as the basis for most games, but also an infinitely expanding intertext.

In "Characterization and Emergent Narrative in *Dwarf Fortress*", an analysis of his open-world game, Tarn Adams evokes the realm of the "power of games as storytelling companions". Narratives also arise here from the interaction with the game and the retelling of it. The inhabitants of *Dwarf Fortress*, who can only be controlled indirectly, become the protagonists, and thus, their core identity and their psychological and social make-up become the raw material for narratives.

In his essay "On the Evolution of Narrative Mechanics in Open-World Games", Ulrich Götz examines some of video game history's famous artifacts such as the *Colossal Cave Adventure*, and proposes that "it is not narrative, but rather, rule-oriented game forms that are dependent upon visual representation". Analyzing spatial design and mechanics in different open-world games, Götz concludes that the reduction of exploration in favor of intensifying the narrative aspects seems advisable.

With "Open-End Storytelling in Pinball Machines", David Krummenacher dives into the world of the open narrative mechanics of the beloved pinball machine. The pinball box itself consists of a variety of visual narratives. These offers are continued in the pinball gameplay, where the player can unlock the various nested narratives. Therefore pinball machines appear as narrative open-world game systems "avant la lettre", with a lot of potential also for today's (digital) open-world games.

Considering *Superbrothers: Sword & Sworcery EP* as an heir of the Sword & Sorcery genre, being heavily influenced by the US pulp fiction author Robert E. Howard, Florian Faller emphasizes its "Mechanics of Inspiration". Creativity is understood as a process of referencing, copying, transforming and combining which utilizes, mirrors, reflects and subverts narrative tropes, genres and ultimately mechanics.

As video game journalist Robert Glashüttner reveals in his contribution about "Narrative Approaches in Contemporary Video Game Reviews", there are several strategies in the framing of game reviews dependent on the narrative features, following either holistic or personal approaches. Glashüttner investigates the motivation behind these approaches, and the resulting perception of the readers and its impact on their own gaming experience, as reflected in studies of *Death Stranding*, *Animal Crossing: New Horizons* and *The Last of Us Part II*.

The third book section, "Games, Politics and Society", deals with narrative mechanics in society and politics. In "'We're not murderers. We just survive!'", Eugen Pfister takes a closer look at the ideological function of game mechanics in zombie games. How is societal collapse depicted in their narratives? How sophisticated is the political self-awareness in these games, and in how far are discursive rules disclosed?

Discussing the game mechanics and autopoetic strategy in his science fiction novel *Quiz*, Günter Hack reflects on how, in a dystopian world, Situationist strategies have been implemented to consolidate the power of the spectacle in today's mass culture. In his "What if?" thought experiment, corporations use the spectacle "in order to monetize the smallest movement of their subjects", and work itself has become a *dérive*.

Margarete Jahrmann anchors her essay close to contemporary real-world events. "Ludic Meanders through Defictionalization: The Narrative Mechanics of Art" addresses highly topical developments during the Covid-19 pandemic. By staging interventions such as the "Social Distancer" in public space – which she defines as narrative space –, Jahrmann coins and subversively reframes "pandemic mechanics".

Aiming to create games that have a positive impact on the world, Mary Flanagan discusses the ways in which embedded design facilitates and measures how game stories become real. Her text "If You Play it, Do You Believe It?"

identifies obfuscating, intermixing and psychological distancing as the three main methods of effective narrative mechanics for that purpose.

The last essay of this book section on society and politics consists of the radical semiotic reading "Ball Games and Language Games". Martin Lindner discusses how Wittgenstein, football fan culture and pop culture come together, and how there cannot be any "empty signs", and no escape from social meaning and consequences.

The essayistic discourse of narrative mechanics is followed by a fourth and last section with seven case studies of specific games. Six authors perform an analysis of the narrative mechanics of a particular game or game genre – contrasting and complementing the discussed theoretical explorations with a hands-on approach: "*Florence*" (Mela Kocher), "*The Last Guardian*" (Beat Suter), "Murder at the Museum" (Stefan Schmidlin), "Even *Missile Command* Tells a Story" (Beat Suter), "*Shave*" (Sonja Böckler), "The *Twitter* Game" (René Bauer) and "Commander Kurz" (Eugen Pfister).

The case studies also reflect on interconnections between games, the real world and our increasingly virtual real world. René Bauer analyzes the communication platform *Twitter* as a game and Eugen Pfister compares the Austrian chancellor to Commander Shepard from the video game *Mass Effect*. This may seem a bit odd at first, but today, the world is very much intertwined with games. We are in fact rather familiar with game mechanics and narrative strategies and apply them when playing games as much as when using (and abusing) social media, advertising a product, telling friends about a movie, communicating at work or being active in politics. It helps us paint a distinctive image of ourselves. At the same time, when we play or tell stories, we create an aesthetic construct, in our minds or in shared discourse, omitting things or emphasizing specific meanings.

Narrative mechanics thus contribute a temporary sense of meaning by bringing stringency to an increasingly complex and seemingly contradictory world. They can be used to create new access to the world, to pull things together, or to create entirely new "Magic Circles", from playgrounds to cities to political constructs. Therefore, the world (like the games) appears more manageable and controllable again, or in other words, more rule-based. This is what makes narrative mechanics so attractive today, but equally dangerous, because they have long since become dispositives of power. And here, too, we need to look closely – which we aim to do, with the book at hand.

Zurich, February 2021

REFERENCES

Literature

Barthes, Roland/Duisit, Lionel (1975): "An Introduction to the Structural Analysis of Narrative." In: New Literary History 6/2, On Narrative and Narratives, pp. 237-272.
Eskelinen, Markku (2001): "The Gaming Situation." In: Game Studies. The International Journal of Computer Game Research, volume 1, issue 1, july 2001 (http://www.gamestudies.org/0101/eskelinen/).
Punday, Daniel (2017): "Narrativity." In: Tabbi, Joseph (ed.): The Bloomsbury Handbook of Electronic Literature, London: Bloomsbury, pp. 133-149.
Ryan, Marie-Laure (ed.) (2004): Narrative across Media. The Languages of Storytelling, Lincoln and London: University of Nebraska Press.

Games

The Last of Us, Naughty Dog, Sony Computer Entertainment, 2013.

Playing with Narratives

Narrative Mechanics

Strategies and Meanings in Games and Real Life

René Bauer and Beat Suter

Narrative mechanics have many "faces", displays and interfaces. They occur as texts, recipes, stories, dramas in three acts, movies, videos, tweets, journeys of heroes, but also as rewarding stories in games and as narratives in society (such as a career from rags to riches, the concept of modernity or market economy) and are increasingly used in politics. Below their surface, however, narrative mechanics are a special kind of motivational design, or more precisely: a special kind of game mechanics. In the same way as classic game mechanics, they consist of rules and rule sets for control cycles that contain challenges, provide options, make decisions possible, and then reward or punish, thereby creating a magic circle. As in all game mechanics, everything that is possible in the system may be used. Most narrative mechanics, however, use a narrative structure (rule set mechanics), narrative rewards and punishments. Often, rules with linear connections are employed for this purpose.

Figure 1: Linear narrative mechanics are simple motivational mechanics. Most challenges are not overly complex. and are often built as basic rules.

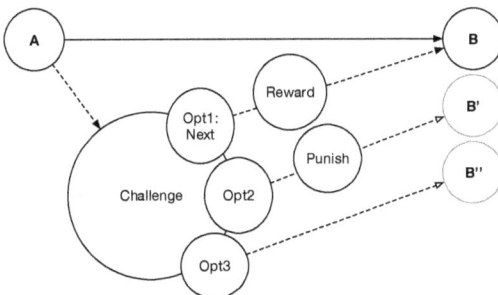

A → B

Opt1: Next — Reward — B'

Challenge — Opt2 — Punish — B''

Opt3

Source: René Bauer (all vector graphics in figure 1-6 and 17)

Linear links usually correspond to linear rules. From an "A" follows a "B" (A->B) and from that "B" a "C" (B->C). Of course, complex systems can be created even with such simple connections, for example when "C" refers to "B". Narrative mechanics are not limited to language or text, they can also be visually narrative (with developing and recurring forms and patterns) and they can be auditory or tactile. A film, for example, contains formal rules pertaining to images (Image1->Image2, Image2->Image3). However, this can also become complex for the viewer, for example, if the last frame of a film corresponds to the first, but the film breaks off afterwards. In terms of content, the images again contain rules relating to figures and symbols.

Like games, narrative mechanics can also adapt to their rules, whether these concern the behavior of the reader or player or the environment of the reader or game. Even in texts, adaptive mechanics are possible. Initially, a text consists of a string of rules, respectively sentences, for a human interpreter. These rules can be used adaptively: a text provides different readings and can be written in a formulaic way so that the reader has to fill in the blanks. It can even be highly generalized, so that the reader interprets the same text in a different way depending on its use. In games, much more is possible in narrative terms. The story may depend on the player's decisions and may lead to prefabricated multilinearity.

Simplified, this leads to a whole set of basic narrative connections from simple links to explicit decision lines or associative linkages.

Figure 2, table 1 and 2: Six narrative mechanics. Each linkage is different, no matter if the result of the linkage before the decision is clear or not. These different narrative links can be combined. The representation below excludes reward mechanisms.

Simple mechanics	Conditional mechanics	Explicit decision mechanics
Stories in which the next section follows by necessity	Images are shown after a certain time	Go to x or to y or press the button yes/no, choose your next step out of more than one option; often visualized and clearly shown
Visual novel, non-fiction, story, news	Film, anime, cutscenes in games	80 Days, Choose your own Adventure, quick-time events

Optional mechanics	Implicit decision mechanics	Associative mechanics
Games in which the player can do something extra	Texts in which the reader decides on a reading by presuming something and continues reading under this assumption	Stories are shown in excerpts or only implied; player's interpretation as a personal decision
GTA, Minecraft, pinball machines, playground, city, special quests	Braid, Limbo, Textadventures, literature, poetry	Another World, FAR: Lone Sails, advertisements, pop songs

In more complex cases, the game generates a story that is specific to each player and each traversal of the game. This can turn narrative mechanics into storytellers or storytelling machines.

In many cases, narrative mechanics can become so strong that they function as containers or systems that absorb other narrative mechanics and thus turn into complex narrative mechanics with their own names or are associated with simple claims such as: "from rags to riches", "anyone can be successful (and rich)", "free market", "we are the people", "liberté, égalité, fraternité". At this point, narrative game mechanics become actual narratives. These complex narrative systems are in constant competition with other narrative mechanics and their spectacle.

Figure 3: Narratives as complex narrative mechanics containers or mechanics systems. Different narrative mechanics can be combined and appear as containers of various mechanics that mostly support each other and make up an elaborate mechanics system.

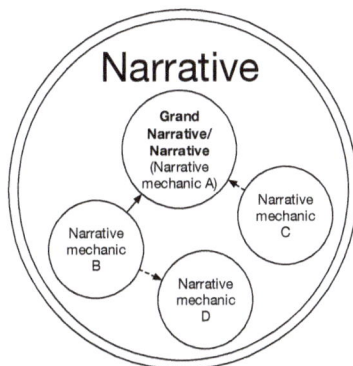

Just as with games, in politics especially the attempt is made to strengthen one's own narrative mechanics through rewards and punishments, so that it slowly displaces the other narrative "realities" and finally makes an absolute claim.

Rewards in particular serve as welcome confirmations in everyday life and are thus well anchored in the world we live in. They can be seen as part of a selective narrative spectacle that generates a strong immersive force. The narrative mechanics then become the only rewarding extension of our perception of the world and the basis for action (for everything). In certain methods of politics, narrative mechanics are defictionalized and at the same time become motivational mechanics for society. This means that narrative mechanics use their gamelike rewards and punishments in an incredibly tangible way in the analog world.

Below is a compilation of various narrative mechanics in a matrix of structure and involvement. These narrative mechanics will be examined in more detail in the following sections of this essay.

Figure 4: A compilation of various narrative mechanics from loosely structured mechanics (bottom) to highly structured mechanics (top), and from independent of recipient (left) to heavily involving recipient (right).

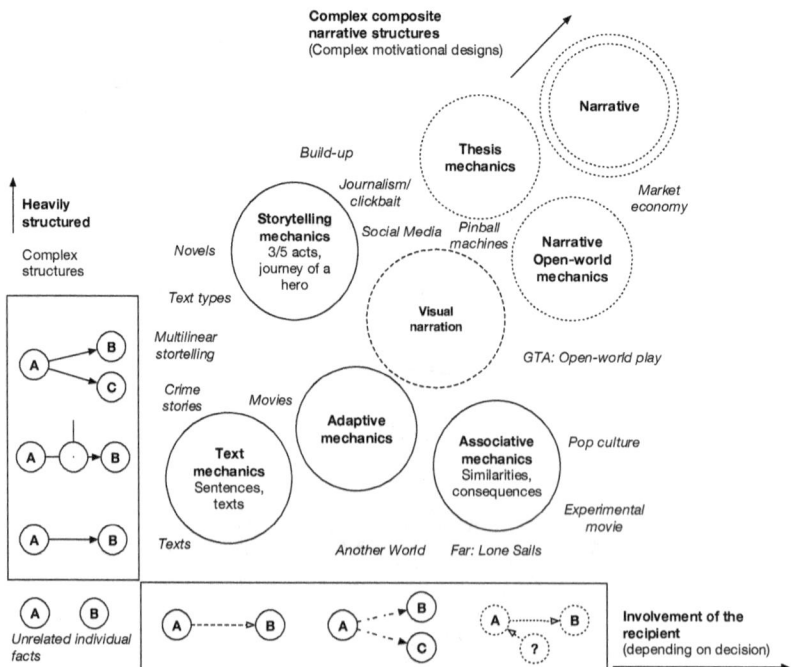

TEXT AS AN IMMERSIVE NARRATIVE MECHANIC WITH TRADITION AND POTENTIAL

Even the simplest texts work as game mechanics with sets of rules. They show decision-making processes and reward and punishment mechanisms on different levels of their motivation design. The reader is permanently challenged at the level of the reading process. As readers we have to understand sentences. Every single sentence is a challenge and a short-term motivation. We have to translate the rule set of a sentence into our mental system. There are paradigmatic rules (as meaning) and syntactic rules (as logical or associative linking). The simplest reward is that we understand each sentence and therefore the entire text. We are punished with non-understanding, i.e. an impaired reading process.

Figure 5: Text as narrative mechanics. Sentences consist of words that are linked with syntagmatic and paradigmatic challenges; semiosis creates meaning or a construct. You are rewarded if the syntax is right, when your words fit into the construct, a witty syntax, a humorous choice of words. You are punished with not understanding.

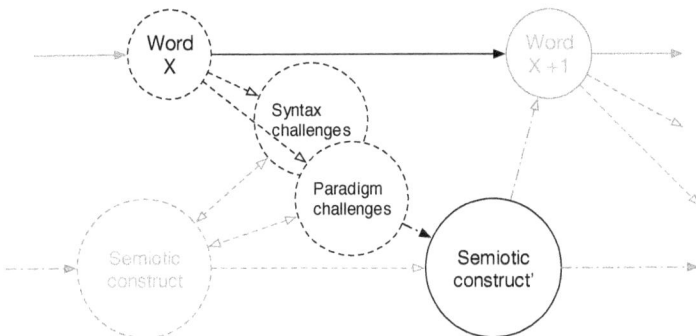

Source: René Bauer (all vector graphics in figure 1-6 and 17)

As readers we transpose texts, imagine our own memories and ideas in semiosis, and create our own "illustrated" story. We try to understand texts and must constantly fill the spaces or voids in the text (cf. Iser 1972), and decide on how to read and interpret the text. In doing so, we form our own assumptions that are rewarded or punished by the progression of the text. Building on this fundamental reading process, the text keeps us "in the game" in the medium term with refined word choices and interesting descriptions, and punishes us with short- and medium-term twists and ugly details.

Figure 6: Connected sentences become one text. Filling voids and creating meaning by semiosis is a constant challenge to the reader or player.

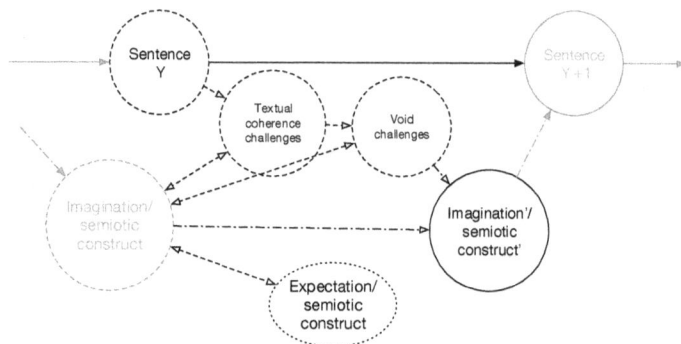

In long-term motivation, texts often use existing motivational structures such as closed dramaturgical three-act or five-act progressions or the hero's journey as the unconscious (developmental) story of the protagonist. This keeps us moving forward as readers. When we read, we link the current text back to the larger text, perhaps even rewriting the read text already, or creating expectations for the future of the text or fiction. As in classic games, we dive into the immersive world of the magic circle and its own rules. All too often texts let us consistently collide with our own moral presumptions: Do we "survive" the pervertedly ugly but logically stringent passages in Marquis de Sade's *Justin and Juliette*? Can we tolerate the twist in Rimbaud's poem with the person stretched out peacefully in the field, or the brutal mechanics of the gatekeeper, the penal colony or the trial in Kafka's text? All of which is nothing more than game mechanics applied in writing.

TELLING STORIES WITH NARRATIVE MECHANICS

In terms of narrative mechanics, text types are particularly striking. Each type of text seems to have its own narrative mechanics to motivate readers. The text type structures the way in which the text is composed and processed. Modern cooking recipes are a good example: the ingredients and quantities are listed at the beginning, and only then the text about the food preparation starts.

In storytelling, predetermined narrative mechanics are often used and modified, such as the three-act and the five-act structure, the hero's journey or Vladimir Propp's deep structure of fairy tales (1968). These dramatic structures are both analytical and narrative tools. They help to tell stories in an exciting way, or in other words: they motivate readers and keep the story rolling (cf. Suter: 62ff.). In games this is often done with exaggerated, dangerous jobs that keep up the tension. In 1967, Erving Goffman commented on the illusory world of the novel, providing what could be regarded as a pointed picture of narrative games with hero stories. In a footnote, he writes "criminal jobs (as well as the structurally similar secret operations of various government agents) are carried out despite a long sequence of threatening and actual disturbances, each of which carries a high probability of ruining everything." Despite its unlikeliness, "the hero manages to survive from episode to episode, but only by roughly breaking the laws of probability" (Goffman 1986: 183), which may be motivating for most players, but could well be a little discouraging for players that are fully aware of the unlikeliness of the events and outcome.

Figure 7: Star Wars' dramaturgical arc shows how rising tension and short breathers between confrontations structure and move the story forward; the three-act structure is as classic as it gets – with a slow setup, a long and arduous second act and a short, explosive and cathartic third act.

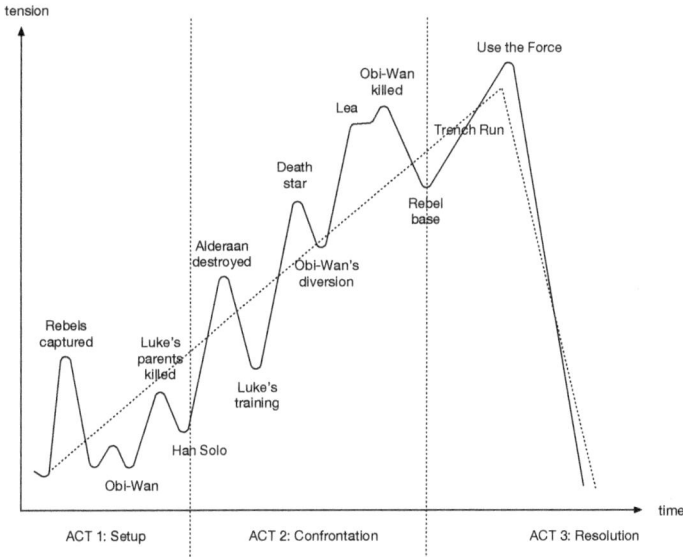

Source: Wesolowski/Gamasutra

Besides such dramatic structures, there are also specific types of texts that structure not only the formal composition, but the content too. A good and popular example is the crime thriller.

Crime thriller as narrative mechanics

In a crime thriller and a crime novel, two narratives work towards each other: the actual story of the crime and the investigative story which is written by the detective, policeman or player-avatar through their actions over the course of the presentation of the fiction. The challenge is clear: Can we complete our own detective work and with it our investigation story before we have been told the entire crime story? As readers or players, can we find the murderer in the crime fiction before the text reveals it? If we are not fast enough, we can read the revelation again as our punishment. A reward would then be the earliest possible identification of the perpetrator in the crime story. Psychological insights, in-depth character descriptions and descriptions of the crime scene are as much a part of the sophisticated narrative micro mechanics of a crime novel as are the private conflicts and moral dilemmas of the investigator-avatar. And it becomes even more exciting when the investigative story has a direct impact on the crime story and is supplemented or expanded by the intervention of an investigator with action elements, pursuits and follow-up crimes.

STORIES AS NARRATIVE MECHANICS IN GAMES

Generated and procedural stories

Games such as *Don't starve* (2013), *No Man's Sky* (2016), *The Forest* (2014), *Eco* (2018) and, to an extreme degree, *Dwarf Fortress* (2006) do not use a given story, but a set of rules to create the world in which the game starts. In the beginning – on old computers an endless ten minutes long – unique tectonics are created, a story about every tree, every creature and every path is rendered over 1000 or more years. And then you step into this story of your own, ready to face any challenge, ready to play.

Stories as part of the motivational structure of games

Games use narrative mechanics such as stories and interactive storytelling as part of their motivational strategies. Starting with cultural embedding, games frame their content by using advertising and covers to create a world in which we want to play. Games often suggest that we are in a much larger and more important story, taking place in a much more significant and exciting world than the one we live in.

Figure 8: Asteroids for Atari 2600 with cover illustration on its game box and on the cartridge; the third picture shows the in-game world with asteroids and spaceship.

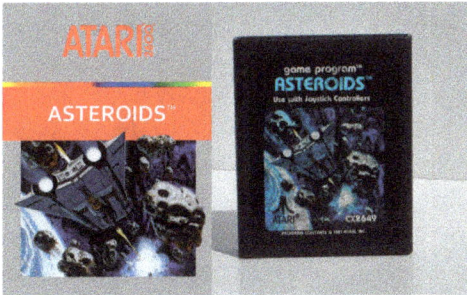

Source: screenshots (Bauer)

We don't just see pixels when we play an Atari 2600 game like *Asteroids* (1981), but view these pixels through the lens of advertising, posters and the illustrations on the cartridges (if they are available). Good examples for other consoles and PC are *Worms* (1995), *Donkey Kong Country* (1994), *PacMan* (1980) and *Tomb Raider*'s (1996) Lara Croft. The illustrations always showed a more detailed and exciting world than technology was able to produce in-game. But it spurred the players' minds. Players who spin this framing further are rewarded with faster progress because they can read the connections better. In terms of the progression of the game itself, we will be rewarded with the continuation of the story or be punished if an inglorious end awaits us. Both are mostly used in long-term motivation and include intros, in-game cutscenes, scripted sequences of voice-overs and other narrative tools. Gameover is actually always the first step towards the extended potential of games as a supermedium. This can be seen especially well in interactive adaptive stories and multilinear games. Each game that is played generates its own story or story version of the respective generic game. And players may experience slightly different or even very different stories according to their choices and semiosis.

THE STORY WORLD AS COMPREHENSIVE MECHANICS

Open-world mechanics

Narrative mechanics can also be found in open-world games. There are three main narrative mechanics (e.g. in *GTA: Chinatown Wars* 2009): the main narra-

tive mechanics of the world that tells you what it is all about, the story mode mechanics as linear mechanics of the protagonist(s) and a large number of smaller
narrative mechanics that are "inserted" into the playground-like, designed game
world. These smaller mechanics are usually tied to specific locations and areas.
They often form their own small mini-worlds within the larger open world and
have their own corresponding narrative mechanics.

GTA: Chinatown Wars (2009) is a clear example of how narrative mechanics
in open-world games can interlock. The franchise of *Grand Theft Auto* was created in 2009 for the portable Nintendo DS console which had fairly modest 3D
graphical capabilities. This means that the game is limited to its essentials and
looks and works in a similar way to older versions of *Grand Theft Auto*. The
game's main narrative mechanic is Liberty City, an invented city that is modeled
after New York and could be anywhere in the USA. The main story is set in a
framework that is open for any kind of criminal activity: any gangster can make
it in this town. Liberty City is a narrative "playground" that was not only used in
Chinatown Wars but also in *Grand Theft Auto V* (2013).

The main story comes as a linear narrative mechanic and is quickly told: A
gangster, whose father has just been murdered in Asia, lands in Liberty City in a
private jet in order to hand over a sword to his uncle, who is also a serious criminal. This is where the interactive story begins, with missions that are supposed
to improve the situation of the player-avatar who has to complete these missions
to slowly but surely climb the narrative ladder of organized crime in Liberty City
with all its twists and turns. Players can opt for this grand narrative that consists
of 58 main missions and 5 extras, or just go for it and get lost in the city and
choose to do some of the many quests and 13 side missions. They can also just
roam the streets, go sightseeing or steal a car and write their own story of escape
and pursuit or stunts and races. (cf. rrvirus 2019)

An open world usually contains many embedded stories, missions and quests
that are all a possibility for the player to engage in. Liberty City is such a huge
(open) world with almost endless possibilities for smaller jobs and opportunities,
in which you can immerse yourself narratively. The jobs are clearly arranged and
mostly very linear, but can be combined in different ways. You don't have to
follow the main narrative mechanics, the main quest line. Instead, you may want
to take on an assignment to transport drugs from A to B or you may want to buy
drugs cheaply and spend a lot of money on the other side of town on a luxury
lifestyle, or you may want to defuse bombs or perhaps buy lottery scratch tickets
– or indeed, you may not want to be criminal at all. Even the trophies on the trophy shelf in your apartment are all collectable achievements like the "Jeweled

Key to the City". You can earn this key if you own all of the 21 safe houses in Liberty City.

These possibilities were subsequently expanded in many open-world games in series such as *Grand Theft Auto* and *Red Dead Redemption.* So today, there are an enormous number of possibilities, side quests, and areas for actions and events on the fringe of an open world, all with their own narrative possibilities. It is also not surprising that there are fan-made interactive websites such as rdr2map.com on the internet, which show you all locations, quests, treasures, etc. of the vast *Red Dead Redemption 2* (2018) world.

Figure 9: Interactive Map of all Red Dead Redemption 2 Locations, showing side quests, treasures, weapons, campfires, hideouts and all points of interests, stores, etc.

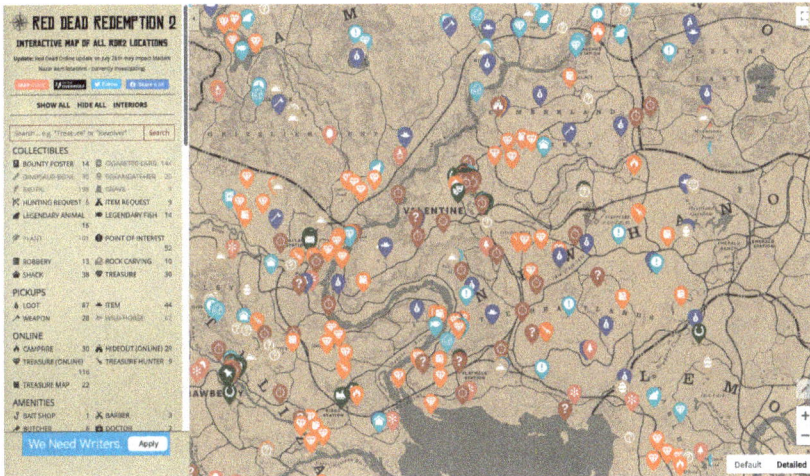

Source: screenshot by René Bauer

Open-world constructions also play an increasingly important role in the specific design of cities. In this context, some city districts are designed like modern playgrounds. The urban playground is a narrative framework which sits at the top of the urban planning process. This can be seen in Zurich's "Europallee" and "Zurich West", Vienna's "Museumsquartier", Paris' "Les Halles", London's "Embankment", New York's "High Line", San Diego's "Gaslamp Quarter" or Sidney's "Darling Harbour" and other locations. Stores, clubs, museums, restaurants and outdoor areas unite under the umbrella of a narrative theme that serves as a framework to them and holds everything together.

Figure 10: Urban playground embedded in the city. Darling Quarter in Darling Harbour area in Sidney, Australia.

Source: Darling Quarter website

Pinball machines feature different simultaneous narrative game mechanics

Pinball machines work in a similar way: they have a superordinate narrative, such as an amusement park in *Funhouse* (1990), or twilight and horror as the theme for the pinball machine *Twilight Zone* (1993). What lies behind this narrative is the mechanism that allows a player to control two flippers inside the glass-covered box. Players can shoot up a metallic ball and hit targets by operating two buttons on the outside of the box using their fingers. Pinball machines simultaneously offer various subordinate narrative mechanics with many targets, blinking eyes, small animations, etc. In his thesis *Storytelling in Pinball Machines* (2018), David Krummenacher investigated storylines in pinball machines and found four complementary narrative zones and three distinct narrative mechanics for the player. Sequential order and time play a major role in those narratives. Unlike classic games that give the player minimal control, the basic game mechanics of a pinball machine become different with every shot, because the ball rolls and bounces off differently each time.

Figure 11: Bally's advertisement for the pinball machine Twilight Zone: an open-world game with story quests?

Source: Bally/screenshot (Bauer)

Only gradually does the player gain partial control over the pinball machine, allowing them to interact in a more controlled manner and to advance the main narrative mechanics further. For the corresponding (local) story to continue, the player must consciously and sometimes randomly hit and trigger individual narrative options ("Hit the head", "Hole in another ball") (cf. Krummenacher: 177-195). Thus, different narrative options can be open simultaneously and may develop as events at the same time. This is a feature that years later became common in open-world games. A pinball storyworld is similar to analog social reality, where different narrative game mechanics are also open at the same time and are only triggered over time or not at all – depending on the skills of the player or the randomness of the event. The player generates 'new' stories of their own, or in other words, the narrative becomes a storytelling machine. In today's politics, narrative mechanics work in a similar way – just not everyone has access to the flipper buttons.

Narrative adaptive game mechanics

Adaptive games fit in with their worlds, begin to incorporate the environment, such as *Boktai: The Sun is in Your Hand* (2003), in which daylight must be used for certain moves. The mobile game *Wardive* (2009) uses hotspots as opponents while walking or driving through the city, creating a dynamic game. In the Augmented Reality game *Pikselbacteria* (2010) (also by AND-OR), digital creatures are embedded in the game screen and eat the buildings and objects the player targets in the photo viewfinder. And in *Koko's Curse* (2018) by Geneva-based game studio apelab, a tree stands in the middle of the real living room, on which the petrified guardian of the forest, the owl Koko, sits. Now you have to help her find the lost feather that was stolen by one of the little birds. The forest environment in the living room changes with the actions and the original state of the forest can be restored.

The prime example of adaptive interactive storytelling is still the game *Façade* (2005) in which the player visits a married couple and is drawn into their relationship problems in a conversational manner. With strategic answers the player can mediate or stoke the relationship dispute. The two game characters react to the player's input with dialog and with facial expressions and gestures. The game adapts the further course of the conversation with the help of a drama meter and finally makes five different narrative endings possible. (cf. Suter: 71)

The fictional quiz machine in Günter Hack's real-sci-fi novel *QUIZ* (2018) may be even more adaptive and radically embedded in everyday life. The handheld device generates adaptive challenges as quiz questions from its respective environment. It includes what is currently being said, what time of day it is and what mood the player is in. The quiz machine generates specific questions with four multiple-choice answers – and it does it all the time and wherever it is. (cf. Hack: 250)

Associative narrative mechanics

If the concept of voids or blanks in texts is radically expanded, a kind of associative narrative mechanics emerges. The rules used in this case are mostly associative links, sometimes loose strands that the user can link and extend with their own links.

In *Another World* (1991), for example, lightning strikes a particle acceleration facility during an experiment, catapulting the protagonist, a professor, into another strange world whose logic he does not understand and into which he can only enter by trial and error.

This well-known narrative mechanic of being thrown into another world is even more radicalized in *Another World*, as the entire story functions as a kind of visual film without a GUI and without any written or narrated text accompanying it. The story is told purely through visuals and animations and the player has to make sense of how the story is connected with its visual scenes and events. (cf. DOS Nostalgia 2016)

The associative chain already starts with the first encounter scene, where our protagonist raises his arm as a sign of welcome and is then shot and stunned.

Figure 12: Another World (1991) is told only through associative visuals – the protagonist waves to the discovered creature (left), his gesture is ignored, and he is then shot (right).

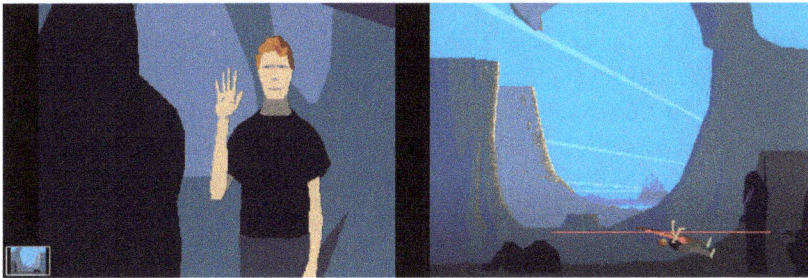

Source: screenshots (Bauer)

Later, you escape with another prisoner of this world without knowing why he was imprisoned or what his intentions are. Again, no communication is possible and you don't get to know any more narrative content than what can be guessed from the immediate area you are in. Nevertheless, this Non-Player-Character (NPC) is rather important because he demonstrates certain moves and explains the functions of various things you are going to encounter in his company. A relationship is established by interacting with objects in this world and by interacting with this NPC. And even the ending remains open: the two ride on a dragon into the sky. Another World works with associative visual storytelling and associative interactions. Most things are left to the imagination of the player, which successfully establishes a very immersive game.

Figure 13: Another World (1991): Finding a companion in prison with no known history (left), riding on a dragon into the sky towards an unknown future.

Source: screenshots (Bauer)

More radical yet is *Far: Lone Sails* (2018). Whereas the opening sequence of *Another World* (1991) still contains a few spoken in-game texts like "Welcome, Professor", *Far: Lone Sails* has no words and starts with an ambiguous scene. An undefined figure (is it a child, is it male or female, or does this even matter?) stands next to a grave or a monument with a small wind wheel under a severely cut tree. What is the relation between the small figure dressed in an orange safety jacket and hat and the person in the picture, a man?

Figure 14: Opening scene of Far: Lone Sails, suggesting a vast landscape, man-made interference, some sort of remembrance and a lonely child in safety attire.

Source: screenshot (Bauer)

All these questions remain open, though there are some more hints, small scenes that can help you imagine a (back)story, if you wish. The following scene shows an enigmatic house with construction plans and notes and more portraits. In the attic, there is the child's bedroom. Our character must be familiar with all this. A short time later, this part is resolved when the player's character finds the vehicle that is shown on the plan some distance away and begins the journey. (cf. Indie James 2018)

Figure 15: Second scene of Far: Lone Sails. The player finds construction plans and more portraits in a house that must be familiar to the child (left). Some distance away, there is a vehicle constructed according to the plans (right).

Source: screenshots (Bauer)

This is followed by an almost endless journey through a vast world that the player has to get to know themselves. The images are interpretable and open and ask the question: What happened here? It is an invitation to fill in the voids.

Figure 16: Stranded container ships, planked paths, scaffolding and undefined landscapes hidden through weather patterns. Where are we? On a dried-out seabed? What happened?

Source: screenshots (Bauer)

Open and interpretable images aren't only to be found in the background, but also in the world your avatar travels through. They don't seem to have a fixed story, and you can give them some meaning yourself.

Games like *Another World* (1991) and *Far: Lone Sails* (2018) mostly work with allusions. The story is told without text, and the story of the world is conveyed in the background through pictures, stranded objects and the vastness of the landscape. The players assemble their story from these finds and voids, adapt them and get rewarded with the finding of the next supposed puzzle. In this way the players generate their own interpretations and backstory for the game while striving to establish progression for their avatar's story.

Visual narratives

All media using forms of visual display, from posters to images to interactive games, employ visual narrative mechanics, because the individual images or image sections have to be linked together somehow. Images can be linearized and serialized and thus transformed into simple narrative mechanics. But this of course takes the complexity out of an image which is always also a narrative mechanics link of itself.

At the same time, the first step in the semiosis of images works like the semiosis of texts. The signs must be interpreted and put together to form a whole. This is a complex challenge: to begin with, shapes and colors must be decoded and transformed into signs, and these in turn must be assembled and condensed into larger units of meaning. It is always about the question: Does the picture make sense, does it rewrite the rest?

Figure 17: Visuals as narrative mechanics. Visual display consists of forms and colors which are grouped and read and recognized as signs. They form bigger complexes of signs and are again recognized as signs.

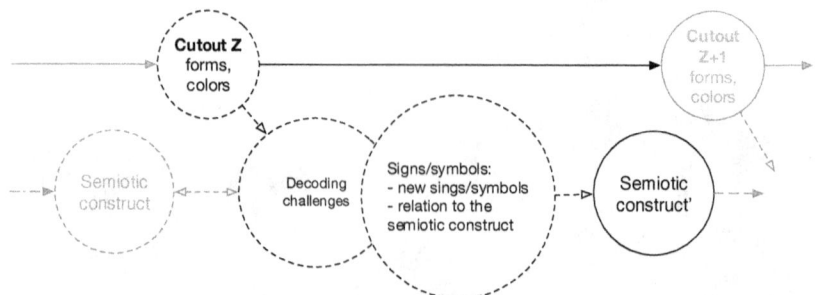

Source: René Bauer (all vector graphics in figure 1-6 and 17)

Interesting visual narrative mechanics are: copy, variation, enlargement, reduction, doubling, similarity and patterns of colors, shapes, space, movement and multitudes.

In films, concrete temporal coding is added and the expected construct (future) plays a much greater role.

Visual narrative mechanics in games

In games, visual narrative mechanics play a major role. It is always important to find out how individual signs and representations relate to each other. In most cases, visual rules are simply a reflection of the game mechanics. But there are also more complex visual rules in the service of game mechanics, where the visual itself actually becomes a mechanic. The rhythm space game *REZ* (2001) is a well-known example. Its linear visual mechanics are not developed according to the space requirements on the screen but through graphic styles in the development history of computer graphics. But not everything works with simple rules. The avatar goes through a change that is synonymous with the graphics evolution in games. It is kind of a metanarrative of computer graphics history that is cleverly told through a progressively changing player-avatar.

Figure 18: The growing avatar in REZ (2001), from Wireframe all the way to a shaded 3D model.

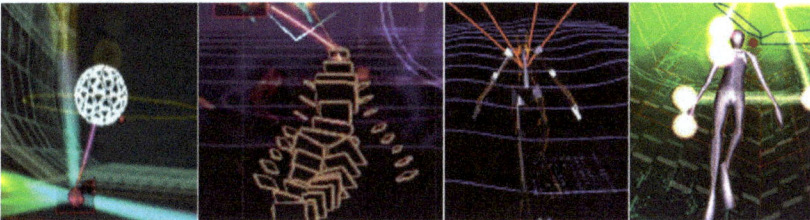

Source: screenshots (Bauer)

Visual mechanics not only in the service of game mechanics

In addition to this classic use of visual mechanics as a reflection of the game mechanics, there are games that function purely through visual narrative means.

The head in Vectorpark's *Feed the Head* (2011) wants to be manipulated and fed from time to time. The basis is to find out what to do. In the beginning you receive a pointer to tear off the nose, but soon it is all about simple manipulations that lead to rather unexpected results. (cf. WithPCGame 2011)

Figure 19: Feed the Head (2011). "Tear off the nose."

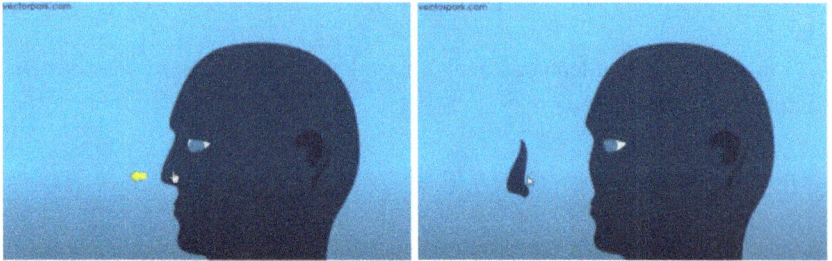

Source: screenshots (Bauer)

Following suit, the eye falls out of the mouth. The attempt to insert it fails. Only eating it leads the player to the next level of the head. The interactions nevertheless follow a certain visual logic but the further you get, the weirder they become and the head turns out to be filled with witty little objects.

Figure 20: Feed the Head (2011). "Help, the eye fell out through the mouth. How do I put it back?" (left) Further into the game, you can open up the head's top and juggle a ball (right).

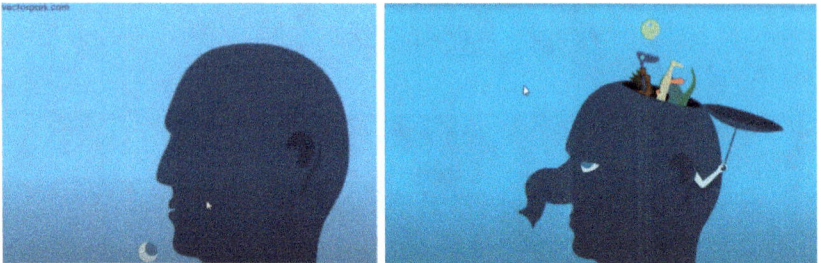

Source: screenshots (Bauer/Suter)

Osada (2011) by Amanita Design is also a trip through a world of its own with its own visual rules. Again, the interactions are very linear and the visual adventure only progresses forward to the next scene when you find out what interaction is needed in order to solve the current scene. Often, similarities and changes of shapes and objects are utilized here. In the first scene, there is a UFO. It turns out that the flying object has a similar shape to a sombrero. When it changes into a sombrero, the silhouettes of singing Mexicans with their hats on, gathered around a now lit campfire, appear in the foreground of the hilly sunset environment. (cf. Fmips 19 2012)

Figure 21: Osada (2011) is an interactive music video with linear visual puzzles. Shapes and side characters turn into characters, make music and sing a song.

Source: screenshots (Bauer)

In *Kids* (2019) simple visual narrative rules again play a leading role. Masses of people have to be managed. They have to be pulled into a hole or diverted. This causes others to fall into the hole as well. More humans then follow this rule. They behave like lemmings. You are rewarded with a huge number of falling "kids". In the next scene you try to find out what is to be solved, and how to manage the crowds there. The game uses simple linear visual mechanics, it is about how to control the human figures in a certain space, how to get rid of them, divert them, make them run in the same direction, make them swim down a tube, make them wave etc., and how to reach the goal, the next scene. (cf. Nathan-BlakeGames 2019)

Figure 22: Kids (2019) is a game in which the player controls either individual humans or whole crowds. Here they all fall into a black hole.

Source: screenshot (Bauer)

In *LIM* (2012) you are a block on your way through an abstract world of other blocks, and have to find out what is possible and how you can establish it. This is, how meaning in form of game mechanics is created. Despite the abstract world, complex narrative mechanics await you. You can flash your colors. The other blocks react to you according to your and their color and movements. You can be trapped for some time by the other blocks. Sound and shaking make this rather unpleasant. You may even be thrown out of the labyrinth (cf. Solonface 2013). It is inevitable that you ask yourself: What am I experiencing here? What am I? Who am I? What is my relationship to others? I can move and change my color, but what does it mean? What narrative rules are hidden behind the basic visual elements such as form, color and behavior? *LIM* is a game that tries to convey the experience of violence in a liminal social space. Developer Merrit Kopas explains: "With Lim I wanted to portray a kind of violence less obvious and familiar than that normally portrayed by games, and to place the player in the position of a person experiencing it without the usual defenses games offer (weapons of their own, agile movement, magical powers, etc.)." (Kopas 2012)

Figure 23: LIM (2012) is an abstract game with different layers of expression. The player's avatar is a block that can change colors and fit in but experiences adversarial behavior by some other blocks.

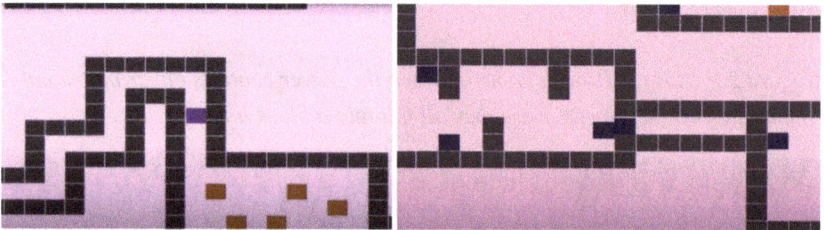

Source: screenshots (Bauer/Suter)

NARRATIVE MECHANICS IN CULTURE (BEYOND GAMES)

Mechanics of assertion and counter-assertion in journalism

Interesting adaptive narrative mechanics can increasingly be found beyond games in fields such as journalism or politics. Journalistic texts are more and more often being formulated and published as assertions. In this respect, the chosen narrative mechanic is an actual game mechanic and at the same time a business model. These assertion-based texts attract readers by means of their radically phrased headlines. This ensures that they are clicked on by opponents and supporters alike. And both sides rush to the forum and run riot with their comments, generating more online attention (clickbait) that can be monetized several times over. Wait for the next day, and you will be guaranteed to be rewarded with a counter-assertion to keep the "debate culture" going. But that's not all, even if the assertion cannot be proven or is rejected, it remains active as narrative (game) mechanics. As in the novel *Der Verdacht* (Suspicion) by Friedrich Dürrenmatt (1953), a suspicion remains that it could be correct. Even the most improbable assertion may be used here as game mechanics. The proponents as well as the opponents live from finding new "evidence" for or against the assertion. And the longer the time of argumentative abstinence, the higher the gain of pleasure is; the deeper the fall is, the bigger the challenge becomes. With each fact found, the mechanics of the assertion are strengthened and the magic circle that was created or found together becomes more consistent and more immersive. This can be observed particularly well in social media like Facebook, Twitter, Instagram, TikTok, etc., with their "like"-mechanisms that create own magic circles for each of their many users.

Narratives as solidified narrative mechanics containers and systems

Politicians apply this kind of adaptive narrative game mechanics far more radically. Here, language is used openly in texts and conversations. Words appear as variables that can mean anything and that can always adapt to anything. Words are here for manipulating. Who is on the right, who is on the left? Who is a do-gooder? Who is an upright person? Who is a refugee? Shared creativity in this context entails filling the variables as creatively as possible, enriching them with one's own experience, one's own life and being rewarded through narrative mechanics. A special form of narrative mechanics: narratives or *grand récits*. Narratives are meaningful and rudimentary, they are formulaic and transport certain values and emotions, and refer to a certain (political or historical) environment. Although they contain all the possibilities of rewards and punishments, they are often perceived as still and preserved stories. As in games, one enters the magic circle created by specific rules and accepts the fiction of a specific narrative.

The narrative can be understood as a concept of life: a symbolic framework such as "The American Dream" or a motto such as "Just Do It". It does not care about what is true and what is not. It is the design of a fictitious world. It doesn't necessarily have a clear beginning, a clear middle and a clear ending like a story, but begins with rudimentary recordings and metaphors and evolves over the course of time and is able to generate more and more stories. In video games, the narrative can often be equated with the concept of the lived-in world, which serves as the framework for the story world. Open-world games in particular have to use such narratives. In the game *Grand Theft Auto V* (2013), it is the narrative of the gangster metropolis that serves as the framework for the game world as a kind of playable 3D architecture of Los Angeles or New York. The world is designed with rather realistic visuals and some important landmarks from reality, but serves as a surface and reduced space for all the player interactions and challenges. In turn, individual stories are embedded in it. And the individual quests and missions that slowly take over the lives of the main characters serve as a link between these stories. (cf. Suter: 60ff., 70)

Narrative mechanics in politics

In politics, narrative mechanics and narratives are often used to set an emotional framework of meaning for your supporters. In this context, the narrative is to be understood as an overarching formulaic narrative, a mechanism which creates meaning and motivates in its essence. A narrative is a narrative mechanic that brings together and coordinates other narrative mechanics. The narrative mechanics appear as the dispositif of a narrative. And simplified narrative mechanics are mostly perceived as linear stories and are thus easier to communicate in society.

The term "the narrative" appears in Jean-François Lyotard's work *La condition postmoderne* from 1979 in which he identified as part of his theory on postmodernism two *méta-récits* of Western philosophy by which modernity legitimized itself: Immanuel Kant's "self-liberation of the individual through enlightenment" and Georg Wilhelm Friedrich Hegel's "gradual self-enlightenment of the mind as the goal of history". The term *méta-récits* was translated into English as *grand narrative* – from which the German neologism *das Narrativ* was derived. It describes a fundamental motto of a concept, or rather the established narrative of a cultural circle with a certain legitimacy. This becomes clearer in two popular and somewhat less intellectual examples: The French Revolution was able to inspire with its grand narrative "liberté, egalité, fraternité" and to shape an entire epoch, while American capitalism has been able to keep its citizens at bay for decades with the grand narrative "from rags to riches", meaning that everyone in society has the chance to become rich in a system assumed to be full of opportunities, even though you may have to start as dishwasher. And this narrative was labeled with the patriotic term "the American Dream".

A political narrative today often corresponds to an easily understandable fictional feel-good narrative that increasingly attempts to suppress or displace other political narratives and their mechanisms.

The parallel with games is obvious, because that is exactly what games always have to do. They must make their narrative mechanics far more attractive and rewarding than reality. They must be very pointed, they must exaggerate, they must do the improbable. Egoshooter mechanics are a prime example. With a short story using pictures and animation and a specific war setting, a distinct magic circle is established. Through clear challenges ("They want to kill me") and approaches ("I have to kill them", for example), moral concepts are consciously narcotized in "action" and taken out of the game. This provides us with more "action". And paradoxically, we seem to feel liberated under such rule sets even though they are much more restrictive than we assume.

When Donald Trump promised to build a wall to prevent Mexicans from crossing the border illegally and repeated this over and over again, and finally "illustrated" it with detention camps and the tearing apart of immigrant families when they were crossing the border, he used a narrative mechanic that deliberately plays with the American fantasy that Mexicans would steal jobs of "good Americans". Therefore, the land has to be safeguarded against the (job) invaders from the South. Whether this was true or false did not matter at all. The narrative is simple, symbolic, coherent, and takes the form of a mechanic for Trump's followers. It is a character-fitting propaganda that served the purpose of establishing Trump's election and reign. And as it is the major rhetoric of a political backlash, it didn't stop with the election. The pursuit goes on, the wall is being designed and built. Parts of it are built in reality too, but above all in the heads of many people, the wall has been erected and established as a permanent feature. And the narrative mechanics turn into charades and games that have severe consequences for many people. Even inside the United States, Immigration and Customs Enforcement (ICE) units have been making arrests of unauthorized immigrants, deporting them immediately without granting them a hearing. At the border itself, the situation is one of constant farce with immigrants getting funneled to certain parts of the border where they are more likely to be picked up and turned around or put in detention or die in the hostile border area. In 2019 smuggling gangs in Mexico repeatedly sawed through new sections of Trump's border wall with commercially available power tools, opening gaps large enough for people and drug loads to pass through. When the border patrols see this, they send out welding crews to fix the steel pillars of the border wall. A few days later, the smuggling gangs work on the same pillars again.

Figure 24: Wall as a narrative defining politics. Reagan's open-up motto "Tear down the wall!" against Trump's border closure motto "We build a wall"; the fall of the Berlin wall (left), Trump border wall samples (right).

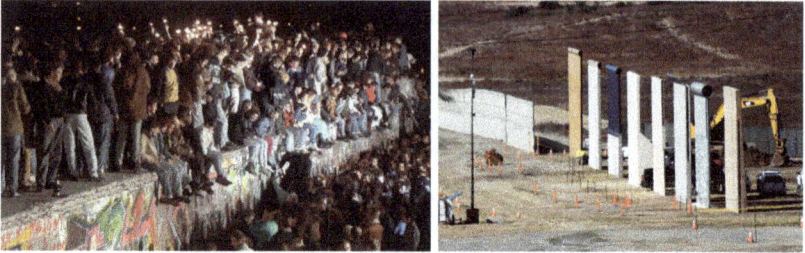

Sources: DPA/Reuters

Ironically, 35 years earlier, Ronald Reagan had established a similarly pervasive narrative mechanic with the opposite message "Mr. Gorbachev, tear down that wall!" After the Berlin wall went down, it seemed that the time for separating walls was over. But division and propaganda are never far away. The communication theorist Walter R. Fisher used the term "Homo narrans" (1987) to emphasize his point that humans are essentially storytellers. For him communication is, in effect, the exchange of stories. He argued that "the world is a set of stories which must be chosen to live the good life in a process of continual recreation."(Fisher 1985) His theory may be a bit short-sighted but stories certainly are important for communication and decision-making because they are able to establish coherent connections between events. The listeners evaluate these stories on the basis of their understanding of the world. In other words, a populist like Trump tells stories that enable his followers to understand the world because those stories are linked to their knowledge and identity. Reagan had done the same, but with reversed premises in relation to a defining wall.

Thus, Trump does not propose that Americans adapt their knowledge to reflect the new social and economic reality of their country, but instead offers to change the world so that it ultimately matches the knowledge of his followers. This continues in many other areas of Trump's politics. He tries to rewrite events like his own inauguration, the white supremacy rally in Charlottesville in 2017, the demonstrations for the Black Lives Matter movements in 2020, and even the history of the Covid virus. He does this in a way that corresponds to his own knowledge and that of his followers, and persists stubbornly in his world view without listening to counter-arguments and facts – in some areas probably until the bitter end.

From this perspective, various conspiracy theories have appeared in recent years as narrative-mechanical containers that can neutralize any "attack" with their narrative mechanics, supporting the narrative as a simple story system. The Flat Earth Society believes that the earth is not a sphere but a disc of an infinite plane. Apollo conspiracies state that there never was a moon landing and the astronauts staged it on a movie set. 9/11 conspiracies usually center around a deliberate controlled demolition of the towers by the state. Global warming conspiracy theorists want to believe that scientists invented global warming or distorted data for financial reasons. And QAnon is an absurd conspiracy that alleges that a cabal of satanist pedophiles run a global child-sex-trafficking ring and plot against President Trump. It seems anything works as a conspiracy narrative.

Narrative mechanics of the market economy

And yet, cleverly constructed adaptive narrative mechanics themselves are already actual systems of rules that create stories. The best and most influential example are the narrative mechanics of the (neo-)liberal market, which as a kind of mechanics (of absolute benefit and profit maximization) can be used and adapted anywhere, solves every problem at any level and on any topic, and creates the same individual success story for any (life) story. It is always possible to find an example in everyday life that supports the assertion of these narrative mechanics and confirms it to the reader. No statistical substantiation is required; it is enough for the narrative mechanics to hit the nail on the head every now and then. This seems to be reward enough. In this way, the narrative of the market and its current power-political use opposes the achievements of mankind. If, for example, truth, human rights and justice are evaluated on the market, all mechanisms and narratives so far developed lose their significance.

Culture as narrative mechanics and its Homo Cyberneticus

Narrative and narrative mechanics do not exist forever, of course; they must be fed and kept alive. The "thousand-year Reich" only managed 12 years. In itself a long time, because narrative mechanics must always be kept alive as long as the term of office of a politician or dictator or a certain economic cycle lasts. But the feeding is important, because only when people believe they can profit from them are narrative mechanics also meaningful, implemented and usable as a means of power. That is why politics and business try to convince as many people as possible of their narrative. The narrative of "Modernism" shows this very well. It has been alive for hundred years, but today, it has to share space and time with several other narratives like "Postmodernism", "Hypermodernism" and "Nonmodernism" or "Antimodernism". According to Bruno Latour (2018), the narrative of "Modernism" for a better common future is important for science and technology and therefore for acknowledging the issue of climate change. We have not reached this better future yet, still aspire to it, but it has been increasingly denounced and set under attack by politicians who ignore and devalue science in order to re-establish the old ways of exploiting the planet. Their underlying credo is: "There is simply not room and resources for everyone. But there is enough for us. Let's take what we need."

Culture as narrative mechanics needs the mechanics to organize, motivate and ultimately reproduce society. The members of such a system and society, however, think in terms of "stories" and "histories". They deal with texts, facts, stories in conversation, in traditional media as well as social media. They have long since ceased to think in terms of stories, and are guided instead by narrative mechanics, i.e. complex narrative game mechanics. The actors of such a society are no longer linear storytellers and consumers. They have become specimens of the "Homo Cyberneticus" type. For quite some time now, they have been acting *with* narrative mechanics and *in* narrative mechanics. Their tools are cybernetic circuits, programs and algorithms that come across as narrative mechanics.

Figure 26: Absurd and extreme narratives dissipated by Twitter, from "flat earth" (left) to "all mainstream media are a fake" (right).

Source: Twitter

Homo Cyberneticus now also tosses these narrative messages into habitats, into experimental vats. In those echo chambers such as Twitter, Facebook, Instagram, Reddit, Twitch, TikTok, etc., the narrative mechanisms can multiply epidemically depending on time, place, content, sender and references, by spreading via other users or via algorithms and infecting others (literally "going viral"). These narrative messages create their own furrow or reinforce the fairway of an existing narrative or even a combined stream of several narratives. This new culture comes across more as a fluid network than a hierarchically fixed system. Even if individual narrative mechanics contradict each other within their own narratives, this is where people play, fight, cheer, pay and motivate each other with their narrative mechanics. Only on the surface does this culture of narrative mechanics and narratives look like the culture of the last 80 years; further in or deeper down it is more cybernetic, more technical, more self-generating and therefore more feedback-driven, prone to manipulation and distortion, and more explosive.

REFERENCES

Literature

Dürrenmatt, Friedrich (1953): Der Verdacht, Einsiedeln: Benziger.

Fisher, Walter R. (1987): Human Communication as Narration: Toward a Philosophy of Reason, Value, and Action, Columbia: University of South Carolina Press.

Fisher, Walter R. (1985): "Homo Narrans. The Narrative Paradigm: In the Beginning." In: Journal of Communication (pre-1986); Fall 1985; 35/4; ABI/INFORM Global, p.74.

Goffman, Erving (1986 [1967]): Interaktionsrituale. Über Verhalten in direkter Kommunikation, Frankfurt a. M.: Suhrkamp.

Hack, Günter (2018): QUIZ. Roman, Berlin: Frohmann.

Iser, Wolfgang (1972): Der implizite Leser. Kommunikationsformen des Romans von Bunyan bis Beckett, München: Wilhelm Fink.

Kopas, Merritt (2012): "The Aesthetics of Gameplay: LIM." In: ACM SIGGRAPH Digital Arts Community (http://gameartshow.siggraph.org/gas/lim/).

Krummenacher, David (2018): Storytelling in Flipperautomaten. Eine Beschreibung der narrativen Elemente und Strukturen in Flipperautomaten. Unpublished Master thesis (ZHdK), Zürich.

Latour, Bruno (2018 [2017]): Das Terrestrische Manifest, Frankfurt a. M.: Suhrkamp.

Lyotard, Jean-François (1982 [1979]): Das postmoderne Wissen. Ein Bericht, Bremen: Impuls & Association.

Propp, Vladimir (1968 [1928]): Mythology of the Folktale, Austin: University of Texas Press.

Games

Another World, Eric Chahi, Delphine Software, 1991.
Asteroids, Atari, Atari, 1981 [1979].
Boktai, The Sun is in your hand, Konami, Konami, 2003.
Donkey Kong Country, Rare, Nintendo, 1994.
Don't Starve, Klei Entertainment, 505 Games, 2013.
Dwarf Fortress, Tarn Adams/Zach Adams, Bay 12 Games, 2006-2020.
Eco, Strange Loop Games, Strange Loop Games, 2018.
Façade, Michael Mateas/Andrew Stern, Procedural Arts, 2005.
Far. Lone Sails, Ocomotive, Mixt Vision, 2018.
Feed the Head, Vectorpark, Vectorpark 2011.
The Forest, Endnight Games, Endnight Games, 2014.
Funhouse Pinball, Pat Lawlor, Williams Electronics, 1990.
Grand Theft Auto: Chinatown Wars, Rockstar North, Rockstar Games, 2009.
Grand Theft Auto V, Rockstar North, Rockstar Games, 2013.
Kids, Playables, Double Fine Presents, 2019.
Koko's Curse, apelab, apelab, 2018.
LIM, Merritt Koppas, merritt k., 2012.
No Man's Sky, Hello Games, Hello Games, 2016.
Osada, Amanita Design, Amanita Design, 2011.
Pac-Man, Namco, Midway Games, 1980.
Pikselbacteria, AND-OR, and-or.ch, 2010.
Tomb Raider, Core Design, Eidos Interactive, 1996.
Twilight Zone (Pinball), Pat Lawlor, Midway, 1993.
Vib Ribbon, NanaOn-Sha, Sony Computer Entertainment, 1999.
Wardive, AND-OR, and-or.ch, 2009.
Worms, Team 17, Team 17, 1995.

Videos

DOS Nostalgia (2016): Another World playthrough, YouTube (https://www.youtube.com/watch?v=awQwSXwNWCw).
Fmips 19 (2012): Osada – Amanita Design – Walkthrough, YouTube (https://www.youtube.com/watch?v=QBIvq3g0ky0).
Indie James (2018): FAR: Lone Sails – Full Game & Ending (Longplay), YouTube (https://www.youtube.com/watch?v=nIV-6kwEBL8&t=1506s).
NathanBlakeGames (2019): From the Makers of *Plug & Play/Kids*, YouTube (https://www.youtube.com/watch?v=Xp-wHPwC9uk).

rrvirus (2019): GTA: Chinatown Wars, YouTube (https://www.youtube.com/watch?v=wNspLeF1cUo).

Solonface (2013): Lim – A Loving Review, YouTube (https://www.youtube.com/watch?v=Dr0LdXhSnFk).

WithPCGame (2011): Feed The Head – Walkthrough, YouTube (https://www.youtube.com/watch?v=f8vUnArRFAo).

Narrative Patterns in Video Games

Narrative Mechanics and Its Rules and Rule Sets

Beat Suter

Storytelling in video games can take very different forms and encompass a variety of values. Whether as a small backstory for the game world, as detailed life stories of individual characters or as the dominant narrative of a complex epic, storytelling always has to interlock with game mechanics and the game world in such a way that the player can easily cope with logical interactions. Since a game is a framework of game rules, storytelling does not have a superordinate role, but acts as a game mechanic and is therefore integrated into a set of rules (Suter/Kocher/Bauer 2018: 31). In a role-playing epic (*Final Fantasy* series) it can be a principal macro mechanism of the game, in a platformer (*Super Mario* series) it can be one mechanism among many, often formulaically rendered. And in a puzzle game, it may merely serve as an accessory or a decorative frame (*Gunpey* 1999, *Candy Crush Saga* 2012). The most exciting game stories are probably those that, rather than just laying out a narrative, rely more on hints and have to be discovered or playfully and actively worked out by the player (*Inside* 2016, *The Last Guardian* 2016).

But even in a game with a dominant narrative storytelling is often accompanied by a second macro mechanic such as exploration or solving puzzles. These second-tier dominant mechanics then serve as the key to building sets of supporting micro mechanics. Consequently, the narrative is often used as a targeted game mechanism. Progress in the form of solving a puzzle or finding a new space leads to narrative progress, adds a scene to the story, reveals more of a character's personality and takes the story one step further. For example: In *The Last Guardian* (2016), the narrative is built gradually through the relationship between the two characters and their exploration of the world in which they are trapped. The boy and the beast develop minor skills that allow them to advance into the next room and open up new realms both spatially and narratively.

Many developers, however, do not (only) identify storytelling as a game mechanic, but rather as a method of structuring games into storylines that allow them to organize the flow of a game. In addition, they see storytelling as a way of conveying meaning (Fabricatore 2018: 86). But meaning can also be conveyed through motivating game mechanics, as evidenced by so-called emergent storytelling, which has become important in many newer games. Wolfgang Walk puts it clearly: "Game and story are not separate aesthetic categories." (Letsch 2018) Ludic and narrative elements should not simply be thought of separately or as one after the other, but should be planned in a networked way with the best possible interaction. Our starting point (for this chapter) therefore is narration as a networked interaction of game and story, in conjunction with the question of how to develop stories for video games that can be experienced by the players.

HOW DO YOU DEVELOP STORIES FOR VIDEO GAMES?

Should you proceed in a similar way as in films or novels? Should you follow the patterns of television series? Should you base your approach on animes? Is it preferable to simply write down the stories or rather to draw and create a rudimentary storyboard? How are emotions conveyed in a way that can be (actively) experienced? And how do you start the process – by designing a character or a setting? These questions can't be answered easily, because stories in games can be set up in many different ways. Therefore, it is important to study the functions and structures of these narrative units more closely in relation to video games. The range is enormous, and the approaches could not be more different. We will focus on a few important patterns and use examples to find out how such stories are developed and how they are interwoven with the mechanics.

MOVEMENT AND CHARACTER

First and foremost, we need to take a closer look at the set of rules pertaining to mechanics and narration. Our main focus is on movement and character, which means that we will try to define the behaviors of objects and their interactions. How does the object (the avatar) move and what happens when it encounters other objects, boundaries, etc.? The design process starts with the development of basic mechanics as already described in the introduction of *Games and Rules*

(Suter/Kocher/Bauer 2018: 7). At the same time, however, we need to develop a narrative mechanic for our game, which is generally an outline of what may happen to our avatar during the time of play. Many game designers carry out this step rather unconsciously at first. The approach of using a backstory as a framework for the game mechanics probably demonstrates this most clearly.

BACKSTORY AS A FRAME

One of the most famous examples of this approach is the arcade game *Space Invaders* (1978). Mechanically it is about shooting pixel sprites which advance threateningly from above and can also shoot. The narrative revolves around aliens threatening Earth and having to be fended off by protected anti-aircraft guns. The formula "Save the World" was transferred into the contemporary context of space travel and thus transformed into a very comprehensible narrative mechanic of an attack from space, which was immediately recognizable in the era of NASA's Apollo space program and contemporary popular entertainment like the TV series Star Trek and the first Star Wars movie. The contextual narrative of *Space Invaders* functions as a social framework that paves the way for understanding the events in the game. It provides "guided doings" in "a serial management of consequentiality" (Goffman 1974: 22f.). According to Goffman, a social framework, usually in the form of the presentation of information, is a communicative aid which influences the way data is interpreted, processed and communicated and makes it memorable. In games like *Space Invaders*, the narrative frame takes over the presentation part and the framed information becomes the interactive playground for the player's actions and decisions.

While the backstory of *Pac-Man* (1980) seems even more rudimentary – Pizza Pac-man has to eat his way through the labyrinth (reminiscent of pinball machine patterns) and is haunted by ghosts (including a short role reversal) – the arcade game *Donkey Kong* (1981) develops in its narrative frame a dichotomy between the giant ape King Kong and the insignificant plumber Mario, thus making the fairy tale formula "Save the Princess!" usable in an everyday superhero setting. This means that a well-known fairy tale formula is being transformed in a different context and narratively disrupted with a slight nod to comedy. Instead of striving for a game with complexity and new story elements, designer Shigero Myamoto chooses the iteration of a known process. He constructs a clear and simple narrative mechanic that subordinates itself to the mechanics and interactions of the gameplay. He reduces the plot to the rescue of the princess from the urban scaffolding and makes this his frame and the goal of the game, adding short cutscenes at the beginning and end of each level as narrative accompaniment (2-5 seconds) and leaving the player to concentrate on the iterative gameplay.

Figure 1: The backstory functions as a frame for the gameplay: borders are permeable and the contexts of society, history and entertainment influence both gameplay and backstory and allow them to link up well.

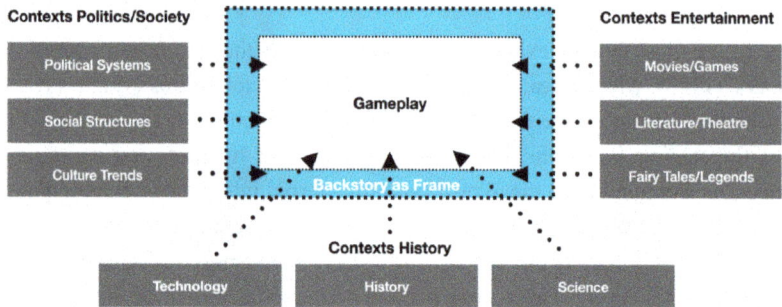

Source: Beat Suter

BACK(GROUND) STORY AS SUPPLEMENT

The backstories in the games above are well interwoven, but there are also often those, especially in puzzle games, which are probably best described as background stories. This is the case when a game designer creates a puzzle game first and looks for a story afterwards. The designer devises a background story for the fictional world of the puzzle; thus, puzzle and story become separate entities. Or the designer supplements characters with background stories; this is often done in fighting games and sometimes in role play games. Popular puzzle games that work with (separate) background stories are for example *Puyo Pop Fever* (2003) and *Gunpey* (1999). Gameplay and plot are separate units in those games, but nevertheless a plot is integrated as a progression and can only be unfurled by completing individual puzzle levels. *Puyo Pop Fever* creates a minimal narrative scenario in which the teacher Ms. Accord has lost her flying stick (magic wand). Two of the students of the magic school go on a search. The plot is told in slightly animated pictures with the cartoon characters and text represented by subtitles and voice-over. After each level, the plot is continued in another picture-text cutscene in the style of a visual novel – right to the end. The puzzle levels, however, take place in a container with two playing fields of 6x12 units, into which colorful blobs fall. These have to be arranged in the same manner as in *Tetris* (1989). The player has to defeat another player or an AI. Narrative scenes and puzzle levels are completely separated from each other, the only connection is the player character (Amitie or Raffine) who occupies one of the two containers.

Puzzle and narrative are even more blatantly separated in the game *Gunpey*. The gameplay consists of arranging fragments of lines to create a left to right connection. The playing field is made up of 5x10 cells. There are different modes for players to choose. In Story Mode they play against the CPU and make progress in the story by winning. The story revolves around a frog named Vincent who saves a cat called Sherry from a group of outlaws. It is set in an imaginary Wild West, but in the original game version, this is only shown in a short intro and at the end of the game – and barely so with some slightly animated pictures. The combination of gameplay and plot doesn't seem to follow any logic, except that it could perhaps be conceivable that by connecting the lines a path may be opened for the character. Because it is so unimportant, the background story could easily be regarded as a decorative element, one that helped introduce the game to the market. But nevertheless, in its light-hearted way, this game presents itself as a crazy funny product and may be classified as an interesting example of a Mukokuseki (cf. Kato/Bauer: 113-150). In later versions of *Gunpey* (2006), single animated scenes take place in the actual (visual) background of the puzzle while you are playing. Thus, the story becomes a literal "background story".

While the selection of characters in *Gunpey* are backed up by a comic-style name and a drawn portrait, Beat 'em Ups, for example, develop more detailed background stories for the characters you can fight with. *Tekken* (1994), *Street Fighter* (1987) etc. offer CVs for the fighters and opponents to give the player more information about the game world. This may not interest every player, but it makes the game world more credible. *Tekken's* background story is a violent conflict in the Mishima family, which provides the basis for the Iron Fist tournament organized by the Mishima Corporation (Zaibatsu). Whoever wins the tournament will also control the company. The player can choose from numerous characters. Each of these characters has a short biography to narratively embed them into the fictional world and link them with other characters.

Traditionally, games have usually been designed to enliven the physicality of their characters. Some older characters, for example, follow dominant movement patterns: Super Mario (originally Jumpman) jumps, Solid Snake sneaks, Lara Croft climbs. The personalities and background stories of these characters are side issues or flimsy marketing exercises. The characters lack substance. Their motivations are rather obscure. However, this mechanism of narrative restraint or reduction does not have a negative effect on the player. On the contrary: they identify with their avatar through movement patterns and are provided with ficti-tious void spaces which they can fill with their own interpretations – which may well be self-referential. As soon as a character is predetermined down to the last detail, the player has less opportunity to fully identify with the avatar.

ENVIRONMENTAL STORYTELLING

Besides back stories for individual characters, there are also background stories for the fictional world of a game. This is also called environmental storytelling or spatial storytelling and can be understood as an expanding backstory in the setting of a game. It involves the design of the environment and the architecture of individual buildings, cities, objects and boundaries within a game world. In most cases, this environmental storytelling is designed as a parallel or tangential narrative. This means that the aim is to tell non-player-driven stories and thus give the player more of a sense of the motivation of the characters. (cf. Heussner 2019: 38) The mysterious ruins made of rock in *The Last Guardian* (2016) tell of an unknown culture that bears witness to knowledge and power. The island in Jonathan Blow's *The Witness* (2018) was even designed with the help of an ar-chitectural firm that, in constructing the buildings on the island, tried to conjure up a cultural history of bygone times which would be perceptible in individual locations. In *Journey* (2012), it is not only the buildings and bridges, but also the murals, carpet-like paths and scarves with symbols on them that seem to repre-sent traditions from another time – they add to this game world a unique and dis-tinctive historical layer. Tobias Heussner (2019: 37) describes this as lore, "composed of traditions, knowledge, and beliefs as held by a particular group".

In itself it is an extended part of world building. World building in the sense of: we need to have an economy for our game world. We must have a cultural history for this world. We have to know what the driving forces are in this eco-system. We need to have an idea of how this world or its current state was creat-ed. We need not only terrain, but also suitable flora and fauna. We need social systems, communication systems, transport systems, guidance systems, etc. This world building is, of course, very important, but it also differs considerably from game world to game world in terms of its layout and diversity.

It doesn't help much if we recreate a real city, but then can't enter the famil-iar buildings, so they don't tell us anything because only the facades are there. And it doesn't help much when, as in Tom Clancy's *The Division 2* (2019), the

Martin Luther King Library in Washington DC is recreated and serves as a shooting location (with books piled up to form protective walls), but the whole social background of the building is hidden. A good example, however, is the completely fictional world of *The Legend of Zelda: Breath of the Wild* (2017), which provides a kind of story sense for the player with its landscapes, individual locations, huts, villages and strange communities and cultures. The game creates a narrative ambiance rich in exciting events and encounters in a vast, varied, attractive landscape. Individual areas such as the desert (the Gerudos) or the water world (the Zoras) are self-contained regions with matching cultures and architecture, right down to the individual rooms, signs, food and objects.

The game critic Mark Brown uses the game *Bioshock* (2007) to illustrate how environmental storytelling permeates the various levels of world building. The entire environment of the underwater city of Rapture is permeated by narration. The city is located on the seabed and seems to have been built primarily for high society with fancy bars, apartment complexes and a theater district. "A place built on lofty philosophical ideals." (Brown 2020) But also a place of ruin and despair. Rapture's decline began on New Year's Day 1959, as a neon sign suggests. The environment here functions as an effective method of storytelling. Narrative elements are embedded everywhere in the spaces and places we visit over the course of the game. We thus understand more and more of this world without the need for more traditional ways of storytelling. Brown believes that level design can drive our understanding, feeling and identity. It is a participatory approach to creating an overall story through deductive thinking as we connect the details. By investigating, exploring and deducting, we become an active participant in the narrative process and are no longer passive spectators. Often it is simply a matter of static objects, but it can also mean that we accidentally overhear something, that a certain animation provides us with new information or that we find texts such as books, letters, item descriptions, scans, graffiti or the like. The transfer of information may also happen through small- or large-scale location evolvement, when previous actions have influenced the environment and we are now confronted with the consequences as we visit the location again. Or we recognize, for example when we encounter an electrified grid, that danger awaits us, or there may be clues such as light, fog or symbols for what could happen next, where to go next, or perhaps hints for the game or for puzzles are provided.

Figure 2: Environmental storytelling as an effective way of conveying a narrative at all levels of development, as seen by Mark Brown (2020). Most effective at the highest level with embedded objects, traces of events and history.

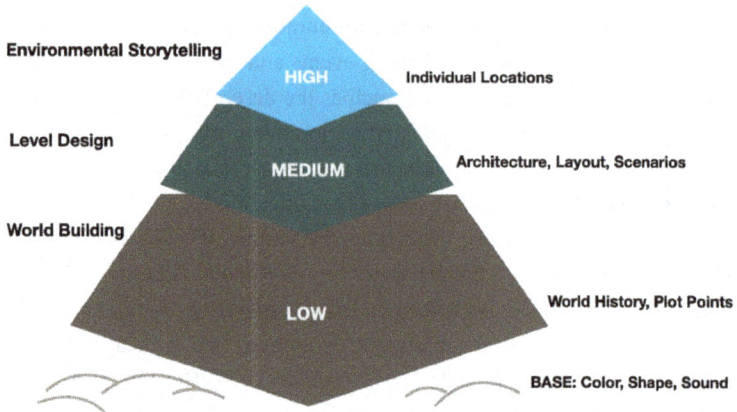

Source: Mark Brown (adapted)

In the games mentioned above, the game designer can be seen more as a narrative architect than as a storyteller. Henry Jenkins (2003: 12) was already convinced of this when he analyzed the narratological consequences of game spaces and described the game world as an information space or memory palace (ibid: 10). Like Jenkins, Brown (2020) divides the development of a narrative landscape in a game into three areas: firstly, environmental storytelling, in which micronarrative vignettes and individual locations such as bars, markets, squares are developed; then, the level design with its architecture, layout, materials and scale; and finally, the world building, where the plot points for the story of the fictional world as well as the factions have to be set, and the main actors for the story have to be determined. According to this concept, environmental storytelling is responsible for the narrower contexts, but depends on good networking or embedding in the wider contexts. There are games in which these areas flow smoothly into one another and trigger an intuitive feeling in the player. In these games, color, shape and size as well as sound and music are the main elements. They are often used specifically as emotional triggers and motivators. Thatgamecompany, for instance, in games such as *Journey* (2012), mainly work with light, sound and flowing animated environmental designs which are influenced by the weather.

But sometimes it is just single objects and ambient scenes that provide us with more information and more immersion concerning the game. In *Mario Kart 8* (2014), for example, an ice cream truck with cheerful toads stands at a central point of the circuit at Peach's castle, which underscores the game's party mood. In the game *Inside* (2016) the player has to pass through a field of very tall corn when it rains. The rain becomes visible under the light beam of the street lamp and together with the misty gray background lends the game a soft horror mystery atmosphere, while the player with their avatar of a frightened boy sneaks past in direction of the barn.

QUESTS – EVENTS, TASKS AND MISSIONS

Narrative games often use the proven system of quests as a bridge between story and interactivity. In these, simple narrative mechanics tend to be extended into complex quest systems and more complex network storyworlds, such as in open-world games and MMORPGs. Quests have the advantage that they can transform narrative structures into activities. This has always been the case with quest narratives, except that authors (of legends and books) could only encourage their readers to engage in interpretative activities and imaginary interactions with and in their fictional world. Practical activities, however, were not possible for them. This has changed fundamentally. Now that media and interactive options are available in addition to oral and written narratives, the author can offer action and behavior patterns and invite the player to perform practical actions in simulated rooms or participate in interactive events by means of targeted actions. It is therefore possible to translate narrative quest structures in video games into activities that can be performed in practice by the player (avatar).

Recombined characters and functions

Vladimir Propp's *Morphology of the Fairy Tale* (1968), a formalist study from 1928, provides the basis for the examination of game theoretical narrative structures. In his study, Propp refers exclusively to Russian fairy tales and develops a theory of forms of the fairy tale that comes close to the idea of narrative mechanics. It is based on the extraction of narrative rules deployed by these fairy tales. Starting from the forms and structures of the fairy tale rather than the content, Propp shows that the different elements of a fairy tale are assigned to each other according to a specific logic and can be reduced to a basic structural principle. In other words, he understands a narrative as a sequence of rigidly defined transformations through which elements are recombined according to strict rules of substitution and linking – just like the grammar of a language (Howard 2008: 9). Propp argues that the elements in a fairy tale narrative are thus a series of recurring characters that perform certain functions or prototypical actions, such as giving a character a talisman, hexing someone or saving someone from danger. According to Propp, these characters and functions are recombined countless times in magical fairy tales.

A player in a video game is now able to perform exactly these actions, which Propp refers to as "formulaic functions" (1968). If we add the countless recombination possibilities, we have a working action and behavior pattern for narrative games. Some of the functions are activities to be carried out as actions in short sequences. Other functions immediately become the macro mechanics for the whole game. Super Mario runs and fights his way through a world of enemies and rescues the princess (*Super Mario Bros.* 1985), the Prince of Persia must free himself from the dungeon and rescue the princess and marry her (*Prince of Persia* 1989), Link explores the world and must find the parts of an artifact to free the kidnapped Zelda (*The Legend of Zelda* 1986). Lara Croft climbs acrobatically through jungles and ruins and has to destroy a mystical artifact (*Tomb Raider* 1996), the witch Geralt must overcome his amnesia and uncover a conspiracy (*The Witcher* 2007), Joel and Ellie have to fight their way through a post-pandemic world to become a resistance group in order to secure the survival of mankind (*The Last of Us* 2014). The latter two and many other games contain not just one or a few of these narrative formulas, but numerous such action and behavior patterns, each of which dominates individual sections and chapters, each of which asks the player to complete a specific task such as killing a monster or finding a specific berry or liberating a village before the adventure can continue. For example, *The Witcher 3: Wild Hunt* (2016) features about 50 main quests with numerous side quests, which of course require their own backstories that interweave with each other and keep the player busy for hours.

Quest

The quest as a long and arduous search for something is a narrative mechanic often used in games. It doesn't require long explanations, as we know it from ancient, medieval and modern legends, fairy tales and movies which involve a search for the Holy Grail, an ancient artifact, a secret manuscript or a spell book. In his book *Quests* (2008: 10ff.) Jeff Howard impressively presents the history of quest games and shows the connections between narrative patterns from antiquity and the middle ages and from fantasy literature to the narrative development of Dungeons & Dragons, Interactive Fictions, the first graphical adventure games like the *King's Quest* (1992) series, action-adventure games and online RPGs. The deployed patterns are rather similar, but still very diverse in their application. Quests are stories that are mostly built from sets of mechanics. A story is a collection of experiences and adventures of a character in the form of events. On their journeys, the characters now have to overcome obstacles. Quests are these obstacles in a story that must be overcome. It is important in this context to distinguish between missions, tasks and quests. The assignment and usage of these terms is not always clear among game designers and game studies scholars.

Basically, individual tasks are the smallest elements in the structure of a quest. Supporting this view, Tobias Heussner provides the following definition: "Tasks are single objectives and the smallest element in quest design. They describe exactly one goal linked to one activity." (Heussner 2019: 126) Consequently, a quest is a collection of one or more of these tasks, which receive a narrative framework in this way. (ibid: 126) However, missions can also be described as a collection of tasks. "Missions are a collection of tasks, usually featuring primary and secondary objectives from which only the primary tasks must be completed." (ibid: 126) What distinguishes them from quests is the way their instructions are outlined. Missions are introduced during a break in the gameplay and don't necessarily have a clear narrative framework, but usually focus on action-intensive gameplay. Especially in open-world games we encounter numerous missions that do not continue the narrative. Nevertheless, missions in themselves are an important element for quest game structures.

Quest design can vary greatly: from very simple obstacles and enemies that need to be skipped or competed, to very complex puzzles (and challenging boss fights) that require hours of collecting and figuring out the pieces. This becomes clear when the different functions are compared in a table: A task sets the player a single goal, which can be achieved with one or more actions in an event of a relatively short time (chunk). The assumption of a time frame of 15 seconds is only for comparison with the other functions. A mission is to be understood as a chain of events (with actions by the player), i.e. a story, which only corresponds to a section of maybe up to 15 minutes, for instance, when the player has to cross a river and accept some detours. A quest corresponds to a story with a clear narrative framework and is usually equivalent to a level. In *The Legends of Zelda: Breath of the Wild* (2017), for example, Link has to recapture the elephant automaton Vah Ruta (one of the four Divine Beasts) and complete various complex tasks to do so. *The Legends of Zelda: Breath of the Wild* is particularly convincing because of its clear chains of quests (or quest lines), such as the recapture of the towers and temples, which open up further territories and continue the main plot, finally leading to the victory over Calamity Ganon and the resurrection of Zelda. And of course, the game also has some delightful side quests like finding, catching and taming the giant horse, discovering and using the climbing gear to be able to scale all mountains or finding the Master Sword in the middle of The Lost Woods. These side quests do not need to be completed to continue the main plot, but they are so attractive that the player most likely does not want to miss them.

Table 1: Summary of quest game structures showing the different quest functions, their respective narrative elements and their approximate assembly and duration.

Quest Game Structures			
Function	**Goal**	**Narrative Element**	**Timeframe/Length**
Task	single objective	event	chunk, c. 15 sec.
Mission	collection of tasks assigned in-between gameplay	story as chain of events	section, 1 - 15 minutes
Quest	collection of one or several tasks	story with narrative framework	level, 3-45 minutes
Side Quest	collection of tasks not connected with main plot	side story	quasi-level, 3-45 minutes
Chain of Quests	combination of quests	adventure as chain of stories	chapter(s), bunch of levels, several hours
Main Quest	goal to complete main plot and game	main plot	full game

EPIC STORY

The story itself is a collection of the experiences and adventures (chains of events) of our character(s). Our avatar has to overcome obstacles of all kinds. Literally and psychologically, the avatar covers a long journey, which brings us straight to the classic narrative mechanics of the hero's journey. It is now so well known in the game scene that it no longer requires a long explanation. It is still the most-used narrative strategy for role-playing games, action-adventure games and shooters as well as some other genres. Typically, it is linear and informal with twelve scenes divided into three acts (Campbell 1949). It primarily shows the personality development of the protagonist and his or her torturous adventures to save the world. Conflict, struggles and emotional immersion are developed into effective patterns of medial storytelling that unfolds in a cycle. The hero's journey has become a template for dramatic (digital) entertainment for the masses. It is based on the Aristotelian three-act cycle and incorporates actions and events as well as themes and characters which, as Jungian archetypes and classical legends, are part of our cultural heritage as well as our unconscious (Suter 2016).

Last but not least, modern heroes were introduced by comics. Superheroes like Superman, Spider-Man and Batman reached a growing fan base in the 20th century. The film industry took up the trend and gladly helped to spread the word about these modern heroes – it still does so today with successful blockbusters. In essence, these superheroes – for example, Iron Man and Captain America – are transformed into mythical gods and champions of modern culture. They replace the ancient myths of all cultures and serve as role models across all borders. And sometimes even ancient and classical mythical heroes are transformed into comic and film heroes. Fans no longer celebrate these role models from a religious perspective, but rather from an aesthetic and action-packed and even cathartic perspective, or the more superficial perspective of role-playing, mimicry and imitation aesthetics (like cosplay), which seems to contain less archetypal potential but is capable of generating great cultural resonance and presence. Although these stories are rather escapist and excessively simplistic in terms of behavior and social actions within cultural patterns, they also have a great potential for emotional immersion. This is especially true for video games that capture the archetypes and dramatic structures of the hero's journey – for example, RPGs such as the *Final Fantasy* series, *the Legend of Zelda* games series, *The Last of Us*, *Superbrothers: Sword & Sworcery EP*, or even the more contemplative and atmospheric indie game *Journey* (2012).

The hero's journey

As we have seen, the epic story or the hero's journey is an important narrative mechanic for games. Its dramatic structure consists of the twelve stages of the plot (with possible deviations). These stages are arranged in a circle and at the end bring the hero back to a normal life: 1. Premonition, 2. Call to Adventure, 3. Refusal, 4. Mentor, 5. Crossing the First Threshold, 6. Test, Allies, Enemies, 7.

Progress to the Deepest Cave, 8. Decisive Test, 9. Reward, Grabbing the Sword, 10. Way Back, 11. Showdown, 12. Return with the Elixir. (Vogler 1992, Suter 2016) In classic stories, the dramaturgical arc spanning the twelve action scenarios usually reaches its climax at stage 11, the showdown. Video games that are played over many hours adjust this dramaturgical arc in such a way that individual chapters or individual quests are given their own, adapted arc – similar to the way TV series employ this. In-between scenarios, there are often larger open spatial areas that remain dramaturgically open as well. They are purposely designed as mechanic and narrative playgrounds or open (explorative) grounds and motivate players to design their own scenarios with individually chosen actions within the big(ger) story frame.

Figure 3: Epic stories are commonly outlined as a journey of a hero: the plot comes in a cycle of twelve stages.

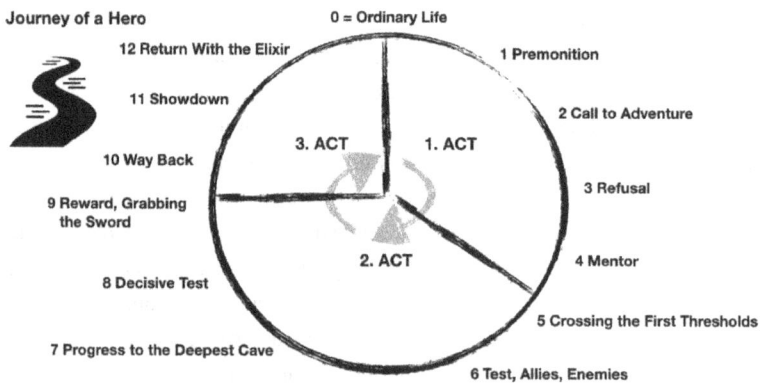

Source: Campbell/Vogler

The absent object

An important part of the narrative mechanics of the hero's journey has crept not only into 20th and 21th century film, but also into video games: the absent object. Propp already used this term for the objects coveted by the heroes. They were either searching for them on their journey and had to bring them back home, or it could be an item that had been lost in the first place and now needed be recovered, or an item given by a mentor (Propp 1968: 34f.). Howard (2008: 83f.), on the other hand, points out how unimportant these objects themselves actually are, but at the same time he emphasizes how important their absence is. Their narrative mechanics only work through their absence from most of the narrative or play; they are motivation and emotional identification and the driving force for the narrative. A good example of this is the Triforce artifact in *the Legend of Zelda* series. The in-game legends refer to it as "The Golden Power" which created the realm of Hyrule. It consists of three pieces, three equilateral triangles that fit together with a recessed fourth equilateral triangle in the middle, and is central to some games in the Zelda series. The common hero Link has been assigned the task of finding the pieces and putting them together to save Hyrule. The absence of the object initiates the narration and is a constant incentive for the player to solve the numerous tasks and complete the adventures.

Thus, the absence of the object has a direct effect on narration and gameplay. This idea is already present in Vladimir Propp's *Morphology of the Fairy Tale* from 1928. He speaks of a deficiency or an insufficiency. This situation of deficiency could be seen as the equivalent of a robbery. It provokes a quest. Propp provides an example with a brief comment: "A princess seizes Ivan's talisman. The result of this seizure is that Ivan lacks the talisman. And so we see that a tale, while omitting villainy, very often begins directly with a lack: Ivan desires to have a magic saber or a magic steed, etc. Insufficiency, just like seizure, determines the next point of the complication: Ivan sets out on a quest." (Propp 1968: 34f.) Propp further defines the function "The hero acquires the use of magical agent" (ibid: 43f.). A magical agent can be any of the following four things: an animal with magical powers, an object out of which magical helpers appear, objects possessing magical properties and qualities, or capacities which are directly given, such as the power of transformation into an animal. Propp further outlines the different types of transmission of the object (or magical agent), such as transference, sale or find (nine in all), which in Campbell's (1949) and Vogler's (1992) works are reduced to only one form of transmission, the "seizing of an object". These two authors speak of the "Magic Sword" or the "Elixir", which is sought by the hero throughout the entire narrative and is finally returned home or brought back to the place of origin.

Howard (2006: 84) points out that in film, Alfred Hitchcock had already regarded the idea of an absent object as the driving force for narration in the 1930s. With his customary sarcasm, he called objects of this kind a "MacGuffin", meaning an object that can drive the plot forward but is unimportant as an object in the film itself – for example, a murder weapon, a murder object or a suitcase with unknown contents that everyone is after, but in the end, the content may not even be revealed. What in Hitchcock's case could be a kitchen knife that loses its importance after being discovered, or in a James Bond film an atomic missile or a test tube with a virus, would find its equivalent in ancient legends in, for instance, the Holy Grail or King Arthur's sword. There are also ironic variations on the serious use of a "MacGuffin", as shown for example in the film *Monty Python and the Holy Grail* (1975). The film structures its narrative around a knightly quest for the Holy Grail, which takes place at different times and is hilariously out of control. The online game *Kingdom Loathing* (2003) also takes a critical and humorous approach to this theme. When players give themselves a name and for example go on a quest called "TallRigatoni and the Quest for the Holy MacGuffin", they do this in the role of a 'pastamancer' called TallRigatoni.

Breaking the hero pattern

From there, it is only a small step to the many indie games of the last twenty years, in which various strategies are used to undermine the stereotypical pattern of a hero myth. In the adventure game *The Journey of the Roach* (2013), for example, two cockroaches are humorously introduced as hero and sidekick, who then deliberately go through all twelve stages of the hero's journey and always encounter rather clumsy animal contemporaries that have survived the nuclear war in the ruins of a department store. The satirical pattern of anti-heroes has been used frequently in point'n'click adventures, starting with *Maniac Mansion* (1987) and continuing through to the latest adventures such as *Psychonauts 2* (2020).

Jonathan Blow's adventure platformer *Braid* (2008) takes a different approach. Our avatar plays a hero who has to fight his way through a world of obstacles, enemies and puzzles in a jump'n'run manner to save his kidnapped princess. The game is a pastiche of Super Mario at first, but otherwise, the plot seems serious. Blow, however, hides a second layer of meaning in the game, which becomes more and more apparent over time, leaving the player wondering who the avatar really is. Finally, the player may wonder if they have been misled and have not played a hero after all, but unknowingly a criminal, who has done nothing but abuse his girlfriend. The suspense is not completely dissolved, and a further layer is revealed, which deals with the ethical behavior of science and its consequences. For a jump'n'run game this is quite a lot of food for thought. In *Braid*, Blow basically uses the hero pattern to take it to a point of complete absurdity.

Davey Wreden achieves a similar result with *The Stanley Parable* (2011). He uses a narrator from offstage to tell the player the story of Stanley. Stanley works in an office building and has the task of monitoring incoming data on a computer and pressing the appropriate buttons without asking any questions. But one day no more data arrives on the computer and Stanley doesn't know what to do. Perplexed, he starts to explore the office space and realizes that there is no-body else in the building. At this point, the story splits into different paths according to the player's choice. Players can follow the instructions of the narrator, or not. If they do not follow the instructions, the narrator will try to put them back on the right path. Further on, the narrator gets angry, doors slam in Stanley's face or he is presented with wrong clues. Stanley is the confused anti-hero who is led around by the narrator. He is given the superficial choice to take the right or the left door, but the narrator immediately takes away control of his actions. The multilinear game has a total of 19 endings, one more abstruse than the other, so that in the end more questions remain than are answered. The heroic image is broken here more than once, and the most important element in all this, besides the divisive storyline, seems to be the commenting narrator who can send Stanley astray at any time.

PATHS, STORYLINES, DECISIONS

What the *Stanley Parable* (2011) does with naturalness is not always so easy to implement in other games. The principle in *The Stanley Parable* is that each path taken finds its own end and in turn motivates the player to start the game all over again and find a different story path next time. *The Stanley Parable* (2011) achieves this on the one hand by focusing on the character Stanley, who is played from the first-person perspective after the initial cutscene, and on the other hand by focusing on the mystery of unusual situations and an extremely unreliable and bossy narrator who constantly confronts the player with the unexpected and carries them to yet another different ending.

If we want to create a multilinear story for our game, the first thing we need to be clear about is whether the player's decisions are not only meant to be cosmetic, but can have direct effects and long-term consequences on the game's story and gameplay. Or do we follow the example of many games and just pretend that the player can choose and determine the story? An important narrative mechanic for this is the planning and delimitation of the storyline: should it be linear, multilinear or nonlinear? Multilinearity is aspired to by some narrative games but claim and reality are often rather far apart. This was already apparent in point'n'click adventure games such as *The Secrets of Monkey Island* (1990), which functioned exclusively via interactive dialogs and, with up to four choices of answers in each case, suggested to the player that they hold the story in their hands and can determine the outcome. However, many dialogs led back recursively, and different endings of the story were also very rare. Nevertheless, the sequels of *Monkey Island* did indeed have short alternative endings and thus contained a pinch of multilinearity, at least in their final sequences.

Periodic attempts to establish multilinear film over the years have vividly shown how much effort is really needed to be able to tell good multilinear stories. As soon as the story fans out (*Late Shift* 2016) or is told from different perspectives (*I'm Your Man* 1992), the individual story strands become shorter, the interweaving of the strands more complex, the work more fragmented, and the flow of the storyline is no longer guaranteed in all parts of a film. *Bandersnatch* (2018) shows this in a relatively extreme form with very short sections. It builds the story around the creation of a game and makes several passes necessary in order to understand it. Games have it a little bit easier. Their decisions don't have to be so set up and immediate. But they often fail to introduce clear paths and communicate them to the player. And in most cases, the decisions made are ineffective, even meaningless and fizzle out in the end. Only open-world games offer more possibilities here, because in these fictional worlds, besides the quest lines, the player gets the option to experience stories that are not prescribed.

Some major productions of narrative games offer multilinear sections for the player or they offer different endings, such as *Resident Evil* (1996), *Heavy Rain* (2010) or *Detroit Become Human* (2018). Generally speaking, these games are difficult to make because it also means that more content has to be produced so that the connections work logically. The immediate solution is to offer certain sections of a game as multilinear areas with some diverting paths and a convergence point where the lines flow back into one storyline.

Figure 4: Multilinear areas are often simply designed with individual side quests and sections providing two or more parallel storylines that soon lead back to the main storyline.

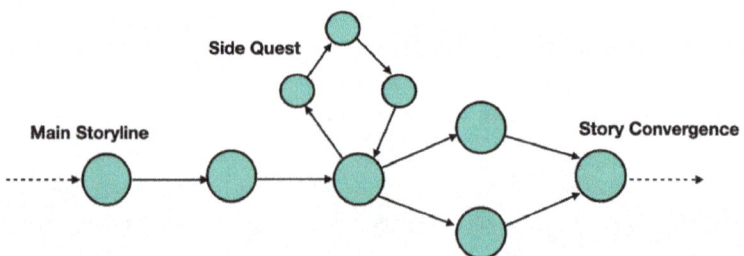

Source: Beat Suter

Among indie games, on the other hand, there is a cluster of games that have made multilinear storytelling the focus of their game. In them, the player has to make decisions all the time and each decision has a clear impact on the story. The narrative mechanics of decision-making becomes the most important mechanics of the game. In *Reigns* (2016) we swipe the respective character card to the left or right. Each card is a replication of a non-player character (NPC) with their statement or question. And this is how we generate the story of our reign, which will be shorter or longer depending on the cleverness of our decisions. In turn, the reigns become embedded in their own history of thousand or more years, thus closing the narrative framework for the individual short stories of the player avatars' reigns.

The thoroughly multilinear game *80 Days* (2014) goes one step further and offers a stringent world the player must travel through as servant Passepartout. His master Phileas Fogg has placed a bet at the Reform Club in London. The basic story is taken from Jules Verne's novel *Around the World in Eighty Days* (1872). One game round corresponds to a journey around the world that should last 80 days or less. But the travel choices made in conversations with other passengers and with residents of the places visited, about timetables and about choosing the next possible routes on the map, turn each game round into a different journey. The decisions not only have immediate consequences, but often also some that cannot be foreseen and only become apparent later, when certain travel options open up for the player or when detours via other countries and continents have to be accepted. Each run lasts between four and six hours for the player, is unique and reveals only two percent of the whole game content. Each run may differ considerably in time and place, since it is very likely that you encounter new transport vehicles, new characters and new interlocutors. In total, the game consists of 750.000 words and over 150 cities and thus confirms the assumption that real multilinear games require huge amounts of content for the individual stories to be longer, rounded and of equal value.

Figure 5: 80 Days: each city offers several possibilities to travel further. On a round-the-world trip, you will certainly visit 50 cities, each with several route options, all of which lead to different routes around the world.

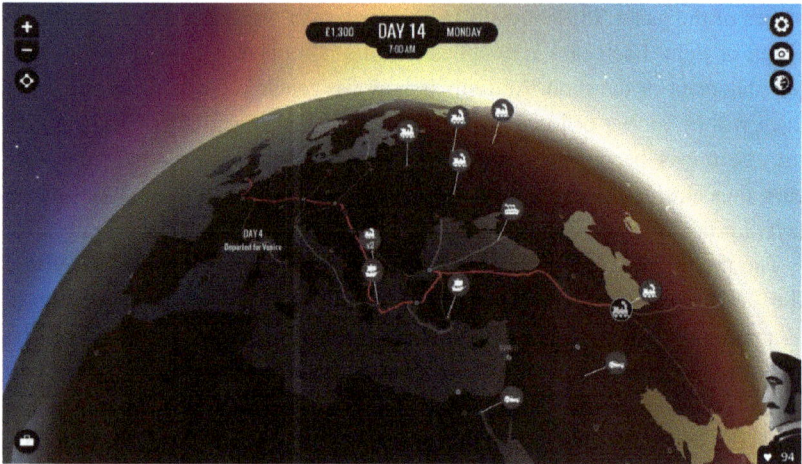

Source: screenshot (Suter)

TOP-DOWN AND BOTTOM-ALONG STORYTELLING

In many narrative games the traditional hierarchical storytelling with a plot still dominates. But generative storytelling is increasingly intervening, creating a variety of story possibilities in the form of different small segments. For the game designer, this means that top-down storytelling mixes with bottom-up storytelling. So, there is still a main plot, which in principle consists of an exposition, a main part and a conclusion, but on the other hand, bottom-along storytelling has become more important, especially in open-world games like *Grand Theft Auto V* (2013), *Red Dead Redemption 2* (2018) and others. This means that functional and narrative mechanics are "decided, processed and performed" by the player scene by scene. The player is given decision points at (almost) every step and can now not only choose the storyline, mission and path they want to follow, but also the time and space. In some games such as *Grand Theft Auto V* it is also possible to not accept missions and quests and instead go and explore the game world on your own. However, there are limitations such as barricaded city districts that are supposed to lead you back to the path of the quests, but even the limited game-world areas offer enough possibilities to play and experience a story for yourself.

Still one of the clearest examples of successful mixing of top-down and bottom-along storytelling is the experimental game *Façade* (2005) by Andrew Stern and Michael Mateas. The two developers built an extensive architecture with a behavior language, a drama manager and a structure of "beats". Not all of the beats can be placed nonlinearly, but most of them are put together in new and different ways each time the game is played. And the beats have nonlinear bottom-along substructures: "Most beats internally have a good deal of variety of behavior, as well as the ability to mix in a large pool of global mix-ins, which comprise a full third of the overall dialog content in Façade." (Stern, August 10, 2005, 2:14 am) The player of *Façade* thus gains the ability to experience a high degree of local action at any given moment. The developers succeeded in doing this through the versatile possibilities for the composition of the beats. The characters develop credible independence in their (conversational) actions and reactions. In addition to this, the player was also supposed to have a high degree of global capacity to act. But this goal could only be achieved to a modest degree. Nevertheless, *Façade* is still considered an outstanding example of an interactive drama. In retrospect, Stern recognized that the real solution to more global agency would have been to produce more generative content. "The need for generativity and procedurality – that's probably the biggest overall lesson learned on the project." (Stern, August 10, 2005, 2:14 am)

And this brings us closer to the next narrative mechanics, generative story elements or emergent storytelling, a narrative pattern that is the current and future hope for game designers and players alike.

EMERGENT STORY

In a so-called emergent narrative, the story is no longer created by the developers, but by the system. Looking at this process from the player's perspective, it seems fair to say that the story is constructed by the player themselves through their interactions and explorations within a particular game world or environment. This type of narrative is influenced by various random game-specific factors. It is "emergent" in the sense that a narrative is created by the player as they continue playing. It is thus a kind of writing down (or recording) of the path the player takes during the game. To put it more succinctly: the narrative emerges from the gameplay. The player does not receive a prescribed story, but rather the game allows them to develop their own story based on their own experiences. This is also the big advantage of emergent stories in games: The player develops their story virtually by themselves, and they then feel like they are in charge, even if the individual characters react differently than expected or desired. Even without noticing it, the player performs interpretation work in order to distill their storyline from the individual actions and plots. This means that they are also thinking actively as they create and develop their own story.

Emergent storytelling in a game means that intricate nested systems of behaviors, relationships, events and processes must be developed. These complex systems must fit together well, but they are difficult to control because they are partly filled with random content which constantly creates new relationships. As a result, often unpredictable actions and unforeseeable events arise – with surprisingly positive but also negative outcomes.

Figure 6: Emergent storytelling is not a story written by a developer, but a set of complex intricate systems. The story emerges from the player's interactions with different subsystems that are connected to each other.

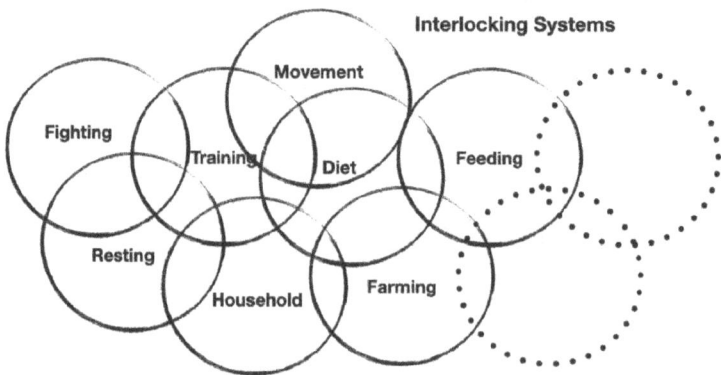

Source: Beat Suter

In the *Civilization* series, history is rewritten each time in a random world. The player can build cities and decide whether the people will live peacefully together or wage war against each other. To a certain extent, the player controls this world. They can set their own goals and progress with a chosen nation through the centuries. This seems so appealing to many that they share their experiences in the form of stories in forums. In *Civilization V* (2010), for example, you can even dominate the world from Polynesia and share this with the community in rhyme (ThatOther Jake, 2014). Each of these game stories is unique and cannot be experienced a second time in the exact same way, even if the initial parameters are set precisely in the same way. Of course, individual events and reactions of individual leaders of other nations will be similar, but the player's own experience of the storyline will not repeat itself, as it is in effect organically produced in the game rather than being prescribed in all its details by the game designers.

Minecraft (2011) is a systemic random world of blocks which is all about survival. The game doesn't come with a ready-made storyline; the player instead creates their own storyline. To survive, the player's avatar must make tools, collect food, mine resources, explore areas, construct buildings and create structures. The game does not take the lead; players set their own goals and ambitions. If they remain inactive, nothing happens. Within the crafting parameters, they create their game world and can even implement small systems like a roller coaster. While progressing through the game, the player creates more and more content for their own world and thus a story for their *Minecraft* character, which of course also contains some formative random events. Basically, games like *Minecraft* and *Civilization* provide the player with a setting of complex world systems and leave them alone with these, so that they can build their own world in peace and experience their own story. In this way the player is responsible for their own story and can identify more strongly with it. However, to an outsider, the narrative interpretations sometimes remain rather hazy.

Somewhat less imagination is needed for a narrative in *Dwarf Fortress* (2006) and *Crusader King II* (2012). Here, emergent storytelling is an important part of the gameplay; the story is written directly into logs and can be read. *Crusader King II* does this in small portions with clear descriptions of the characters and the individual events and their narrative consequences in a kind of biography of a noble family. Thus, without a predetermined plot, it is possible to build a stable prosperous republic with a dynasty in a few decades, for example, starting from Venice in the 15th century and covering the entire Dalmatian coast of Croatia. Or it is possible to conquer all of Britain from Ireland and write a successful history for an Irish dynasty. Clear story-generating mechanics and carefully incorporated historical events and references provide great support. *Crusader King II* essentially creates a generative story like the simpler *Reigns* (2016) does, but the randomness is less noticeable here and the historical lines are longer, more consistent and more credible.

The stories of *Dwarf Fortress*, on the other hand, offer no such support and achieve greater abstraction and vagueness along the lines of epic fantasy stories. Randomness as a creative force comes into play even more strongly here. And the game designer no longer has direct control over the stories, but indirect control via the content-generating systems. *Dwarf Fortress* is a hybrid simulation or roguelike that procedurally generates entire continents, populated by characters with histories stretching back centuries. It uses numerous networked systems;

with each update they become more extensive. The individual events are described with individual sentences, which are always formulated in the same way syntactically and semantically and require a high degree of adjustment for outsiders to get used to. An example:

In 362, the dwarf Kel Caastlecudgels confronted Omsos.
In 362, Omsos struck down the dwarf Kel Caastlecudgels in Oakenchannels.
In 367, the dwarf Zon Curledhandle confronted Omsos.
In 367, the dwarf Zon Curledhandle's left upper arm was ripped by Omsos.
(Kruggsmash, January 23, 2020)

Ultimately, this means that the emergent narrative flows along the mechanical connections of the game – for example, the dwarves' aggression and combat, the objects and their use, or the production of individual resources. The developers work hard on interlocking mechanics which are resonant and consistent with the outside world. This is supposed to make sure that the player can investigate almost anything. It is a bold attempt to strive for accretion and replayability. The game now contains so many networked systems that the developers have to check again and again why individual systems remain inactive in individual actions, so that they can reactivate them with a small change. Finally, the game can give rise to stories that are passed on by the community in documents of up to three hundred pages. The best example of this is the document on *Boatmurdered* (Various authors 2006-2007), which was created in effect as a Let's Play of the game *Dwarf Fortress* (2006), on the epic dwarf fortress "Boatmurdered" in which each ruler was given a single year of game time to manage the fortress before they had to hand over the reign to the next player. Visually, a game like *Dwarf Fortress* with its complex interlocking systems was only possible in a greatly reduced form. The developers Tarn and Zach Adams had decided to use a full Ascii character set. This gave and gives the game a special singularity and made it possible to connect complex systems with each other (cf. Adams: 151-160). This may discourage the uninitiated, but nevertheless, after 18 years of constant development and playing time, *Dwarf Fortress* is still a trendsetter and experimental benchmark for emergent storytelling.

However, more and more visually sophisticated 3D games are also orientated towards emergent storytelling and introduce individual complex systems that allow partial emergent storytelling. A good example is the weather system of *The Legend of Zelda: Breath of the Wild* (2017), which can not only change the environment significantly, but also has a lasting effect on individual events. When it rains heavily, the slopes become so slippery that Link can no longer get up the mountain and has to find another route. Also, some weapons are then no longer usable or have to be discarded immediately to prevent them from attracting lightning. A system like the Zelda weather system therefore influences other networked systems and makes some events more unpredictable and diverse. Players like to research this kind of unpredictability and use it to their advantage. For example, in *The Legends of Zelda: Breath of the Wild*, as in other games, it is possible to lure individual opponents within reach of each other and when they meet, they then fight each other and the player is able to just watch and move on unscathed. The game is full of such complex systems that can change the respective current events in a lasting way. Nevertheless, this doesn't alter anything about the epical framing story around Zelda, which the player is allowed to uncover with their avatar Link.

CONCLUSION

The patterns of storytelling in video games can be very different as these games have their own mechanics, formats, premises and structures. Over the years, more and more patterns have been added. However, the use and strategic application of individual patterns are always connected with the choice of genre or the approach to a genre for the game that is to be developed. While a game like *The Witcher 3: Wild Hunt* (2016) uses all the patterns and strategies mentioned above, indie games apply individual patterns or put them in the foreground in a very specific way, thus creating a clear narrative focus for the player. For instance, *80 Days* (2014) puts the choice of the itinerary at the center of the storytelling process, *Braid* (2008) focuses on rewinding actions for gameplay and story, *The Stanley Parable* (2011) tries to destroy the hero myth by means of a commentator and show different outcomes, *The Last Guardian* (2016) focuses on empathy and cooperation between humans and animals and an intuitive environment design as a guidance system, *September 12* (2010) addresses the moral dilemma of fighting terrorists, *Crusader King II* (2012) generates entire histories for royal families and nations in the style of a narrative simulation, and *Dwarf Fortress* (2006) focuses on the dynamic generation of life stories of individual (dwarf) avatars with a strong random component.

Therefore, this article can only provide an overview and a brief introduction to the most important of the many possible narrative patterns for games. These are patterns that can also be combined and expanded and may include, for example, music and sound as narrative mechanics (cf. Polus: 91-110) or emotional character design, or even the targeted narrative use of game mechanics itself (cf.

Kocher: 299-306) – all of which outlines a topic that may need to be explored much further and more deeply.

REFERENCES

Literature

Campbell, Joseph (1949): The Hero with a Thousand Faces, New York: Pantheon Books.

Fabricatore, Carlo (2018). "Underneath and Beyond Mechanics. An activity-theoretical perspective on meaning-making in gameplay." In: Suter, Beat/Mela Kocher/René Bauer (eds.), Games and Rules. Game Mechanics for the "Magic Circle", Bielefeld: transcript, pp. 86-111.

Goffman, Erving (1986 [1974]): Frame Analysis. An Essay on the Organization of Experience, Boston: Northeastern University Press.

Heussner, Tobias (ed) (2019): The Advanced Game Narrative Toolbox, Boca Raton, Florida: CRC Press Taylor & Francis Group.

Howard, Jeff (2008): Quests. Design, Theory, and History in Games and Narratives, Wellesley, Massachusetts: A.K. Peters.

Jenkins, Henry (2004): "Game Design as Narrative Architecture." In: Noah Wardrip-Fruin/Pat Harrigan (eds.), First Person. New Media as Story, Performance, and Game, Cambridge, Massachusetts and London: MIT Press, pp. 118-130.

Letsch, Hannes (2018): "Wolfgang Walk: Storytelling in Videospielen." Interview. In: Pixelwarte, 15. September, München, 01.07.2020 (https://www.pixelwarte.de/gespraech-wolfgang-walk-storytelling-in-videospielen.html).

Propp, Vladimir (1968 [1928]): Mythology of the Folktale, Austin: University of Texas Press.

Stern, Andrew (2005): "A Few Façade Post-Release Comments." August 10, 2005, 2:14 am. In: grand TEXT auto, a Group Blog, August 9, 2005, accessed via Archive.org, 01.07.2020 (http://web.archive.org/web/20051103091712/http://grandtextauto.gatech.edu/2005/08/09/a-few-facade-post-release-comments/#more-889).

Suter, Beat (2016): "The Collective Unconscious as culprit – Archetypal projections from the unconscious (per Carl Jung and Joseph Campbell) in video games (and film)." In: Steven Brock Schafer (ed.), Exploring the Collective Unconscious in a Digital Age, Seattle: IGI Global.

Suter, Beat/Kocher, Mela/ Bauer, René (eds.) (2018): Games and Rules. Game Mechanics for the "Magic Circle", Bielefeld: transcript.

Various authors (2006-2007): "Dwarf Fortress – Boatmurdered." In: Let's Play Archive, 01.07.2020 (https://b.goeswhere.com/Dwarf_Fortress_-_Boatmur dered.pdf).

Verne, Jules (1874 [1872]): Around the World in Eighty Days. Project Guten-berg Ebook, released May 15, 2008 (http://www.gutenberg.org/files/103/ 103-h/103-h.htm).

Vogler, Christoph (1992): The Writer's Journey: Mythic Structure for Storytel-lers and Screenwriters, Studio City, California: Michael Wiese Productions.

Games

80 Days, Inkle, Inkle, 2014.

BioShock, 2K Boston and 2K Australia, 2K Games, 2007.

Braid, Jonathan Blow, Number None, 2008.

Candy Crush Saga, King, King, 2012.

Civilization V, Firaxis Games, 2K Games, 2010.

Crusader Kings II, Paradox Development Studios, Paradox Interactive, 2012.

Detroit Become Human, Quantic Dream, Sony Interactive, 2018.

Donkey Kong, Nintendo, Nintendo, 1981.

Dwarf Fortress, Tarn Adams/Zach Adams, Bay 12 Games, 2006-2020.

Façade, Andrew Stern/Michael Mateas, Procedural Arts, 2005.

Gunpey, Koto Laboratory, Bandai, 1999/2006.

Grand Theft Auto V, Rockstar North, Rockstar Games, 2013.

Heavy Rain, Quantic Dream, Sony Computer Entertainment, 2010.

Inside, Playdead, Playdead, 2016.

Journey, Thatgamecompany, Annapurna Interactive, 2012.

Journey of a Roach, Koboldgames, Daedalic, 2013.

Kingdom Loathing, Asymmetric Publications, Asymmetric Publications, 2003.

Maniac Mansion, Lucasfilm Games, Lucasfilm Games, 1987.

Mario Kart 8, Nintendo, Nintendo, 2014.

Minecraft, Mojang Studios, Mojang Studios, 2011.

Pac-Man, Namco, Midway Games, 1980.

Prince of Persia, Jordan Mechner, Broderbund, 1989.

Psychonauts 2, Double Fine, Xbox Game Studios, 2020.

Puyo Pop Fever, Sonic Team, Sega, 2003.

Red Dead Redemption 2, Rockstar North, Rockstar Games, 2008.

Reigns, Nerial, Devolver Digital, 2016.

Resident Evil, Capcom, Capcom, 1996.

September 12, Gonzalo Frasca, Newsgaming, 2010.

Space Invaders, Taito, Midway Games, 1978.

Street Fighter, Capcom, Bandai, 1987.

Super Mario Bros., Nintendo, Nintendo, 1985.

Tekken, Bandai Namco Studios, Bandai Namco Entertainment, 1994.

Tetris, Nintendo, Nintendo, 1989.

The Last Guardian, Team Ico, SIE Japan Studios, Sony, 2016.

The Last of Us, Naughty Dog, Sony, 2014.

The Legend of Zelda, Nintendo, Nintendo, 1986.

The Legend of Zelda: Breath of the Wild, Nintendo, Nintendo, 2017.

The Secret of Monkey Island, Lucasfilm Games, Lucasfilm Games, 1990.

The Stanley Parable, Galactic Café, Galactic Café, 2011.

The Witcher, CD Projekt Red, CD Projekt, 2007.

The Witcher 3: Wild Hunt, CD Projekt Red, CD Projekt, 2016.

The Witness, Jonathan Blow, Thekla Inc., 2016.

Tom Clancy's The Division 2, Massive Entertainment, Ubisoft, 2019.

Tomb Raider, Core Design, Eidos Interactive, 1996.

Videos

Brown, Mark: How Level Design can tell a Story, YouTube, 11.03.2020 (https://www.youtube.com/watch?v=RwlnCn2EB9o).

Kruggsmash: Dwarf Fortress: Legendary Stories, YouTube, 23.01.2020 (https://www.youtube.com/watch?v=98CnBDoyS5I).

ThatOther Jake: Civ 5 in 5 Mins: How to Get Happiness – Polynesia Civilization V BNW LP Summary, YouTube, 30.03.2014 (https://www.youtube.com/watch?v=UDFJx2HJ8RM).

Movies

Bandersnatch (2018): David Slade, House of Tomorrow, Netflix.

I'm Your Man (1992): Bob Bejan, Interfilm Technologies.

Late Shift (2016): Tobias Weber, CtrlMovie, Wales Interactive.

Monty Python and the Holy Grail (1975): Terry Gillian and Terry Jones, Python Pictures.

Teaching Narrative Design

On the Importance of Narrative Game Mechanics

Teun Dubbelman

INTRODUCTION

For fifteen years now, I have been teaching the design and analysis of computer games. Although my approach and focus have changed over the years, I have always had a strong interest in the narrative potential of game mechanics. In my 2016 paper for the annual ICIDS conference, I coined the term *narrative game mechanics* to describe mechanics that "invite agents, including the player, to perform actions that support the construction of engaging stories and fictional worlds in the embodied mind of the player" (Dubbelman 2016: 43). The reason why I have developed the idea of narrative game mechanics can be found in my teaching experiences.

In my narrative design classes, I have noticed that students are not used to looking at mechanics from a narrative angle, and often expect lessons on game writing instead of game design. Also, when a team of students want to create a narrative game on their own, they often struggle. Without guidance, the following usually happens: Within the team, one or two students are *into* narrative, meaning, they like to write. These students work on the game script and the worldbuilding bible. They write the storyline, create the characters with their backstories and work out the details of the game's imaginary world. Other students, often designers without a specific interest in storytelling, take the responsibility for designing the mechanics. In most cases, they copy mechanics from a genre they love, and add some novel twist.

When designing the mechanics, the narrative, created by the other students, is never really taken into account. Frequently, the narrative is developed separately from the mechanics, and is simply added to the game, at some point in time, through (spoken) in-game texts and cutscenes. In this way, narrative becomes an afterthought, or simply a nice but expandable add-on. The mechanics do not really rely on the narrative; one can simply change the backstory, and the mechanics will still make sense.

For me as a teacher, this situation poses a considerable challenge. I want my students to come up with unusual designs, but with their design approach, the resulting games are often similar to existing games, just with different (and interchangeable) narrative backdrops. It is important to teach students a more integrated approach, showing them how mechanics can be used as a dynamic narrative device, alongside other narrative devices, like dialogues or cutscenes, to create engaging narrative experiences. I want them, for example, to discover how, in the design process, original storylines could lead to unexpected mechanics, and vice versa, that novel mechanics might produce surprising storylines.

To accomplish this, I have built my classes around the notion of narrative game mechanics, and developed tools to help students connect mechanics and authored narrative in practice.

As argued in previous publications, narrative design is still underdeveloped as a creative discipline, and lacks shared vocabulary, methods and tools (Koenitz/Dubbelman/Knoller/Roth 2016; Dubbelman/Roth/Koenitz 2018). By sharing my approach, I hope to inspire other teachers, and by doing so, contribute to their educational efforts and the advancement of the discipline in general.

First, the article will discuss the notion of narrative game mechanics, and its theoretical groundings. Second, it will showcase the Narrative Design Canvas as a practical instrument for teaching narrative design. This canvas can be used by students to analyze and design narrative games. It helps them to recognize and establish a connection between a game's written narrative (expressed for example in dialogues and cutscenes) and a game's mechanics. The article concludes with a closer look at the game *Brothers: A Tale of Two Sons*. Using the canvas, the game's narrative design will be analyzed. This analysis reveals how the game succeeds in creating an engaging narrative experience by articulating developments in the authored storyline through changes in the game mechanics.

COGNITIVE NARRATOLOGY

To understand how mechanics can function as a narrative device, it is important to first explain my understanding of the term *narrative*. Following the work of cognitive narratologists like Marie-Laure Ryan and David Herman, I approach narrative as a cognitive frame for meaning-making. This cognitive understanding allows me to address the arguments from ludologists in game studies against theorizing games as a narrative medium. One of the most convincing arguments is based on the apparent differences in formal properties between games and established narrative media, like books or movies (Eskelinen 2001; Juul 2001). Games are interactive systems, and consequently produce dynamic output. In contrast, books and movies lack this interactivity, and have static output. To put it simply, a movie shows the same images every time it is played, and a game, through system and player, does not.

When you look at these differences from a traditional understanding of narrative, one could indeed make the argument that games are unsuitable as a narrative medium. According to Marie-Laure Ryan, in traditional narratology, the term *narrative* is seen as being synonymous with the term *recounting* or "telling somebody else that something happened" (2004: 13). Ryan recognizes this traditional approach to narrative in the work of many ludologists (2006: 184). Indeed, with this particular understanding of narrative in mind, the formal properties of books and movies are better suited for narrative purposes. That is, their static output makes it easier to recount; to communicate 'this happened, then this happened, then this happened, etc.'.

However, when embracing an alternative, cognitive understanding of narrative, this argument no longer holds. If you understand narrative as a mental process of meaning-making, the output of a narrative medium does not necessarily have to be static. The formal properties of a medium do not have to be suited for explicitly communicating 'this happened, then this happened, then this happened, etc.', because the causal connections between events can be made cognitively by the user. The player is actively constructing a narrative, based on their personal engagement with the game's imaginary world. Again, my understanding of narrative stems from cognitive narratology, and echoes the work of David Herman, who understands narrative as a "forgiving, flexible cognitive frame for constructing, communicating, and reconstructing mentally projected worlds" (2002: 49). In order to make sense of the presented world, the characters that inhabit it, the events that take place, and the player's own goals, roles and position, the player is actively constructing and re-reconstructing a meaningful, mental narrative.

It is important to emphasize that this construction does not happen after the fact (retelling), but in real time, in the moment of acting (Graesser/Olde/Klettke 2002). As emphasized in narrative comprehension theory, mental narrativization is a real-time process in which readers are continuously accessing how the status of the narrative (of the world, the characters, the conflict, etc.) changes through the depicted events: "[…] the mental representation of a narrative can be thought of as a complex network of states and events tied together by causal relations." (Fletcher/Lucas/Baron 1999: 195) Likewise, when playing a game, players are continuously updating their understanding – their narrative – of the game's imaginary world.

To sum up, although there are apparent differences in the formal properties of movies and games, both can trigger processes of narrativization. Whether I watch a movie or play a game, in both instances, a narrative can be constructed in my mind. Indeed, these narratives are not necessarily similar and can have different qualities, but they can both be engaging and recognizable as narrative. Thus, from a cognitive perspective, narrative is not in the work itself, but in the mind of the user. Users are actively constructing a narrative while mentally (and physically) engaging with a specific work (Herman 2009). This process of narrativization happens even when there is no authorial narrative intention behind a work. One can find a story in a painting, even though the painter never aspired to tell it.

But are all games narrative games then? According to Ryan, we can still describe certain works as narrative works, or better, as being more narrative-driven, because they – often deliberately, but sometimes unintentionally – trigger more narrativization than others. Ryan calls this the property of "possessing narrativity" (2004: 9-10). For games, the same applies. When playing a game, a narrative can be triggered in my mind's eye, even though the designers never had any narrative intentions. We should, however, reserve the term narrative games or narrative-driven games for those games where the design is (intentionally) catered towards triggering an engaging narrative in the player's embodied mind.

NARRATIVE GAMES

When looking at narrative games, we can observe a great variety in how these games try to evoke mental narratives. Some games rely heavily on a pre-authored storyline, taking the player through a more or less predefined narrative path (e.g. *Last of Us*). Other games leave more room for the player to explore and to direct the course of the narrative, for example through branching structures (e.g. *The Walking Dead*), or alternatively, through emergent structures (e.g. *Middle-earth: Shadow of Mordor*).

Regardless of how games try to trigger processes of narrativization, in each case, mechanics and rules play a key role. As also recognized by Salen and Zimmerman: "[...] it is the dynamic structures of games, their emergent complexity, their participatory mechanisms, their experiential rhythms and patterns, which are key to understanding how games construct narrative experiences." (2003: 382-383) Whether a game relies on a predefined narrative path, or uses branching storylines, or creates a narrative experience through emergent structures, in each case the mechanics, in tandem with other narrative devices, are responsible for the overall narrative experience.

When we look at the current game industry, some of these narrative devices have already been brought to fruition. For example, many of the existing critically acclaimed narrative-driven games have perfected the device of environmental storytelling, also known as narrative architecture (Jenkins 2004; Nitsche 2008). In games like *Firewatch*, *What Remains of Edith Finch* and *Everybody's Gone to the Rapture*, the environment is cleverly used to communicate relevant narrative information, such as backstory, conflict and character personalities.

Alternatively, popular games like *Until Dawn* or Telltale's *Game of Thrones* make extensive use of on-screen choice prompts. At specific moments during the game, the system presents the player with a limited set of predefined choices in form of prompts on the screen. These can be mundane, like choosing which road to take, or they can be more dramatic, like deciding which character perishes.

Unlike environmental storytelling and on-screen choice prompts, narrative game mechanics are still underdeveloped in the industry, and underexamined in academia. To counter this, I have conducted additional research on the topic (Dubbelman 2017), and used the outcomes to develop the aforementioned tools for aspiring game designers. One of these tools, the Narrative Design Canvas, is discussed below.

NARRATIVE DESIGN CANVAS

The Narrative Design Canvas (Figure 1) has been developed to facilitate discussions between students about the design of narrative games, specifically regarding the connection between the intended player experience, the interaction possibilities and the written narrative. The games under scrutiny can be either existing games, analyzed in the classroom, or games that the students work on in their projects. By facilitating design discussions, the canvas tries to break the students' habit of focusing solely on the written narrative, or alternatively, solely on gameplay, as explained in the introduction.

When working on their own projects, students mainly use the canvas during the concepting phase. Before turning to the canvas, students have already gone through an ideation phase, and have chosen the most promising idea. This idea is then written at the top of the canvas. Subsequently, students start working on the canvas, following this basic rule: they can start on any field of the canvas, but are required to fill in the other two fields on the same horizontal level, before moving up or down the canvas.

Figure 1: Narrative Design Canvas.[1]

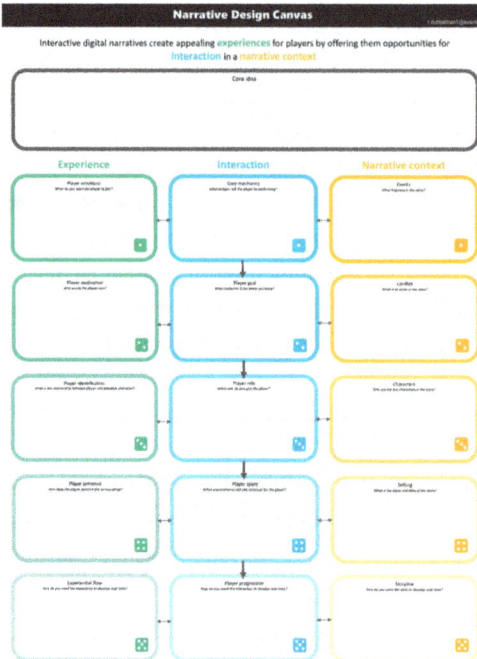

Source: Teun Dubbelman

The canvas has three pillars: experience, interaction and narrative context. Each pillar has five key elements. In the experience pillar they are: player emotion, player motivation, player identification, player presence and experiential flow; in the interaction pillar: core mechanics, player goal, player role, player space and player progression; and in the narrative context pillar: events, conflict, characters, setting and storyline.

---

1   For the pdf and the instructions, see: https://www.researchgate.net/publication/3438
     58640_Narrative_Design_Canvas.

As mentioned, students are only allowed to work horizontally, not vertically. For example, students with an interest in narrative must not work solely on the narrative context and only write down the events, characters, conflict, setting and storyline of the game. They may start with one of these elements, but before continuing to another narrative field, they need to fill in the adjacent fields of the experience and interaction pillar. For example, students may start by writing down the main events of the game, but before moving on to another narrative field, they need to write down the core mechanics and the core emotional experience of the game first.

In this way, the canvas tries to guide the creative thought process of students towards a more integrated approach. Other teams might start with the core mechanics or the core emotional experience. Regardless of this, in each case, students are invited to think about the interconnection between the three pillars, asking themselves questions such as: what kind of emotions do we want to evoke; what kind of mechanics do we need for this; and what kind of events do these mechanics imply? Or, what kind of events do we want in our game; what kind of mechanics do we need to create these events; and what kind of emotions could these events carry?

As such, the canvas is primarily an educational tool, not a design tool. Although the canvas may also support the actual design process, the purpose of the canvas is to teach students a creative mindset that helps them to create engaging narrative games; games in which the narrative experience as envisioned by the students is not only expressed in dialogues or cutscenes, but also arises from the interplay between mechanics and the other narrative devices in the game. When explaining the canvas to students, it helps to show them examples of such games. It goes beyond the scope of this article to address each field on the canvas, and the interconnectedness between these fields, in detail, so I will only discuss the bottom of the canvas, using one game as an example.

At the bottom of the canvas, we find the following three fields: experiential flow (the experience pillar), player progression (the interaction pillar) and storyline (the narrative context pillar). Although the connection between these three horizontal fields might not be immediately obvious, upon closer examination the connecting element appears to be time, or more precisely, development over time. To make this clear to students, each field contains a short question for them to answer, namely:

- *Experiential Flow: How do you want the experience to develop over time?*
- *Player Progression: How do you want the interaction to develop over time?*
- *Storyline: How do you want the story to develop over time?*

Students need to answer all three questions before moving further up or down the canvas. Again, by asking the students to answer all three questions, the canvas lets them consider the interplay between experience, interaction and narrative; something they probably would not do without the canvas. For example, it has become common practice in game design to give players more gameplay possibilities as a game progresses, mainly to keep them interested and challenged (Björk/Holopainen 2005). Because students are used to this convention, they copy it, often without really considering why they incorporate it into their designs. With the canvas, they are invited to reflect on their design decisions. It allows them to consider that changes in gameplay might also be employed for narrative purposes, and that changes in gameplay can carry narrative meaning and create emotional impact.

A game that does this particularly well is *Brothers: A Tale of Two Sons*. When discussing the bottom of the canvas in class, I usually examine the game together with students. In the next section, I share this analysis and explain how the game succeeds in creating an engaging narrative experience by articulating developments in the authored storyline through changes in the game mechanics.

BROTHERS: A TALE OF TWO SONS

Brothers: A Tale of Two Sons is a third-person adventure game released in 2013 by Swedish game company Starbreeze Studios. Since it appeared, the game has received strong critical acclaim, particularly because of its unorthodox narrative design (Roth/Nuenen/Koenitz 2018). As will be shown, the game cleverly uses game mechanics to express narrative meaning, in tandem with cutscenes and spoken text. It deliberately changes the mechanics over time to articulate key moments in the authored storyline, and by doing so, heightens their emotional impact.

The story of the game deals with two brothers who leave their village on a quest to find a cure for their dying father. At the start, the player is introduced to the controls of the game. The controller's left thumbstick and trigger button are used to direct the older brother, while the controller's right thumbstick and trigger button are used to direct the younger brother. With the thumbsticks, the player guides the movement of the brothers, and with the triggers, their interaction with the environment. To overcome obstacles in the game, the player needs to control both brothers at the same time and make use of their unique abilities. For example, the older brother is strong and can move objects, while the younger brother is little and can pass through small openings. It soon becomes clear that the two brothers need each other in order to survive and fulfil their quest.

However, at some point in the storyline, the older brother dies (mainly shown in a cutscene). Instead of using the two sides of the controller, the player now only uses the right side, and the left stick and trigger of the older brother become obsolete. Later in the storyline, the younger brother needs to cross a river but is scared to go into the water by himself (shown in a cutscene). When the player directs the younger brother into the water, he refuses to swim. Before losing his older brother, the younger brother crossed water by climbing on his older sibling's back. Only when the player presses the left trigger again (belonging to the older brother), does the younger brother find the courage to cross the river.

Table 1: Progression in Two Brothers: A Tale of Two Sons.

Chapter	I	II	III
Storyline	Brothers on quest to rescue father (brothers physically together)	Older brother dies (younger brother alone)	Younger brother crosses the river to complete quest (brothers spiritually together)
Mechanics	Swim-mechanic I	Deprivation of swim-mechanic I	Swim-mechanic II
Controls	Left stick and trigger to control the older brother; Right stick and trigger to control the younger brother	Right stick and trigger to control the younger brother	Right stick and left trigger to control the younger brother

As can be seen in the figure above (Table 1), the game deliberately changes its mechanics (and associated control scheme) to articulate key moments in the storyline. At the beginning of the game, the repetitive act of simultaneously manipulating the left and the right side of the controller in order to navigate the two brothers through various perilous environments, like rivers, becomes synonymous with the close bond between the two and their mutually dependent relationship. When the older brother dies, the younger one suddenly finds himself alone. The feeling of loss and loneliness felt by the latter is communicated to the player by taking away the need to control the left stick and trigger. Having become accustomed to operating both the left and the right side of the controller, and both characters, this change can indeed evoke a strong sensation in players that something is missing. When the player finally reaches the river, and the younger brother does not want to continue alone because he fears the water, the loss of the older brother is again emphasized. When the player finds out what to do – namely, that they need to press the left trigger – the older brother becomes present again, not in body, but in spirit. This marks an emotional moment in the storyline, where the younger brother through the memory of his older sibling, finds the strength to continue and complete their joint quest. Although the older brother is not physically there, the younger one, with the spiritual guidance of his older brother, succeeds in crossing the river by himself. This moment is emphasized by spoken text: the younger brother briefly hears the voice of his departed sibling. Shortly after this, he finishes the quest they embarked upon together.

To summarize, *Brothers: A Tale of Two Sons* deliberately utilizes game mechanics for narrative purposes. By changing the controls and mechanics over time, the game moves towards an emotional climax in the authored storyline, where the younger brother, by remembering his older sibling and feeling his presence, finds the strength to continue.

CONCLUSION

In this article, I have discussed an approach to teaching narrative design for games that is centered around the notion of narrative game mechanics. The purpose of this approach is to teach students a creative mindset that helps them to create engaging narrative games; games in which the narrative experience as envisioned by the students is not only expressed in dialogues or cutscenes, but also arises from the interplay between mechanics and the other narrative devices in the game.

Not only in education, but also in the game industry, the attention to game mechanics in narrative design is still too limited. Narrative design as a distinct practice is relatively new, and with it, the position of narrative designer. Many of the larger companies today employ narrative designers. Their responsibilities differ from studio to studio, but generally focus on game writing or quest design, and not on the design of mechanics. Although some companies try to align gameplay and narrative by establishing a close collaboration between game designers and narrative designers, this approach is vulnerable. Especially in the case of companies who set out to create narrative games, it is almost impossible to separate the process of designing mechanics from the process of developing a game's narrative (or quests for that matter).

An important step towards a more integrated approach of narrative design in the industry would be to make future game developers (game designers as well as narrative designers) more sensitive to the narrative potential of game mechanics. In this article, I have shared ideas and tools for achieving this, with the hope of making a minor contribution to the promising practice of narrative design for games.

REFERENCES

Literature

Björk, Staffan/Holopainen, Jussi (2005): Patterns in Game Design, Boston: Charles River Media.

Dubbelman, Teun (2016): "Narrative Game Mechanics." In: Frank Nack/Andrew S. Gordon (eds.), Interactive Storytelling, Heidelberg: Springer, pp. 39-50.

Dubbelman, Teun (2017): "Repetition, Reward and Mastery: The Value of Game Design Patterns for the Analysis of Narrative Game Mechanics." In: Nuno Nunes/Ian Oakley/Valentina Nisi (eds.), Interactive Storytelling, Heidelberg: Springer, pp. 286-289.

Dubbelman, Teun/Roth, Christian/Koenitz, Hartmut (2018): "Interactive Digital Narratives (IDN) for Change: Educational Approaches and Challenges in a Project Focused on Migration." In: Rebecca Rouse/Hartmut Koenitz/Mads Haahr (eds.), Interactive Storytelling, Heidelberg: Springer, pp. 591-602.

Eskelinen, Markku (2001): "The Gaming Situation." In: Espen Aarseth/Jessica Enevold/Markku Eskelinen/Maria Gedoz Tiep (eds.), Game Studies: The International Journal of Computer Game Research 1/1 (http://www.game studies.org/0101/eskelinen/).

Fletcher, Charles/Lucas, Sarah/Baron, Corinne (1999): "Comprehension of Mathematical Proofs." In: Susan Goldman/Arthur Graesser/Paul van den Broek (eds.), Narrative Comprehension, Causality, and Coherence: Essays in Honor of Tom Trabasso, London: Lawrence Erlbaum Associates Publishers, pp. 195-208.

Graesser, Arthur/Olde, Brent/Klettke, Bianca (2002): "How Does the Mind Construct and Represent Stories?" In: Melanie Green/Jeffrey Strange/Timothy

Brock (eds.), Narrative Impact: Social and Cognitive Foundations, Mahwah: Lawrence Erlbaum Associates, pp. 229-262.

Herman, David (2002): Story Logic: Problems and Possibilities of Narrative, Lincoln: University of Nebraska Press.

Herman, David (2009): Basic Elements of Narrative, Chichester: Wiley-Blackwell.

Jenkins, Henry (2004): "Game Design as Narrative Architecture." In: Noah Wardrip-Fruin/Pat Harrigan (eds.), First Person: New Media as Story, Performance, and Game, Cambridge, Massachusetts: MIT Press, pp. 118-130.

Juul, Jesper (2001): "Games Telling Stories? A Brief Note on Games and Narratives." In: Espen Aarseth/Jessica Enevold/Markku Eskelinen/Maria Gedoz Tiep (eds.), Game Studies: The International Journal of Computer Game Research 1/1 (http://www.gamestudies.org/0101/juul-gts/).

Koenitz, Hartmut/Dubbelman, Teun/Knoller, Noam/Roth, Christian (2016): "An Integrated and Iterative Research Direction for Interactive Digital Narrative." In: Frank Nack/Andrew S. Gordon (eds.), Interactive Storytelling, Heidelberg: Springer, pp. 51-60.

Nitsche, Michael (2008): Video Game Spaces: Image, Play, and Structure in 3D Game Worlds, Cambridge, Massachusetts: MIT Press.

Roth, Christian/Nuenen, Tom/Koenitz, Hartmut (2018): "Ludonarrative Hermeneutics: A Way Out and the Narrative Paradox." In: Rebecca Rouse/Hartmut Koenitz/Mads Haahr (eds.), Interactive Storytelling, Heidelberg: Springer, pp. 93-106.

Ryan, Marie-Laure (2004): Narrative across Media: The Languages of Storytelling, Lincoln: University of Nebraska Press.

Ryan, Marie-Laure (2006): Avatars of Story, Minneapolis: University of Minnesota Press.

Salen, Katie/Zimmerman, Eric (2003): Rules of Play: Game Design Fundamentals, Cambridge, Massachusetts: MIT Press.

Games

Brothers: A Tale of Two Sons, Starbreeze Studios, 505 Games, 2013.

The Narrative Role of Sound in Games

Chris Polus

Sound is a weird beast. You mostly can't see it. It is not really tangible. Yet, it is everywhere. It is much easier to close your eyes if you don't want to see something than to close your ears if you don't want to hear something. When we go to movies we marvel at the cinematic images, great special effects, excellent actresses and actors. Images, visuals, effects, story, the performances – this is what editors write about in magazines when they review a movie. Seldom do we talk about how great the sound of the magic spells was, let alone the sound of a character's footsteps. Sound, for the most part, is just there. Invisible. Unnoticed. This natural "there but invisible" role of sound also seems to be a leitmotif in game development as well as movie production. Sound in many cases is merely an afterthought. Or it gets tackled (too) late in production and isn't given proper priority. And yet, try watching a movie with the sound turned off. It seems distant. Uninteresting. Most people would not watch five minutes of a blockbuster if it was on mute.

Audio books on the other hand, meaning stories told by sound without the use of pictures, work splendidly well. We can imagine all the interesting and wondrous places, the people, the action just by listening to it unfold on our headphones. Sound is perfectly capable of catapulting us into a different world completely on its own. No images needed.

Why is that so? Why does sound work on its own while a movie on mute does not? What is the narrative power of sound? How does it work and why does it evoke the power of imagination?

This chapter is about getting to the bottom of this mystery by analyzing the narrative power of sound. Before we do though, I want to clarify that by sound I mean sound effects, sound ambiences. Things, places, motions that make sound. I explicitly exclude music from this analysis. That is a totally different beast and chapter altogether.

To further our understanding of both sound and the following analysis, I will start with a topic we are all well familiar with: movies. From that common ground our journey continues to games and what it is that sets them apart from movies. We will then look at the practical functions sound fulfils and why it is able to do so. This understanding will help us to see the narrative qualities of sound in a new light. I am excited to take you on this journey, let's go.

SOUND IN FILM VS. SOUND IN GAMES

Although sound in film is a hugely complex manual as well as artistic undertaking, it makes a good starting point for our journey to understand sound in games.

In movies, sound mostly represents what is on the screen. Sound documents the action the audience sees. Sound in film is very direct. Only on very rare occasions would one hear sounds that are off to the side or behind the audience, given a properly equipped 5.1 sound system. The reason is that sound attracts attention. If there was a significant sound behind the audience, people would want to turn around and see what is there. But in a film, there is nothing behind them. So these sounds only confuse the audience and are therefore omitted.

As far as documenting the action goes, sound engineers sometimes go too far. There are running jokes that everything entering the screen should make a sound to "announce" itself. And sometimes this is taken to extremes. Pay attention next time you watch a movie. If there is a scene on a street and someone drives by with a bike, you will probably hear the bike bell. Even though nobody would ring the bell in that situation. If a cat enters the picture, you will hear a meow. If a car drives by, it honks. And so on.

A big advantage of sound in movies is that every sound can be hand-crafted to fit the scene, the moment, the individual event down to the millisecond. Foley artists in sound studios often perform sound with objects in the same way that musicians perform music with their instruments. Making every sound unique. This only needs to be done once as the movie sounds identical every time somebody watches it.

This is not the case with games. Games not only provide a suitable sonic ambience and document the action on a computer screen. Sound in games has a very active role in directing players and making them aware of their surroundings.

Unlike in movies, in games players *can* turn around and investigate an odd sound. As such, sound is used to communicate many things. Odd sounds draw the players' attention and guide them to a spot they might have missed. Monsters vocalize to make players aware they are around so they don't walk into a fight unprepared. The user interface sometimes triggers sounds when the health bar drops to a low level in order to signal danger. These sounds carry information and tell players what is about to happen so they in turn can decide what to do next. If a low-health warning is played, they might turn around and try to flee the fight. On the other hand, when they have just consumed a double-damage power-up they might want to make use of the time it is active. When there is a magical sound, they might want to investigate to find a hidden collectible.

Furthermore, sound cannot be performed, recorded and placed once in the right spot in time. In an interactive medium such as a computer game, players are the directors. They trigger scenes, sounds and events by their immediate actions. Players could decide to do nothing and stand still for hours. The ambient sound for standing around for hours cannot be recorded. It would be a huge sound file. Instead, it is made up of multiple bits: wind, random bird calls, crickets, and other environment sounds. Those bits are looped at different intervals in such a way that players have the perception of a never-ending, ever evolving and changing soundscape. If they stand around long enough and the game allows for it, they might even hear the soundscape change from day sounds like birds to night sounds like owls and frogs. It is all a question of the rules put into place that allow sounds to transition from one soundscape to another. From day to night. From sun to rain. Sounds in games are shorter and put together with multiple rules to create the illusion of a living, breathing world that never sounds the same twice. In fact, every sound probably only has a handful of variations and is played over and over – but in such a way that players don't notice.

Now that we have established the difference between sound for film vs. sound for games, let's look at the types of sounds in games and their influence on an interactive medium such as games.

SOUND MOTIVATORS AND HYGIENE FACTORS

During my economy studies I came across Herzberg's motivation-hygiene theory (Herzberg/Mausner/Snyderman 1959). Although partly outdated today, this theory makes some valid points, stating that job satisfaction in the workplace is dependent on motivational factors as well as hygiene factors.

Motivational factors (e.g. recognition by a superior, fulfilling work, responsibility, etc.) increase your satisfaction and give you joy and pride in your work. If these factors are present and strong, they create a sense of happiness and make you want to stay in the company. If those factors are lacking, you are neither happy nor satisfied.

Hygiene factors (e.g. the salary, working conditions, vacation etc.) are merely what you expect. Their presence does not lead to higher satisfaction. But if absent, they drag your satisfaction down.

Think about this for a minute. When hygiene factors are all present and you have a super-shiny and clean workplace, coming to work is simply "OK". Nothing more. If you are thinking about getting another job anyway, that clean workplace is not going to be high on the list of advantages that keep you in the current company. But if the workplace is really dirty, it significantly lowers your motivation to come to work at all.

On the other hand, if you are seldomly recognized by your superior, that is no reason to quit your job straightaway. If the hygiene factors are satisfactory, you might consider staying in the company. However, if you are recognized and you feel that you are making positive contributions within your team, your morale gets a substantial boost. You are working in a company that can probably count on your loyalty for a long time.

I believe these categorizations are also applicable to sound. There are hygiene sounds that have to be there because their absence would adversely affect the perception of the game. On the other hand, there are motivational sounds. If executed well, these sounds significantly boost immersion and the player's perception of the game. Additionally, there also are the "nice to have" sounds. These are sounds that are completely optional and might have a positive effect if noticed, but go unnoticed if they are not present.

HYGIENE SOUND

Hygiene sounds constitute the vast majority of sounds in a game. They absolutely have to be present in order to keep players immersed in the game. In my opinion, this is the primary goal of hygiene sounds: to maintain immersion.

Games are masterpieces of engineering and artistry. A huge amount of work goes into every discipline: game design, story, art, animation, programming, sound and music, each of them utilizing countless iterations. All these disciplines have a common goal: creating a great game. And games are great when players are able forget reality. Just like a book. Once you start reading you become so immersed you can't stop and thus totally forget time. Great games might have great gameplay, a story well told, an unforgettable experience, magical moments when you finally win a hard, epic fight. But if one aspect in this mechanism of all these game development disciplines is out of place, players are quite literally jolted out of the experience. The whole building of immersion falls apart. The magic of being absorbed by a game, forgetting time: gone. All because of one element. This may be a graphical glitch. For example, in *Assassin's Creed: Unity* (2014), heads of characters disappear and you then talk to floating wigs with eyeballs. Or maybe a voice-over glitch where one of the recorded voice lines was a temporary placeholder meant to be replaced, but was accidentally retained. Thus, a character suddenly talks with a completely different voice for one sentence and then returns to normal.

Some sounds start to become annoying after a time. There may be a tiny mistake in the editing, or the repetition pattern. Or they sound great at first but are ever so slightly over the top that, after enough repetition, their effect of sounding great turns into the opposite. They start to sound annoying. As stated above (cf. "Sound in film vs. sound in games"), games heavily rely on repeated sounds, sprinkled with variations to cover that fact. The goal with repeated sound is to have enough of a variation to make it seem different, while at the same time having enough of a similarity for it to be recognizable by players as the same type of sound.

Diablo 3 (2012), for example, has excellent sound in general, but in swamp levels, when player characters walk through shallow water, there is one footstep sound which sounds dramatically different from the others in that repetition group. If a player pays attention to details such as the sound of footsteps, the immersion may potentially be broken every time this strange footstep sound is triggered.

These glitches remind players that they are not really in that fantasy world. That the thing in front of them is just a computer game.

Keeping up this immersion is what hygiene sounds are about. Every ambience, every door, every footstep has to "sound just right". It has to sound believable, realistic, as if a sound engineer was there – in the game! – and recorded the sound as it happened. If such a thing was possible …

The sad truth is, if the sound team manages to do a good job, nobody will probably notice. As noted above, "it sounds just right". Hygiene sounds don't make players feel special, they primarily prevent players from losing immersion. Allowing them to stay in the illusion. Enjoying themselves.

MOTIVATIONAL SOUNDS

Motivational sounds are rare. They are the highlights of sound work. A sound so well made that it feels great to hear it, which results in players wanting to repeat it. For example, an awesome sound of a very powerful weapon, a magic spell or a hard-to-pull-off move in a fighting game. These sounds, if designed correctly, placed correctly, catapult players into an emotional high, sometimes accompanied by thoughts such as "Whooa what just happened?! Haha, crazy! Awesome!" This type of sound.

Although I was not going to talk about music in this chapter, I shall make an exception here. *Doom* (2016) had one of the greatest intros in the history of games, combining storytelling, cutscenes, music and sound into a magical moment. After about eight minutes of gameplay, after the first few fights, seeing the Mars Station destroyed, all scientists dead, the Doom Marine (the player) steps into an elevator. During the ride, the well-known Doom theme starts playing faintly in the background and an NPC explains that he takes full responsibility for the catastrophic events on that station. The Marine, he says, has to understand that everything was done for the betterment of mankind. At this moment, the camera pans down casually to the floor of the elevator, where one of the scientists lies dead, covered in blood. Betterment of mankind, the irony! In the cutscene the Marine then destroys the screen through which the NPC talks. Publisher and developer logos fade in. Then the Doom logo, and a heavily modernized Doom theme by Mick Gordon played in full force. After the logos, we are back in the elevator, hearing the last raging beats of the music. The Doom Marine lifts up a shotgun and cocks it. This cocking is in-sync with the last beats of the music, creating an intertwined link between story, music and sound.

Star Wars Battlefront (2015), *Star Wars Battlefront 2* (2017) and *Star Wars Jedi: Fallen Order* (2019) all contain extraordinary weapon and explosion sounds. Of course, a lot of the credit has to go to Ben Burtt, the main sound designer on the original *Star Wars* movies, but the sounds were masterfully modernized and optimized for maximum impact, as well as newly created for these games. Lightsabers, laser cannons, explosions – many of them sound so good, impactful and powerful that you will want to hear them over and over. It makes you feel very powerful as a player. A big plus in a game where one is supposed to wield "The Force".

Sometimes ordinary sounds slowly make it into the realm of motivational sounds by virtue of repetition. *World of Warcraft* (2004) had distinct "quest completed" and "level up" sounds heard frequently by the players. Probably everybody who has played the game at one point would still recognize them as they are tied to the positive experience of having completed a quest or gained a level.

Baldur's Gate (1998) did not only have the sound effects of its D&D spells. Before every spell, the in-game character uttered magical words to conjure it up. Thanks to an echo effect and being spoken with great pathos, it became a landmark sound which is easily recognizable even today.

NICE-TO-HAVE SOUNDS

Sometimes I notice sounds that are nice and add to an existing atmosphere, but whose absence would not be missed. If a game already features a dense sonic atmosphere, say crickets at night, a lush wind, some owls and so on, a dog barking on a faraway farm might be added for flavor, but if it was not, nobody would notice.

So there is this category of surplus sounds that add to a certain atmosphere, yet are only small factors within an overall, greater picture. They are not crucial for its maintenance.

CONCLUSION

Putting sounds into these categories supports the notion that sound plays a very active role in games. Not only does it work as a guiding system, directing players to certain locations, it also evokes feelings of immersion. And while hygiene sounds mostly work in the same way in movies, destroying a believable illusion if they are missing, motivational sounds have a far greater effect in interactive mediums such as games. There is something about controlling the action that is absent from movies. And when there are moments in games supported or induced by motivational sound effects, it feels like one's own success. I did that. I beat the boss. I fired that big-ass gun. I did all of this!

Figure 1: Sound categories and their influence on feeling and immersion in video games.

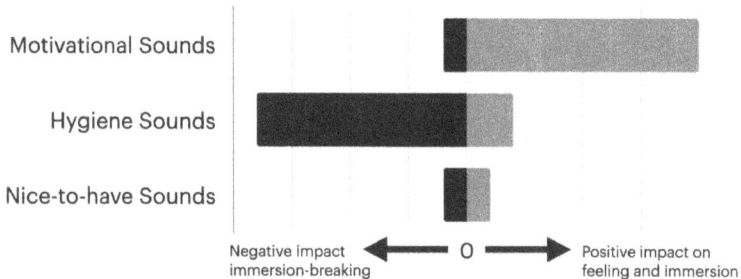

Source: Chris Polus

Every sound helps the narrative

Thus far, we have established the active role of sound in games as it guides players through a level. We have seen that sounds can be roughly categorized into hygiene sounds, motivational sounds and nice-to-have sounds, and that motivational sounds have an extraordinary power in games, a power not found in movies because they lack the interactive qualities of games. The player causes these sounds to appear, which creates a connection not possible in linear media.

Our focus in this section will be on all the things sound can tell us just by being heard. Most of the points made here will be fairly obvious. We are enveloped in sound all the time and gather information from our surroundings without even thinking about it, so that we are not aware of the extent of information we are actually obtaining through it. We take it for granted.

In my opinion, every sound adds to a narrative. A sound that does not have anything to say does not exist. Everything that happens in the physical world emits a sound. And thus, every sound tells us something about what happens. Consequently, every sound can and should be used to evoke a small, particular story.

Books are prime examples of storytelling, with a significant amount of space dedicated to descriptions of the surroundings. What time of day it is. The weather. What shoes somebody is wearing. If they are too tight. What material they are made of. If they creak or not. Sound has the power to tell this, too. Through hearing. How is sound able to do that? Let's uncover it in this part.

I will refrain from using formulas or technical terms and instead try to describe sound and what it means using examples.

Physical properties of sound

Sound has a very simple underlying physical concept. You hit your hand on a desk. The desk vibrates. The vibration is transmitted to the air. Air molecules vibrate. They travel like waves in water and reach your ear. You hear your hand hitting a desk.

Interestingly, with all the complexities and capabilities sound has in regard to storytelling, it only comprises two dimensions. One of them is the frequency, or speed, at which air vibrates. We perceive that as pitch. The higher the frequency of vibration, meaning the quicker something vibrates, the higher the pitch we hear. The other dimension is the amplitude, or force of vibration. We perceive this as loudness. The higher the amplitude of vibration, meaning air molecules moving back and forth a longer distance, the louder the sound. An explosion for example pushes air molecules a long way, even blasting away physical objects in its path. Hence an explosion is really loud.

Another well-known fact is that sound loses energy the further it travels through the air. The greater the distance from the sound, the quieter it becomes. Equipped with this knowledge, we can already make some assumptions about sound:

- *Only big things can move a lot of air to make loud sounds. Something very loud is either very close or it is very big.*
- *Something very quiet tells us it is something small or something very far away.*

Depending on how a sound changes over time, we can also perceive motion:

- *If something becomes louder, it probably comes closer.*
- *If it gets quieter, it moves further away.*
- *We can hear something passing by like the siren of an ambulance (Doppler effect).*

Information transported by the physical properties of sound:

size, distance, direction

SOUND DEFINES THE ENVIRONMENT THROUGH REVERB

When we jump into a pool on a hot summer's day, the waves we produce travel outwards in circles from the point we jumped in. When the waves hit the walls of the pool, they are reflected by the walls and move back. In that sense, just by looking at the waves and their reflections, we would be able to deduce the size and shape of the pool.

This happens to air waves in the same way. Sound is reflected by any surface it hits. A feature bats famously use to navigate in absolute darkness. The interesting part is that the surface significantly alters the properties of the sound waves. Some surfaces are highly reflective to sound, such as metal or stone. Some reflect lower frequencies and absorb higher frequencies, such as wood, thereby altering the reflected sound dramatically. Or they can absorb sound altogether, such as thick layers of cloth.

If we listen carefully, we can deduce by hearing what kind of a room we stand in. Imagine somebody talking in a bathroom with its highly reflective tiles, and you will probably know how it sounds. We can not only gauge what material the walls of a room are made of, but are also able to guess how big the room is. The bigger the room, the longer sound waves take to travel through the air, be reflected by the walls and come back to our ears. Imagine somebody talking in a bedroom vs. in a cathedral. You would most likely know which one is which.

Information transported by reverb:
material of the room's walls, size of the room

RECOGNITION OF SOUNDS

Our ears are amazing instruments that can perceive all frequencies of vibration transported through the air at the same time. The example earlier of a hand hitting a desk was simplified. In fact, the desk will not vibrate at only one frequency, but the event will spawn many frequencies simultaneously at different amplitudes.

This particular event, meaning the combination of frequencies and their loudness, forms a fingerprint of this sound. Everything that happens in our physical world produces a specific pattern of different frequencies at different levels of loudness that also change over time. However, the same things generate more or less the same frequency patterns and changes over time.

Figure 2: The frequency chart of an organ-like sound (top); you see frequency spikes at 110Hz (meaning the sound creates 110 air vibrations per second as a fundamental frequency), 220Hz, 440Hz, etc., as additional upper frequencies. The simplified fingerprint showing the frequencies and their loudness (bottom); this forms the fingerprint of an organ-like sound.

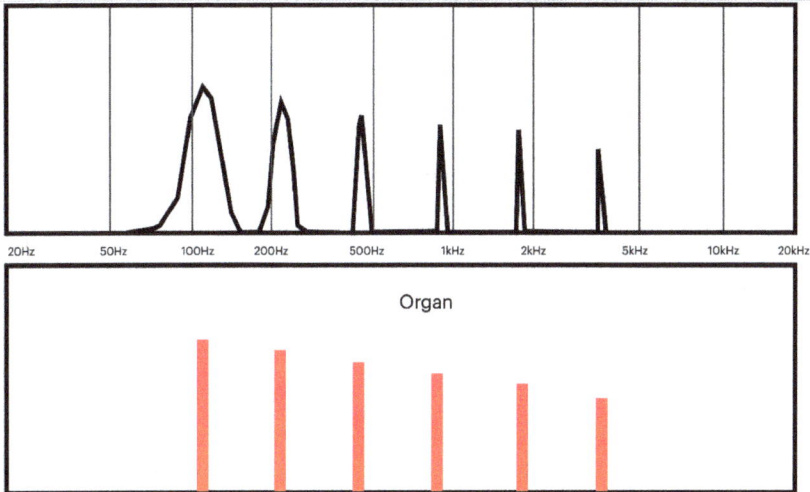

Source: Chris Polus

Figures 3-5. Simplified frequency fingerprints of a piano, flute and horn respectively. You can clearly see the differences and sometimes similarities.

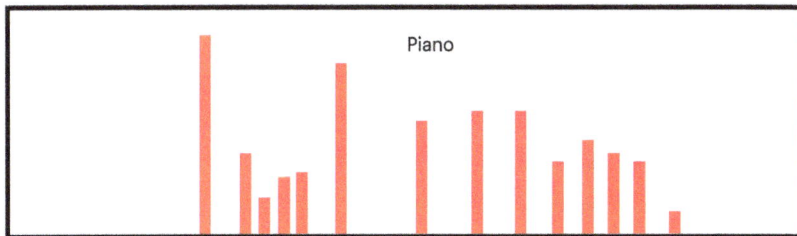

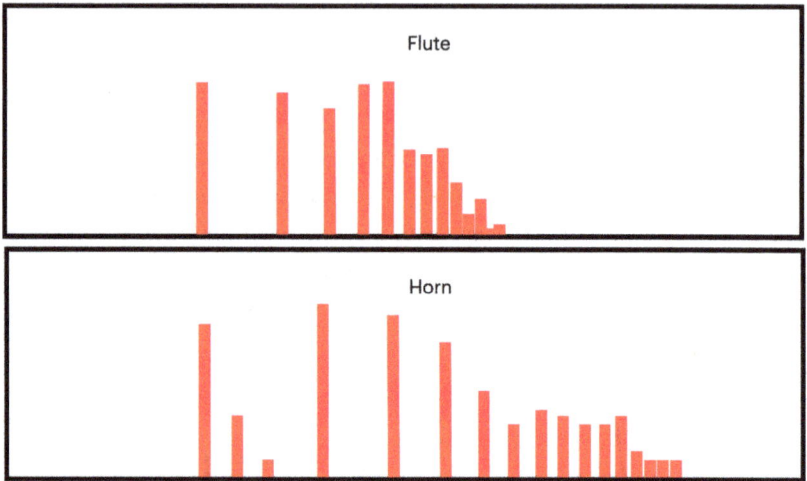

Source: Chris Polus

Now, think of somebody jumping into a pool. We can all imagine what the resulting splash could sound like. And every time a person jumps into a pool, the splash will be different. But we recognize the pattern of frequencies and can identify this sound as splashing water.

And this is what happens with everything we hear. From the moment we are born our brain perceives those frequency patterns of things happening. The voices of our parents, people walking through the room, doors opening and closing, cooking in the kitchen, people getting closer or moving away into the next room. Our brain learns to connect the sounds to what the eyes see, to the extent that we can close our eyes and still say with fair accuracy what is happening. It is something that required a lot of training in the beginning and works almost without having to think the older we get.

This means that we are able to recognize sounds because all sounds have an individual frequency pattern. A sound consists of multiple frequencies specific to this sound, and every frequency has an amplitude specific to this sound. Both frequency and amplitude change over time, sometimes significantly, but always in a similar fashion for similar kinds of sounds. This combination then makes up a fingerprint which we can distinguish from other sounds. Or to put it bluntly: We recognize sounds because we have heard them thousands of times.

Information transported by the sound event itself:

identity of the object that makes the sound

MATERIAL

Closely tied to the recognition of a sound is the identification of the material. Every material produces its own set of frequencies and amplitudes by the way it resonates. Its own sonic fingerprint! And with our growing experience we are more and more capable of recognizing what material something is made of.

Is it a wooden or plastic pen that fell on the ground? Is it a wooden or metal stick? Is it a plastic or paper sheet being shaken? Next time we hear a sound we are very likely able to tell.

Information transported by sound:

type of material

ACTIVITY

Sound carries a lot of information about what is happening. We have saved so many sound fingerprints in our heads that we recognize distinct events. We can tell if a door opens or closes. Whether it is an entrance door or a car door. Or a window. When something falls down and breaks. Or doesn't break. When there is water running in the kitchen. Or somebody takes a shower. We know exactly what context a sound originates from and can deduce what is happening.

Information transported by sound:

what happens around us

ADDITIONAL MEANINGS OF SOUND

There is yet another layer of meaning which plays a part in the recognition of sounds. It is dependent on the context we hear sounds in. We know that certain sounds only occur in a specific place. Or at a specific time.

Let's take crickets as an example. We never hear crickets in the winter. Thus, crickets tell us we must be in a warm season, and usually somewhere outside town. Birds mostly sing during the day. Owls call at night.

Church bells ring in the context of calling people to a church service. In Switzerland typically on a Saturday evening and Sunday morning. When we hear church bells we know which countries we are most likely to be in, as church bells are not common in Muslim countries, to take just one example. This means specific sounds help us determine time of day, season and place.

Let's look at another type of sound: alarms. Alarms are used to make us aware of something. Danger, a threat, or that it is time to wake up. Old-fashioned wind-up alarm clocks with mechanical bells come to mind. Or more modern digital alarm clocks with their penetrating fast-paced "beep beep beep beep". And by using the words "old-fashioned" and "more modern" respectively we again can gather information as to which decade or century we operate in. As digital or radio alarm clocks were invented around the 1940s, it is clear its sound should not be used before that time.

So, this is one alarm sound we know the meaning of – "get up for work" – but there are many other alarms. Those in buildings which give the signal to leave the premises immediately. Or the wailing alarms that are heard throughout a whole city to warn of bigger threats. This list can be expanded infinitely. We learn the context of sounds we hear and can then deduce a wealth of information from them.

Information transported by sound events:

time of day, season, place, time, decade, century, alarm types, and much more

ARTISTIC CHOICES CONCERNING SOUND

We have seen how sound is created and what kind of information and properties it carries with it. This knowledge can now be used to manipulate sound.

As stated before, we can identify sounds because we have heard them thousands of times: in different variations. We have heard thousands of different doors closing: small doors, huge doors, flimsy doors, wooden doors, creaking doors, metal doors. We know what a closing door sounds like.

And once we have learned the rules of sound, we can start bending or using them, breaking them, and expanding on them. We can alter the sound of a door to make it more menacing. Adding more rumble and deep frequencies. Or we can give it a friendly touch by adding a short wooden creak. We can add mechanical sounds to the closing mechanism to "make it more secure".

Footsteps are another famous example. Foley artists, who recreate sounds for film in a studio, usually have a whole wall of different shoes and boots, every one of them producing a different sound. Some sound light and clacking. Others deep and firm. Some sound menacing, like the footsteps of a villain. Others resolute like the footsteps of a hero. Footstep sounds are meticulously chosen to tell the story of who is wearing them.

This can be said about all sounds. Not only is it important to choose a physically probable representation of sound for an object. Within those boundaries of possible sounds, sound designers choose a sound that adds an extra layer of feeling. Threatening, friendly, uncertain, funny, gritty, and many more.

In the indie game *Inside* (2016) by Playdead, the sound was extremely well chosen from an artistic perspective. Some people, when asked, would say *Inside* has no sound, that it is a quiet game. But Inside is full of sounds. There are even sounds that are a key to the puzzle that needs to be solved. Players have to listen for a certain sound event to traverse a bridge. If they don't listen, they are blown away by a mysterious shockwave. Only by listening and timing the character's steps can the bridge be traversed. All those sounds blend perfectly with the dark, sinister atmosphere of the visuals, making them virtually "invisible".

In *Far: Lone Sails* (2018), players control a tiny red character. The character travels through a beautifully abandoned world in a huge machine which they need to operate and keep running. The machine feels almost alive. It has various needs: power to set itself in motion, pressure that needs releasing through a valve. Sometimes a system overheats and develops a fire that needs extinguishing. With all the machine's quirks, very nicely represented by its many sounds, creaks and metal impacts, it comes alive and becomes a friend on the long journey. Artistically, the choice was made to create a machine with many quirks and imperfection: something that is represented in the sound layer of the game. Sound here tells the story of a journey, of a friendship, a symbiosis. The little red character needs the machine to travel, and the machine needs the red character to function.

In the creation process of all games, it is the responsibility of the sound artist to make a decision as to how something should sound, and to find, recreate or design the perfect sound for that purpose.

CONCLUSION

Looking at the examples above it is clear that every sound holds the key to what happens in the physical world. Because we have heard everyday sounds thousands of times, we are able to tell the size of an object, how close it is, if it moves, what material it is made of, what room we are in, what it is that makes the sound, and even a mood or a feeling. We have been learning these properties throughout our lives.

That means that every sound tells a story and hence is deeply relevant for storytelling. If sound is to represent something in a movie or game, all of the aforementioned aspects need to be represented "just right". In other words, the size, material, type of sound, etc., need to be correct to create a believable illusion, or you run the risk that your audience will see through the smoke screen and drop out of the experience.

SOUND AS A COMMUNICATIONS DEVICE

I have already mentioned some of the relevant aspects in the section on "Sound in film vs. sound in games". In an interactive medium, sound is a very strong communications device. Because we have come to know what certain sounds mean, if they happen in a game world, players can react to them. Every sound has a meaning. So let's look at the communication aspects sounds have.

Simulation of the physical world

On a basic level, sound represents the physical world of the game. Objects players can interact with should produce expected sounds. When players throw a glass bottle, the glass should shatter. When players open a door, the door should make the respective sound. They are the hygiene sounds of the world and are needed to keep up the illusion. These sounds communicate what is going on.

Feedback from an activity

Players constantly perform actions in the game world. They walk, open doors, interact with objects, or fight and shoot. Every action should result in some kind of sound, otherwise players will get confused and suffer a disconnect in the immersion.

Imagine a game where you are in a room you have to escape from. You look around and see a door. You walk up to that door and click on it. But nothing happens. The problem is not that the door does not open, but that literally nothing happens, you don't even hear a sound.

As a result, many players are not sure if they really clicked the mouse button. After all you could have missed it or the mouse didn't register your click.

At this point, the immersion is already broken and players are thinking about the technology rather than how to escape the room. Often they click a second and third time. More sophisticated players know that sometimes you have to click in the right spot. Maybe you have to click on the doorknob instead of the door itself? And so players click everywhere on that door, leaving the immersion far behind.

Had the game integrated just one feedback sound, like the rattling of a doorknob, indicating *something* happened, telling the player, yes, the game did register the click, the disconnect could have been averted.

Feedback of this sort is incredibly important as it is high on the list of immersion-maintaining hygiene sounds.

Orientation in the game world

Most people have gone sightseeing at some point in their lives. Most of them probably didn't think of sightseeing as "sighthearing". But sound takes an important part in one's orientation: This is the place where there is a lot of traffic. That's the place where you hear the bazaar ...

In games, sound not only plays an active role in making players curious about what is behind the next corner, directing or luring them to a specific location. It also helps to passively pinpoint locations. When you roam through endless corridors in *Bioshock* (2007), for example, it helps when there are some orientational sounds. The restaurant where a broken radio still plays music, the room where water leaks in. It enables the brain to make more connections to the virtual map in your mind, and not only through visual means but also through a secondary channel, hearing.

Environment

We have looked at the informational payload about the environment which is transported by sound. How we can deduct from environmental sounds like animal noises what time of day it is. Thus, for a specific location and time, sound artists utilize a deliberate selection of sounds to communicate to players what environment the game is set in.

Some sounds are more omnipresent background ambiences like wind noises or tree leaves rustling. Others are more in the foreground, carrying information relating to birds, crickets, wolves, dogs, traffic, or people.

Changes in the game state

All games react to player actions in some way. When a puzzle gets solved, a music stinger is played, telling players they have solved the puzzle. When they explore a vast world and an enemy creature attacks, combat music begins. When the game character is low on health points, not only might vision become clouded, but hearing might be impacted as well. Low health points could be represented by making all sounds dull, filtering out higher frequencies, as if a grenade exploded nearby and you heard everything through a thick layer of cloth. Maybe some sine beep rings in the character's ears.

Information about the state of the game is very important. Especially because in a 3D game world things can happen *behind* the player character. Nobody wants to be surprised by an enemy from behind. It is not fun and it is also frustrating. Therefore, enemies often telegraph where they are by issuing a short sound from time to time, revealing their location. This way, players don't accidentally run into them. If enemies attack, they issue another short sound communicating the changed state of the game (from exploration to fight). This indicates that at least one enemy has spotted the player and is running towards the player's character to attack it. Often this is also accompanied by a change in music.

Reducing the cognitive load

Sound is like a separate channel to the brain. We can see only so much with our eyes. But we can take in additional information through our ears and our other senses. In that respect, sound can help reduce an overload of the visual channel.

Think of a hectic battle situation in a more complex strategy game. You have to keep all the stats, units, resources and more under control. Your eyes would need to scan the whole screen all the time and read health bars and other information.

But when designed in a good way, sound can support gameplay by reducing the load. Sounds that inform players of depleting resources, of low health of important units, or that a fight has started somewhere on the map. In this way players don't need to constantly check all the stats but can concentrate on the most important task at hand and only need to react when something important happens.

This is even used in games with minimal UIs, like *Doom* (2016). The UI doesn't consist of much more than a health and armor bar. And yet, in hectic fights players have to concentrate so much on aiming, evading attacks, and killing demons that there is almost no time left to keep checking the bars. But if health drops below a critical level, a distinct "beep beep" is triggered, and you still have a chance of breaking away from the battle, looking for health kits.

Narrative elements

Sometimes sound supports the storytelling in more direct ways. If a stressful event is triggered in the game world and chaos breaks out in the streets, sound can try and underline the situation from the main character's perspective. It creates a subjective reality bubble for the game character. Environment sounds could deliberately be filtered out and the sound of people screaming altered to sound far away, with plenty of reverb. This could emphasize the helplessness of the main character. The state of mind of not knowing what is going on. Being distant. Not being in control.

A stereotypical use of this would be an explosion impacting the hearing of the game character. When something explodes, all high frequencies are filtered out, only a very muffled sound remains. Sometimes the effect is further improved by adding a very high ringing in the ears. This, too, helps to experience the world from the perspective of the player character. Perceiving the virtual world through their eyes and ears.

CLOSING THOUGHTS

Many of the elements I have presented over the course of this chapter overlap. Some are clear and obvious, others more obscure. But it is remarkable that we rarely think about sound in our day-to-day lives. It is just there. Yet, it functions as a complete channel with a direct connection to our brain, just like the eyes. And we have seen how many aspects are transported through vibrations of air molecules. They are packed with information and meaning.

Sound has a gigantic potential to add immersion, define places, introduce a light and happy mood or cover everything under a dark, sinister layer.

When the various aspects examined in this chapter are understood, artistic choi-ces can be made. A player's perceptions can be played with. Rules can be bro-ken. If sound artists omit all animal noises, birds, flies, frogs in a forest, some-thing sounds "off" immediately. Rules we are used to are broken because when we see a forest and daylight, we expect birds and other animals. This expectation can be manipulated to induce an uneasy feeling.

It is all about one's personal experience. The game world developers want to take you on an exciting journey. So go and listen carefully to the sound of the next game you play and immerse yourself in the audible world that was created for you. Enjoy :)

REFERENCES

Literature

Herzberg, Fredrick/Mausner, Bernard/Bloch Snyderman, Barbara (eds.) (1959): The Motivation to Work, New York: John Wiley & Sons.

Games

Assassin's Creed: Unity, Ubisoft Montreal, Ubisoft, 2014.
Baldur's Gate, Black Isle Studios/Bioware, Interplay Entertainment, 1998.
BioShock, 2K Boston/2K Australia, 2K Games, 2007.
Diablo 3, Blizzard Entertainment, Blizzard Entertainment, 2012.
DOOM, id Software, Bethesda Softworks, 2016.
FAR: Lone Sails, Okomotive, Mixtvision, 2018.
Inside, Playdead, Playdead, 2016.
Star Wars Battlefront, EA Dice, Electronic Arts, 2015.
Star Wars Battlefront II, EA Dice, Electronic Arts, 2017.
Star Wars Jedi: Fallen Order, Respawn Entertainment, Electronic Arts, 2019.
World of Warcraft, Blizzard Entertainment, Blizzard Entertainment, 2004.

Expanding the Narrative

Mukokuseki and the Narrative Mechanics in Japanese Games

Hiloko Kato and René Bauer

> "In fact the whole of Japan is a pure invention. There is no such country, there are no such people."[1]

> "I do realize there's a cultural difference between what Japanese people think and what the rest of the world thinks."[2]

> "I just want the same damn game Japan gets to play, translated into English!"[3]

Space Invaders, Frogger, Pac-Man, Super Mario Bros., Final Fantasy, Street Fighter, Sonic The Hedgehog, Pokémon, Harvest Moon, Resident Evil, Silent Hill, Metal Gear Solid, Zelda, Katamari, Okami, Hatoful Boyfriend, Dark Souls, The Last Guardian, Sekiro. As this very small collection shows, Japanese arcade and video games cover the whole range of possible design and gameplay styles and define a unique way of narrating stories. Many titles are very successful and renowned, but even though they are an integral part of Western gaming culture, they still retain a certain otherness. This article explores the uniqueness of video games made in Japan in terms of their narrative mechanics. For this purpose, we will draw on a strategy which defines Japanese culture: *mukokuseki* (borderless, without a nation) is a concept that can be interpreted either as Japanese commodities erasing all cultural characteristics ("Mario does not invoke the image of Ja-

---

1 Wilde (2007 [1891]: 493).
2 Takahashi Tetsuya (*Monolith Soft* CEO) in Schreier (2017).
3 Funtime Happysnacks in Brian (@NE_Brian) (2017), our emphasis.

pan" [Iwabuchi 2002: 94])[4], or as a special way of mixing together elements of cultural origins, creating something that is new, but also hybrid and even ambiguous. We opt for the second reading as this provides us with instruments that help us to look under these games' (seemingly) nationless surface, analyzing their narrative mechanics.[5]

We start by focusing on one specific way to metaphorically cope with Japanese games by looking at statements of Let's Players while playing Japanese video games ("1. Japanese video games: Drugs!"). We then introduce the notion of *mukokuseki*, by examining the contexts in which it was first used as well as explaining why the interpretation of it as a mingling of cultural traits is more useful for understanding Japanese games ("2. *Mukokuseki*: Japaneseness under the surface"). This also reveals our phenomenological and semiotic method of dealing with video games in general. By looking at different cases, we then discuss how the mukokuseki principle is inherent in Japanese games and their narrative mechanics ("3. *Mukokuseki* as narrative technique: Cases"), the principle of mixing becoming a general technique that also thrives as a unique feature of Japanese games ("4. Absurd overcomplexity, intriguing simplicity and mixing of everything: *mukokuseki* as catalyst").

JAPANESE VIDEO GAMES: DRUGS!

```
                music of Katamary Damacy in the background
PA_01   P:   hey GUYS-
PA_02        PANdacard here-
PA_03        and NOW it_time for me to start a nEw let_s play.
PA_04        this game is called katamari <<len> daMAcy>;
PA_05        i know i never mentioned ANY of this to ANYone-
PA_06        beCAUse (.) i wanted it to be a surprise;
PA_07        cause THIS game,
PA_08        let_s just say it_s JApanese innovAtion mixed in
             with-
```

---

4   28 years after its first appearance, *Super Mario 3D* (Nintendo, 2013) featured a Japanese-inspired level for the first time, the action taking place in the localities and on the rooftop of a Dojo. The level is labelled "Hands-On Hall", which refers to the gameplay: the traditional Japanese sliding doors have to be opened by a swiping movement, combining narrative and gameplay mechanics.

5   This article is a shortened and revised version of our exploration on Japanese games and gaming culture, in which we focused on game mechanics and furthermore employed the term *magic cone*, a concept of the appropriation of Japanese gaming culture in the West, based on the notion by Johan Huizinga (cf. Kato/Bauer 2020).

```
PA_09        <<len> DRUGS>.
PA_10        like (.) this game is <<len> SO trIppy>;
```

The above transcript quotes from a Let's Play (Pandacard 2014, transcript starts right at the beginning of the video),[6] in which the presenter Pandacard plays the beginning of the game *Katamari Damacy* (Namco, 2004). He kept it as a surprise (L PA_05-06) as the game seems to be something special to him, the prosodical emphasis underlining the uniqueness of "THIS" game (L PA_07). The reason for keeping it a surprise is then qualified by introducing the expression "let's just say" (L PA_08), this hedging indicating some difficulty in explaining the matter easily as well as signaling a certain caution concerning the statement that follows. By then describing the game as "Japanese innovation mixed in with drugs", the Let's Player hits the nail on the head: the weirdness of the game is right away located in the otherness of the Japanese. Pandacard takes this in a benevolent way as he retrospectively calls it an "innovation" (the game came out 10 years prior to the Let's Play). Furthermore, the provocative comparison to psychoactive substances is clearly staged by emphasizing it prosodically with special syntactical structure (L PA_08) and slower and stressed pronunciation (L PA_09). Following this forthright opening, the reason for the comparison is provided, but a certain difficulty in describing it remains, as the phrase "this game is so trippy", even with the heavy stress on "so" (L PA_10), is still rather vague and redundant.

Of course, no Japanese game is better suited to be compared with drugs than *LSD: Dream Emulator* (Asmik Ace Entertainment, 1998). Let's Player Pewdiepie, who mistakenly had taken it for a horror game, replays it in one of his Reminisce-Let's Plays and instantly refers to the association of the game title (Pewdiepie 2017, the transcript begins at 00:00:14, L PE1_06):

```
PE1_01  P:   there is one (-) <<len> i !REAL!ly want to revIsit.
PE1_02       EL ES DEE (-) dr!EA!m emulator.>
PE1_03       this game has a kind of a CULT following,
PE1_04       because of how much it STANDS (.) OUT.
PE1_05       there_s really NO gAme Like (.) THIS.
PE1_06       it_s basically (--) <<distorted voice with echo>
```

---

6 The transcript has been created on the basis of the transcription system *Gesprächs-analytisches Transkriptionssystem 2 (GAT2)*, cp. Selting et al. (2009). For the transcription conventions of this system or the meaning of individual symbols please refer to the key at the end of this article. The letter "L" is used to refer to specific lines.

```
!DRUGS!.>
\____/
 /
```
*Pewdiepie stares into the facecam, screen is
distorted in terms of color, long pause*

At the beginning of this Let's Play, the references to the game being Japanese
are scarce. Later in the game, it is revealed by Pewdiepie's actions, that he actually plays *as being in Japan*, trying to imitate the Japanese way of communicating – even including an opening politeness formula in Japanese ("hajime-
mashite", how do you do, L PE2_04). He even bows in the local greeting manner, the camera pointing downwards for a brief moment before the greetings are
uttered:

```
PE2_01       <<disguised voice> let me just walk in this e
             wonderful REStaurant.
PE2_02       well hello there kind SIR,
                  _____/
                    \
             positioning face-to-face with the NPC
PE2_03       WOW,
PE2_04       EE: <<scratchy voice> ee> <<staccato> hajimeMAshite.>
                                  \__/
                                    \
             for a brief moment, the camera points downwards
PE2_05       uu how you_re DOin.
PE2_06       i wanna give me some fine (--)↓‾WHISkey.>
```

It seems to be obvious that experiences of Japaneseness, and even that of Japan
itself (as a travel destination), are related to drugs in a metaphorical sense. This
can be seen in the YouTube video by the "Game Grumps" (Let's Players Arin
[A in the transcript] and Dan [D]) with the title "Learning About Japan! – Game
Grumps Compilations" and labelled with hashtags "#gaming #japan #culture"
(Game Grumps 2019, transcript starts right at the beginning of the video):

```
GG_01  D:    so what did you think in (sic!) jaPAN arin,
GG_02  A:    <<p> i dunno it was GREAT,>
GG_03  D:    was it was it better than the OTHer trips?
             (1.0)
GG_04  A:    uuh ACID,
GG_05        elesDEE,
             ((both laugh))
GG_06  A:    no no nothing can comPAre-
GG_07  D:    yeah it_s TRUE; (--)
GG_08        i didn_t SEE shit the way i thought i would when i
             was (-) ON jaPAN-
             ((both laugh))
((...))
GG_09  D:    it_s VEry strange;
```

Dan and Arin are talking about their experiences – the reason being their recent trip to Japan – interestingly though not while playing "LSD" (L GG_05), but *Super Mario 64* (Nintendo EAD 1996). Japan is so overwhelmingly impressive, that it becomes the drug itself ("when I was on Japan", L GG_08) and Dan sums up his experience as "very strange" (L GG_09).

The comparison of Japanese games and of Japan itself to drugs is clearly an approach used by dedicated players to be able to understand and grasp the otherness that cannot be explained by putting it into their own words. And it is a way of dealing with the perception of cultural differences.

Another way to handle this topic is that chosen by big gaming companies: For big triple X productions, which are designed to serve an international audience, terms and guidelines as regards *culturalization* or *glocalization* seem mandatory because "cultural mistakes often prove to be costly for game developers and publishers" (IGDA 2012: 2).[7] However, this method of adapting Japanese games frequently does not meet the approval of Western players. A very prominent example is *Xenoblade Chronicles X* (Monolith Soft, 2015), where the adaptation was made – amongst other things – on the skimpy clothing of the Japanese PCs (e.g. of the 13-year-old Lin Lee, but for the male characters as well, see Figure 1).

Some avatar adjustments were also eliminated (e.g. the breast slider determining the chest measurements of the female characters). In the debates that followed, player communities spoke of censorship, and the casual comments by *Monolith Soft* CEO, Takahashi Tetsuya,[8] added fuel to the flames:

---

7 Very often, the case of *Kakuto Chojin* (Dream Publishing, 2002) is mentioned, where a single, randomly and carelessly chosen background audio file caused the recall of the whole, ready-for-sale project. In addition to the concept of *localization*, the paper *Best Practices for Game Localization* (IGDA 2012) by the *International Game Design Association* (IGDA) addresses the topic of *culturalization*, which comprises more than just translating the verbal material: "It's important to consider this fact when thinking about a local market's reaction to game content; not everyone is reacting in the same way and for the same reasons. So what does 'culture' mean for game content? First consider these two simplified definitions: Content: Information created for perpetuation and dissemination; in game titles, it's basically anything a player will see, hear or read. Context: The circumstances or events that form a unique environment in space and time, within which information is created and managed." (Edwards 2011: 21-22)

8 Japanese names will be cited here in the Japanese order (family name, first name).

For example, there was a discussion about the breast slider. Jokingly, I said, "Well would it help if we had a crotch slider for the male?" Obviously it was a joke, but they responded obviously it's not gonna work out. I do realize there's a cultural difference between what Japanese people think and what the rest of the world thinks. (Takahashi Tetsuya in Schreier [2017])

Figure 1: Culturalization in terms of men's clothing in Xenoblade Chronicles X.

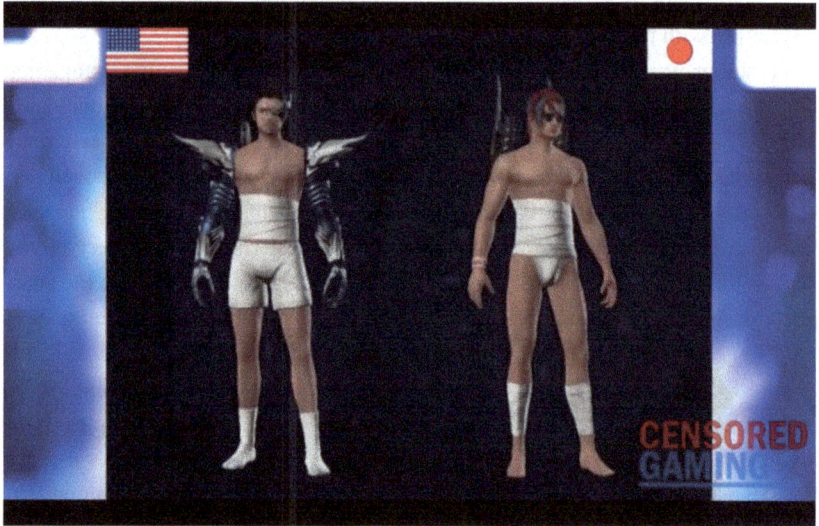

Source: Censored Gaming 2017

There are two interesting points in this statement by Takahashi: First, he does not seem to be concerned by the *culturalization* measures taken, but appears rather indifferent to this matter: "I really didn't mind much at all, actually." (Schreier 2017) Second, he confirms the existence of cultural differences, underlining this by speaking of the divide between "Japanese people" and "the rest of the world". Nonetheless, the handling of cultural differences by means of *culturalization* is not the solution players want. As reader comments show, players prioritize preservation of originality over cultural adaptation:

I know Nintendo is a business and that our ratings system is different. But I don't know how it is so hard for them to understand, we buy Japanese games because we like Japan! I don't buy JRPGs for some overly-sensitive Treehouse [name of the American *localization*-team] hipster's interpretation of Japanese content, watered down or sterilized for Western consumption. *I just want the same damn game Japan gets to play*, translated into English! (Funtime Happysnacks in Brian [@NE_Brian] [2017], our emphasis)

It is also uncertain whether the majority of Japanese games can be adapted to Western conceptions at all. Their core seems to remain Japanese no matter what.

MUKOKUSEKI: JAPANESENESS UNDER THE SURFACE

Coping with different cultures of origin is a precarious matter. In general, it brings forth fundamental incommensurable differences. Using drug analogies and arguments in favor of or against culturalizability are strategies to handle these difficulties and somehow describe the helpless out-of-control-state of mind (while being drugged with Japan). And even after the localization process, Japanese games still seem to remain Japanese under the modified surface. One term that helps to understand Japanese commodities is *mukokuseki*:

The term *mukokuseki* is widely used in Japan in two different, though not mutually exclusive ways: to suggest the mixing of elements of multiple cultural origins, and to imply the erasure of visible ethnic and cultural characteristics. (Iwabuchi 2002: 71, original emphasis)

The term is a composition that consists of two parts: *mu* (無, without, negation of) and *kokuseki* (国籍, nationality), so literally reads as 'without nationality' or 'nationless'. As Iwabuchi explains, there are two ways of understanding this term: One of them – the second in Iwabuchi's definition – outlines the fact that Japanese commodities often do not display their origins on the surface, so that for example characters in mangas, animes or video games are not depicted as Japanese:

The characters of Japanese animation and computer games for the most part do not look 'Japanese'. Such non-Japaneseness is called *mukokuseki*, literally meaning "something or someone lacking any nationality", but also implying the erasure of racial or ethnic characteristics or a context, which does not imprint a particular culture or country with these features. (Iwabuchi 2002: 28, original emphasis; he cites the film producer and director Koi)

Mukokuseki in this sense was used to explain the rising international popularity of Japanese commodities since the 1990s, especially of manga and anime, but of video games as well: it was argued, that the products – commodities of popular culture – were becoming unproblematic and more digestible for Western audiences as their nationality had been erased, enabling a so-called seducing *soft power* ('soft' compared to the already established *hard power* of technological

export goods).[9] Concurrently, this national pride about the international eupho-
ria for Japan was heavily criticized through the same term of *mukokuseki*:[10] As
the products lacked the characteristics of nationality, their influence on Western
culture was nothing but an illusion, conveying no Japanese values at all.[11]

As we would like to show in greater detail, this understanding of *mukokuseki*,
and the ways in which cultural markers are analyzed in this respect, are too blunt
and superficial.[12] Most of these examples exclusively concern the external and
visual appearance of characters in manga and video games. On closer inspection
though, the communication of cultural markers and characteristics is far more intricate than the mere display of Japanese facial features:[13]

From our point of view, the complexity of culturality exceeds the narrow
perspective on the surface of things. Its manifestation goes deeper and has to be
treated more on a phenomenological level. As Cohn shows in his analysis of the
visual language of comics, the visual classification allows us to identify manga
and anime characters as Japanese even if they do not look like real Japanese
people (cf. Figure 2):

At this point, people around the globe can easily identify Standard JVL [Japanese Visual
Language] unconnected to any particular author's manner of drawing. The 'style' has
transcended individuals to become a visual vocabulary representative of Japan as a whole.
Indeed, JVL is not constrained to manga, and recurs ubiquitously in cartoons, advertise-

---

9   Citing the political scientist Joseph Nye, Napier notes the uniqueness of soft power:
    "[...] soft power is seductive. It attracts; it 'co-opts people rather than coerces them'."
    (Napier 2007: 6). Iwabuchi describes this as "a shift from techno-nationalism to soft-
    ware-oriented, 'soft' nationalism" (Iwabuchi 2014 [2002]: 22). Interestingly, the lack
    of national identity was already discussed in connection with technological goods
    made in Japan, e.g. the Sony Walkman (Iwabuchi 2002: 28).
10 This cultural debate is known as the *Nihonjin-ron*, "'treatise on what makes Japan
    separate'. The form had its origins as far back as the seventeenth century but reached
    an apogee in more modern times" (Pilling 2014: 36), culminating in the 1990s (cf.
    Iwabuchi 2002: 6-7; 213-214).
11 Iwabuchi cites the cultural critic Otsuka Eiji (cf. Iwabuchi 2002: 33).
12 Furthermore, the notion of *mukokuseki* is often diluted by the use of metaphors, as in
    the case of Iwabuchi himself, who points out the lack of any "Japanese bodily odour"
    (Iwabuchi 2002: 28).
13 As a public survey shows, the subject of depicting the nationalities of anime charac-
    ters is quite a delicate matter, cf. That Japanese Man Yuta (2017).

ments, emoticons, and visual culture generally. One is pressed in Japan to *not* find this style in graphic representations. (Cohn 2013: 156, original emphasis).

Figure 2: Despite mukokuseki: Eyes as typical recognition features.

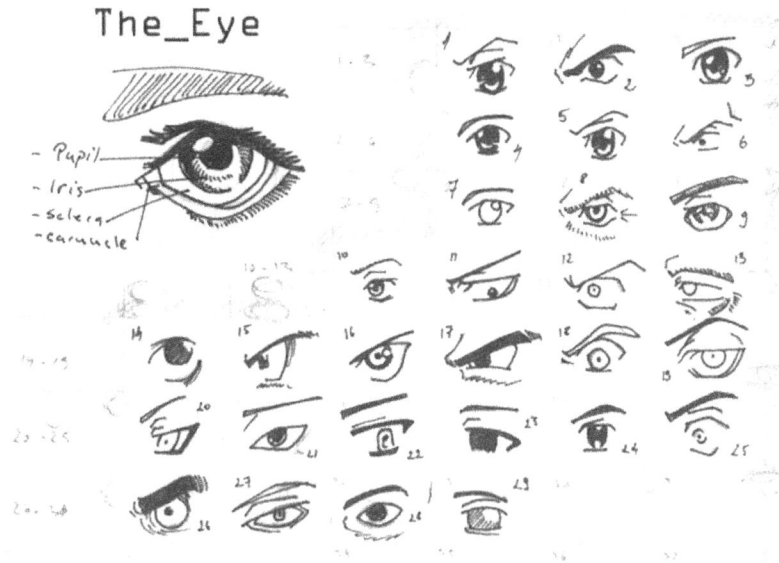

Source: Aoi-Ne-Blue 2009 [14]

This semiotic example is useful for understanding the first part of the notion of *mukokuseki* as in the definition by Iwabuchi (see citation above): the Japanese way of creativity lies in indigenization, taking patterns and traces from foreign culture and mixing them with domestic elements to create something completely new and, paradoxically, Japanese through and through. Cohn's example of JVL is telling, because on the one hand, contemporary manga cannot be understood without its origins in traditional illustrated handscrolls (the so-called *emaki*, which have existed since the 12th century), but on the other hand, it is heavily influenced by the visual language of American comics as well (cf. Cohn 2013: 153). This and many other established cultural characteristics of commodities are therefore a hybrid mixture – a blend of the Japanization of Americanization, so to speak. In this mixed state, these commodities are not genuinely Japanese nor simply coated with Western properties and values so as to disguise the original

---

14 This image is reproduced with the kind permission of the artist.

Japanese traits – they become a whole new amalgamation of cultural origins that is neither purely Japanese nor, in a sense, 'colonialized' by the West. Napier in her analysis on the Japanese influence as a fantasy and a fan cult states it accurately:

The characters in anime and manga are both 'Japanese' and at the same time 'nationless'. Or, more accurately, they belong to the world of animation and caricature, of fantasy and unreality to the highest degree. Thus, when a non-Japanese enjoys or identifies with a character, he is identifying within a highly distinctive fantasyscape that combines elements of 'real' Japan within a cartoon imaginary. (Napier 2007: 210)

The fact that "Hello Kitty and the Pokémon characters still possess certain distinctively Japanese characteristics, even if they are not as obvious as facial or landscape features" (Napier 2007: 130), remains unnoticed at first sight. For more dedicated observers, its otherness is nonetheless perceptible:[15]

Not knowing that the programs they loved were Japanese but simply aware that they [Japanese animes in this case] seemed 'different' (Napier 2007: 176).

As for American children themselves, all whom I interviewed knew that *Pokémon* came originally from Japan. [...] [M]any said that, as a result of *Pokémon* and other 'cool' Japanese goods, they have developed an interest in Japan. (Allison 2014: 140-141)

Figure 3: Mukokuseki as de- and reculturalizing strategy.

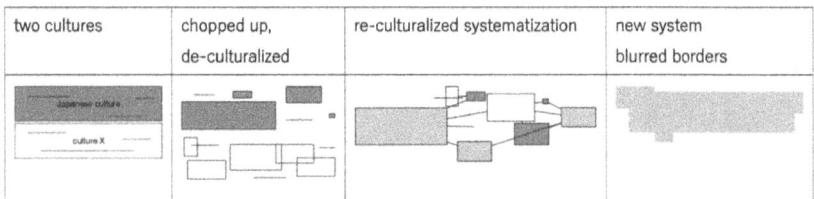

two cultures	chopped up, de-culturalized	re-culturalized systematization	new system blurred borders

Source: Hiloko Kato and René Bauer

---

15 In a similar way, Consalvo (2016: 1) states: "I never thought about where the games or consoles came from or who had made them. Yet even the few games and systems that I was familiar with reveal a mixture of American and Japanese games and systems comingling at the beginnings of a global game industry."

The otherness, which obviously cannot be found on the immediate surface of things (e.g. of *Super Mario Bros.* or *Pokémon*, see below), in our opinion becomes tangible through the second way of understanding the notion of *mukokuseki*: it is a unique cultural technique that chops up cultural features and reculturalizes them by mixing in known domestic features, thus creating a new system (cf. Barthes 1983 [1970]), with whole new possibilities (cf. Figure 3).

The context in which the concept of *mukokuseki* was first introduced helps to understand it better. It initially served as a description for a new genre of Japanese action movies, which was created in the 1960s.

For Japan's oldest film studio Nikkatsu, the late 50s and early 60s represented a rapidly evolving, cosmopolitan playground in which Eastern and Western influences could be collided together in an explosive mix that ultimately resulted in movies that felt quite apart from either. These were the *mukokuseki eiga*. (Green 2018: 41)

The first movie of this new genre – as part of a series of nine with the *wataridori* (渡り鳥, wanderer) theme – was *The Rambling Guitarist* (ギターを持った 渡り鳥, 1959) by Saito Buichi, which clearly refers to the lone gunslinger in the genre of Westerns. The plot centers on the titular young wanderer Taki Shinji who becomes embroiled with the local *yakuza* of the northern port town of Hakodate, embarks on a romance with the *yakuza* boss's daughter and has awkward encounters with acquaintances of his mysterious past. On the surface, this star-vehicle movie is Japanese, but – in line with the term of *mukokuseki* – an amalgamation of Japanese and Western culture can be seen throughout the entire movie. It includes the titular guitar ("ooz[ing] Western style", "the most overt signifier of an old-school cowboy feel, but crucially, the song he's singing is in Japanese", Green 2018: 43), the Westernization of the name of the main antagonist (George, who in the course of the plot turns out to be morally complex, even more so than the hero), the depiction of the modern Japanese woman (wearing Western clothes but living Japanese womanhood), and the unabandoned pursuit of a Japanese sense of morality and traditional values (the 'good' yakuza, tied both to conflicting concepts of *giri* [obligation] and *ninjo* [compassion]) – all this tying "into a deep-rooted system of signs and symbolism" (ibid 44).

From a more historic and diachronic point of view, the strategy of *mukokuseki* – prominently emerging in the light of actual globalization – is in fact a very old and mostly successful Japanese method of coping with foreign influences: "Japan's long tradition of cultural indigenization is celebrated as the secret of Japan's prosperity and the core of Japan's national sense of Self" (Iwabuchi 2002: 59). This strategy of indigenizing characteristics of foreign cultures not only pertains to the Americanization after World War II, or, further back, after the forced opening of the country by Commodore Perry's steamed *kurofune* (black warships) in 1853.[16] It can also be applied to the importing of features from the more advanced Chinese civilization, a process beginning at the end of the 6th century. From 600 to 838, diplomatic missions of the reigning imperial dynasties were sent to China to learn from their successful neighbor about a range of subjects, including the written language (with all its consequences), rules concerning the structures of government, historiography and how to legitimize it, religion, and cultural assets like art and architecture.[17] "Of course, the Japanese adapted all that they learned to their own needs and tastes" (Vogel 2019: 2), and "[s]ometimes, what it brought was so altered as to become unre-

---

16 In 1878, therefore 25 years later, the first Japanese warships arrived in Marseille: "This is nothing more than an exchange – Japan borrows from us our mechanical arts, our military art, our sciences [and] we take their decorative art" (critic Ernest Chesnau, cited by Napier 2007: 28). Cf. also McLuhan, for whom Japan was – in his understanding of "tribal ways" – a largely successful counterexample to the West: "Long centuries of tight tribal organisation now stand the Japanese in very good stead in the trade and commerce of the electric age. A few decades ago they underwent enough literacy and industrial fragmentation to release aggressive individual energies. The close teamwork and tribal loyalty now demanded by electrical intercom again puts the Japanese in positive relation to their ancient traditions. Our own tribal ways are much too remote to be of any social avail." (McLuhan 2006 [1964]: 256)

17 "During this period, the Japanese mastered a written language, Chinese characters, that allowed officials to communicate over a broader geographical distance and to provide greater consistency in contacts among the highest officials in the capital and officials who served elsewhere. Japan developed standardized rules to clarify what local officials were expected to do and a specialized administrative staff to manage a larger and more complex organization. The Japanese learned how to write histories of former rulers to support the legitimacy of the current ones. They also learned about Buddhism and strengthened the legitimacy of their rulers by linking them with the natural order. They learned how to plan large communities in a systematic way and how to build large Buddhist temples. Furthermore, they imported Confucianism, which reinforced the importance of the loyalty of the subjects to their leaders and emphasized the rules of propriety to maintain a stable organization. They developed new art techniques and poetry styles after studying Chinese culture, and they imported musical instruments." (Vogel 2019: 1-2)

cognizable" (Braudel 1993: 281).[18] This is best shown by the development of the Japanese tripartite writing system, consisting of Chinese characters (Kanji) and two syllabaries (Hiragana and Katakana) which were adapted from Kanji to match Japanese phonetics, as Japanese and Chinese do not have a genealogical relationship.

Against this backdrop, it is interesting to realize how deceiving these indigenized cultural artifacts and assets are: At first sight (or seen by an ignorant foreigner), these everyday artifacts – written language, but also cultural buildings like temples or everyday goods such as chopsticks –[19] are not distinguishable or do not look unquestionably Japanese (they could also be Chinese). But a deeper look under the surface reveals the unique mixture of unprejudiced appropriation of foreign culture and self-confident adaptation to Japan's own cultural needs.[20]

Mukokuseki in this wider context is the modern synchronic form of indigenization with an even more deceiving strategy, as the cultural traits in the mixture

---

18 Pilling (2014: 33-34) is more cautious, but his examples point in the same direction: "This cultural appropriation and subtle subversion of outside influence is hardly unique to Japan. But the distance between Japan and the outside world, both physical and psychological, perhaps exaggerated the phenomenon. The Japanese adapt what comes from outside. They mix strips of seaweed or sea urchin in their pasta. They use the term sebiro to mean suit, mostly unaware that the word is a distortion of Savile Row, a London street famed for its men's tailors. More recently, they have taken western technology and modified it. In the inventive hands of Japanese engineers, trains became bullet trains, and mobile phones morphed into powerful computers (and electronic wallets) well before the onset of Apple's iPhone."

19 Depending on the country, chopsticks vary in size (the Japanese use shorter chopsticks for eating than their Chinese or Korean counterparts, but long ones for cooking), shape (Japanese chopsticks are often pointier than Chinese ones), material (Japanese chopsticks are mostly made of wood or bamboo, ones made of melamine or porcelain are common in China, Korea favors stainless steel), and in terms of their combined use with other eating utensils such as spoons (not common in Japan or Vietnam). On the chopsticks culture sphere, cf. Wang (2015).

20 From a historical perspective, it is interesting to see that Japan also dared to reject foreign techniques and influences later on after having gained a national self-confidence so to speak (for example Christianity, firearms [cf. Perrin (1979), but also Howell (2009)] or letter press [cf. Giesecke (2007), especially 432-441] and of course in the case of the seclusion of the entire country [*Sakoku* 鎖国, "closed country"] in the Tokugawa period [cf. Pilling (2014: 59-61)]).

do not appear to be visible on the surface anymore (other than in such cases as chopsticks, temples or written language). This also applies to video games, where characters do not look Japanese (*Mario*, characters in *Pokémon* or *Devil May Cry*). Narrowing the focus down to the narrative, we will show in the following case studies how the very Japaneseness of these *mukokuseki* examples can be brought to light.

MUKOKUSEKI AS NARRATIVE TECHNIQUE: CASES

Arcades as *loci mukokuseki* – the birthplace of new techniques, themes and Mario

Japanese arcade halls or game centers (jap. ゲームセンター), are the places where *mukokuseki* has been existed since the first game center opened on the rooftop of a department store in 1931 (cf. Smith 2020). Of course, this amusement park did not yet offer games or arcades, but mainly catered for sports activities like archery, roller skating, bowling or bicycling (cf. Eickhorst 2006: 16) – strikingly, the latter all being Western sports activities. Today, game centers are a heterotopia, a world made of different motivational design and game mechanics: there is tinkering around, as well as try and error (play), but also earnest rule-based play (game), an exotic ambience and the performances of players, solo or in groups, regardless of gender (*Pac-Man* released in 1980 was especially designed for a female audience) or age (the same kind of equality applies to *Pokémon*, see below) – and all in a manner that, from a Western perspective, could be called uncommon, exaggerated or even freaky. Additionally, playing games often does not seem to be the main activity. Instead, visitors turn the place into their second home by doing homework together, eating or even napping.[21] In game centers, a world with strange rules is forged, a culture of otherness *par excellence* (cf. Figure 4).

---

21 Cf. the insightful studies by Pellétier-Gagnon (2019), by Tobin (2016) and (2015), as well as by Guins (2014).

Figure 4: Loci mukokuseki – Japanese Game Center.

Source: screenshot (Kato/Bauer)

Other than in America, the land of origin of the modern arcade,[22] in Japan, these machines and their gathering places have survived despite home entertainment systems and smartphones. The amalgamation of cultures is most apparent in Okinawa, where game centers prospered from the beginning because of its American military base (cf. deWinter 2015: 332). Nowadays, the large concentrations of game centers in urban regions like Tokyo emphasize how firmly anchored in culture they are.

This development is remarkable as it was not clear initially if Japan would invest in coin-op games at all, given that they were a competitive threat to the existing *pachinko* halls: [23]

---

22 See Huhtamo (2005) for the archeology of arcade games, which of course goes back to European roots.

23 *Pachinko* are pinball machines originating from the French table game of the early modern period, *bagatelle*. In the 1920s, an altered form of these table games called the "Corinth game" was imported from America. These could be found especially as an attraction for children in candy-shops (cf. Sedensky 2012: 16); here the "pleasure and play"-background is prominent again (see below, 3.2). The first official pinball machine was introduced in 1929 and named *Pachi-Pachi* describing the noises it made. Due to space restrictions, the Japanese transformed them "by mounting them vertically rather than horizontally and borrowing elements from the European coin-operated

However, the Japanese government did express doubt that game centers, and later computer games, were a good cultural investment in a society that worked 6.5 days per week. David Rosen, a founding member of SEGA (SErvice GAmes) argued successfully with the Ministry of International Trade and Industry (MITI) that coin-op arcade games would provide an emotional release, and in 1957, was granted a licence to import coin-op games. (deWinter 2015: 321) [24]

As it turned out, the import of arcade games strengthened the already operating game hall community and *pachinko* culture even more, instead of diminishing them. One explanation can be found in the already existing technological and economical requirements that helped to boost the native arcade industry with clones of imported games and also with creations of their very own:[25] "The Japanese video game industry is one of those industries in Japan that was imported from the United States during the twentieth century, but that was able to somehow 'improve' the model." (Picard 2013)

One factor in the success of these games also lies in the – again borderless – understanding of hardware and software as being an inseparable unity. This holistic approach resulted in the never-ending creation of innovative interfaces, always on the lookout for transformations of the arcade-machine itself, and enabled intricately new game experiences, first by enhancing the simulation of real life activities, e.g.: *MotoPolo* (Sega, 1968, a soccer game with motorcycles, therefore a very early form of *Rocket League* [Psyonix, since 2015]); *Periscope* (Namco, 1965/Sega, 1966, a game with submarines which included looking through a periscope); *Stunt Car* (Sega, 1970, a combination of traditional arcade and racing games); *Wild Gunman* (Nintendo, 1974, with light guns and full-motion videos),[26] *Speed Race* (Taito, 1974, the very first game with a back-

---

gambling device called allwin such as a lever in place of a plunger and circular tracks to supplement the traditional bagatelle pins." (Smith 2020: 103)

24 Cf. also McLuhan (2006 [1964]: 255, our emphasis): "As extensions of the popular *response to the workaday stress*, games become faithful models of a culture." On the Western founders of Taito and Sega, cf. Smith (2020).

25 This strategy compensated for lack of sponsorship from the armaments industry, e.g. in comparison to the USA. On further influences in terms of socio-economics, cf. Picard (2013) and deWinter (2015).

26 On the development of electric rifle games, which originated in the United Kingdom in the late 19th century, cf. Smith (2020: 110): "In Japan, gun games became the premier coin-op amusement through the efforts of David Rosen."

ground that scrolled vertically and the first arcade game that was exported to the USA),[27] and other play items such as *Love Tester* (Sega 1972).[28]

Figure 5: Space Invaders: new technology and themes.

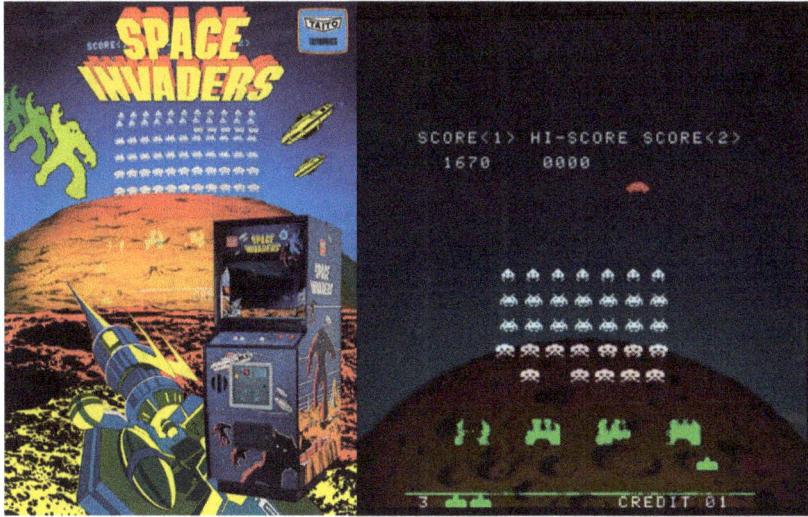

Source: screenshots (Kato/Bauer)

After the first imports of Western arcade games like *Pong* (Atari, 1972), the Japanese game developing scene started to make their own mark. An innovation both in terms of technology and narrative was *Space Invaders* (Taito, 1978, cf. Figure 5).

This arcade game used microprocessors instead of electric circuits and cleverly took advantage of already known technologies that electromechanical arcades provided, adding something new in terms of technology: "That was the first game in Japan to use a CPU with joystick. It was after that when Sega started making similar games, with a CPU and a joystick." (Szczepaniak 2014b: 272) Furthermore, it is a game that makes one thing clear: you are alone, against the rest of the universe. A complex setting, which might even be called theatrical, creates a world with graphics and animations that seem to be inspired by manga: the aliens of the game look more cute than scary, and they explode radially according to the usual manga style.

---

27 Other noteworthy titles: *TV Basketball* (Midway, 1974), *Sea Wolf* (Midway, 1976).

28 For an overview, see https://segaretro.org.

With *Galaxian* (Namco, 1979), similar game mechanics were technically as well as thematically refined by Namco: it was the first arcade game in color, and the player was confronted with insects instead of aliens (cf. Figure 6).

Figure 6: Galaxian: invasion of the insects from outer space.[29]

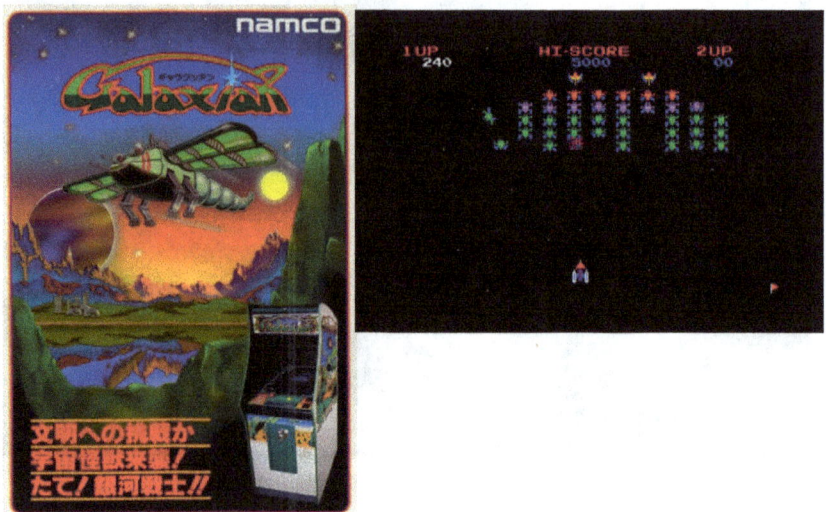

Source: screenshots (Kato/Bauer)

While the outer-space theme was retained, the adversary is not an unknown extraterrestrial species, but originates from the familiar home planet, reminiscent of radioactively mutated monsters like *Godzilla* (1954) or *Mothra* (1961).[30] Thus, the Japanese arcade has emancipated itself, creating its very own imaginative space where the development of every narrative and visual idea now seems possible.

One important difference to Western game development lies in the creation process, with the existing technology as starting point. This is also expressed by designer and producer Inafune Keiji (*Mega Man* series [Capcom, 1987]):

---

29 The inscription in red characters reads: "Is this a challenge to civilization?! – Invasion of the monsters from outer space! Defy them! Galactic warrior!"

30 Linking the monster invasion to nuclear weapon testing is of course meant as an allegorical take on the atomic bombings of World War II. Cf. Coulmas (2014) for the corresponding events of the *Daigo Fukuryu-Maru* incident on March 1, 1954.

I think for example with Mega Man, we looked at the colours and we said: 'OK, what does this colour limitation mean for our character? How can we make the best character from this limitation?' Whereas my image with maybe some Western developers is that they drew a picture of a character's design, and they said to their programmer or whoever: 'Right, now put this in the game.' (Inafune in Szczepaniak 2014a: 497)

One famous example is Mario's red cap: "[...] his red cap was there so his hair wouldn't have to fly around when he jumped" (Kohler 2016 [2005]: 34). *Donkey Kong* (Atari, Nintendo R&D1/Nintendo, 1981), where Mario made his first appearance (by his original name of Jumpman that indicated his main action), "was the first game project in which the design process began with a story" (ibid). Seen through Western eyes, the handling of the narrative seems strange: the story is named after an ape that clearly resembles the movie monster King Kong,[31] with the absurd name of "Donkey Kong". Understandably, the American sales managers were perplexed:

'Donkey Hong?', 'Konkey Dong?', 'Honkey Dong'? It made no sense. Games that were selling had titles that contained words such as mutilation, destroy, assassinate, annihilate. When they played 'Donkey Kong', they were even more horrified. The salesmen were used to battle games with space invaders, and heroes shooting lasers at aliens. One hated 'Donkey Kong' so much that he began looking for a new job. Yamauchi (CEO Nintendo) heard all the feedback but ignored it. 'Donkey Kong', released in 1981, became Nintendo's first super-smash hit. (Sheff 1993: 49)

Despite the name, it was not King Kong that served as the blueprint for the game story, but Popeye. And even though efforts to obtain a license did not work out, the nature of the relationship between the protagonists – seen through Japanese eyes – remained the same, as Miyamoto Shigeru explained later:

Even after the Popeye license fell through, I was still thinking about the relationship between Popeye, Bluto, and Olive Oyl. Their relationship is somewhat friendly. They're not enemies, they're friendly rivals. (Kohler (2016 [2005]: 36)

---

31 Of course, Nintendo was sued by Universal Studios. The renaming of the player character as "Mario" goes back to Mario A. Segale, who was the owner of the warehouse in a suburb of Seattle where Nintendo stored their arcade games that were sold in America (cf. Nintendo UK 2015). See also the homage to King Kong combined with Godzilla in *Bayonetta* (Platinum Games, 2009).

In retrospect, this friendly rivalry makes perfect sense as narrative groundwork for the expansion to an immense story universe that still goes on today: the success of the *Mario* series shows in the impressive number of more than 200 games that feature the short, friendly plumber, making it the most successful Nintendo game series.[32] The infinite seriality is reflected in the unlimited nature of the playable game world in *Super Mario Bros.* (Nintendo, 1985): "The 'Mario' games were more interesting because there were always new worlds to conquer, each one more magnificent than the last." (Sheff 1993: 50) The disparate thematic settings – the world of the princess (castles, walls and moats) and that of the plumber (sewer system), animated with diverse animals and plants (tortoise, mushrooms and the piranha-plant *pakkun*) – are mingled to form a new, family-friendly (represented by Nintendo's Famicom) *mukokuseki* game world:

Adults enjoy Mario too. They respond, Miyamoto feels, because, the games bring them back to their childhoods. 'It is a trigger to again become primitive, primal, as a way of thinking and remembering.' Myamoto says. 'An adult is a child who has more ethics and morals. That's all. When I am a child, creating, I am not creating a game. I am in the game. The game is not for children, it is for me. It is for the adult that still has a character of a child.' (Sheff 1993: 50-51)

One reason for the worldwide success of these games arguably lies in the (superficial) *mukokuseki* interpretation: "Mario does not invoke the image of Japan." (Iwabuchi 2002: 94) By looking under the surface and taking into account the design of Mario's appearance, the groundwork of a different relationship between hero and villain that was borrowed from the West, as well as the reactions of the sales managers, the fundamental Japaneseness of the game's narrative structure and design is revealed.

Pokémon: Japanese ambiguity and nostalgia

Alongside the *Super Mario* series, *Pokémon* (Nintendo, since 1996) is one of the most mentioned titles in the *mukokuseki* discussion. With its multiverse expand-

---

32 An offshoot is the *Kaizo-Mario* genre, also known as *Asshole-Mario*. These fan projects use hacks of *Super Mario World* to create unique, extremely difficult levels: "Behind these Kaizo games lies a certain mentality: they are about challenging the player's skill and patience, but also try to balance this with a sense of fun, mischief and discovery" (Lipscombe 2018) – a very own world of *mukokuseki*, so to speak (on mastering as a Japanese game mechanic cf. Kato/Bauer 2020).

ing crossmedially into nearly every form of entertainment commodity (games, manga, anime, movies, collector's cards, merchandise) and being integrated into everyday life in many different ways,[33] this global phenomenon is indeed the figurehead of *mukokuseki* Japan. Again, it seems fair to assume that the unproblematic renaming of the human protagonist boy from Satoshi to Ash in the Western localization process proves the odorlessness of the narrative, where it does not appear to matter whether the characters are Japanese or not. However, it is a fact that the structure and dynamics of the character's development had to be altered and localized for the Western audience. This is strong evidence that a unique cultural manifestation exists underneath the neutral surface:

When Pokémon entered the marketplace of the United States, the image given it was more dynamic and bolder than the cuteness accorded it in Japan. Brighter colors have been used in the advertising, for example. And instead of making Pikachu the central character, Ash has been forefronted, under the assumption, not entirely borne out, that American kids need a heroic character with whom to identify [...]. In *Mew Two Strikes Back*, for example, the US director, Norman Grossfeld, altered the storyline to make the cloned Pokémon, Mew Two, clearly evil, and the battle Ash waged against it, definitively 'good' – two features that were much hazier in the Japanese original. (Allison 2014: 142)

As Allison has shown in her analysis, ambiguity "in the sense of a murkiness that blurs borders rather than gets contained by them (good/bad, real/fantasy, animal/human)" (2014: 143), is a central aspect in the Japanese understanding of things, even being reflected in the Japanese understanding of 'cuteness'. Pokémons, or pocket monsters, are the prototype of these ambiguous *kawaii* (cute) beings, strong and dangerous, but tamable, faithful and constant companions of human kids, which transform into a handy pocket size within the pokeballs.[34] Here, the border between imagination and reality starts to blur as well: Pokémons are not only to be found on portable consoles (Game Boy, Nintendo DS), but, especially in Japan, also in manga books, on collector's cards, as merchandising and therefore are, in fact, portable companions. In this way, these "children's mass fantasies" become an incarnation of a postmodern-capitalistic materialism in a culture where "the border between play and non-play, commodity

---

33 Cf. also the extensive analysis by Allison (2006).

34 Cf. also the possibility of playing Dark Sonic in *Sonic Adventure 2* (Sega, 2001): "What our six-year-old discovered was that there are (besides still others) two different models of what counts as being or doing 'good'." (Gee 2006 [2003]: 613)

and not, increasingly blurs." (Allison 2014: 137; 150)[35] Allison introduces the notion of *polymorphous perversity* ("mixing, morphing, and moving between and across territories of various sorts" [ibid]), and thus makes this hybrid structure tangible for a Western audience.

The recent hype around *Pokémon Go* (Niantic, 2016) has clearly shown: the whole *Pokémon* series crosses age boundaries, in defiance of Western unambiguousness; four-year-olds are hooked by the games and the animation series in the same way as teenagers, older players looking for nostalgia can catch the monster in the real world with the now available pokeball accessories (Pokéball Plus). And the involvement strategies also prove to be gender-neutral, reminiscent of the Japanese game centers (see above, 3.1). It is well known that the inventor of *Pokémon*, Tajiri Satoshi, was an arcade maniac, spending hours and days with games like *Space Invaders*.[36] Besides these arcade origins with their age- and gender-crossing structures and the beating of highscores and adversaries, the narrative mechanics of collecting and stock taking that dominate the *Pokémon* world with its countless monsters can be seen as uniquely Japanese: collecting as an activity is omnipresent in Japan and reflected, for example, in the *Otaku* culture,[37] in other game titles such as in the *Katamari* series or in general in the *Gacha* genre, where the collecting of real and virtual collector's cards is used as a fan-based expansion of successful games. Stock taking of countless entities on the other has a highly educational value: "Pokémon is centrally about acquiring knowledge", as part of an almost 'Bildungsroman'-like journey of learning from a Western perspective (cf. Buckingham/Sefton-Green 2004: 21).

In 1999, a Time magazine cover story titled *Beware of the Poke-Mania* was dedicated to the hype coming from overseas. It provided some telling background information about Tajiri Satoshi, who at the beginning of the article was depicted as an outcast, making even his parents cry because of his childish pas-

---

35 Cf. also Napier (2007: 131).

36 "He was such a fanatic that one arcade gave him a Space Invaders machine to take home" (Chua-Eoan/Larimer 1999: 84). None other than Shigeru Miyamoto says about him: "Mr. Tajiri didn't start this project intending to make something which would become very popular. He just wanted to make something he wanted to play himself", Kohler (2016 [2005]: 228).

37 This *Otaku* culture was, for example, also integrated in the *Katamari* series (Namco, since 2004), cf. Jones (2008: 66).

sions.[38] His intentions behind creating such a game also became more understandable from a cultural point of view:

Yet collecting Pokémon and pitting them against one another is not a new kind of quest, simply one tweaked with technology. In Asia, fathers and grandfathers still tell of growing up in the midst of World War II, of nights of not knowing what to do with yourself except sneak into the tall grass of the countryside to catch crickets, then take them home, cupped in your hand, to raise in the dark of matchboxes, training the insects for fights with the crickets of other boys who have been on the same nocturnal hunt. The more experience each cricket has had, the better a fighter it becomes – the tiny surrogate for the boy unable to fight in the war going on all around him. Pokémon is that kind of game. (Chua-Eoan/Larimer 1999: 86)

As for today, collecting living insects still is a nostalgically beloved activity of kids in their summer holidays, also being used as a narrative element in anime, television drama or games such as the *My Summer Holiday* series (Millennium Kitchen, since 2000). In Tajiri's case, the solitary concentration on collecting and taking stock of insects as well as cracking highscores was balanced nonetheless against the desire to interact with others.[39] Thus, the 'Game-Boy Link Cable' not only provided the possibility of trading with other pocket monster owners, but was even designed to be mandatory for the completion of one's own collection, making interaction a congenial core activity of the game. Here again, the subtle and skillful interconnection between game and narrative mechanics emerges clearly.

Cutscenes: Narrative motivation, background information and entertainment made in Japan

Japanese games have always been described as being narration-heavy when compared to Western genres: the game action is embedded in stories and thus provides narrative depth to the ludic actions. Of course, the crossmedial over-

---

38 Before that it reads: "In Japan, where the Pokémon were born, Ash is called Satoshi; and Satoshi was made in the image of his creator, Satoshi Tajiri, a young outcast who, as a boy living just outside Tokyo, collected insects and other tiny creatures of field, pond and forest." (Chua-Eoan/Larimer 1999: 83)

39 "Since the late 1980s, the trend in game design has been towards greater complexity that, demanding intense concentration, pulls players into solitary engagements with their virtual gameworlds." (Allison 2014: 145)

flow into story universes (e.g. of *Pokémon* or *Mario*, see above) nurtures and ex-pands this affinity already inherent in individual game stories even more. In this context, cutscenes are an often used narrative mechanic.

First introduced in arcade games, the so-called intermissions that were born *ex negativo* – Western arcades did not at that time provide any narrative ele-ments – already comprise all of the three main characteristics of modern cutscenes: narrative motivation, expansion of background information and con-text, and supply of reward and entertainment at the same time.[40] *Space Invaders Part 2* (Taito, 1979) first introduced these intermissions, which can be described as transitions that secure a narrative sequentiality: instead of exposing the player seamlessly to the next wave of adversary alien spacecrafts, the intermissions show how the alien mothership escapes while transmitting distress calls. This provides the player with useful information (the next attack is impending!), not only based on logical consequences but also on narrative motivation.

Pac-Man (1980) also uses intermissions, but rather than motivating the ongo-ing game action as in *Space Invaders Part 2*, they primarily serve as entertain-ment and provide additional information about the characters: the ghost called Blinky gets caught on a pixelated nail and tears his robe, and reappears in the next intermission with patches, before dragging the cloth behind him in the third. These intermissions expand the narrative in a more humoristic and nonsensical way, underlining the ambiguity of the cuteness of deadly ghosts (similar to *Pokémon*, see above, 3.2).

The very first title that uses a cutscene as an introduction came out only one year later at the very beginning of the *Donkey Kong* series: significantly, the kidnapping of Jumpman's girlfriend not only serves as background and motiva-tion for starting the game action, but also introduces, in a very subtle manner, the micromechanics of climbing up the ladder, which is key to the gameplay.

Meanwhile, 40 years after their first appearance, cutscenes are not always a po-pular feature in games:

We love to play the game, and not waste 15 Minutes during the first time skipping all those cutscenes. (setsunaaa 2015)

i've done plays through while skipping all cut-scenes and, while it can feel disjointed […] i think it's a better experience overall. (LoG-Sacrament 2013)

I get it when it's a cutscene heavy game (Japanese games especially). (csward 2016)

---

40 Cf. Klevjer, who speaks of "reward by entertainment" (2002: 195).

In these cases, cutscenes are not taken as motivating, informative, rewarding and entertaining elements, but as a waste of time that luckily can be avoided by skipping them. The perceived cutscene-heaviness of Japanese games in fact can be seen in the 141 answers on an internet forum, replying to the question "What game has the longest intro cutscene?" (Menitta 2016). The games that stand out are *Ōkami* ([Clover Studio, 2006] referred to 31 times; in fact being 18 min long), *Metal-Gear-Solid* series (17x; 7-16 min), *Persona 4* ([Atlus, 2008] 16x; 20 min) and *Xenosaga* ([Monolith Soft, 2002] 10x; 13 min). It does not seem necessary for a game to have intro cutscenes that long, but the only positive answer addresses the reason:

this thread made me realize that I really like long intros, world setups that bring me into the world before even doing anything. Never really thought of it before, guess I treated it as a given. (WilyRook, #59 in Menitta 2016)

In the case of *Ōkami*, the long, even doubled-up narration at the beginning is clearly intended to help the player adapt to the world of ancient Japanese folk tales and myths: "The passive role of the player in this sequence, merely clicking on the screen to progress through the text, heightens the feeling of being told a story." (Hutchinson 2019: 48-49) From a Western viewpoint, this large number of cutscenes combined with an abundance of text is somewhat difficult to digest. It also suggests that game genres such as visual novels are clearly meant to be popular in Japan only, given its strong culture of writing (*Hatoful Boyfriend*, see below).

ABSURD OVERCOMPLEXITY, INTRIGUING SIMPLICITY AND MIXING OF EVERYTHING: *MUKOKUSEKI* AS CATALYST

The world record for the longest cutscenes is held by *Metal Gear Solid 4* (Konami, 2008, 27 min at a stretch, and 71 min combined). In general, the whole *Metal Gear* series comes up with a unique amount of cutscenes, nonetheless enjoyed by the gamer community. This is corroborated by an article entitled "Which game has cutscenes you actually enjoy watching? Tell us about the ones you don't want to skip", in which video game journalists name their favorite cutscenes. Andy Kelly associates the cutscenes in *Metal Gear Rising: Revengeance* (Platinum Games, 2013) with a kind of jolly absurdity.

You know when a cutscene starts in a Platinum game you're gonna be entertained. And *Rising* is the peak of their powers when it comes to daft cinematics. To the point where they're almost more fun than the actual game at points.

Fusing the most indulgent theatrics of anime with the outrageousness of Japanese video-games, *Revengeance* is a celebration of the absurd. Which is amazing considering it's a game based on the dull co-star of MGS2. (PCGamer 2019)

The *Bayonetta* series (Platinum Games, since 2009) is another well-known celebration of the absurd. In a forum on steamcommunity.com, users Cake and Setnaro X exchange their thoughts about this:

Cake: RIDICULOUS. I don't think I've ever rolled my eyes as much as I have whenever there's a cutscene in this game. Why is there so much nonsense?
Setnaro X: Story purposes. You can easily skip through all the non-interactive cutscenes instantly by holding the right trigger and select button at the same time if it's really that bothersome to you.
Cake: It's not bothersome, it's just . . . weird. Almost as if they went out of their way to make it as silly as possible.
Setnaro X: Bingo. Welcome to PlatinumGames' storytelling. Their writing is pretty much the usual tongue-in-cheek shenanigans you'd expect from an over-the-top Japanese action flick. (Cake/Setnaro X 2017)

For Cake, the nonsensical cutscenes are not "bothersome" and therefore not to be skipped. However, it does not seem so easy for him to cope with the otherness of *Bayonetta*'s cutscenes, and he searches for a word to describe it (shown by the dots: "just … weird"). Setnaro X's explanation for the underlying absurdity is twofold: it refers to the storytelling of a game production company ("Welcome to PlatinumGames' storytelling"), and the fact that it clearly serves Japanese narrative mechanics ("from an over-the-top Japanese action flick").

For other Western players though, the exaggeration and absurdity of Japanese games can take on unacceptable proportions. YouTuber TheGamerTron, who in general loves to play Japanese games, explains in his video "Why I dislike Japanese Storytelling in Video Games" that these absurd insertions are the "biggest issue" for him and make him feel as if he is on drugs:

The pointless bullshit, the pointless weird shit [...] the weird out of nowhere shit. [...] I swear, watching some anime, it makes me feel like, am I under the influence, did I actually drink some alcohol or do some narcotics before watching this, because it doesn't seem right. (TheGamerTron 2017, at 00:09:36)

TheGamerTron talks of animes here, but the video shows cutscenes from *Bayonetta* and *Vanquish* (Platinum Games, 2010) during his discussion of this, in his opinion, tiresome topic.

As we have seen in the case of the Let's Play of *Beautiful Katamari* (see above, chapter 1), the strategy of comparing Japanese games to a drug trip seems helpful for coping with the excessive absurdity and strange mixture of things. In that sense, *Beautiful Katamari* is the perfect example, where story, absurdity and the simplest mechanics are mingled to perfection: "[…] the story's premise is a more or less transparent pretext for gameplay that is non-narrative with a vengeance — you just roll a ball." (Jones 2008: 52)

With the Platinum Games titles and the *Katamari* series, we have already digressed from the pool of examples that are based on the *mukokuseki* principle, by dealing with games that are Japanese through and through. Still, the fundamental mechanic seems to be the same: unceasing and unabashed mixing of everything at every level. Seen in this light, the *mukokuseki* principle that first helped to establish a Japanese game industry in its own right has become an independent catalyst for creativity of its own. Our last three examples will focus on the mixture of deceptive simplicity, nonsensical joy and uncanny narrative continuity.

Simplicity as a narrative mechanic seems to be one answer to this often excessive mixture of over-exaggeration and absurdity. Nonetheless, the nonsensical aspect still remains an important part of these games. *Frogger* (Konami/Sega, 1981), for example, is one of the oldest arcade games in which the rules of the real world do not apply anymore: the goal is to achieve a happy ending (albeit endlessly postponed) by guiding a frog over a multi-lane motorway and a river. On the micro level, the cars drive in opposite directions in each of the lanes, and – even more irrational – safe places like logs and water lilies may float down the same river, but on different currents. The fact that the frog dies if it falls into the water, is the high point of the nonsense.

ママにゲーム隠された (*Mama ni gemu kakusareta*, hap inc., 2017) is a novel "casual yet surreal escape game" (description on Google Play). Already the title is more complex than it might seem and is in fact difficult to translate: on Google Play, the title is stated as *Hidden my game by mom 3* (Hidden 2018), Wikipedia labels it as *Mom Hid my Game* and also Let's Players refer to it in the latter way. The literal translation is "by my mom the game has being hidden", the passive voice underlining the abnormal might of mom and the importance of the gaming device in contrast to the helplessness of the boy, who is desperate to find it.[41] The visuals and point-and-click design are very simple, but the appeal and the suspense of the game lie in a rather subtle narrative mechanic, of finding out where mom has hidden the device and where she has hidden herself – bumping into her before getting the console means a fail – mixed with a nonsensical touch. First, her hideouts are almost ridiculously easy to find, but gradually, they become more and more disguised, making the atmosphere of the game fun and uncanny at the same time. Later on, the measures taken to prevent the boy/the player from getting the device grow highly absurd. The more or less obvious hideouts are for example guarded by crocodiles and motorcycle acrobats, which need to be outwitted. This basically never-ending story of the boy outsmarting his mom contains a surprising twist after 49 levels, which represent days: the boy barricades himself in his room for the next 950 days, and the solution of the last level is to release him from his *hikikomori* state (social withdrawal syndrome), uniting him with his mom and family.

It is a narrative strategy that emphasizes the bittersweetness of things and merges play-and-pleasure with tragedy and sadness in a sudden, unabashed manner. Often, the (Western) audience is caught on the wrong foot, lulled in by the blithe Japanese game world of the hilarious and easy-going absurd.

This is also the case with *Hatoful Boyfriend: A School of Hope and White Wings* (PigeoNation Inc., 2011). Here, the mixing strategy seems to go over the top by mixing everything at every level. The game's genre is the visual novel, in which lavish images and a great many textual inserts are combined into a multibranched narrative. The player takes the role of the story's protagonist, interacting through extensive text-based conversations with various characters and altering the story's ending by making different choices (prompting an invitation to replay the game after the first playthrough).

Of course, the visualizations clearly refer to manga, with the player clicking through images that are not animated in general, only "[a]t certain pivotal moments in the story, more detailed images drawn especially for those scenes and enhanced by more cinematic camera angles and CGI are included." (Cavallaro 2010: 90-91) From a Western perspective, visual novels are often falsely equated with dating sims, where the player controls a usually "male avatar whose goal is to date, and converse with, various female characters in order to form a romantic relationship" (ibid 94-95) in a high-school environment. In Hatoful Boyfriend, this is indeed the case, but with important twists: the avatar is a female and the dating sim mode is only the first round of the game. The setting of the game is

---

41 On the concept of self, represented by the structure of Japanese language, cf. Hasegawa/Hirose (2005).

fairly nonsensical: In an alternate world taken over by sapient birds (the dystopian background is not fully revealed in the first round of the game), the player – a
human named Hiyoko, meaning 'chick' – starts college at St. PigeoNation's Institute, an elite school for birds that has invited her as human liaison to prove the
possibility of peaceful co-existence and even friendship between birds – mainly
doves – and humans. The title of the game is already highly ambiguous and os-
cillates between different readings – in Japanese, 'hato' means dove, but the often inconclusive Japanese pronunciation of the English words results in further
different possibilities, playing with its contradictive meanings: heartful vs. hurtful (and even hateful). And this is not a coincidence: if the player has completed
four specific endings (out of thirteen) of the first part and is willing to 'fulfill the
promise' (instead of living a normal life), the second round of the game is un-
locked, known as *Bad Boys Love* (or *Hurtful Boyfriend*).

*Figure 7: "Kawaii!" – Pewdiepie as 'weabitch' during his Let's Play of Hatoful
Boyfriend.*

Source: Pewdiepie 2014, screenshot (Kato/Bauer)

In this storyline, the protagonist soon goes missing, with the game turning unex-
pectedly from a drippy love story into a veritable murder mystery mixed with
horror. *Hatoful Boyfriend* is in this sense a deceptive game, as the pinkish background and the purple text box invoke a lavish atmosphere of easy-going romance (cf. Figure 7). But a closer look at this introduction of a character already
reveals an excessive, almost uncanny mixture of things: the quail (a photo of a

real bird) is depicted as it would look in human form (a manga character). It is difficult to tell from the bird's appearance, but all the human forms of the male love interests of the female protagonists look rather feminine, blurring the gender lines. And in the case of Kazuaki Nanaki, the name is Japanese, but the character is not (cf. Figure 7).

Hatoful Boyfriend is a prototype of the otherness of Japanese games, playing excessively with the blending of oppositions: non-Japanese and Japanese, text and image, human and animals, male and female, friendship and cruelty, romance (dating simulator) and murder mystery, mellow schooldays and postapocalyptic background. Many Western players were set on the wrong track by this game – one of them summing it up as follows:

Here's what I expected from Hatoful Boyfriend: a lighthearted dating sim filled with bird puns and typical Japanese high school tropes. I got that. I also got punched in the gut with emotions many times. As a result of playing this game, I am now suffering from PTSD: Pigeon Tragedy Shock Disorder. (Ali 2014)

CONCLUSION

Hatoful Boyfriend was positively received in the West in general, but in the case of Pewdiepie's Let's Play, it could not win the audience's favor. Against his will, the Let's Player had to drop it after only one part, as a result of generating too few likes. This example shows that some of the Japanese games and narrative mechanics might be just too weird to be easily watched by a Western audience. Of course, this underlines the incommensurability of different gaming cultures.

However, this should not to be seen too negatively. As Bhabha (e.g. Bhabha/Rutherford 1990) has shown in his critique of multiculturality and by providing an alternative way of dealing with otherness – by accepting it and creating a third space instead of incorporating or colonializing it –, it is essential to be able to accept and acknowledge the other culture. Against this backdrop, the Japanese strategy of *mukokuseki* can be regarded as a solution that was perfected by and for Japanese culture, driven by the fundamental principle of pushing the home-grown gaming culture to its limits. And this strategy could serve as a mirror to reflect Western ways of dealing with other cultures as well.

In this article we used the concept of *mukokuseki* as an instrument for comprehending the otherness of Japanese games and for understanding some of the narrative mechanics that are to be found under the surface, which so often appears to be non-specific in terms of nationality. This comprised the intertwined approach of game and narrative mechanics (soft- and hardware, so to speak), the mixture of old and new dealing with the desire for innovation together with the urge for nostalgia, the unflinching copying or even plagiarization of the best practices and the already known, blurring the lines between real and digital, the overflow of stories and their incorporation into ever more expanding crossmedial story universes, the coexistence of contrasting narrative topics and excessive use of absurd and nonsensical storylines, always serving play-and-pleasure, but also hiding surprising twists that break with traditional narrative patterns. It appears that the de- and reculturalizing *mukokuseki* strategy, with its mixing of own domestic elements with ones borrowed from the West, has become a fundamental principle of Japanese game design. Western players try to cope with these strategies by using drug metaphors or by immersing themselves into the game world by acting out their own idea of Japaneseness. Nonetheless, as the example of Pewdiepie shows, his gestures and prosody when expressing the exaggerated *kawaii* feelings still remain that of a foreigner: "sorry, my weabitch took over" (cf. Figure 7). It is clear though that playing Japanese games affects Western players as well, as they subtly become a part of the *mukokuseki* machinery.

Key to GAT2 transcriptions

(the list below only contains the conventions relevant to this article)

°h	breathing in
(.)	micro pause, estimate, up to approx. 0.2 seconds
(--)	medium-length pause, estimate, approx. 0.5 to 0.8 seconds
(1.0)	timed pauses
robert_s	words joined together within units
((coughs))	para- and extralinguistic actions and events
<<whispers>>	para- and extralinguistic actions and events accompanying speech
((...))	gap in transcript
=	fast, immediate follow-on contribution by speaker
:	extending, lengthening by approx. 0.2 to 0.5 seconds
acCENT	focal stress, accentuation
accEnt	secondary stress
ac!CENT!	pronounced stress

Fluctuations in pitch at the end of intonational phrases:

?	steep rise
′	medium rise
–	even level
;	medium drop
.	steep drop

Intralinear notation of fluctuations in stress and pitch:

^SO	rising-falling
′SO	rising
↓⁻SO	jump in pitch to a noticeable low and constant accent

Changes in volume and pace of speech:

<<ff> >	fortissimo, very loud
<<p> >	piano, quiet
<<len> >	lento, slow

REFERENCES

Literature

Ali (2014): "It's a Hatoful Life: The Deep, Dark Story of Hatoful Boyfriend", November 10, 2014 (https://miscellanyali.wordpress.com/2014/11/).

Allison, Anne (2006): Millennial Monsters: Japanese Toys and the Global Imagination, Berkley: University of California Press.

Allison, Anne (2014): "Portable Monsters and Commodity Cuteness. Pokémon as Japan's new global player." In: Matthew Allen/Rumi Sakamoto (eds.), Japanese Popular Culture. Critical Concept in Asia Studies 4. Globalizing Japanese Popular Culture: The Coolness of Japan, London: Routledge, pp. 137-154.

Aoi-Ne-Blue (2009): "REFERENCE-Manga eyes", January 29, 2009 (https://www.deviantart.com/aoi-ne-blue/art/REFERENCE-Manga-eyes-111 141658).

Barthes, Roland (1983 [1970]): Empire of Signs, New York: Hill and Wang.

Bhabha, Homi/Rutherford, Jonathan (1990): "The Third Space. Interview with Homi Bhabha." In: Jonathan Rutherford (ed.), Identity: Community, Culture, Difference, London: Lawrence and Wishart, pp. 207-221.

Braudel, Fernand (1993): A History of Civilizations, New York: Penguin Books.

Brian (@NE_Brian) (2017): "Monolith Soft on Xenoblade X western changes, Nintendo Europe handling Xenoblade 2, Nintendo's localization process", June 16, 2017 (https://nintendoeverything.com/monolith-soft-on-xenoblade-x-western-changes-nintendo-europe-handling-xenoblade-2-nintendos-localization-process/).

Buckingham, David/Sefton-Green, Julian (2004): "Structure, Agency, and Pedagogy in Children's Media Culture." In: Joseph Tobin (ed.), Pikachu's Global Adventure: The Rise and Fall of Pokémon, Durham: Duke University Press, pp. 12-33.

Cake/Setnaro X (2017): "Bayonetta – Ridiculous", July 19, 2017 (https://steamcommunity.com/app/460790/discussions/0/1458455461472520344/).

Cavallaro, Dani (2010): Anime and the visual novel: narrative structure, design and play at the crossroads of animation and computer games, Jefferson: McFarland & Co.

Censored Gaming (2017): "How Video Game 'Culturalization' Differs From 'Localization'", June 17, 2017 (https://www.youtube.com/watch?v=bqvkbDqtRY8).

Chua-Eoan, Howard/Larimer, Tim (1999): "Beware of the Poke Mania." In: TIME Magazine November 22 154/21, pp. 80-89.

Cohn, Neil (2013): The Visual Language of Comics: Introduction to the Structure and Cognition of Sequential Images, London: Bloomsbury Academic.

Consalvo, Mia (2016): Atari to Zelda. Japan's Videogames in Global Contexts, Cambridge: The MIT Press.

Coulmas, Florian (2014): "Das Monster aus dem Meer". In: nzz.ch, February 21, 2014 (https://www.nzz.ch/feuilleton/das-monster-aus-dem-meer-1.18247790).

csward (2016): "I hate cutscenes in video games so much" (https://www.gamespot.com/forums/games-discussion-1000000/i-hate-cutscenes-in-video-games-so-much-33278480/).

deWinter, Jennifer (2015): "Japan." In: Mark J.P. Wolf (ed.), Video Games Around the World, Cambridge: The MIT Press, pp. 319-343.

Edwards 2011: "Culturalization: The Geopolitical and Cultural Dimension of Game Content." In: TRANS 15, pp. 19-28.

Eickhorst, Eric (2006): Game centers: A historical and cultural analysis of Japan's video amusement establishments (MA thesis), Kansas: The University of Kansas.

Game Grumps (2019): "Learning About Japan! – Game Grumps Compilations", August 16, 2019 (https://www.youtube.com/watch?v=tshNA5HdSjE).

Gee, James (2006 [2003]): "Cultural Models: Do You Want to Be the Blue Sonic or the Dark Sonic?" In: Katie Salen/Eric Zimmerman (eds.), The Game Design Reader. A Rules of Play Anthology, Cambridge: The MIT Press, pp. 610-639.

Giesecke, Michael (2007): Die Entdeckung der kommunikativen Welt. Studien zur kulturvergleichenden Mediengeschichte, Frankfurt a.M.: Suhrkamp.

Green, Laurence (2018): "The Rambling Guitarist: Gender, Genre and Archetypes in Nikkatsu Action's Mukokuseki Eiga." In: The SOAS Journal of Postgraduate Research 12, pp. 41-53.

Guins, Raiford (2014): Game After: A Cultural Study of Video Game Afterlife, Cambridge: The MIT Press.

Hasegawa, Yoko/Hirose, Yukio (2005): "What the Japanese Language Tells Us about the Alleged Japanese Relational Self." In: Australian Journal of Linguistics 25/2, pp. 219-251.

Hidden (2018): "Hidden my game by mom 3", July 31 (https://play.google.com/store/apps/details?id=air.jp.ne.hap.mom3&hl=en).

Howell, David L. (2009): "The Social Life of Firearms in Tokugawa Japan." In: Japanese Studies 29/1, pp. 65-80.

Huhtamo, Erkki (2005): "Slots of Fun, Slots of Trouble. An Archaeology of Arcade Gaming." In: Joost Raessens/Jeffrey Goldstein (eds.), Handbook of Computer Games Studies, Cambridge: The MIT Press, pp. 3-21.

Hutchinson, Rachael (2019): Japanese Culture Through Videogames, London: Routledge (e-Book).

IGDA (2012): "Best Practices for Game Localization", February 1, 2012 (https://cdn.ymaws.com/www.igda.org/resource/collection/2DA60D94-0F74-46B1-A9E2-F2CE8B72EA4D/Best-Practices-for-Game-Localization-v22.pdf).

Iwabuchi, Koichi (2002): Recentering Globalization. Popular culture and Japanese transnationalism, Durham: Duke University Press.

Iwabuchi, Koichi (2014 [2002]): "'Soft' Nationalism and Narcissism. Japanese popular culture goes global." In: Matthew Allen/Rumi Sakamoto (eds.), Japanese Popular Culture. Critical Concept in Asia Studies 4. Globalizing Japanese Popular Culture: The Coolness of Japan, London: Routledge, pp. 18-39.

Jones, Steven E. (2008): The Meaning of Video Games: Gaming and Textual Strategies, New York: Routledge.

Kato, Hiloko/Bauer, René (2020): "Magic Cone – der erweiterte Magic Circle. Japanische Spielkultur und ihre Aneignung im Westen." In: Martin Hennig/Hans Krah (eds.), Spielzeichen III – Kulturen im Computerspiel/

Kulturen des Computerspiels, Boizenburg: Werner Hülsbusch Verlag, pp. 277-340.

Klevjer, Rune (2002): "In Defense of Cutscenes." In: Frans Mäyrä (ed.), Proceedings of Computer Games and Digital Cultures Conference, Tampere: Tampere University Press, p. 191-202.

Kohler, Chris (2016 [2005]): Power-Up: How Japanese Video Games Gave the World an Extra Life, New York: Dover Publications.

Lipscombe, Daniel (2018): "Kaizo: The Dark Side of Super Mario", April 11, 2018 (https://www.kotaku.co.uk/2018/04/11/kaizo-the-dark-side-of-super-mario).

LoG-Sacrament (2013): Most cutscene-heavy video game you've played, December 4, 2019 (https://www.gamespot.com/forums/games-discussion-1000 000/most-cutscene-heavy-video-game-youve-played-29337000/).

McLuhan, Marshall (2006 [1964]): Understanding Media. The Extensions of Man, London: Routledge.

Menitta (2016): What Game Has The Longest Intro Cutscene?, April 27, 2016 (https://www.neogaf.com/threads/what-game-has-the-longest-intro-cutscene. 1212133/).

Napier, Susan J. (2007): From Impressionism to Anime. Japan as Fantasy and Fan Cult in the Mind of the West, New York: Palgrave Macmillan.

Nintendo UK (2015): "Mario Myths with Mr. Miyamoto", September 10, 2015. (https://www.youtube.com/watch?v=uu2DnTd3dEo).

Pandacard (2014): "Let's Play Katamari Damacy Episode 1: Japanese Drugs!!", March 25, 2014 (https://www.youtube.com/watch?v=gXofi752lms).

PCGamer (2019): "Which game has cutscenes you actually enjoy watching?", January 19, 2019 (https://www.pcgamer.com/which-game-has-cutscenes-you-actually-enjoy-watching/).

Pellétier-Gagnon, Jérémie (2019): "Players, Cabinets, and the Space In-between: Case Studies of Non-ludic Negotiation of Video Game Cabinet Spaces in Japanese Game Centers." In: Replaying Japan 1, Kyoto: Ritsumeikan Center for Game Studies, pp. 29-39 (http://r-cube.ritsumei.ac.jp/repo/repo sito-ry/rcube/11679/rcgs_1_pelletier gagnon.pdf).

Perrin, Noel (1979): Giving Up the Gun: Japan's Reversion to the Sword, 1543-1879, Boston : D. R. Gordine.

Pewdiepie (2014): "PIGEON BOYFRIEND SIMULATOR! – Hatoful Boyfriend – Gameplay – Part 1", September 5, 2014 (https://www.youtube.com/ watch?v=GCst68yJ7co).

Pewdiepie (2017): "L-S-D.", September 16, 2017 (https://www.youtube.com/ watch?v=GrVpSMIWK50).

Pilling, David (2014): Bending Adversity. Japan and the Art of Survival, London: Penguin Books.

Picard, Martin (2013): The Foundation of Geemu: A Brief History of Early Japanese video games, September 13, 2013 (http://gamestudies.org/ 1302/ articles/picard).

Schreier, Jason (2017): "Xenoblade Chronicles X's Director On Localization Changes: 'I Didn't Mind Much At All'", June 16, 2017 (//kotaku.com/xeno blade-chronicles-xs-director-on-localization-change-1796157409).

Sedensky, Eric (2012): Winning Pachinko: The Game of Japanese Pinball, Tokyo: Tuttle Publishing.

Selting, Margret et al. (2009): "Gesprächsanalytisches Transkriptionssystem 2 (GAT 2)". In: Gesprächsforschung – Online-Zeitschrift zur verbalen Interaktion 10, pp. 353-402.

setsunaaa (2015):c"TOO MANY CUTSCENES you are forces through at start...", September 2, 2015 (https://steamcommunity.com/app/287700/discus sions/0/527274088385015737/?l=portuguese).

Sheff, David (1993): Game Over. Nintendo's Battle to Dominate an Industry, London: Hodder & Stoughton.

Smith, Alexander (2020): They Created Worlds. The Story of the People and Companies That Shaped the Video Game Industry 1: 1971-1982, Boca Raton: CRC Press.

Szczepaniak, John W. (2014a): The Untold History of Japanese Game Developers 1 [self-published].

Szczepaniak, John W. (2014b): The Untold History of Japanese Game Developers 3 [self-published].

That Japanese Man Yuta (2017): "Do Anime Characters Look White to Japanese People?" August 15, 2017 (https://www.youtube.com/watch?v=q_Xd2x LAjDM).

TheGamerTron (2017): "Why I dislike Japanese Storytelling", June 16, 2017 (https://www.youtube.com/watch?v=Bc2PjlGV124).

Tobin, Samuel (2015): "Cocktail Cabinets: A Critique of Digital and Ludic Essentialism?" In: Evan Torner/Emma Lee Waldron/Aaron Trammell (eds.), Analog Game Studies 2, Carnegie Mellon University: ETC Press, pp. 175-179.

Tobin, Samuel (2016): "Hanging in the Video Arcade". In: Journal of Game Criticism (http://gamescriticism.org/articles/tobin-3-a).

Vogel, Ezra F. (2019): China and Japan: Facing History, Cambridge: Harvard University Press.

Wang, Q. Edward (2015): Chopsticks. A Cultural and Culinary History, Cambridge: Cambridge University Press.

Wilde, Oscar (2007 [1891]) "The Decay of Lying." In: David Richter (ed.), The Critical Tradition: Classic Texts and Contemporary Trends, Boston: Bedford, pp. 478-496.

Games

Bayonetta, Platinum Games, Sega/Nintendo, 2009.

Beautiful Katamari, Namco Bandai Games, Namco, 2007.

Donkey Kong, Nintendo R&D1, Nintendo, 1981.

Donkey Kong Jr., Nintendo R&D1, Nintendo, 1982.

Frogger, Konami, Sega, 1981.

Galaxian, Namco, Namco/Midway Games, 1979.

Hatoful Boyfriend, PigeoNation Inc., MIST[PSI]PRESS, 2011.

Kakuto Chojiin, Dream Publishing, Microsoft Game Studios, 2002.

Love Tester, Sega, Sega, 1972.

LSD: Dream Emulator, Asmik Ace Entertainment, Asmik Ace Entertainment, 1998.

Mega Man, Capcom, Capcom, 1987.

Metal Gear Rising: Revengeance, PlatinumGames, Konami Digital Entertainment, 2013.

Metal Gear Solid, Konami Computer Entertainment Japan, Konami, 1998.

Metal Gear Solid 4, Kojima Productions, Konami, 2008.

Mom Hid My Game, hap inc., Kemco/hap inc., 2017.

Motopolo, Sega, Sega, 1968.

My Summer Holiday-series, Millennium Kitchen, Sony Computer Entertainment, since 2000.

Ōkami, Clover Studio, Capcom, 2006.

Pac-Man, Namco, Namco, 1980.

Periscope, Namco, Namco, 1965/Sega, Sega, 1966.

Persona 4, Atlus, Atlus/Square Enix/Ubisoft, 2008.

Pokémon, Nintendo, Nintendo, since 1996.

Pokémon Go, Niantic/The Pokémon Company, Niantic/The Pokémon Company 2016.

Pong, Atari, Atari, 1972.

Sea Wolf, Dave Nutting Associates, Midway, 1976.

Sonic Adventure 2, Sonic Team USA, Sega, 2001.

Space Invaders, Taito, Taito/Midway, 1978.

Space Invaders 2, Taito, Taito/Midway, 1979.
Speed Race, Taito, Taito/Midway, 1974.
Sports Fishing, Sega, Sega, 1994.
Stunt Car, Sega, Sega, 1970.
Super Mario Bros., Nintendo EAD, Nintendo 1985.
Super Mario 3D World, Nintendo EAD Tokyo, Nintendo, 2013.
Super Mario 64, Nintendo EAD, Nintendo, 1996.
TV Basketball, Taito, Taito/Midway, 1974.
Wild Gunman, Nintendo, Nintendo, 1974.
Xenoblade Chronicles X, Monolith Soft, Nintendo, 2015.
Xenosaga, Monolith Soft, Namco, 2002.

Movies

Alien (1979), Ridley Scott, Brandywine Productions, 20th Century Fox.
Godzilla (1954), Honda Ishirō, Toho Studios, Toho.
Mothra (1961), Honda Ishirō, Toho Studios, Toho.
The Rambling Guitarist/ギターを持った渡り鳥 (1959), Saitō Buichi, Nikkatsu.

Characterization and Emergent Narrative in Dwarf Fortress

Tarn Adams

When people play games, they tell stories about their experiences. A tale might concern the tactics used in a chess game or be part of a multi-part series recounting the generations of a family in *The Sims* (Maxis 2004). If we view games as a storytelling companion, we can think systematically about what sorts of game mechanics encourage player stories of a certain kind or make the storytelling process easier for players, and we can think about utilizing traditional authorial techniques toward these ends.

In *Dwarf Fortress* (Bay 12 Games 2006), a fantasy settlement simulator, we attempted to provide players with a game to tell generic but intricate stories in a fantasy setting. Most elements of *Dwarf Fortress* are procedurally generated by the game itself, so we could not rely on writers to produce elements of the stories for players to incorporate into their retellings. However, we were still able to improve our players' ability to tell stories and to increase their enthusiasm for doing so by employing methods of characterization.

WHERE WE STARTED

When *Dwarf Fortress* was released in 2006, we had a basic approach to characterization. Each of the player's dwarves was given a name, had work and combat skills, a sex and a specific age, could form family relationships and take a position in the fortress (such as manager or broker), and had likes and dislikes. They had bodies which could be injured, as well as clothing and a few other possible items like weapons and shields.

We came to this list in a variety of ways. Sometimes elements drive mechanics, like skills and preferences, sometimes elements are required to provide crucial information to the player about underlying mechanics, such as injury descriptions, while other elements like names have no mechanical purpose and are used purely as storytelling aids.

As we developed the game toward emergent narrative and the creation of player stories, each of these systems was expanded, as we will discuss below. At the same time, the initial selection provided a scaffold for what constitutes a "*Dwarf Fortress* story" that still exists to some extent in new stories, as part of the culture of the community surrounding the game, so it is important to be thoughtful about the first features which are provided to the player even in ongoing projects.

DIRECT PHYSICAL CHARACTERIZATION

The most straightforward method of characterization is simply to provide a description of a character. Reliance on this method is sometimes discouraged in writing ("show don't tell"), but most games sidestep this concern through the use of graphics. For the first decade and more of its existence, *Dwarf Fortress* relied on text and ASCII glyphs, so we had to use paragraphs of text for this purpose. Dwarves have eye colors and hairstyles, and much more. They can have scars from old injuries and gain age markers as the years pass by.

Notably, in player stories, wounds and scars figure most heavily, as well as the strength and other physical attributes of the dwarves. The reason for this is that these descriptors are related to game actions and player choices, and also to system mechanics. We saw these elements used in stories even though the text medium requires the player to seek out this information rather than absorbing it passively through graphics in the main play mode (Figure 1).

Figure 1: The beginning of the fortress "Pickenjoy" in blossoming springtime. What could possibly go wrong?

Source: screenshot (Ulrich Götz)

Beyond the body itself, direct physical characterization encompasses the outfit and mannerisms of a character. Dwarves have a variety of clothing and tools, and they can also collect personal trinkets and trophies from hunts. They use medical equipment such as crutches, splints and sutures. Not surprisingly, again, these personal trinkets, trophies and medical equipment figure into player stories more than standard elements of clothing, as these are linked to action in the game and sometimes reflect the consequences of player decisions.

We also briefly attempted to give the dwarves mannerism descriptions, such as "She taps her foot when she is nervous". As catalysts for emergent narrative, these were a failure, and this can be traced to the lack of a mechanical link to either mechanics or player choices. Emotional states and conversations are hard to model, and we did not link these mannerisms to what systems existed there. The mannerisms were just simple descriptions, and while this can carry weight when done well, as in regular writing, a kind of "show don't tell" principle still exists, with game mechanics being the analogue to illustration through character action. The descriptions most likely to be incorporated into player stories are reflected mechanically. In a way, direct characterization merges with indirect characterization because words potentially become actions when they describe system elements.

We can see this by comparing the mannerisms to our most effective early characterization method, the system of likes and dislikes. Dwarves have favorite foods, gems and pets, and fear vermin, to name just a few examples. When a dwarf produces an engraving, evaluates their living quarters, chooses personal treasures or their next meal, or shrieks in terror at the sight of a rat, this system comes into play, and has an impact on the course of the game as well. The player made or traded for those treasures, and the player carved those living quarters. Player stories and fan art incorporating the likes and dislikes of dwarves turned out to be disproportionately frequent, more common even than stories incorporating wounds or family. Thus, description, mechanics, and player agency all come together to produce emergent narrative.

However, the descriptive paragraph (the direct characterization) is still crucial as it confirms what the player is seeing or may not have noticed. In fact, screenshots of the descriptive paragraphs, with the relevant sentences highlighted, often accompany related player stories.

EXPANDING THE LIKES-DISLIKES SYSTEM

Seeing this initial success, we decided that expanding the interior life of individual dwarves would be an important focus of further additions. Games, notably strategy games, have incorporated visible, mechanically-realized personality traits into rulers and other characters to diversify play experiences, and these also have the effect of encouraging player narratives in these games. A personality trait here is generally an adjective such as "Wise" or "Cruel" that has an impact on AI decision-making or overall statistics. A character with two or three of these becomes more distinct as a story entity and a game object.

Ultimately, we decided that using a few distinct traits would not work in *Dwarf Fortress* because characters in the game need to respond to a diverse set of circumstances on an ongoing basis, and employing only a few traits would not differentiate characters in stories enough. We therefore decided to use a more general set of personality facets and intellectual values. Every character is rated on a 100-point scale in roughly 50 facets and roughly 30 values. For instance, a dwarf might be rated "Merciful +10" on the "Merciful-Impartial-Cruel" facet, and +25 on the value of "Scholarship". Numbers are not shown to the player, but the dwarf's personality is described in text, as stories without numbers are generally more compelling and shareable beyond the confines of the game's knowledgeable community.

When work on the personality expansion began in 2007, we started with the 30-facet NEO PI-R inventory based on the Big Five (OCEAN) model (Costa and McCrae 1992). This was adequate to start, but ultimately, we found this system of characterization was not narrative enough; in some cases, we wanted dwarves and others to be judged harshly. This inspired us to derive some additional facets from collections of literary character archetypes. We also drew from a variety of related lists, such as Thomas Aquinas's virtue and vice inventories from *Summa Theologica* (Aquinas 1920: II, Q1-170), culling improper elements and molding the material to fit the fantasy setting and our narrative goals. Intellectual values were cobbled together through simple brainstorming.

DEALING WITH LACK OF STIMULUS

The new personality system was an immediate success, with facet descriptions finding their way into player stories regularly, relating an interior life for characters often well beyond what the game was actually modeling.

Despite this progress, there were flaws in stories where dwarves were left by themselves or did not participate in any positive events. These dwarves could still be entirely happy, which caused some stories to feel odd. We eventually addressed this by adding a set of needs derived from every character's personality facets and intellectual values. Dwarves that did not meet their needs would complain and suffer from stress and distraction, and we further encouraged player engagement with needs by making dwarves that met their needs more satisfied and focused in their work.

THE ROAD TO CHARACTER ARCS

Emergent narrative is bolstered by the interplay of presentation, system mechanics, player investigation and player agency (Adams 2019: 149-158). We add new systems and expand existing systems in ways that the player can see and interact with, in ways that align with the story types and qualities we want to arise. The needs system addressed a particular problem in this way. But our player stories to this point had broader characterization problems in that, mentally, dwarves never really changed. Physical trauma could change a dwarf, and they could form social relationships, attain a position in society, or craft a masterwork, but they had the same essential personalities at age 20 as they did at age 130.

We arrived at character arcs in *Dwarf Fortress* in a roundabout way. After the initial release in 2006, player stories often revolved around a phenomenon the community came to call a "tantrum spiral". These were caused by the model for dwarven happiness. Each event a dwarf experienced in a season was assigned a happiness or unhappiness value. These were added up, with the unhappiness values considered to be negative, and the sum represented the dwarf's current happiness. Dwarves that were sufficiently unhappy could throw a tantrum. The problem was that after the first tantrum, the resulting bad events caused unhappiness levels to rise among all those affected, leading to further tantrums, and the eventual fall of the fortress (Figure 2).

Figure 2: The soon fall of the fortress "Pickenjoy", with significantly increased unhappiness values among all dwarves affected.

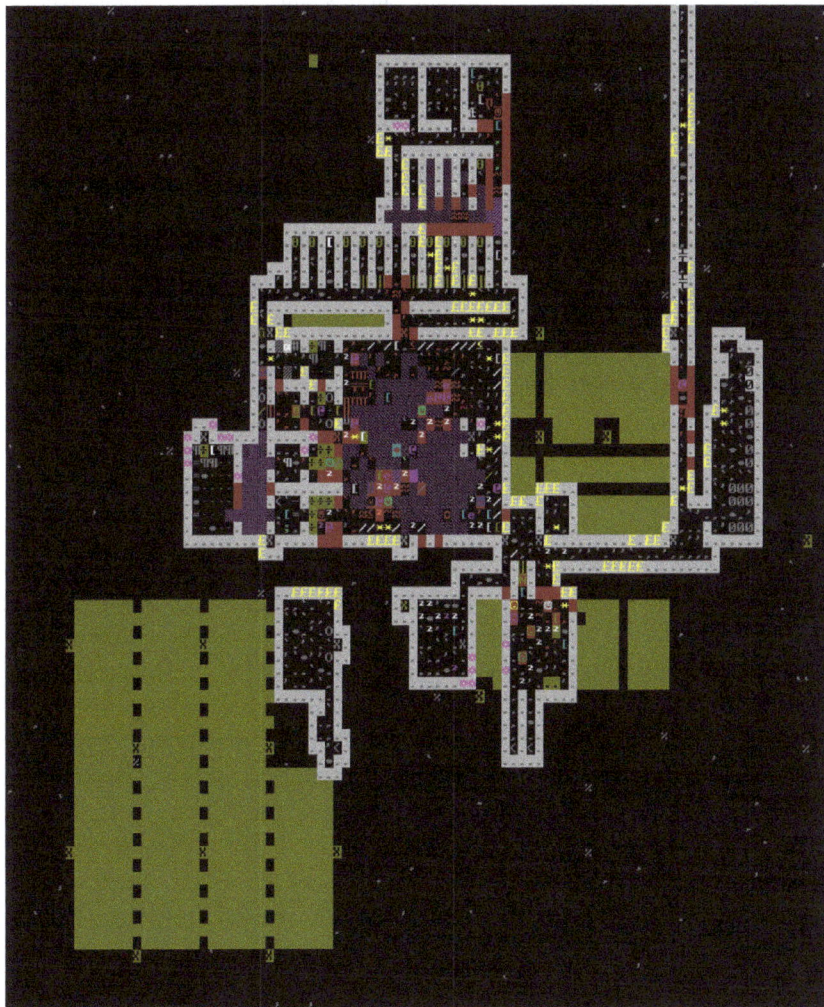

Source: screenshot (Ulrich Götz)

Our first attempt to address this problem was the stress system. Instead of a dwarf's emotional state being determined by the season's events, the old happiness number was repurposed into a stress number which was added to a dwarf's total stress over time. Only dwarves that accrued enough stress would throw tantrums. To increase the story potential of this new system, we also added 120 emotion glosses to the events, filtered through the dwarf's personality. For instance, one dwarf whose masterwork is ruined might feel vengeful and gain some stress, while another dwarf might feel depressed (while gaining a similar amount of stress), whereas a third dwarf in this situation might simply feel resigned or accepting of the misfortune and gain no stress at all. These circumstance and emotion pairs are displayed for the player, again without any numbers. The total stress level of the dwarf is also described.

This process caused us to reflect on memories. With the needs system, we solved the problem of dwarves not minding total neglect. With the stress system, we solved the problem of them living entirely from moment to moment. But they were still creatures that did not much appreciate their pasts, and their pasts did not provide any kind of buffer for the stress that accumulated in their lives. So we decided to give them memories.

The strongest events in several categories, such as "work" or "family", are selected and stored into a first layer of memories each season. Any existing weaker memories here are overwritten (that is, forgotten). Dwarves, at random, can remember any memory in the top layer, and reexperience the emotion they felt when it happened, often with less severity. This adds or subtracts stress from the dwarf in the standard way. The player can see this happening along with the current season's regular circumstance-emotion pairs.

After more time passes, any top layer memory that has survived the overwriting process passes to a deeper layer of permanent memory. This process always causes personality changes in the dwarf, related loosely to the circumstance and which emotion it produced. The game allows this to be cathartic. A dwarf who was deeply humiliated might find that the memory is now freeing, for instance, and that they no longer care as much about the opinions of others. The personality change and the date and circumstance that caused it to occur is recorded for the player to see in the dwarf's personality readout. In the example above, occasionally remembering the permanent memory causes the dwarf's stress to be reduced rather than increased. Other unfortunate dwarves have permanent harmful memories. The personality changes affect play on an ongoing basis. This has been recorded in player stories, complete with screenshots of the personality and memory text.

This system is still imperfect, naturally, as the character arcs can often be about trivial matters if the dwarf has not experienced sufficient situations. A common problem is dwarves upending their whole life outlook due to being caught in the rain! This can be addressed through some additional gates and other checks, though we might keep some of this behavior to allow seemingly unimportant circumstances to be touchstones for characters on a rare basis.

CHARACTERS IN SOCIETY

Characters are not defined in isolation. Events are not just experienced internally but can be witnessed and talked about. Relationships can change and rumors can pass through communities. Dwarves have family, friendships, grudges, citizenship, religious affiliations and positions in society. Spies and vampires can adopt secret identities, and evidence might be given on the grounds of appearance alone. Agents can manipulate dwarves by appealing to their ideology or their greed. All of this contributes to characterization. It is clearly a broad topic, but in *Dwarf Fortress*, we have not spent quite as much time on this as on the physical and interior life of individuals. Here we will present a few decisions that made a difference.

In the original 2006 release, when a fortress reached a certain level of prestige, a baron or baroness would be installed, traveling to the site from the larger world. The noble needed to be taken care of, causing a drain on fort resources and a distraction from the player's goals. This did have a large impact on stories, but the repercussions were mostly of the variety "noble inexplicably drowns in magma". In order to address this, we instead allowed the player to elevate one of their own dwarves to the position of baron when the time came. The dwarf selected is likely one they have a history with, possibly a favorite or one with a story rationale for attaining the position. The dwarf's story advances, and the overall stories diversify (though "noble accidents" are still a common theme in player stories).

The addition of taverns and libraries also had an oversized impact on emergent narrative and the characterization of dwarves. Most activity in the fortress is inward-facing, as treasure is mined and crafts are produced, and up to this point, trade and warfare were the most realized activities relating to the rest of the world, and, as implemented, they did not contribute much to social ties. Taverns were different. Travelers could come, speak to dwarves, be served by the dwarven bartender, make friends, get into fistfights, and even ask to become permanent residents or eventual citizens of the fortress. Existing dwarves had their character elucidated and changed by the proceedings, and new residents became new characters with an entirely different aspect to them, such as "resident human poet in the dwarven fortress". Migration and travel are resonant themes with a lot of people, and diverse and enthusiastic player stories were immediate.

PROCEDURAL AUTHORING AND COLLABORATIVE STORYTELLING

Emergent narrative relies on the ability of players to form stories from partial information, imagining connections, investigating details, and then using words artfully and sharing their tales. But none of the stories arising from video games rely on these player abilities alone, and developers can increase both the quantity and quality of narratives emerging from their games through their designs.

Beyond characterization, one can imagine every tool in a traditional author's toolbox as being at the developer's disposal, once the developer finds a fitting transposition of the underlying concepts. This is a difficult process, human authors are not replaceable, and the results are imperfect at best, but consideration in this direction can only strengthen the power of games as storytelling companions. And just as the author respects the reader, the developer must respect the player. This is done by valuing the player's choices and time, giving them the ability to find the information they are seeking, providing them with resonant material and connecting mechanics into a coherent whole.

REFERENCES

Literature

Adams, Tarn (2019): "Emergent Narrative in *Dwarf Fortress*." In: Tanya X. Short/Tarn Adams (eds.), Procedural Storytelling in Game Design, Boca Raton, Florida: CRC Press/Taylor & Francis, pp. 149-158.

Aquinas, Thomas (2008 [1920]): Summa Theologica, trans. Fathers of the English Dominican Province (https://www.newadvent.org/summa/3.htm).

Costa PT, McCrae RR (1992): Rev. NEO Personality Inventory (NEO-PI-R) and NEO Five-Factor Inventory (NEO-FFI), Professional Manual, Odessa, Florida: Psychological Assessment Resources.

Games

Dwarf Fortress, Tarn Adams/Zach Adams, Bay 12 Games, 2006.

The Sims, Maxis, Electronic Arts, 2004.

On the Evolution of Narrative Mechanics in Open-World Games

Ulrich Götz

SAME MESSAGE, DIFFERENT BOTTLE

Experiencing and propagating narratives is an essential component of cultural history. Although this process has changed over the course of centuries, its basic principles persist. Regardless of eras or means of transmission, it is a primordial human instinct to want to communicate real or imagined experiences, and experience them oneself. How deeply rooted this can be is reflected in a wide variety of social endeavors, demands and circumstances, which underscore the central importance of storytelling to our social fabric. The value of narrative and performative acts manifests itself in the layout of human settlements, which are oriented towards meaningful landmarks. New narrative styles intertwine themselves closely with the most advanced technologies, which they either advance as a driving force, or rapidly incorporate.

The communication of narrative content may have altered its external appearance, but its essence has been preserved. Printing made it possible to replicate texts, replacing the oral transmission of poems, songs or performances. Contemporary technological innovations further expanded narrative possibilities: today, these range from audiovisual compositions and three-dimensional projections to hybrid performances that fuse real and virtual space. This change of narrative modes distills existing methods down to their core and creates new genres, until they, too, are subject to this process of reduction. At the heart of these continuing cyclical mechanisms lies the moment of narrative transfer. What was once conveyed through interpersonal contact is now amplified by highly diverse forms of media and performative practices. Despite radical changes in form and a tremendous increase in reach, some content has lasted over great lengths of time: the dramas of the ancient Greek writer Sophocles are still being performed, and German publisher Reclam Verlag presents world literary classics as internet films featuring Playmobil figurines.[1] The continued existence of established content, considering these shifts in the form of communication, proves that what endures is the content, not how the message is conveyed.

BIRTH OF NARRATIVE MECHANICS

The anchoring of video games into mainstream society marks another tremendous change in narrative methods. Some cultural critics today state: "Those who do not play video games … ignore the great narratives of our present." (Hugendick 2020) This level of societal significance was inconceivable and unexpected during the first decades of computer-based game development. At the time, there was a stark division between the fields that would later combine to generate the cultural significance that is now attributed to digital games.

Comparable to the importance of narrative content, rule-based games have always held a prominent socio-cultural status, in the form of competitions, sports, board games, dice or card games. Such concepts were consolidated under the term *ludology* as the result of a factional dispute within the emerging field of game studies. (cf. Frasca 1999) By using this term, 'ludologists' attempted to distinguish themselves from 'narratologists' who explained the phenomenon of computer games from a narrative perspective. The ludologists rejected this perspective; for example, Markku Eskelinen noted: "If I throw a ball at you I don't expect you to drop it and wait until it starts telling stories." (Eskelinen 2001) Jesper Juul (2001) emphasized that: "Narratives may be fundamental to human thought, but this does not mean that everything should be described in narrative terms." Ludological, or strongly rule-based game concepts, in particular represent what was understood as *gaming* before the era of video games. These games primarily differed from narratives in that they consisted of a sequence of rules, yet contained hardly any narrative content. This is in contrast to the way in which the narrative manifested itself other cultural formats, such as literature and poetry, singing, theater or cinema. So what kind of new thinking was required in order to conceive video games such as *Dear Esther* (The Chinese

---

1   Michael Sommer, "Sommers Weltliteratur to go" (http://sommers-weltliteratur.de).

Room 2012), in which large-scale game worlds are traversed in search of a story, like in a 'walking simulator'?[2]

The first computer games did not yet aspire to renew narrative strategies. Instead, in the 1950s, emerging computer technologies began to reflect analog, ludological games due to their well-defined sequences of rules, which is why digital versions of such games were used for demonstration purposes. As such, the first computer games to result from this were all "transformations of existing games" (Suter 2018: 36). Their rules for gameplay, known as game mechanics, were simple to comprehend. The first graphically visualized computer game *OXO* (Douglas 1952) was a direct adaptation of tic-tac-toe – thus, while it had ludological qualities, its narrative qualities were practically non-existent.

In the decades that followed, rapid progress of computing technology made increasingly complex interactions possible; computers were used for an ever-expanding number of fields and range of applications. William Crowther utilized these new opportunities in 1975, when he created a milestone for the future of game design with *Colossal Cave Adventure* (Crowther 1975). In this game, players navigate through the rooms of a cave system using interactive commands, all of which are purely textual. The gameplay was therefore the sum of the individual actions that determined the plot. Crowther thus transposed a concept into the realm of digital games which became popular at the time. Separately but simultaneously in 1975, Gary Gygax continued to develop the role-playing game *Dungeons & Dragons* (*D&D*), in which the participants verbally improvise the actions of the game characters they are assigned. Gygax's developments "made it possible to play D&D in Solitaire[3]", thus "blurring the lines between board games and RPGs" (Arnaudo 2018: 71-72).[4] In this same period, beginning in 1969, Edward Packard sought a publisher for his book *The Adventures of You on Sugarcane Island*, and eventually published it in 1976. The concept of the book was to let readers themselves decide the course the story by giving them the option of following several possible storylines. This became the successful *Choose-Your-Own-Adventures* book series[5]. The parallel development of these three approaches in different media demonstrated a newly emerging narrative practice: "Independently from one another Gygax, Crowther and

---

2 The term *walking simulator* was originally intended as a derogatory term for extensive game worlds with a predominant narrative element. However, game distribution platforms such as www.steampowered.com use the term today as a genre filter.

3 Solitaire: a board game for one person

4 RPG: role-playing game

5 See: https://en.wikipedia.org/wiki/Choose_Your_ Own_Adventure

Packard came to the same conclusion that stories were something that the audience could co-create, not just receive, and such parallel developments go a long way to show the time was ripe for this type of audience engagement." (Arnaudo 2018: 74)

In Crowther's *Colossal Cave Adventure* and subsequent, similarly structured computer games, a new genre grew out of the narrative principles more closely associated with the field of "narratology" (Frasca 1999), in which the "interactive storytelling constituted the actual mechanics" (Suter 2018: 42). *Colossal Cave Adventure* thus pursues an idea that is fundamentally different to that pursued by *OXO*, so that these two early video games can be regarded as reflecting the often-discussed dichotomy between narratologically- and ludologically-based game concepts. It is fascinating how these once disparate concepts eventually coexisted, and then coalesced with one another over the history of video game development, until they were considered to be the same. As such, one of the most significant cultural achievements of digital games as a medium is to have overcome the historical, fundamental separation of ludological and narratological approaches, uniting them in a new medium and making them accessible to a broader audience.

ENTERING NARRATIVE VISUAL SPACE

This convergence has far-reaching consequences for the visual appearance of computer-based games. As *Colossal Cave Adventure* demonstrates, in principle, narrative games do not require visualization. Narrative aspects of games can be reduced to spoken or written texts[6], for example, leaving it up to the player to flesh them out using their own imagination. Narrative aspects could be envisioned, but sequences of strategic moves, dependencies on resources, situations of competition, and so forth, require dynamic visualizations in the course of the game. It is virtually impossible to control games with a pronounced rule-oriented (ludological) focus without a form of visual representation for the components of the game. Interestingly, it is not narrative, but rather, rule-oriented game forms that are dependent upon visual representation.

---

6   A number of computer games designed for the blind utilize this approach, as described in "Computer Games and Visually Impaired People" (Archambault et al. 2007).

This observation reveals a paradox. The rapidly increasing computing power of personal computers and game consoles led, from the 1970s onwards, to ever-more detailed graphic visualizations. Although rule-oriented game elements in computer games must be depicted, this requires relatively little computing power. The rapid increase in the capacities of imaging calculation methods would therefore not have been necessary to depict the game mechanics at all; as such, this change primarily took the form of creative embellishment, and thus, contributed to the expansion of the visual-narrative quality of games. Accordingly, Stephan Günzel notes that "due to advances in hardware and software development, a general aesthetic change from the symbolic to the representative" (Günzel 2012: 111) occured. Due to technological developments, the two-dimensional representation that characterized early video games became a three-dimensional representation – even if this 'representative' turn often means that "game productions organize their work for the visual plausibility of the supposedly real, and not for the qualities of the fictional in the virtual." (Götz 2019: 207) Thus began a narrative mode of unwritten laws which still dominate the design of digital games today: in the vast majority of cases, progress in the plot of a digital game is equated with progress in spatial environments.

THE WAY WE SEE IT

This new combination of narration and experiential virtual space has allowed games to permeate narrative disciplines that also rely on spatial scenarios to convey stories. In searching for the rules with which to construct a virtual space of high narrative quality, the emerging medium of games embraces many approaches from cinematography. There are remarkable parallels with the development of animated films which matured to perfection at Walt Disney Studios, among others. As in games, the principles developed can be described "as the creation of fictional spaces imbued with seamlessly plausible, self-referential narration" (Götz 2018a: 241). Animated films began to visualize narrative space by first constructing the scenery with background images that shift behind the characters. This spatial model was later expanded by the ability to use a one-point perspective animated camera, in which staggered layers were laid out "similarly to the spatial configuration of theater backdrops" (Girveau/Diederen 2008: 124), to zoom into the background. The spatial representations of animated films imitated the zooming perspectives that had already long been introduced into real films. But also in real films, the complexity of narrative spatial representations increased steadily: spatial expressions transitioned from rigidly mounted cameras to curving movements along rails, from shots on swivel arms to film sets in which the entire set moved around a permanently installed camera.[7] These increasingly sophisticated three-dimensional film sets corresponded to audacious narrative content. They demonstrated the growing complexity of the relationship between the camera and the staged space, both of which were continually evolving, but also emancipated themselves from one another.[8] The final phase on the path to the independence of camera and set was, however, pioneered by animated films and later adopted by real films: in compositing spatial scenarios whose origins lie in 3D modeling, animation and rendering, hybrids are created through virtual reality, augmented reality, and CGI (computer-generated imagery). Their narrative representations of space are no longer subject to the restrictions of physical film sets.

The cinematic connection between narration and space paved the way for corresponding approaches in the creation of narrative visual space in video games – almost as if video games had to relive the process of cinematic camera development all over again. *Defender* (Williams Electronics 1981), which is representative of similarly visualized games, utilizes a horizontal camera to show the action as if it were in an endless 'tracking shot' on rails. The central-perspective racing games of the arcade era look like time-lapse camera shots of animated backdrops being pulled apart. While the spatial scenarios in games have become more and more complex, their virtual cameras have gained in narrative quality and taken on a life of their own, directly based on the cinematography of real films: depending on the situation, virtual camera angles swivel from wide-angle shots to close-ups, or change their camera lenses interactively to match the action.

Although such cinematic approaches would not necessarily be relevant to the narrative in games, they shape the conventions of how something can be presented in a continuous sequence of virtual spaces, and thus, what can even be told at all. Within this self-imposed restriction, entire game genres have been derived directly from existing film genres. (cf. Rauscher 2014) However, this filtering of what video games visualize based on real filming conventions is not

---

7   See, for example, the film sets for *2001 — A Space Odyssey* (1968). They were created to realistically depict the crew of a spaceship suspended in weightlessness.

8   There is hardly a more iconic film scene encapsulating such possibilities for cinematic narration than the famous "Copa Shot" in *GoodFellas* (Scorsese 1990) by Martin Scorsese (Director) and Michael Ballhaus (Cinematographer), in which a steadycam floats from the back entrance and through the hustle and bustle of the club's kitchen into the Copacabana nightclub, without any cuts.

only apparent in the final results of game productions. Typically, such constraints are already inscribed in the programs used to produce video games as presets – for example, in the simulation of real camera lenses for virtual cameras. Within these conventions, games such as *Antichamber* (Demruth 2013) remain an exception; in it, non-Euclidean spatial sequences question the construct of game space itself. The potential of narrative space in video games therefore appears to be far from fully exhausted. It remains an open question whether, over time, games will produce their own narrative space constructs which are only possible in the virtual realm, or whether they will primarily adopt spatial-narrative methods from other disciplines.

THE DOUBLE AVATAR

As far as other aspects of narrative mechanisms are concerned, the interactive nature of video games has engendered at least one crucial innovation. For protagonists, actors, mediators or other narrative entities, gaming invented a new vessel: the avatar. Whether in first- or third-person perspective or in axonometric view, the gaming avatar has become a universally applicable, omnipresent tool of narration. The avatar is a representative proxy whose appearance can be adapted according to personal preferences. It provides a surface upon which to project from a necessary distance, allowing the narrative experience to emerge. The avatar is the shield with which negatively connotated action can be endured in the course of the game, and the disguise with which such actions will be carried out. Thus, it functions as armor, ambassador and scout when venturing into the realm of fictional portrayal and experience.

The construction of an interactive avatar transforms the role of the audience. Before the era of video games, an intensive experience of narration was expressed through admiration for actors or authors, and it turned the audience into fans. Experiencing narration intensively through a gaming avatar means controlling the action of the role play itself. Interestingly, controlling an avatar seems to generate such high-quality experiences that it not only ensures participation in interactive narration, but also sustains the passive role of the audience. Watching other players play publicly has long been a mass phenomenon, with millions of followers on the internet.[9] In so-called *Let's Plays*, the Double Avatar is created: the audience follows and interacts with players live, who in turn control their avatars through virtual game worlds.

OPEN WORLDS FOLLOW LIMITING PRINCIPLES

The combination of narrative and rule-oriented systems in gaming represents a novel construct. It combines features of existing narrative disciplines with the rule mechanics from the fictional environment of game space. Narrative actions occur only at defined positions in the virtual sphere, and are therefore clearly located. At the same time, narrative and rule mechanics are intertwined in such a way that conditions must be fulfilled in order to experience the narrative, or narratives will follow different paths when conditions are altered. *Fable 2* (Lionhead Studios 2008) explored such sophisticated possibilities of storytelling in one of the first ever reputation games: the "system is directly tied to the character development, such that actions that are evaluated by the game from an ethical perspective" defining "how the NPCs react to the protagonist" (Christen et al. 2013: 73).[10]

As a result, this association means that "a video game is a set of rules as well as a fictional world" (Juul 2005: 1). The radical nature of this statement deserves consideration: In games, the action is structured, but in contrast to other narrative disciplines, it is not performed. Rather, it is deliberately concealed by the mechanical constraints of the game. The motivation thus awakened by games creates an incentive for players to experience the plot individually. In this way, rule-based functionality, interactivity and narrative are merged – and narrative mechanics emerge as a result. These narrative mechanics essentially prevent, in carefully metered degrees, a general accessibility in terms of the narrative. In fact, the narrative is only revealed to those who strive particularly hard to find it. Sometimes games take this to the extreme: well-hidden and almost undetectable 'Easter eggs' contain additional gameplay that is withheld from most gamers and only discovered by the most tenacious players.

---

9   Although this may initially seem surprising, it is ultimately nothing new: the observational role of a public audience in analog, rule-based games, such as in team sports games, is commonplace.

10   NPC: non-player-character or non-playable character

Nowhere are the manifestations of these prerequisites and the successes of narrative mechanics more evident than in the comparatively young genre of open-world games. With its vast, free-to-explore open environments, this genre represents a tentative culmination of what can be told in games, how it must be visualized, and which spatial settings are suitable to do so. To provide some context: the size of the playable open world of *Read Dead Redemption II* (Rockstar Studio 2018) is estimated by fans to be 75 square kilometers[11]; other comparable worlds extend to several hundred square kilometers. The implications for storytelling in virtual worlds of such dimensions are that connections of the highest complexity are required between rule-based concepts and narrative strategies.

In the construction of such worlds, there are systems in place that are rarely apparent to the player. The combination of ludological and narratological concepts optimizes the structure of these virtual environments in order to maximize their playability. For example, the depiction of medieval Florence in *Assassin's Creed II* (Ubisoft Montreal 2009) only follows the historical city map in a few places and otherwise distorts it for dramatic effect: "In this case, form does follow function – but it is reality adapted to the necessities of the game." (Gerber/Götz 2019: 15) The interactivity of the medium requires specialized storytelling strategies to guarantee a dramaturgical narrative, even though the players exercise their own free will. In what order are the main strands of the narrative structured, when are alternatives or multilinear variants possible, and in what way is this main framework supplemented by freely selectable secondary missions? And how does the individually experienced story add up to what is known as emergent storytelling, which is based on rule-based actions (such as those involving the game's resources)?

The scenography of the virtual is conceived to maximize the narrative effect of events, even if their occurrence is not entirely predictable. The overall attributes of play are derived from the set of rules, because "the prevailing rules in games govern the nature of virtual environments – and not the other way around." (Götz 2018b: 260) As a consequence, "such virtual landscapes are precisely scaled to bridge the distances between one event location and the next" (ibid: 262). To foster gameplay, a racing game thus provides drivable surfaces; a hidden object game involves bewilderingly detailed environments; some conflict-based games require arenas, and others hideouts. It is not possible to clearly assign the specific details from the design of such worlds to either narrative or

---

11 "How big EXACTLY is the new map? A detailed analysis", August 2019 (https://www.reddit.com/r/reddeadredemption/comments/9rgmbp/how_big_exactly_is _the_new_map_a_detailed_analysis/).

rule-oriented logic. The forms of cover in a shooting game – are they narrative or rule-oriented elements? As this question demonstrates, it must be acknowledged that design elements in games combine different tasks. They simultaneously assume functions for narration, rules, information, usability, and so forth. This amalgam serves to advance the game and motivation to play.

Successful patterns of design in open-world games culminate in typologies that are regularly applied. While the narrative content varies greatly from game to game, the construction of the worlds follows such universal strategies that they sometimes seem interchangeable. The similarities between these virtual spaces can be traced back to effects that serve to enhance narration and usability. They manifest themselves in virtual worlds that include features such as high points for a better overview, spectacular landscapes underscoring dramatic storylines, prominent locations serving as obvious landmarks, regularly distributed settlements justifying the next resources to procure or missions to execute, and labyrinth-like forests or towering high-rises. In order to make the boundaries of these worlds as plausible as possible, a creative canon of rock chains, gorges, islands, and isolated plateaus in mountain ranges is created. They are perforated with cave systems, subway lines, and tunnel entrances by which the depth of the worlds is extended without having to provide spatial continuity (for example, one enters a tunnel system and emerges at another location).

The design of open-world games involves typological set pieces of natural or artificial landscapes which act as the basic spatial structure for gameplay. They guarantee not only the usability of a particular place, but most importantly, a sensible transition to the next section of a game world, corresponding to the continuation of the plot. In her study on "Nonverbal Guidance Systems", Francine Rotzetter (2018) explains typical guidance systems of open-world games in detail. Apart from distinguishing between different methods of guiding players through virtual worlds, Rotzetter's study shows that the construction of such worlds follows common, comparable design strategies.

NARRATIVE CONTAINERS

The megastructures of open-world games present unprecedented possibilities for narration. However, their spatial designs also inherently introduce both restrictions and problems. Gigantic virtual worlds raise questions about the relationship between storytelling and space, which other narrative disciplines have already long resolved.

Open-world games all too often equate an avatar's movement with the experience of action, which leads to the fallacy that a lot of virtual space also means a lot of storytelling. The opposite assumption would be more logical: that narrative density decreases in relation to the size of virtual worlds. Thus, open-world games have acquired the reputation of requiring players to cover long distances on their way to the next stage of the story, while nothing much actually happens. This fundamental problem of combining space and narration is countered with a number of tricks. Avatars rush through vast digital spaces at absurd speeds on foot to prevent boredom. As soon as any kind of exciting initial exploration is over, shortcuts are revealed to bridge distances more quickly throughout the rest of the game; transport stations, flying objects, fantastical animals, teleportation spells or portals become accessible. These devices aim to support the underlying idea of narrative progress by a change in location.[12]

Other narrative disciplines devised elegant tricks for such matters a long time ago. In order to increase narrative speed, written narratives established a change of scene or narrative perspective; cinematic narration perfected the tool of editing. These fields demonstrate that spatial progress need not be a precondition for coherent narration. In order to negotiate particularly important topics in a concentrated manner, theater developed the *Kammerspiel* – presenting the great questions of humanity in the smallest possible space. In this sense, some open-world games could be described as the opposite of the *Kammerspiel*: simple content in an infinite space.

To depict architecture and virtual landscapes in open-world games, the most advanced technologies are utilized. In comparison, the implementation of storytelling follows relatively simple principles. Action sequences are conceived for NPCs at specific locations and positioned there, as if they were invisible containers activated upon entry. When all the options of the events that can be triggered are exhausted, these virtual counterparts shift into a meaningless, idle state that signals the end of this section of the plot – the narrative containers are now empty. When open-world games promise hundreds of hours of gameplay, this refers to the time needed to experience all narrative events. Once this is achieved, a game world continues to exist, but only as a shell of empty game

---

12 *No Man's Sky* (Hello Games 2016) pursued this idea to an extreme and was correspondingly controversial. Does the possibility of visiting 18 trillion procedurally generated planets really lead to a more interesting plot?

space, in which no further specific action can be expected.[13] Revisiting an 'empty' narrative container reveals a strange side effect: if NPCs remain frozen in a meaningless, Sleeping-Beauty-like state after their action has been completed, this state also applies to the game space itself. Thus, it becomes apparent that, although open-world games are characterized by an immense abundance of sequential or parallel narrative strands, a strange absence of time prevails within these game worlds. Despite all the perfection of their audiovisual appearance, the worlds do not age, but gradually release their prepared contents instead. In place of passing time, a controlled sequence of predetermined events reigns supreme. As a result, the worlds often appear animated rather than alive.

FREEING THE NARRATIVE

Such narrative containers with ready-made content present a sharp contrast to the practice of emergent storytelling, that is, narratives evolving out of a set of rules. A prime example of emergent narration is *Dwarf Fortress* (Adams 2006), which is predicated on the procedurally generated interplay of related processes used to build a fantasy world (cf. Adams: 153, Figure 1). The dynamic entanglements of the physical, historical and social events simulated are so complex that their effects on the game plot are not even foreseeable by the game developers themselves. As an explicit goal for creating *Dwarf Fortress*, Adams (2006) names "the ability to surprise yourself with the game doing things that you did not anticipate", which he achieved by programming "all these little procedural elements to bring out this perpetual state of surprise."[14] To a certain extent, this narration runs autonomously, controlling itself without requiring any further input. In order to pursue their own goals in *Dwarf Fortress*, the players brace themselves against the freewheeling dynamics of the game world and try to maintain an overview among the complexity of interactions and coincidences. At the same time, players adopt the role of observers, and are entertained by these

---

13 In order to ensure that players have experienced all elements of the prepared narrative, the gaming platform www.steampowered.com, for example, reports the status of "Steam Achievements".

14 "Dwarf Fortress: What Happens When It Becomes A Game? The Zach and Tarn Adams Interviews", April 5, 2018 (https://www.youtube.com/watch?v=HtKmLciKO30, min. 9:11-9:40).

unpredictable processes. Although many situations escalate dramatically, the narrative does not follow an intentional dramaturgy.

The much-praised design of *Dwarf Fortress* provides valuable arguments for the discussion of the inherent weaknesses of open-world games. Given the complexity of combining space and narration, it seems advisable to reduce the spatial dimensions of future open-world productions and increase their narrative density. To achieve meaningful narration in games, the exploration of unknown territories should not be the leitmotif. In high-quality narrative video games, virtual spaces should instead act as framework for the plot. In fact, game spaces themselves sometimes seem to be the most important part of the games. Furthermore, game spaces can only unleash their true narrative potential if they change over time. The plot can ultimately evolve at the same location, and the simultaneous change of the place itself can facilitate this process. However, this central narrative technique is undermined by the lack of significant time-based processes in narrative containers.

Many open-world games provide their fan bases with Downloadable Content (DLC) or the possibilities to create their own mods[15], in order to be able to expand game worlds even after they are released. Fallout 4 (Bethesda Game Studios 2015), with its DLC release Far Harbor (2016), included the expanded content of an additional island with more scenery to explore, as well as a variety of other major and minor missions. Instead of such modular world enlargements, the lasting appeal of Dwarf Fortress lies in the dynamic interaction of its narrative agents: the headstrong, free-spirited dwarves. It is therefore worthwhile, when developing strategies for open worlds, to consider shifting narration from the exploration of scenographic locations to narrative agents such as NPCs. The virtual locations of open-world games are by no means exhausted after a single narrative iteration. On the contrary, they could provide the chance of a complete renewal of content, for example, if familiar settings are reinterpreted by the new generations of narrative agents. Would it not be fascinating to witness how the same virtual place is later populated and transformed by newly implemented, intelligent NPCs? Narratively speaking, it would be particularly effective to introduce agents that are not stationary, but move throughout the entire game world in order to ally, exchange, persuade or attack when they randomly encounter each other (Figure 1).

---

15 Mods: modifications of existing games, usually created by fans.

Figure 1: Study by Anna-Lena Pontet at Zurich University of the Arts on group dynamics – mobile agents competing for membership of a given faction.

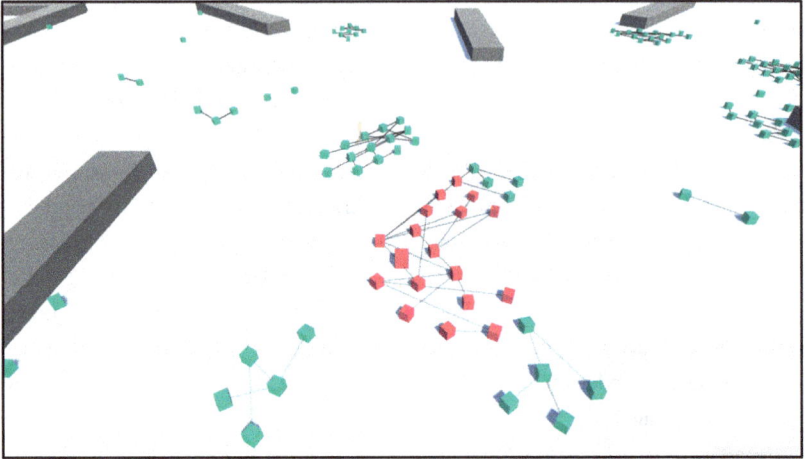

Source: Anna-Lena Pontet

The inner life of open-world games would benefit considerably from this form of emergent narrative because the unforeseen dynamics and singular events create meaningful – and epic – game experiences.

Through the fusing of different disciplines, a transmedial boom in narrative content is emerging. Video games are able to integrate the contributions of performing, narrative and audial media and arts. The development of open worlds has paved the way for making these elements more interactive and experiential in compelling spatial scenarios. It is now up to the games to follow the example of other narrative disciplines, and to create stories that are worth preserving for generations to come.

REFERENCES

Literature

Archambault, Dominique/Ossmann, Roland/Gaudy, Thomas/Miesenberger, Klaus (2007): "Computer games and visually impaired people." In: Upgrade 8/2, pp. 1-11.

Arnaudo, Marco (2018): Storytelling in the Modern Board Game. Narrative Trends from the Late 1960s to Today, Jefferson NC: McFarland.

Christen, Markus/Faller, Florian/Götz, Ulrich/Müller, Cornelius (2013): Serious Moral Games. Analyzing and Engaging Moral Values through Video Games, Zurich: Institute for Design Research, Zurich University of Arts.

Eskelinen, Markku (2001): "The Gaming Situation." In: Espen Aarseth/Jessica Enevold/Markku Eskelinen/Maria Gedoz Tiep (eds.), Game Studies: The International Journal of Computer Game Research 1/1 (http://www.game studies.org/0101/eskelinen/#top).

Frasca, Gonzalo (1999): "Ludology meets Narratology – Similitude and differences between (video)games and narrative." In: Parnasso#3, Helsinki (https://ludology.typepad.com/weblog/articles/ludology.htm).

Gerber, Andri/Götz, Ulrich (eds.) (2019): Architectonics of Game Spaces. The Spatial Logic of the Virtual and Its Meaning for the Real, Bielefeld: transcript.

Girveau Bruno/Diederen, Roger (eds.) (2008): Walt Disneys wunderbare Welt und ihre Wurzeln in der europäischen Kunst, Munich: Hirmer.

Götz, Ulrich (2018): "Zugänge zu Zwischengängen – Konstruktion eines räumlichen Modells." In: Natascha Adamovsky (ed.), Digitale Moderne – Die Modellwelten von Matthias Zimmermann, Munich: Hirmer, pp. 230-249.

Götz, Ulrich (2018): "Rules Shape Spaces – Spaces Shape Rules." In: Beat Suter/Mela Kocher/René Bauer (eds.), Games and Rules. Game Mechanics for the "Magic Circle", Bielefeld: transcript, pp. 259-265.

Götz, Ulrich (2019): "From Asteroids to Architectoids. Close Encounters between Architecture and Game Design." In: Andri Gerber/Ulrich Götz (eds.), Architectonics of Game Spaces. The Spatial Logic of the Virtual and Its Meaning for the Real, Bielefeld: transcript, pp. 201-214.

Günzel, Stephan (2012): Egoshooter. Das Raumbild des Computerspiels, New York/Frankfurt: Campus.

Hugendick, David (2020): "Zu Hause geblieben. Gespielt." In: Die Zeit, May 5, 2020 (https://www.zeit.de/kultur/2020-05/videospiele-gaming-coronavirus-pc-spiele-konsole-erzaehlungen).

Juul, Jesper (2001): "Games telling Stories?" In: Espen Aarseth/Jessica Enevold/Markku Eskelinen/Maria Gedoz Tiep (eds.), Game Studies: The International Journal of Computer Game Research 1/1 (http://gamestudies.org/0101/juul-gts/).

Juul, Jesper Juul (2005): Half-Real. Video Games between Real Rules and Fictional Worlds, Cambridge Massachusetts, London: MIT Press.

Rauscher, Andreas (2014): "Filmische Spielräume." In: Benjamin Beil/Marc Bonner/Thomas Hensel (eds.), Computer | Spiel | Bilder, Glückstadt: vwh-Verlag, pp. 179-197.

Rotzetter, Francine (2018): "Nonverbal Guiding Systems." In: Beat Suter/Mela Kocher/René Bauer (eds.), Games and Rules. Game Mechanics for the "Magic Circle", Bielefeld: transcript, pp. 169-189.
Suter, Beat (2018): "Interaktiver Bildraum in Computerspielen." In: Natascha Adamovsky (ed.), Digitale Moderne – Die Modellwelten von Matthias Zimmermann, Munich: Hirmer, pp. 34-61.

Games

Antichamber, Demruth, Demruth, 2013.
Assassin's Creed II, Ubisoft Montreal, Ubisoft, 2009.
Dear Esther, The Chinese Room, The Chinese Room, 2012.
Defender, Williams Electronics, Williams Electronics, 1981.
Dwarf Fortress, Tarn Adams/Zach Adams, Bay 12 Games, 2006.
Fable 2, Lionhead Studios, Microsoft, 2008.
Fallout 4, Bethesda Game Studios, Bethesda Softworks, 2015.
No Man's Sky, Hello Games, Hello Games, 2016.
Red Dead Redemption II, Rockstar Studio, Rockstar Games, 2018.

Movies

GoodFellas (1990): Martin Scorsese, Warner Bros.
2001 – A Space Odyssey (1968): Stanley Kubrick, Metro-Goldwyn-Mayer (MGM), Stanley Kubrick Productions.

Open-End Storytelling in Pinball Machines

A Summary of the Narrative Elements and Structures in Pinball Machines

David Krummenacher

Pinball machines have long been part of everyday culture. Today, they have almost completely disappeared from public spaces and can mostly be found in closed hobby rooms or in digital form on the players' private devices. A similar situation applies to their description in a scientific context. They let many players live through their story while playing, but so far nobody has described how these stories are structured and how they are received.

This article is based on a master's thesis (Krummenacher 2018) in the subject area of Game Design at Zurich University of the Arts. It examined pinball machines with regard to their narrative elements and structures, utilizing content analysis as a method. The results were mostly limited to storytelling in physical pinball machines and dealt only marginally with virtual pinball machines. Virtual pinball machines that are subject to the restrictions of a physical pinball machine were of course not excluded, but not explicitly investigated. The purpose of the thesis was to open up the field and to give designers of physical and virtual pinball machines a framework in which they can think about storytelling for pinball machines. The following article provides a summary of the findings of this thesis.

DEFINING STORYTELLING AND PINBALL

Stories are told all over the world and by every culture. The object is for the storytellers to pass on information to the listeners. The conveyance of the information follows certain rules of the respective culture so that the information is perceived as a story.

In this article, the term *storytelling* is used to describe how content and concepts are narrated. The conveyance and reception of narrative content is also understood in this work as part of storytelling. This forms the basis for the following definition of storytelling.

Pinball machines are games of skill whose central element is a ball. The ball moves within an inclined, self-contained game space. The object of the game is to collect as many points as possible when the ball hits various game elements. The ball is shot into the playfield by interacting with the machine. This can be done by pulling and releasing a plunger or pressing a button. The presence of a tilt mechanism, which stops the game if the machine moves too much, is not included in this definition.

Furthermore, the game must have at least two paddles, which introduce a further level of skill through increased interaction possibilities. This is necessary to differentiate the pinball machine from the game *Bagatelle*.

As the title of the article indicates, the two previous definitions must be combined. This results in further terms that have to be specially defined in the context of pinball machines.

Storytelling in pinball machines means the process of how the contents or concepts of pinball machines can be narratively charged, communicated and received.

Contents and concepts in this context means the game mechanics, the game goals and the game elements. Furthermore, references to already existing media and the pinball machine as a product are also included here.

Narratively charged means that these contents and concept have been equipped with narrative means. These make it possible to convey and receive the contents and concepts of pinball machines in a non-abstract form.

Conveyance is the process of instructing or guiding players to learn the story of the pinball machine. *Reception* is the activity of experiencing the game from the players' point of view. The players take different roles within the reception. The result is that the conditions for reception are different for each role, which means that the reception cannot always be the same in the different roles.

For readers unfamiliar with pinball terminology the following figure provides a simplified; visual glossary.[1]

---

1   More extensive glossaries can be found online, eg. https://www.ipdb.org/glossary.php

Figure 1: Simplified visual glossary.

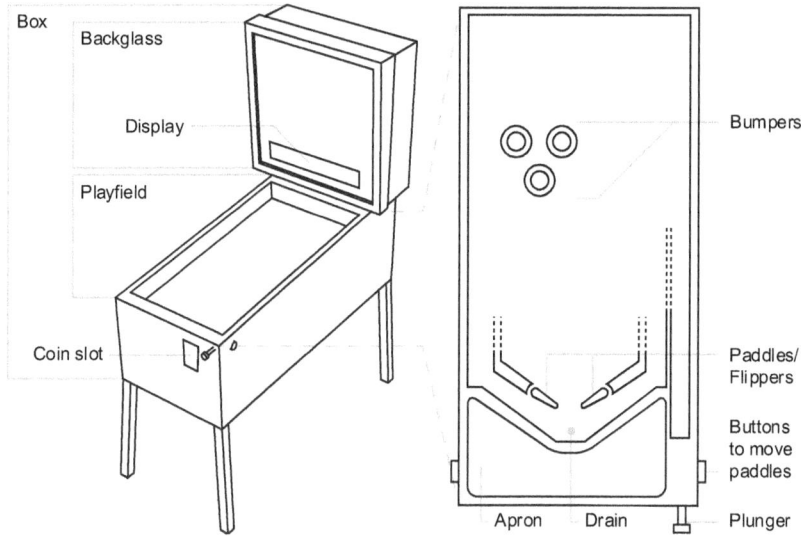

Source: David Krummenacher

THE FUNCTIONAL STRUCTURE

A pinball machine takes on different functions, each of which can be of narrative importance. These functions enable storytelling to frame pinball machines as a game, but also as a product. The following described functional elements are not necessarily always located at the same place, but are present in most pinball machines in some form.

The box as poster

The first function of storytelling in pinball machines is to recruit potential players. Mostly this is done by the visual and auditory design of the box in its idle or dedicated advertising mode. It is intended to generate attention and create incentives for potential players. A narrative function that is performed here is the establishment of the theme. This is particularly relevant in the case of adaptations from other media. The aim here is to establish a connection to the original work as quickly as possible.

The playfield as a stage

The first function of storytelling in pinball machines is to recruit potential players. Mostly this is done by the visual and auditory design of the box in its idle or
dedicated advertising mode. It is intended to generate attention and create incentives for potential players. A narrative function that is performed here is the establishment of the theme. This is particularly relevant in the case of adaptations
from other media. The aim here is to establish a connection to the original work
as quickly as possible.

The display

Another functional level is the playfield. On this level the actual story of the
pinball machine is being told. It is the main area where the game takes place, because the ball is visible for the players. The active game elements are located in
the playfield, which allow the pinball machine to function as a game, even if any
narration is left out. Screens in the upper part of the box or within the playfield
can be used to expand the playfield or the game elements.

Other functional elements

In the following section, further functional elements are described which only
play a lesser role in narrative terms, but can nevertheless be charged narratively.

The coin slot

In the following section, further functional elements are described which only
play a lesser role in narrative terms, but can nevertheless be charged narratively

The game instructions

The game instructions are one of the elements designed to explain the game to
the players. The instructions can be partly embedded in the theme, but partly
completely separated from it. In terms of content, the theme is referenced when
formulating the winning conditions.

Furthermore, the game instructions teach the players the pricing and available game modes. Often the price per ball is indicated and whether these can be
distributed among several players. The game instructions are usually located at
the bottom of the playfield, the so-called apron.

Interaction possibilities

Further functional elements are the interaction possibilities. These are, for ex-ample, the buttons on the side which move the paddles, a start button and the plunger that transports the ball into the playfield. The buttons are usually not in-tegrated into the theme in terms of design, but simply highlighted in color. The plunger can often be pulled up and released to control the force with which the ball is released. Sometimes the plunger is replaced by a button or even integrated into the theme of the pinball machine.

For example, *Indiana Jones: The Pinball Adventure* (Williams 1993) uses the handle of a pistol instead of a plunger or a simple button. The players have to fire the pistol to literally shoot the ball into the playfield. A familiar motif from the film is used here.

Figure 2: Plunger button in the shape of a pistol from Indiana Jones: The Pinball Adventure (Williams 1993).

Source: unknown author, from: "Indiana Jones Williams Pinball Machine For Sale UK", https://www.homeleisuredirect.com/pinball-machines/vintage-pinball-machines/indiana-jones-williams-pinball-machine.html.

Relationships of the functional elements

All functional elements are spatially bound to the pinball machine and are narra-tively united by the given theme or are separated from the theme to achieve spe-cial meaning.

A special relationship is that of the display and the stage. The display is a complementary narrative level to the stage. This means that narrative contents of the stage can be temporarily stored in the display. An object that is on the stage might be taken up again in the display as part of an animation and the stage can thus be extended for a short period of time.

As an example, the genie from *Tales of the Arabian Nights* (Williams 1996) can be mentioned here. He is represented as a figurine within the stage, but also appears in multiple animations.

Figure 3: The genie from Tales of the Arabian Nights (Williams 1996).

Source: screenshot (Krummenacher) from YouTube Video The Pinball Arcade – Tales of the Arabian Nights [98,071,260] (TeaKayKay, March 13, 2014).

Conversely, however, this relationship is also possible if the design of the stage allows for dynamic or interchangeable content. An example of this is *The Machine: Bride of Pinbot* (Williams 1991). Here, the face of a woman is used as a game element but also as a progress indicator. The players have to shoot balls at the face, which then changes.

Figure 4: Progress bar as game element in The Machine: Bride of Pinbot (Williams 1991).

Source: screenshot (Krummenacher) from YouTube Video Pinball Arcade – Bride of Pin*Bot (pinballwiz45b, April 17, 2015).

Conversely, however, this relationship is also possible if the design of the stage allows for dynamic or interchangeable content. An example of this is *The Machine: Bride of Pinbot* (Williams 1991). Here, the face of a woman is used as a game element but also as a progress indicator. The players have to shoot balls at the face, which then changes.

Figure 5: Additional display in the playfield in Big Shot (Gottlieb 1974).

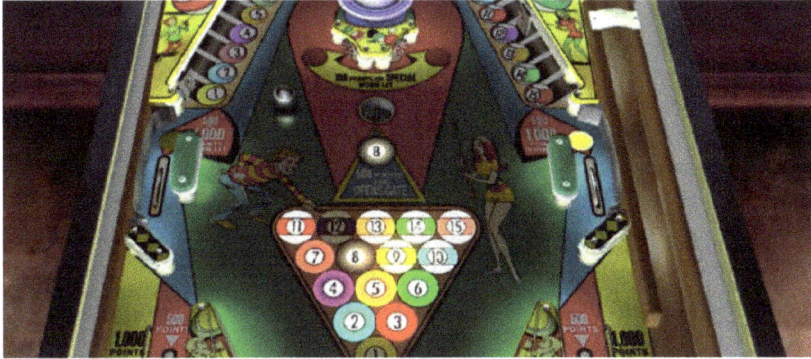

screenshot (Krummenacher) from YouTube Video Pinball Arcade – Big Shot (pinball-wiz45b, April 19, 2014).

THE STRUCTURE OF THE NARRATIVE

Pinball machines have structures in which their stories are told. Structures are understood here to be mechanisms that create content-related framing, time-related sequences and spatial organization for the narrative.

The following chapters show the individual elements of the structure and their relationships to each other.

The narrative framework

As with almost all stories, a narrative frame can be constructed around the stories in pinball machines. The theme is the overriding arc for all the components of a story. It determines the narrative content of all subordinate frames. Three parallel frames can be constructed under the theme.

The first are the primary narrative offers. These contain the overall task that leads to the conclusion of the game, whether by reaching a certain condition or losing the last ball. Primary narrative offers are very strongly tied to the theme and give the pinball machine an overarching tension.

Figure 6: The narrative framework.

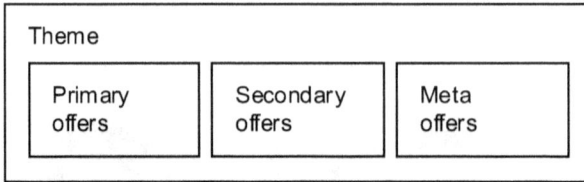

Theme		
Primary offers	Secondary offers	Meta offers

Source: David Krummenacher

Next, there are the secondary narrative offerings. These provide the framework for secondary tasks and serve the logical consolidation of the game world within the theme. Secondary narrative offers can also have informative value.

The last frame contains the meta offers. These serve to consolidate the pinball machine as a product within the theme, draw the player into the story and create motivation to stay in the game.

All narrative offers can be perceived several times. Since a game of pinball inevitably ends with the loss of the ball, this also applies to the main narrative arc in the primary offers. When the main story line is completed without losing the ball, it starts again from the beginning.

Narrative offers

The narrative of a pinball machine consists of narrative offers that can be perceived or not. The acceptance of these offers is not only deliberately caused by the player, but can also happen due to a lack of control of the ball. This makes the reception of these offers more difficult.

Narrative offers consist of a sequence of events that is logically self-contained. The narrative offers themselves are structured and held together by the narrative framework.

The types of narrative offers set by the narrative frame can be spatially assigned to the pinball machine. The box itself mostly contains meta offers. The upper part of a pinball machine usually contains secondary offers, such as the score display or meta offers like the backglass. All types of offers can be found within the playing field.

Figure 7: Types and spatial distribution of narrative offerings.

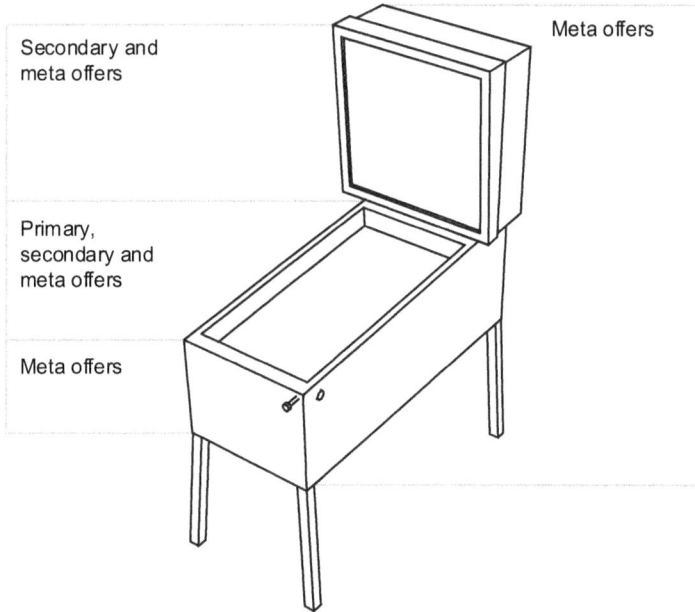

Source: David Krummenacher (figures 7-15)

Temporal logic

Temporally, a story told in a pinball machine consists of a sequence of narrative offers.

A narrative offer dramaturgically consists of a beginning, an end and a continuation or a connecting event of another narrative offer. Narrative offers consist of individual events that can follow one another in a linear fashion and are triggered by the fulfilment of a condition.

Figure 8: Process of a narrative offer.

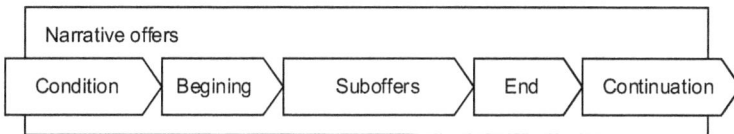

The model of a linear sequence of events can be applied, but it is not sufficient, since offers can also be multilinear or branching.

Figure 9: Linear sequence.

The model of a multilinear structure can also be applied to the individual narrative offerings. This means that decision points are created that lead a single storyline in a new direction. However, a multilinear model cannot be applied to the narrative offerings as a whole, because they are not linearly linked to each other.

Figure 10: Branched sequence.

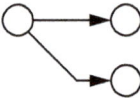

The offers themselves may be non-linear in time and may cause jumps within their own or another storyline. As a result, a new term to describe the process must be found.

Narrative offers run asynchronously and parallel to each other. However, only one narrative offer can always be perceived as active. Therefore, a model is required which allows the narrative offers to be divided into asynchronous parallel narrative or plot strands.

The new model combines the linear and the branched model and introduces a structure of narrative strands. Within the overall narrative, it allows for jumps between the individual strands, which in turn can influence the state of a narrative strand. This means that narrative strands can be moved forward or backward from other narrative strands.

Figure 11: Parallel asynchronous sequence.

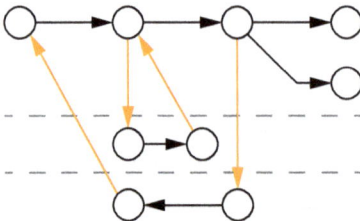

The individual process

Narrative offers consist of a sequence of events. These can only be perceived linearly by a player. Although the individual narrative offers remain the same, the story perceived by a player can be considered individual and emergent.

This individual procedure contributes to the fact that the reception of the story in a pinball machine as a whole is made more difficult. The players are required to engage with the respective pinball machines over a longer period of time in order to be able to perceive and classify the narrative offerings at all. This is also aggravated further by the fact that bad players are denied access to the narrative offerings that appear later.

Spatial logic

The spatial narrative logic in pinball machines is comparable to a stage play or a fairground of narrative offerings. Spatial elements are bound to narrative offers, but can fulfill functions for several such offers. They never perform these functions for several offers at the same time, since only one narrative offer can be the active one.

Spatially the stage is strongly vertically structured. This can be explained by the fact that the ball and gravity are the central elements of the game. At the lower end of the stage there are often meta offers, such as the game instructions. These are immediately followed by the central elements of the primary narrative offerings, the paddles and the drain, which are associated with the loss of the ball. In the middle of the stage there are mostly secondary and meta offers. Secondary and primary offers are at the top. This arrangement reflects the games playing with gravity. The players move up and down on the stage between these narrative offers.

Another spatial element is the display, which can reproduce narrative offers of all kinds.

Figure 12: The vertical structure.

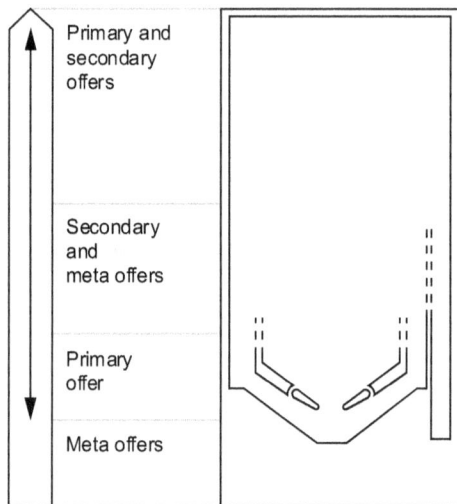

Primary and secondary offers

Secondary and meta offers

Primary offer

Meta offers

Source: David Krummenacher

Conveying the offers

Both visual and auditory channels are used to convey the narrative offers. Often the offers are visually represented as graphics or figurines.

The narrative offerings are supported by guidance and feedback systems, which are designed to be both visual and auditory. Guidance systems can increasingly be found in the playfield and are supported by acoustic indications. Feedback systems are often of an auditory nature and, in addition to the lighting design in the playfield, are often outsourced visually to a screen. Feedback is sometimes also given physically. For example, when a player has won a free game, the so-called knocker within the box hits the inside of the box and lets the player feel the blow as well as the audible bang. Furthermore, due to the physical nature of the pinball machine, the impact of the ball is often felt directly by the players.

ELEMENTS OF THE NARRATIVE

A narrative or narrative offers in pinball machines consist of several elements. However, not all of them are necessarily always present. The elements of the narrative are listed and described below.

Events

Events are the smallest unit of a narrative offer. They are triggered by interactions with the pinball machine by the player or the ball. A narrative offer consists of the concatenation of such events. Events are strongly linked to the tasks within the pinball machine.

Tasks

From a game mechanics point of view, the most important elements are the tasks. They guide the player to trigger certain events and formulate the challenges. In order to use tasks and their completion in a meaningful way, the pinball machine must be able to map the respective states of the tasks. Probably for technical reasons, older pinball machines simplify tasks considerably. In modern pinball machines more complex task sequences occur. These can consist of main and subtasks.

With regard to storytelling, tasks can be structured. In older machines, tasks can be performed without restriction throughout the game.

Figure 13: Task cycle of older pinball machines.

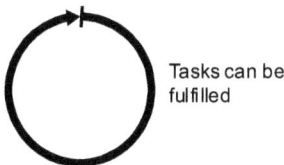

Tasks can be
fulfilled

In more modern pinball machines the tasks follow a dramaturgical sequence. At the beginning the main task is usually established. After that, tasks can be performed concurrently until they come to a head at a certain point at the end of the main task.

Figure 14: Task cycle of modern pinball machines.

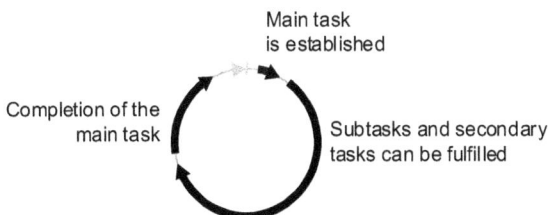

Main task
is established

Completion of the
main task

Subtasks and secondary
tasks can be fulfilled

Tasks can either be formulated explicitly or implicitly. Explicitly formulated tasks are emphasized through narrative means, for example auditively by a voice over of the narrator or visually by the lighting up of a surface or by an animation within the screens. Implicitly formulated tasks are only introduced when they first occur, for example, the bonus points that can often be achieved by hitting the bumpers can be understood as implicit tasks.

The world

Every pinball machine creates a world in which its story is told. The world is defined and held together by the theme or narrative framework. The world is experienced by the player through the design of the individual elements.

Characters

As in most other stories, the stories in pinball machines are also about characters. Characters take on certain roles within the story and these are represented in some form in the machine. The following roles are often given special emphasis.

Narrator
Many pinball machines have a narrator that sometimes is represented in the machine, but often is not. Narrators guide the players through the game and its story. Narrators are also used as a means to advertise a pinball machine that is currently in idle mode.

Protagonist
The protagonist of the story is in most cases the player. Their role is mostly characterized externally. That means, if they have any representation in the game at all, the role they take on is explained by other characters – for example the narrator. A representation of the protagonist is most often found in the display, i.e. in the backglass or in a digital screen.

Antagonist
The antagonist is the opponent of the player, who is often represented by a toy within the stage or on the backglass. A toy is a three-dimensional model that represents an object in the narrative and is placed in the stage. For example a bust, an object or a building. Antagonists are the representation of the main task or the overarching challenge that has to be overcome in the game.

Secondary characters

In many pinball machines you also find secondary characters. These are usually assigned to secondary tasks and provide access to these tasks by personifying challenges or conveying content through them.

The ball

A special case is the figure of the ball. It can take on different roles within the narrative or a narrative offer. For example, in one offer the ball can represent the player and thus become an avatar, in another offer it can represent a projectile with which the player is supposed to hit a certain target.

Since the ball is the central element of the game, because it is directly linked to the win/loss conditions, its relationship to the player is probably the closest.

The creation of meaning

An important part of the narrative in pinball machines is the creation of meaning. Without it, the game of pinball becomes an abstract process in which individual machines can hardly be distinguished from one another and goals can only be formulated in an extremely complicated way.

One requirement for creating meaning is a coherent world logic within the narrative. As soon as this logic is not consistently adhered to, the narrative collapses.

Another aspect that charges the narrative with meaning is the game's inherent struggle against gravity. The players are in constant conflict with it and being defeated by gravity equates to the end of the game.

Significance is also created by the need to pay in order to play the machine at all. Just as with slot machines or digital arcade games, players have to insert money into the pinball machine first and thus put something at stake, which in turn increases the meaning. However, pinball machines differ from slot machines and arcade games, since the game usually cannot be extended by inserting more money, which increases the importance of the individual game. It also increases the importance of free plays or additional balls, which reward especially good players. Since no cash prizes can be won in pinball, the importance of the game itself is further increased.

The individual elements are given meaning by visually highlighting them in the best slot machine manner through lighting, flashing or movement. This is also seen in the feedback systems which give importance to the events and the actions of the players.

The need for points

Points have a special position in pinball machines. They not only measure the players' performance, but also have a narrative function.

Points are an important indicator of how far the player has progressed within the narrative. As a player it is hardly possible to keep track of the different narrative offers due to the narrative structures. The completion of a narrative offer is usually accompanied by an increase in the score, thus making narrative progress readable.

THE ROLES OF THE RECIPIENTS

There are different ways in which recipients can relate to pinball machines. The following describes which roles recipients can take on, how their perception of the pinball machine changes and what effects they have on the narration of the game.

Figure 15: Framing of the roles of the recipients.

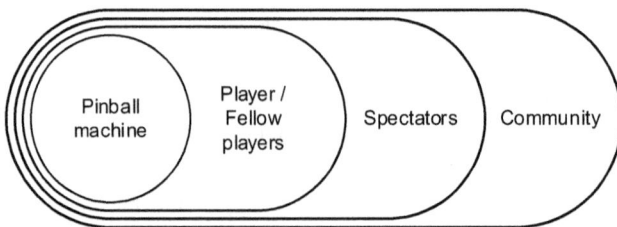

Source: David Krummenacher (figures 7-15)

Around the pinball machine different reception frames can be constructed. In the center is the pinball machine itself, which is directly received by players or fellow players. From the outside the pinball machine is received by spectators. The box directly and the game itself indirectly via the players. The community forms the outermost frame. The community receives pinball machines indirectly via the narration of the spectators and players. Anecdotes are an essential part of this frame. Within the community frame, technical language can also be found. However, due to the widespread cultural distribution of pinball machines, mastery of them cannot be considered a mandatory criterion for membership of this community.

The player

Around the pinball machine different reception frames can be constructed. In the center is the pinball machine itself, which is directly received by players or fellow players. From the outside the pinball machine is received by spectators. The box directly and the game itself indirectly via the players. The community forms the outermost frame. The community receives pinball machines indirectly via the narration of the spectators and players. Anecdotes are an essential part of this frame. Within the community frame, technical language can also be found. However, due to the widespread cultural distribution of pinball machines, mastery of them cannot be considered a mandatory criterion for membership of this community.

Fellow players

Fellow players are players that currently are not actively interacting with the machine, but are still involved in the game.

Fellow players focus on the stage and the display. They have the opportunity to deal with the narrative offerings of the pinball machine much more extensively, since they do not have to concentrate as much on the ball as the active players.

Spectators

A spectator is not actively interacting with the machine and is not involved in the game. They focus on all functional elements of the box and beyond that on the players and fellow players.

Pinball machines as a topic of conversation

Pinball machines not only tell a story within themselves, but also become a narrative subject. The narratively charged game elements make it easier for players to talk about the game mechanics and the rules of the game, because narratively charged game elements do not require technical terms that a layperson is usually not familiar with.

Furthermore, pinball machines are also talked about in the community that is formed around pinball machines. The competition surrounding the games or certain maneuvers are narratively charged by the players. Stories are told about failing or winning at certain pinball machines.

CONCLUSION

The work should be understood as a first proposal for a collection of evidence and a description of structures. This collection and classification can by no means be regarded as final, because only a small part of the whole catalog of published pinball machines was examined. In a further step, other pinball machines would have to be investigated – especially earlier pinball machines manufactured when it was technologically rather difficult to represent complex states.

A point of criticism of the work is certainly that, in the current state of the model, it does not clearly distinguish between narrative mechanics and game mechanics, but a separation nevertheless seems possible and would lead to a clearer terminology. A further point of criticism is that the work tries to cover a very large area and thus remains only superficial at certain points. It should also be investigated whether the developed model can only be applied to pinball machines or whether it is too openly formulated and does not differentiate itself sufficiently from other media.

The topic of how pinball machines tell their stories proved to be extremely profound and entertaining. Pinball machines are a good topic of conversation. Most people who were confronted with the topic during the research had a personal anecdote to tell or a hint of exciting projects in this field. Furthermore, there was no-one among these people who had never played a pinball machine before or perceived the game experience as particularly negative.

Last but not least, a question is raised here which is not completely serious, but also cannot be completely dismissed as a joke. Are pinball machines the leading narrative medium of modern games? Open-world games, for example, give the impression that their narrative structures and elements are closely related to those of pinball machines. Furthermore, their reception is very similar. Narrative offerings are provided in a game world, which are perceived by the player in a temporal arrangement and thus form a user story. The only, but probably rather significant difference is that in open-world games players have more control over whether and when they want to perceive these offers.

REFERENCES

Literature

Krummenacher, David (2018): "Storytelling in Flipperautomaten", unpublished Master thesis, Zurich University of the Arts (https://www.emuseum.ch/en/objects/210550/storytelling-in-flipperautomaten).

Games

Big Shot, Gottlieb, Gottlieb, Chicago, 1974.

Indiana Jones: The Pinball Adventure, Williams, WMS Industries Inc., Waukegan, 1993.

Tales of the Arabian Nights, Williams, WMS Industries Inc., Waukegan, 1996.

The Machine: Bride of Pinbot, Williams, WMS Industries Inc., Waukegan, 1991.

Videos

pinballwiz45b (2014): Pinball Arcade – Big Shot (https://www.youtube.com/watch?v=PxheaPolDio).

pinballwiz45b (2015): Pinball Arcade – Bride of Pin*Bot (https://www.youtube.com/watch?v=zl94pKSpB_w).

TeaKayKay (2014): The Pinball Arcade – Tales of the Arabian Nights [98,071,260] (https://www.youtube.com/watch?v=j5CyPAhTyfI).

Mechanics of Inspiration

A Recursive Play of Reflections in *Superbrothers: Sword & Sworcery EP*

Florian Faller

INTO THE VORTEX

> "In this play of representation, the point of origin becomes ungraspable. There are things like reflecting pools, and images, an infinite reference from one to the other, but no longer a source, a spring. There is no longer a simple origin. [...] What can look at itself is not one." (Derrida 1967: 36)

We are in a bronze age mountain wilderness and follow a bearlike barbarian deep into an ancient forest, where a slow-paced establishing shot starts to unveil a new and secret location. The camera is gently tilting down from the night sky, following a red light beam with no visible origin. Strobe lights are flashing. A heavy drumbeat, a hypnotic bassline and a wailing guitar evoke a dark and mesmerizing vibe, both menacing and seductive. Towering amplifiers manifest themselves in the fog and reveal that this is a diegetic sound: we have stumbled into a modern rock concert. This anachronistic encounter evokes *Twin Peaks: Fire Walk With Me* (1992) and lets us revisit Lynch's movie. The original scene is commonly referred to as the *Pink Room* and borrows its name from the corresponding song by Angelo Badalamenti. The game scene is a subtle but meticulous restaging of the *Pink Room*, including camera movement, light and music. The theme we now hear, not a cover version but a homage, is aptly called *An Ode to a Room*. The name of the game is *Superbrothers: Sword & Sworcery EP*.

Jim Guthrie himself has climbed onto the stage to perform the song, and since the game is labeled like a type of musical recording (*EP* or *Extended Play*), we should probably not be surprised to meet the composer in the dark and orbital center. Yet, the *recursion* (Burns 2006) we are experiencing creates a trace of vertigo, and its infinite mirroring effect gives the *Extended Play* an additional meaning. Also on stage with a pixelated Guthrie are several NPCs from the game, including the narrator and some eerie skeleton warriors. They all have dropped out of their fictional roles like actors in a Brecht play in order to join the party. We might wonder if this dance of death indeed comes from an elaborate design decision or if we are witnessing the shameless reuse of game assets for cost-saving reasons. Nevertheless, the *Verfremdungseffekt* is taking its toll, disrupts the stage illusion, and messes up the game mechanics: The skeletons have abandoned their positions within the gameplay and no longer serve as enemies.

DIGITAL MANNERISM

Superbrothers: Sword & Sworcery EP (2011, *SS&SEP*) prepared its audience early on for its presumptuous mysteriousness and primed future players for an idiosyncratic play with references. Instead of promoting the iPad game with a sober announcement trailer, we are "initiated" by an "audience calibration procedure" that promises a "psychosocial audiovisual experiment" for "touchtronic machinery" and culminates in a nebulous release date: "We will meet again at the appointed time when the day and the night are in balance." "Around the Vernal Equinox", when we get our hands on the indie game, we find ourselves in a meandering fantasy adventure that is simultaneously staged as an 8-bit game, a dream, a theater play (with opening and closing curtains), a counseling session, an analytical test and a double-sided vinyl record.

On the threshold of this *remediation* (Bolter 1999) gone wild sits a narrator, who also acts as a therapist, mythographer, mentor and gatekeeper. The so-called *Archetype* not only mocks Campbell's comparative mythology (Campbell 1949) and Jung's self-experiments with *active imagination* (Jung 2009) but repeatedly pulls us out of the game to dictate periods of rest between the sessions. The gameplay becomes further fragmented as the hypermediated adventure wants to tweet every bit of progression into the social ether, and the switch between game mechanics requires a recurrent rotation of the "machinery". Eventually, we have to wait for a specific moon phase in the real world before continuing our quest. Also responsible for the digression is a narrative device called the *Megatome*. The magical book we have stolen in the fantasy world reads people's minds and writes them into the game log. As the *Megatome* also records the narrator's thoughts, it complements the confusion of *diegetic levels* (Genette 1980) and the disruption of different realities.

In *SS&SEP*, the medial borders are blurred and permeable. The adventure extends the scope of intertextuality, common to the genre (Giappone 2015), as an unbridled number of pop-cultural allusions stray into the mythopoetic landscapes. Our protagonist, the *Scythian*, is battling game references and fencing genre tropes while drawing her strength from cinematic quotations: "Long live the new flesh." (*Videodrome* 1983) The heroine wanders through poetic dreams and loses herself in soundscapes that pay homage to Philip Glass, John Carpenter and *Godspeed You! Black Emperor*, only to bump into wrestling legends and street art: "Last year before the yuletide Andre The Giant assembled a posse & we set out to re-assemble The Trigon Trifecta." (*SS&SEP*) The references come from various media and art forms, but because they span all aspects of the game, they tightly interweave into a captivating and compelling adventure. A tribute to *Zelda* (*The Legend of Zelda* 1986-2015) transforms into a rhythm game. An homage to Al Jaffee's *MAD* fold-ins, which were themselves an ironic reversal of the *Playboy* centerfolds, gives the player the ability to fold landscapes. Since the allusive play is not limited to the usual genre repertoire, it inspires innovative gameplay and contributes to a unique experience.

Figure 1: Superbrothers: Sword & Sworcery EP 2011.

Source: screenshot (Faller)

A consistent visual style maintains the unearthly atmosphere. The pixel art of *SS&SEP* is a highly suggestive aesthetic choice. (Hood 2015) Like low poly art or the so-called silhouette style, it leaves room for imagination. But while a game like *Feist* (2015) uses silhouettes to give an organic feel and hide its digital nature ("It's easy to feel as though you're interacting with a live painting rather than a video game." [Tran 2015]), the pixel style of *SS&SEP* creates awareness of the medium by drawing attention to its digital quality. Of course, this apparent distinctness is pretended and deceptive – the iPad adventure is not an 8-bit game. The result is a kind of stylish artificiality. This artifice is reinforced by lush and static, tapestry-like compositions with illogical compressions of space, elongated character proportions and other elements commonly associated with mannerism. Although *SS&SEP* contributed to a resurgence of pixel art, the game still stands out today as a work of high consistency: The core characteristics of the visual style appear in every other aspect of the game. A scope for imagination, a tendency to deception and nostalgia, a high amount of self-referentiality and artificiality imbue the gameplay, the music, the narrative and the deliberately misspelled name: *Superbrothers: Sword & Sworcery EP*.

DARK MASS

Pop cultural references can give us a sense of belonging, a comforting and soothing sentiment. They can assure us that we have the cultural literacy and proper knowledge of the canon and stand on common and solid ground. They also play an essential role in geek culture, where expertise acts as social currency (McCain 2015), and help cement a fanbase. When a mainstream entertainment industry is committed to the idea that everything needs to be explained and exploited, an abundance of redundant references and worn-out tropes become the cement that suffocates every last spark of inspiration. What we are facing, with a multitude of sequels, prequels, spinoffs, reboots and cinematic universes that aim for the broadest common ground, is "a parody of the world of the imagination" (Baudrillard 1989: 55).

Since *SS&SEP* claims to be an "experimental treatment for acute soul-sickness", it does not shy away from soothing moments. But the explicit hints that give us something to hold onto drift in a vast sea full of vague and oracular allusions. Apparently, references are made out of love (Deleuze 1977), not for clarity. They often *Link to the Past* (*The Legend of Zelda* 1991) and the forgotten: *SS&SEP*'s self-description echoes one of the earliest *Sword & Sorcery* tales. The cover art of *Conan*'s very first adventure (Howard 1932) promised the reader "a soul-searing story". It unmasks the 'soul-curing' game as a remedy against the effects of Howard's fiction. However, the inscription on *Conan*'s cover that exposes *Sworcery* as a kind of inverted *Sorcery* appears only in the original 1932 edition. The reference point is almost untraceable.

Eventually, the game mocks our interpretative efforts: "My logs have many secrets … secrets about sylvan sprites & impossible islands. Unfortunately, I don't speak log-language." (*SS&SEP*) Elsewhere we are warned against excessive interpretation: "In my experience there are times when owls are not what they seem & at other times they're just plain old owls." (*SS&SEP*) Then again, both the mockery and warning are themselves references (*Twin Peaks* 1990) and only draw us deeper into the allusive and self-conscious game. In the heart of its darkness lurks the antagonist, a deathless specter that we have awoken, only to be hunted by him. Its skull-shaped head is a genre trope, but why is the evil creature called the *Gogolithic Mass*? Scholars are in disagreement: "a reference to the Googol, no doubt, or perhaps to Google? The sum of all evil, perhaps an ironic commentary on Google's famous slogan?" (Games on a Train 2015) Likewise, it could be "a deliberate misspelling of the Glagolithic Mass" (No. 6 2016) or an allusion to Nikolai Gogol's Gothic fiction (Gogol 1835). Since the *Gogolithic Mass* allegedly descends from shapeshifters, it must condense all of these explanations and probably more. This "Mass" with its deadly, consuming gravity, awoken by the player and strikingly and self-referentially staged as a black hole, frayed and burned into the otherwise pixelated landscape, was not created by magic but by referential play.

INFINITY MIRROR

This explorative puzzle adventure reminds us to "observe, dream, believe, and reflect". The written words also appear in trailers, where they promise essential features. They refer to general gameplay (observe, reflect) and to specific mechanics like entering the dream state, where they function as subtle but essential clues: The word "believe" appears in the dream world when we reach the lakeshore, an apparent dead end – but we "believe" and walk across the water. The simple but elegant staging reflects a crucial aspect in general game design: creating acceptable level boundaries as part of a believable game world. *SS&SEP* reverses this idea and reminds us that a game is not reality. Instead, we have to believe in the game's dreamlike quality, where waterfalls can be strummed like harps. The word "reflect" surfaces on another shore, where the player character meets his mirror-image in the water. Highlighting a simple mir-

roring effect first appears as a mockery of typical game marketing and its obliga-
tory feature listing. The use of a literal reflection for an ironic reflection of game
traditions has a poetic quality. But as it later turns out, there are more layers: "reflect" was also an instruction to think, and a hint that we need the mirroring in
the water to solve several puzzles.

SS&SEP is a game of waters and a play of reflections, where references appear as distorted mirror images, and genre tropes are consequently inverted. *The
Trigon Trifecta* is literally an upside-down *Triforce* (*The Legend of Zelda* 1986-
2015). Instead of experiencing a worn-out power fantasy, we are on a "woeful
errand" (*SS&SEP*), and our female protagonist is not leveling up, she is weaken-
ing throughout the adventure. The gameplay even reflects its mirror mechanics.
It figuratively stages the reflection of ancestry and raw material when it brings
our heroine to face the *Grizzled Boor* in the dream state. The half bear, half bar-
barian-like creature, which emerges from the forest's depth to enjoy a free-
swinging display of its manhood, is both an embodiment and an archaic remnant
of the *Sword & Sorcery* genre. According to the *Archetype*, the barbarian-bear
helps "to self-identify". Not surprisingly, the name of our *Sword & Sworcery*
heroine is *Ursula*: little bear.

THE MAELSTROM

Players may wonder to what extent the myriads of references are intended or at
which point they "see what isn't even there" (*SS&SEP*). But ultimately, they are
caught in a meticulously crafted mirror maze where the referential play is endless and productive. The narrative mechanics continuously create new points of
reference because *SS&SEP* is both cryptic and self-referential. Eventually, the
game finds a name for this recursive process: "The song of sworcery can be understood as a psionics technique & it allows you to perceive a reality within the
one that you know." (*SS&SEP*) *The Song of Sworcery*'s imaginative potential
and capacity for inspiration manifest themselves in an infinite amount of fan art
and other projects which have followed the game's release. *SS&SEP* has contributed to the revival of an artistic style and inspired countless other titles, including such influential games as *Monument Valley* (2014) and *Hyper Light
Drifter* (2016).

During the adventure, the recursive play with references creates a sense of
wonder and a feeling of being lost. The gameplay made to lose yourself is embodied by a player character that begins to dissolve like a Pynchonesque hero
(Pynchon 1973) and dissipates into the pixelated landscape. In the end, our hero-

ine will deteriorate in a mise en abyme called *The Whirling Infinite*. She will multiply and fade away, eventually die and disappear. But since *SS&SEP* is both a playful homage and a highly inspiring game in itself, it ends in a final act of recursion and a demonstration of respect. In a self-referential closing scene that both reveals and forecasts, the body of the *Scythian* is brought back by the river and recovered. Several characters of the game gather to honor the heroine, while her remains are burned to pixels.

SWORD & SORCERY

> "Our creativity comes from without, not from within. We are not self-made. We are dependent on one another, and admitting this to ourselves isn't an embrace of mediocrity and derivativeness. It's a liberation from our misconceptions, and it's an incentive to not expect so much from ourselves and to simply begin." (*Everything is a Remix* 2012)

Robert E. Howard, who today ranks among the most influential authors of fantasy literature, was already a successful writer in his time in that he could make a stable living. But due to his tragic death at the age of 30, the writing autodidact would never see his work transcend the pulp magazines, which were both devoured and scorned for their lurid and sensational expositions and were printed in huge quantities on the cheapest possible paper. In 1936, when the young Texan shot himself in the head, he left the world more than four hundred stories, full of vigorous men, voluptuous women, vicious beasts and vile wizards. Among these were the adventures of *Conan* (Howard 1932) and a multitude of other scenarios with plenty of violent action. With the decline of the pulp magazines, Howard's work fell almost into oblivion (Dedopulos 2019), but eventually, it would come to define a new and vibrant fantasy sub-genre that would be formative for a wide range of popular media.

This process needed decades, the help of other artistic disciplines and other influential artists. In the early 60s, when *Sword and Sorcery* (*S&S*) was coined (Leiber 1961), emerging art legend Frank Frazetta began to illustrate the covers of Howard's republished adventures. Muscle-bound stallions, callipygian vixens, and, quite literally, big exotic cats, all of them scantily clad, but always maned, sometimes chained and often armored. Frazetta's melodramatic, action-packed oil paintings redefined the genre's style without bastardizing Howard's original work. On the contrary, they introduced a counter-culture vibe with a dash of sex, drugs, and rock 'n' roll, which even amplified its effect. The reinvented imagery of *S&S* would inspire generations of painters, illustrators and designers, while Frazetta's depiction of the barbarian would never again be artistically challenged – probably to the chagrin of historians.

Figure 2: "Chained" by Frank Frazetta (cover art on Conan the Usurper by Robert E. Howard 1967).

Source: Robert E. Howard

TWO SNAKES FACING EACH OTHER, BUT THEY ARE ONE

In the early 80s, Howard's work was finally made flesh – on celluloid, on steroids and in plastic. *Conan the Barbarian* hit the big screen in 1982. Oliver Stone's screenplay had been written under the strong influence of cocaine and depressants and turned out to be "a total drug fever dream" (Riordan 1994: 102). Director John Milius, a gun-loving, self-proclaimed zen-anarchist and Hollywood's man for the rough, apparently valued physicality more than drama school and cast in the leading roles a dancer, a surfer and Mr. Olympia. In the same year that Arnold Schwarzenegger's 'acting' career kicked off, and Frazetta's work was pinned up in the muscle factories, *S&S* was flooding into children's rooms: *Masters of the Universe* (1982), a new toy line launched by Mattel, drew heavily on "Frizetta" [sic] (Seely 2015: 12) and swept the full catalog of genre tropes into the homes of concerned parents – including oversized battle axes, armored bikinis, skull-headed archenemies, skull-faced fortresses, plenty of other skull-shaped items, giant skeletons, enormous snakes and a wild bunch of other monstrosities. As both *Conan* and *Masters* cruised extensively in the genre's primordial waters, they eventually clashed in a lawsuit.

Unlike *Masters*, which would become one of the best-selling product lines in the history of the toy industry, *Conan*, despite its undoubted influence, was a singular and only moderate financial success that was greeted by a storm of negative reviews and lamentations: "more Neanderthal than Nietzsche" (Von Gunden 2001: 15). The Austrian bodybuilder would be back (*Terminator* 1984), but future cinematic approaches to the genre were doomed to become box office flops. There are exceptions. *Mandy* (2019) is substantially (in its narrative core and its orgiastic and visceral imagery) *S&S*, but this highly successful indie film is set in the rural American present.

BARBARIANS AT THE GATE

In other domains, however, no such transformation or relocation of the genre is needed. Pen and paper role-playing games, arcade games, and, later, video games could adopt the pulp fantasy almost one-to-one. The fast-paced scenarios turned out to be a perfect playground and are generally better blueprints for gameplay than the epic, 'unhasty' tales by an English professor at Oxford. In contrast to the slowly evolving stories of the so-called *Epic Fantasy*, which have to conjure up nothing less than a world-threatening battle between good and evil to call the righteous but reluctant hero to a leisurely adventure, the stakes in *S&S* are actually high: because they are personal. The motivational design (often vengeance, mostly survival) is primal and effective. It allows a *show, don't tell* that plays into the hands of game masters and helps arcade games to hook their audience at first glance. The danger is confined to the heat of the moment (Philip 2002: 35) and asks for immediate, but constant action. This ongoing turmoil ensures pure gameplay. Its sequential structure (another pulp heritage) translates into sessions, levels, quests or any other form of breakdown crucial to the game design.

Then there is the perfect protagonist. "They are simpler. [...] They are too stupid to do anything but cut, shoot, or slug themselves into the clear." (Haile: 1982 89) Howard wrote almost lovingly about his heroes. In the same way that the living dead, with their limited abilities and their determined, relentless, Yul Brynner-like behavior, are the ideal embodiment of hostile NPCs, the pulp barbarians from *S&S* are appropriate templates for many player characters. They embody the limitation of possible interactions which have to be accepted and substantiate the lack of knowledge players experience when confronted with a new game world. They represent the players' illiteracy regarding new rules and systems and even justify the inability to speak. (This last point, however, is not pulp heritage, but rather the leftover of a failed logotherapy in showbiz). More importantly, the *S&S* barbarians are morally unbound, socially unattached outsiders. As such, they offer a means of overcoming social restrictions (Crawford 1984) and allow for a freedom of action appropriate to the mechanics (Christen 2012). Not surprisingly, there is a bit of barbarian in many player characters. The tribute to Frazetta on the cover of *Doom* (1992) is apt, and *Dr. Bree*, the antagonist in *Half-Life 2* (2004), has some valid points when he identifies *Freeman* as "Anticitizen One" and accuses him of destructive behavior and throwing civilization into freefall. *Bree*'s problem is that he is in the wrong game genre. If *Half-Life 2* were a strategy game, his fascist and inhuman dreams of optimization would be in line with the goal. Whereas *Freeman*, who does not get the bigger picture, would be doomed to run with the barbarian tribes that usually spawn in random places as a constant annoyance.

S&S's stories of high adventure are set in perilous and dystopian worlds, where civilization is corrupted and in decline, and social structures are either destroyed or an expression of moral decay. The reason why we cannot find the lands of *Howard's Hyborian Age* on the *World Peace Index* is not so much because they do not exist, but because they are totally off the scale. In short: The worlds of pulp are fertile ground for action-packed gameplay. They let the constant spawning of enemies seem plausible and make the player's destructive raids legitimate.

THE WHIRLING INFINITE

Robert E. Howard had to accept countless failures before his first published success – a story about a Cro-Magnon man who had to fight a Neanderthal over a beautiful woman. (Dedopulos 2019) During those years, the autodidact studied the popular pulp stories meticulously, always searching for the perfect narrative formula. In a potentiation process that defied homeopathy laws, he mixed what he found (Martin 2020), until he got a final brew that was fresh, strong and addictive and could hook the readers in seconds. *SS&SEP* is an heir to the *Sword & Sorcery* genre – not because it indulges in the pulp potion, as plenty of other games did and still do, but because it understands the creative process: *copy, transform and combine* (*Everything is a Remix* 2012). *Superbrothers: Sword & Sworcery EP* is a self-referential parable about the inspiration that reminds us that creativity is not a form of exploitation, nor is taxidermy a bedrock for the imagination. When we meet the bearlike ancestor in the ancient wilderness, the adventure gives us a choice: we can slay the primal beast or follow it deeper into the mythic woods – and dive into the vortex.

REFERENCES

Literature

Baudrillard, Jean (1989): America, London: Verso.

Bolter, Jay David/Grusin, Richard (1999): Remediation: Understanding New Media, Cambridge, Massachusetts: The MIT Press.

Burns, Anne M. (2006): "Recursion in Nature, Mathematics and Art." In: Visual Mathematics 29 (http://eudml.org/doc/256575).

Campbell, Joseph (1949): The Hero with a Thousand Faces, New York: Bollingen Foundation.

Christen, Markus/Faller, Florian/Götz, Ulrich/ Müller, Cornelius (2012): Serious Moral Games. Analyzing and Engaging Moral Values Through Video Games, Zurich: Zurich University of the Arts.

Crawford, Criss (1984): The Art of Computer Game Design, Berkeley: McGraw-Hill Osborne Media.

Dedopulos, Tim (2019): The life and death of Robert E. Howard (https://conan.com/the-life-and-death-of-robert-e-howard/).

Deleuze, Gilles/Guattari, Felix (1977): Rhizom, Berlin: Merve.

Derrida, Jacques (1967): Of Grammatology, Baltimore & London: Johns Hopkins University Press.

Games on a Train (2015): Superbrothers: Sword & Sworcery EP Review (https://gamesonatrain.wordpress.com/tag/sword-sworcery).

Genette Gérard (1980): Narrative Discourse: An Essay in Method, Ithaca: Cornell University Press.

Giappone, Krista Bonello Rutter (2015): "Self-Reflexivity and Humor in Adventure Games." In: Game Studies 15/1 (http://gamestudies.org/1501/articles/bonello_k).

Gogol, Nicolai (2015 [1835]): The Viy, Scotts Valley: Createspace Independent Publishing Platform.

Haile, Bartee (2019): Texas Entertainers: Lone Stars in Profil, Charleston: Arcadia Publishing.

Hood, Andrew (2015): Jim Guthrie: Who Needs What, Halifax & Toronto: Invisible Publishing.

Howard, Robert E. (1932): "The Phoenix on the Sword." In: Weird Tales 20/6, Chicago: Rural Publishing Corporation.

Jung, Carl Gustav (2009): The Red Book: Liber Novus, New York: W. W. Norton & Company.

Leiber Franz (1961): In: Amra 2/15, Chicago: Hyborian Legion.

MAD (1952 - 2020). Mad Magazine, New York: Warner Bros.

Martin, Philip (2002): The Writer's Guide to Fantasy Literature: From Dragon's Lair to Hero's Quest, Waukesha: Kalmbach.

McCain, Jessica/Gentile, Brittany/Campbell, W. Keith (2015): "A Psychological Exploration of Engagement in Geek Culture." In PLoS ONE 10/11 (https://journals.plos.org/plosone/article/related?id=10.1371/journal.pone.0142200).

No. 6 (2016): Superbrothers: Sword & Sworcery EP – Meaning? (Spoiler-y Discussion) March 31, 2016 (https://steamcommunity.com/app/204060/discussions/0/412448158145688744/?l=dutch).

Playboy (1953-2020), Chicago: Playboy Enterprises.

Pynchon, Thomas (1973): Gravity's Rainbow, New York: Viking Press.

Riordan, James (1994): Stone: The Controversies, Excesses, and Exploits of a Radical Filmmaker. New York: Hyperion Books.

Seely, Tim (2015): The Art of He-Man and the Masters of the Universe, Milwaukie, Dark Horse Books.

Tran, Chin (2015): Feist (PC) Review, July 24, 2015 (https://www.vgchartz.com/article/260142/feist-pc/).

Von Gunden, Kenneth (2001): Flights of Fancy: The Great Fantasy Films, Jefferson: McFarland.

Games/Toys

Doom, id Software, id Software, 1993.
Feist, Bits & Beasts, Finji, 2015.
Half Life 2, Valve, Valve, 2004.
The Legend of Zelda, Nintendo/Capcom/Grezzo, Nintendo, 1986-2015.
Masters of the Universe, Mattel, Mattel, 1982-1988.
Monument Valley, Ustwo, Ustwo, 2014.
Hyper Light Drifter, Heart Machine, Heart Machine, 2016.
Superbrothers: Sword & Sworcery EP, Superbrothers, Capybara Games, 2011.

Movies/TV series

Conan the Barbarian (1982): John Milius, Universal Pictures, Dino De Laurentiis Company, Edward R. Pressman Film.
Everything is a Remix (2012): Kirby Ferguson.
Mandy (2018): Panos Cosmatos, SpectreVision, Umedia, Legion M.
Terminator (1984): James Cameron, Cinema '84, Euro Film Funding, Hemdale.
Twin Peaks (1990): David Lynch, Mark Frost, Lynch/Frost Productions, Propaganda Films, Spelling Entertainment.
Twin Peaks: Fire Walk with Me (1992): David Lynch, New Line Cinema, CiBy 2000, Twin Peaks Productions.
Videodrome (1983): David Cronenberg, Filmplan International, Guardian Trust Company, Canadian Film Development Corporation (CFDC).

Narrative Approaches in Contemporary Video Game Reviews

Robert Glashüttner

As journalism wants to both inform and engage the reader through telling stories, video game reviews from different outlets have distinct approaches in their narrative designs and structures. Whereas some media, mostly long-running dedicated magazines, prefer a more straightforward and holistic approach for their review style, newer game culture publications tend to adopt a more personal and selective way of writing about video games. This text will analyze and compare these approaches to narrative design. It will tackle the following questions: How do game reviews motivate their readers, not only by presenting an engaging text/story but also in terms of the way in which they influence how a video game will be perceived and played? How do the writers position themselves and their personal preferences in relation to the respective game? And how is the personal act of individually playing a video game reflected in a text that tries to cater to a broader audience?[1]

INTRODUCTION

Since the 1980s, video game journalism has been integral to the perception and the development of interactive entertainment as a medium. Originating in computer culture, video game critics have come a long way from describing a digital

---

1 A personal note: This text is an essay that approaches the topic first and foremost from a journalistic point of view. It draws its sources mostly from other journalistic publications and the author's personal experience as a (video game) journalist and university graduate.

game as a software product to reflecting on video games as cultural artefacts. Multiple steps and milestones have been taken that have led from the early days of digital game criticism in special interest print magazines to texts about video games which use a variety of narrative structures and are now published both in general and special interest newspapers and magazines – in print and online.

While there is a lot that could be said about video game journalism in general, this text will focus on reviews. Specifically, reviews from five different media outlets about three recently released games (November 2019 to June 2020) will be compared with each other in order to demonstrate how different narrative approaches to video games and video game writing can be, and indeed are. While special interest media still reign supreme in today's video game culture landscape, general interest newspapers and magazines have devoted increasing amounts of space to covering video games and video game culture over the last five to ten years. General interest media tend to choose a point of view that compares video games not so much with other games but with other art forms and cultural products such as movies or pop music.

This analysis focuses on (digital) newspapers, magazines and websites written in English and published in the US and the UK.

A VERY BRIEF HISTORY OF VIDEO GAME REVIEWS

Looking back at computer and video game magazines from the 1980s and the early 1990s, it becomes clear that there were no established rules on how to structure a review. A text usually began with an excerpt of the game's story, followed by a description of the interactive elements and a critical subjective statement about the technical and entertaining qualities of the respective game. Sometimes, similar games from the same publishing house were referenced, or a note was added as to whether older titles of the same genre had been better or not. In some cases, this information was provided in separate boxes outside the main text, sometimes it was incorporated. This straightforward reviewing approach was accompanied by rating systems that varied from magazine to magazine. In 1984, *Computer & Video Games* awarded single-digit scores in the categories "Getting started", "Graphics", "Value" and "Playability", whereas two years later, *CRASH* used a more detailed system that also included "Use of computer" or "Addictive qualities" and a percentage rating system (1 to 100 per cent). In 1988 and 1990, *ACE* even used a 1000-point system where a game might, for example, receive a review score of 746. Explanations about what these categories or numbers meant or should describe exactly were not included in the magazines.

It is interesting to note that in some cases, reviews in earlier video game magazines contained elaborate introductions, where one would usually find a summary of the game's story. In hindsight, this seems like a conscious editorial decision to spice up the otherwise rather dry and technical write-up with narrative artefacts that are comparable with the kind of vivid descriptions of scenes and situations one would normally read in a novel.

"Trapped inside a space ship crawling with aliens, the spaceman wants to escape. Robot patrols are on his trail. Somehow the intrepid spaceman must locate his escape shuttle, re-fuel it and crack the code so he can flee from the merciless invaders." – Review of Luna Atac; CRASH August 1986: 18.

Historically, reviews published in ACE magazine stand out because they managed to coalesce the descriptions of a game's setting and those of the interactive elements with the respective writer's critique in a cohesive, surprisingly modern writing style. These texts also always had the writer's name printed next to the review whereas the other historical magazines mentioned above named their writers only in the imprint or within special sections.

MILESTONES OF VIDEO GAME CRITICISM

Computer game and video game journalism started out in form of game reviews around the year 1980, so it is safe to say that the review is the primary and most common text form. The major milestones in the history of video game journalism and criticism are as follows:

(a) Printed computer culture tech magazines and early special interest video game magazines (circa 1980-1993)
(b) The introduction of the CD-ROM as a game changer for video game development as well as for journalistic production methods due to new audiovisual possibilities (1993-2005)
(c) A paradigm shift in narrative writing started by the New Games Journalism movement (2004-2006)
(d) The ubiquity of the internet through fast and stable connections (from circa 2006)

(e) The ubiquity of podcast, video and streaming culture, primarily through YouTube.com and Twitch.tv (from circa 2012)

(f) The Gamergate controversy and backlash (2014-2016)

With each of these milestones, video game journalism underwent a change in character, although in some cases only in minor but still significant form. Let's look at these milestones in a little more detail.

(a) Printed computer culture tech magazines and early special interest video game magazines such as *Compute!* (first issue November/December 1979) or *Computer & Video Games* (first issue November 1981) introduced video games as a certain type of software. Aside from publishing reviews of commercial games, these magazines also printed program listings of non-commercial games that every reader/user could then type up on their computer, enabling them to use the game program for free. This was common content for many years and something that often used up a considerable number of pages within a magazine issue. Reviews were written mostly in a straightforward manner: the game at hand was perceived more as an entertainment product and less as an artistic or cultural artefact. Thus, rating systems were introduced that were added to these game reviews quite early on, with the intention to sum up the "worth" of a video game through certain numbers and very short descriptions. These early, classic texts about digital games and the first rating systems can be considered the genesis of video game journalism as a whole. Other milestones have led to the field branching out and becoming more sophisticated, but many (mostly special interest) publications still stick to this straightforward approach, at least partially.

(b) The introduction of the CD-ROM not only changed the essence of many upcoming video games (for Windows) in the mid-1990s by making it possible for developers to use a lot more disk space than before, but it also changed the monopoly of printed magazines as the only method of media publication. Although the first experiments with audiovisual video game criticism only go as far back as the second half of the 1990s and the first half of the 2000s, videos, podcasts and livestreams have since become ubiquitous and in many cases surpassed the relevance of classic (written) video game journalism. It is important here to note the differences between a person who is a critic and someone who works as a journalist. The difference mostly lies in their respective approach to text creation, with a journalist (who is often part of a larger media house) usually adhering to a list of criteria for their work, whereas a critic (who is often a self-employed internet personality or hobbyist) often does not apply checklists when criticizing a game. A crude way of proving this point and recognizing the differences is by running a Google search for "video game reviewers", "video game journalists" and "video game critics". Although misleading, with the search term *reviewers*, mostly YouTube personalities will be the result. This is in contrast to *journalists*, which returns around 50 to 60 renowned game journalists of the last 30 years. With *critics*, one gets a mixed result comprising both groups.

(c) In 2004, comic book writer and games and music journalist Kieron Gillen published his manifesto for New Games Journalism (a modification of New Journalism applied to video game journalism) in which he pleads for a new form of narrative for video game texts that is more personal and subjective, and more intertwined with other media and art forms. Reviews should thus treat video games less as software products and more like cultural artefacts that deserve more than being mainly put into numbers. Technical aspects should be less important than game design; personal experiences that come up throughout the playing of a game, and the culture of play in general, should be embraced. Although this was a somewhat radical concept in 2004 that was not taken seriously by many mainstream game publications at first, about ten years later, the narrative approach of New Games Journalism was eventually adopted by many modern journalistic outlets that cover video games like *Eurogamer.net* or *The Guardian.com*. It is now as relevant as the classic text structure of video game reviews as seen in (a). Despite the particular orientation and target group of a publication, a personal approach (first-person narrative) became the norm due to the rising demand of personalized game reviews. Today's media consumers are used to storytelling pieces and opinions that are intertwined within a text. Emotionally and narratively, a written video game review can thus be on par with a comparable podcast, video or livestream, as explained further in (e).

(d) Around 2005, the ubiquity of the internet through fast and stable connections and the general sophistication of websites made it possible to publish journalistic content digitally more and more easily than in printed magazines. This led to the rise of online publications as well as a different feedback culture. In forums and comments sections, online readers' feedback was faster, more immediate and also a lot less editorially curated than in a printed magazine or newspaper. In addition, wikis, blogs and social media platforms made (gaming) news public and multiplied it almost instantly. Journalists had to cope with this new situation by differentiating between offline and online content, and their publishing companies had to decide on how to charge money for which content. To this day, both print and online video game publications fight for attention with a slow but steady decline on the side of print media that has been a constant trend for over 15 years now.

(e) First with YouTube and later with Twitch, video game criticism saw a major paradigm shift from written text to audiovisual and audio content around

2010 when these forms of publication started to gain greater popularity. Today's major video game personalities like PewDiePie or Jacksepticeye produce very personal videos about video games, and they can be watched while playing those games live on stream on a regular basis. These personalities have a major influence on digital game consumers that surpasses the impact of written text. As mentioned in (b), the work of a YouTube and/or Twitch personality is more immediate and often does not follow many rules or guidelines. In a written text (within a certain publication), a journalist composing a review often follows a specific structure or checklist or tries to underline a specific point by providing additional explanation. While a video and/or streaming content producer might do the same, in many cases the criticism is presented as a casual, instantaneous opinion that plays out as if it were a personal, informal conversation between two people. This also very much applies to podcast culture where listeners often expect and prefer this interpersonal narrative approach to video game criticism to a more analytically written review piece.

(f) When video game culture became more inclusive and multifaceted at the beginning of the 2010s, this progressivism received a backlash called Gamergate. It started out as a harassment campaign against certain video game developers and activists like Zoe Quinn or Anita Sarkeesian in August of 2014. This cultural war was fought intensely, mostly publicly, for about two years before it started to slowly ebb away in the following months and years. As an excuse for their long-lasting campaign, some harassers would often state that the actual controversy was not about reactionary philosophies concerning the absurd question of who should "own" video game culture and who shouldn't, but rather about the issue that video game publications needed to be more transparent regarding their reviews policy. While many people within digital game culture tried to unmask this argument as a false excuse, a lot of magazines and blogs like *Polygon* or *Kotaku* nevertheless applied new review transparency guidelines shortly after the peak of the Gamergate controversy, for example, requiring the information of whether the reviewer of a video game was provided a free copy (and which one) or not.

RATING SYSTEMS

Throughout the roughly 40 years of video game journalism history, several rating systems have been tried out. While some oddities like the 12- (*ASM /Aktueller Software Markt*) or the 1000-point system (*ACE*) did not last longer than a few years, some other rating systems established in the 1980es are still in use today. In German-speaking countries it became common to use a percentage (or 100-point) system, but many publications written in English eventually settled on applying a 10-point system. Some magazines and game websites alternatively use a 5-star system, yet also award half-stars, which basically again makes for a 10-point system that is only visually different.

It is notable, however, that even though most of the video game rating systems used by different media outlets and publications are easily mathematically comparable to each other, certain ratings within certain systems often have different meanings in practice. This especially applies to the average score which should either be 5 points, 50 points/per cent or 2,5 stars. But when comparing different video game reviews from different publications and periods, it turns out that a purely mediocre game (in the eyes of the reviewer/s) rarely gets these scores. Throughout the last 20 to 30 years, these numbers have experienced some curious kind of inflation process. A mediocre game would therefore mostly receive 6 out of 10 points or sometimes even a 70 per cent rating. As a trend, it can be said that this inflation process is more pronounced when a system is (theoretically) more nuanced. Where 5 out of 10 points is mostly considered only slightly subpar, a 50 per cent rating is perceived worse than that. When looking at scores on the review aggregator website *Metacritic*, which aggregates all scores (rating systems) into a 100-point system, a combined score of around 50 points (+/- three points) is uncommon. In these rarer cases, the games in question are considered bad by the majority of the (professional) reviewers even though the numbers alone would suggest otherwise.

METHOD

For this essay, 15 video game reviews have been analyzed and compared. They had been published online by five different media outlets: *Destructoid*, *TheGuardian.com*, *Polygon*, *Slant Magazine*, and *VICE.com* (United States edition). These media outlets were selected based on diversity in terms of the following parameters: rating system, editorial structure and audience. The five publications include ones with and without (different) rating systems, they are special interest as well as general interest, and they all have different target groups.

The reviews cover three recent video game releases: *Death Stranding* (November 2019), *Animal Crossing: New Horizons* (March 2020) and *The Last of Us Part II* (June 2020). These releases were chosen due to their high public relevance not only for special interest media but also for publications that cover games in addition to other cultural fields. Two of these three games (initially) came out exclusively for Playstation 4, and the third one (*Animal Crossing: New Horizons*) exclusively for Nintendo Switch. This fact is a coincidence; it did not play a part in the selection process and is not considered in the analysis.

First, the chosen games and publications will briefly be described. This is followed by a game-by-game analysis of the five reviews for each of the three games and a comparison of their writing styles and narrative approaches.

THE GAMES CHOSEN

Death Stranding is an action game set in the aftermath of a cataclysmic event where the player takes on the role of Sam Porter Bridges, a courier who carries cargo in a fictional future version of the USA. The game is very elaborate in terms of story and gameplay details. It is special because of its well-known Japanese video game director Hideo Kojima and his expressive ideas which are mirrored in the games he directs.

Animal Crossing: New Horizons is a life-simulation video game that takes place on fictional islands where the player tries to build a settlement and host guests, and interacts with other players. The game is meant to be played regularly over the course of many weeks. What makes it stand out is its release at the beginning of the COVID-19 pandemic, which subsequently turned it into an escapist world for millions of people.

The Last of Us Part II is an action-adventure game that revolves around the relationship of specific characters within a post-apocalyptic world set in the USA of the near future. It is notable and well known for its epic set pieces, technical capabilities and graphic depiction of human violence and madness as the protagonists constantly fight zombies and each other.

THE PUBLICATIONS CHOSEN

Destructoid is a video game-focused website that was founded in March 2006 and is a self-proclaimed "quirky gaming news website for the savvy gamer with a heavy focus on fun." It uses a 10-point rating system for its reviews and allows for half-points (which essentially makes it a 20-point system).

TheGuardian.com is a news and media website launched in 1999 that covers video games as part of their Culture section (as one out of eight categories). It uses a 5-star system for its culture reviews and allows for half-stars (which essentially makes it a 10-point system).

Polygon is a video game website that was launched in October 2012 and covers video game culture in general as well as movies and TV series with a focus on superhero and fantasy themes. It does not use a rating system for its video game reviews.

Slant Magazine is an online publication that was started in 2001. It features stories about music and movies but also covers TV, theater and video games. The website states that it "has become known for its edgy, irreverent, and often funny pop-cultural criticism." *Slant* uses a 5-star system for its video game reviews and allows for half-stars (which essentially makes it a 10-point system).

VICE.com is part of the digital media and broadcasting company VICE Media Group, online since 1999. The site caters to mostly young adults with topics including politics, food and travel. The Games category is one of 16. *VICE.com* does not use a rating system for its video game reviews.

BASIC REVIEW ANALYSIS AND COMPARISON

In general, all reviews chosen here are comprised of one long text each with additional pictures and videos. These visual additions to the reviews are not part of this analysis. All texts are written in a first-person narrative and regularly switch between game descriptions and commentary. None of them try to be objective or try to transparently work from some sort of checklist. The main differences lie within the respective focus, with some reviewers tending to communicate more what the game is about and how it is played, whereas others focus more on the commentary and social or political implications. Reviews written for special interest publications (*Destructoid* and, in parts, *Polygon*) are more likely to thoroughly answer the questions "What do I do in this game?" and "How is this game played?" In contrast, reviews written for general interest publications (*TheGuardian.com*, *Slant Magazine* and *VICE.com*) are more concerned with the question of "What does it mean to play this game?" and are usually more critical towards the object itself. Also, there is a tendency that reviews without a rating system score (*Slant Magazine* and *VICE.com*) are more critical in their analysis and overall verdict.

IN-DEPTH ANALYSIS: *DEATH STRANDING*

Generally, most of the five reviews of *Death Stranding* consider the setting and story of the game very unconventional and therefore tend to be more descriptive than in other reviews. Chris Carter in his *Destructoid* review caters mostly for readers who already have a solid knowledge about the game. Quite early on, he jumps to gameplay details and personal experiences he gained while playing.

"Unless you're a huge Kojima nut you probably came here for an actual gameplay discussion, so let's go to it. No bullshitting around: you run about for most of the game as a postman in a quest to reunite America by reactivating internet terminals. You can scan for packages – that's what the fancy arm-like radar thing does – jump, grab stuff, and occasionally fight."

Similar but less straightforward and more reflective is Dan Dawkins' review for TheGuardian.com. Early on in the text and much like Carter, he refers to basic information about the release of the game which the reader needs in order to fully understand the review. Through comparisons with movies the review becomes embedded into a broader pop cultural context.

"In a recent interview, Mad Max director George Miller suggested Death Stranding was too radical for its time. 'The risk is that people don't accept it', he said."

In a similar fashion to the other two reviewers mentioned above, Russ Frushtick also assumes some basic knowledge of the game and its importance in his Death Stranding review for Polygon. More elaborate in terms of storytelling and often alternating between descriptive elements, gameplay experience and opinion, he delivers a cohesive review in a narrative style.

"The actual walking in *Death Stranding* is incredibly complex: Each small rock or ledge is capable of tripping Sam, sending his packages flying. I find myself constantly scanning the environment, surveying the landscape to find the smoothest possible route through a perilous rocky outcropping."

This type of vivid description that informs and also tells a personal story of the reviewer's experience of events in the game is sustained throughout the entire review. Small puns are incorporated, too. They spice up an already example-laden text that uses figurative language and shows emotional investment.

"I load up Sam's backpack with a ton of materials and hike out with a plan: I'm gonna build a goddamn highway right over these ghosts."

Justin Clark's review of Death Stranding on the other hand is very unconventional in a different way because it is mostly essayistic and analytical in nature. He focuses less on providing a description of the game and turns his attention instead to the political implications that the setting, the characters and the gameplay elements generate for him. When he tells a personal story, which happens only once in the review (at the beginning), he does it in-depth and refers to it again later in the text when the game is interpreted as a metaphor for work, community service and individual effort. According to the reviewer, all of these matters a lot in the greater scheme of things – in the game and also in real life.

"This is a game that values your work. It respects the people that each tiny sparkling dot on that cursed map represents, the need of those people to connect with others to survive, and the fact that that space between matters as well."

Similarly critical, Rob Zacny's review for VICE.com puts the cart before the horse and starts off with a resourceful analysis of the last part of the game. While not written in the most accessible way, the review is elaborate and goes on to detailed descriptions of the game as a whole and also certain events that occur, followed by corresponding critique. There is no clear narrative here, instead the text alternates between covering many aspects of story, setting and gameplay, and what they mean for the player.

"For two-thirds or more of its length, *Death Stranding* is generally that best version of itself. But the last third's focus on grueling boss battles and sudden resource starvation end it on a disproportionately sour note."

IN-DEPTH ANALYSIS: *ANIMAL CROSSING: NEW HORIZONS*

This game was released on March 20, 2020, in the midst of the COVID-19 lockdown, which led to an immense public interest due to the relaxing and welcoming qualities of *Animal Crossing: New Horizons*. Some of the five reviews mention this fact. Another recurring topic, if only touched upon briefly by three reviewers, is the length of time the respective reviewer has played the game. This is noteworthy as this game can't be "beaten" by playing through a predetermined narrative. Rather, it is supposed to be played in brief sessions, day in and day out, over the course of many weeks.

CJ Andriessen delivers a wholly service-related review for *Destructoid*. He is very descriptive, bringing in a lot of comparisons with former *Animal Crossing* games, and also comments on how the game can be played by different types of players. The reviewer also touches on the fact that there are no classic gender identities in this game.

"It's all very positive, and along with the poses your character strikes trying on clothes, easily the queerest the series has ever been."

Keza MacDonald's text about *Animal Crossing: New Horizons* for *TheGuardianan.com* is no review in the classic sense, which is indicated by the fact that it is not accompanied by a rating (ratings appear to be mandatory in the publication's reviews), and the text is comparatively short. The review is mostly personal, referring to the COVID-19 pandemic at the beginning, and overall summing up the basic character of the game and thus catering more to the casual player.

"The absence of noise and urgency on my little island has made it a vital sanctuary, and it looks as if it will be greatly needed in the weeks and months to come."

Also a good read for people who are not that familiar with the game yet is the review from Russ Frushtick for *Polygon*, although his text is more comprehensive. He describes things one can do in the game in some detail through examples, briefly touches on technical aspects when comparing the game to older entries in the *Animal Crossing* series, and also points out an inconsistency in the upbeat and welcoming presentation of the game.

"'Come live here!' he says. The child agrees. It seems nice, after all. But suddenly, the child is saddled with the debt of their first house, and must sell bugs and fish to settle up."

Steven Scaife's review is unconventional in its focus and stands in contrast to the other reviews mentioned above. His text is very political and only provides a broadly outlined description of the game. His quarrel with *Animal Crossing: New Horizons* lies in the game's (virtual) community building which he regards as a step back. He cites older entries in the game series as much more collaborative and also picks up on the fact that you can pillage uninhabited islands for resources. By the way, this review has the lowest score (3,5 stars out of 5; or 70 points) of all 110 professional reviews listed on *Metacritic*.

"The cracks add up, allowing an ugly reality to seep into an otherwise friendly fantasy. The game inadvertently becomes about the cost and upkeep of civilization, about what actions we're willing to turn a blind eye toward just as long as things keep running smoothly."

Gita Jackson's review for *VICE.com* takes the same line as Steven Scaife in terms of the critique of the overall sociopolitical implications.

"You're essentially given a carte blanche to wreck the place."

In addition to that, she goes into more detail when describing her play experience and ends on a personal, conciliatory note about the importance that should be given to community building in the game and in real life.

IN-DEPTH ANALYSIS: *THE LAST OF US PART II*

This game was perceived very positively overall by the press, although it also stirred controversy due to the ambivalence produced by the intense violence depicted throughout the game, and the player's complicity in it. The opinions on what that means for people who play *The Last of Us Part II* differ widely across the five analyzed reviews.

In his review for *Destructoid*, Chris Carter mostly delivers a detailed write-up on what is offered to the player. He describes specific gameplay elements and cites examples, however he refrains from going into narrative details.

Keza MacDonald uses a more narrative approach in her review for *TheGuardian.com*, although she also informs the reader about the gameplay. Her emotional involvement becomes apparent in her take on the grim setting and the corresponding heavy violence, while she manages to avoid any story spoilers.

"No video game has ever gone to these lengths to humanise the enemy, or to interrogate the violence that it asks the player to perform."

The review for *Polygon* by Maddy Myers is very elaborate and reflects thoroughly on the effects that the constant depiction of the intense violence has (on her). Describing many of the game's scenes, she keeps insisting that nothing can be learned through the choices and the tenacity of the game's characters, and that this sets a bad example for our society and humanity in general.

"It's a missed opportunity to explore how the rage of a marginalized character might take on a different form. [...] While the game was made with great skill and craft, we are actually much, much better than [game developer] Naughty Dog thinks we are."

Justin Clark sees more philosophical value in the game's depiction of human madness in his review for *Slant Magazine*.

"At what point do we determine the cost of hate, chaos, death, and vengeance to be more or less than the cost of simply *stopping*?"

This is the only review out of the five selected for *The Last Of Us Part II*, that goes into a remarkable amount of detail when describing the game's story. An editor's note announces these spoilers at the beginning of the text.

In his review for *VICE.com*, Rob Zacny writes about his overall disappointment with the sequel. His write-up makes it clear that he finds the choices and reactions of the main game characters understandable, but the development of the story itself does not surprise him overall. Similarly, he thinks that not much has changed in terms of gameplay compared to the original game from 2013, and thus he ends on a rather sour note.

"It sets out to surpass its predecessor, but the only meaningful contrast between them is in its even more oppressive bleakness and violence."

CONCLUSION

While all the reviews examined here share common traits, such as a first-person narrative and a tendency toward providing a well-readable and engaging text, they differ distinctly in length, style and focus. Whereas some reviewers (and publications) feel obliged to offer first and foremost service-related reviews to mostly keen video game players through elaborate descriptions of contents and gameplay possibilities, other reviewers choose to reflect more on the setting and the most important player choices and ask questions like: What political implications does this game have? What do these gameplay possibilities say about our society? The existence or absence of a rating system also has an effect on the reviewer's verdict, although in the cases at hand, the content of the text always has a bigger impact than its respective rating number.

There is no clear indication that the five publications selected for this analysis use specific review systems that their reviewers must adhere to. Still, the balance between service content and analytical reflection within a text varies between these media outlets. *Destructoid* mostly uses the straightforward (special interest) approach whereas *Slant Magazine*, *VICE.com* and, to some lesser degree, also *TheGuardian.com* and *Polygon*, grant their reviewers more freedom to sometimes also bring their texts up to a meta level that steps away from the question "Is the game fun?" and rather tries to answer the question "What do we learn from the game's setting and its interactive elements?" Reviews from *Polygon*, *VICE.com* and *Slant Magazine* alternate between these two approaches more often and thus create a more sophisticated and varied style of writing.

All of these analyzed reviews only offer the reviewer's perspective on the subject matter – they do not try to compare possible perceptions of different player types. Most reviews require the reader to bring at least some basic information about the respective game with them – this also applies to *VICE.com*, *Slant Magazine* and *TheGuardian.com*, although these publications are general interest and also cater to an audience with less information about video games in general. Overall, the examination and comparison of these 15 reviews show that video game journalism – regardless of where it is published – has become more approachable thanks to its narratively driven writing styles, but still mostly requires an effort, even from a more or less dedicated audience.

REFERENCES

Literature

Glashüttner, Robert (2006): "Das Wesen und die Entwicklung des Computerspiele- und Videospielejournalismus." ("The Character and the Development of Computer and Videogame Journalism."), Vienna: Master Thesis, University of Vienna.

Khaled, A. (2019): "A Much-Needed Crash Course on Video Game Journalism." In: Medium.com, May 9, 2019 (https://medium.com/swlh/video-game-journalism-gamergate-ethics-f88689894b84).

Online Reviews

All online reviews have been accessed on August 20, 2020.
Andriessen, CJ (2020): "Review: Animal Crossing: New Horizons." In: Destructoid.com, March 22, 2020 (https://www.destructoid.com/stories/review-animal-crossing-new-horizons-583381.phtml).

Carter, Chris (2019): "Review: Death Stranding." In: Destructoid.com, November 16, 2019 (https://www.destructoid.com/stories/review-death-stranding-568760.phtml).

Carter, Chris (2020): "Review: The Last of Us Part II." In: Destructoid.com, June 18, 2020 (https://www.destructoid.com/stories/review-the-last-of-us-part-ii-592974.phtml).

Clark, Justin (2019): "Review: Death Stranding Is a Surreal Elegy to the Work that Binds a Broken America." In: SlantMagazine.com, November 18, 2019 (https://www.slantmagazine.com/games/review-death-stranding-is-a-surreal-elegy-to-the-work-that-binds-a-broken-america/).

Clark, Justin (2020): "Review: The Last of Us Part II Is a Gory and Complex Feat of Empathetic Storytelling." In: SlantMagazine.com, June 27, 2020 (https://www.slantmagazine.com/games/review-the-last-of-us-part-ii-is-a-gory-and-complex-feat-of-empathetic-storytelling/).

Dawkins, Dan (2019): "Death Stranding review – Hideo Kojima's radically tough slow-burning epic." In: TheGuardian.com, November 1, 2019 (https://www.theguardian.com/games/2019/nov/01/death-stranding-review-playstation-4-pc-kojima-gameplay).

Frushtick, Russ (2019): "Death Stranding review: Hideo Kojima tries to make fetch happen." In: Polygon.com, November 1, 2019 (https://www.polygon.com/reviews/2019/11/1/20942070/death-stranding-review-hideo-kojima-ps4).

Frushtick, Russ (2020): "Animal Crossing: New Horizons is a much-needed escape from everything." In: Polygon.com, March 16; and March 26 (Update), 2020 (https://www.polygon.com/reviews/2020/3/16/21178911/animal-crossing-new-horizons-review-nintendo-switch).

Jackson, Gita (2020): "Animal Crossing: New Horizons Is a Little Heaven in a World Gone to Hell." In: VICE.com, March 16, 2020 (https://www.vice.com/en_us/article/n7jkd7/animal-crossing-new-horizons-review-building-community-nook-miles-coronavirus).

MacDonald, Keza (2020a): "Animal Crossing: New Horizons is the escape we all need right now." In: TheGuardian.com, March 16, 2020 (https://www.theguardian.com/games/2020/mar/16/animal-crossing-new-horizons-review-nintendo-switch).

MacDonald, Keza (2020b): "The Last of Us Part 2 review – post-apocalyptic game is groundbreaking and powerful." In: TheGuardian.com, June 12, 2020 (https://www.theguardian.com/games/2020/jun/12/the-last-of-us-part-ii-review-zombie-fiction-playstation-4-naughty-dog-sony).

Myers, Maddy (2020): "The Last of Us Part 2 review: We're better than this." In: Polygon.com, June 12, 2020 (https://www.polygon.com/reviews/2020/6/12/ 21288535/the-last-of-us-part-2-review-ps4-naughty-dog-ellie-joel-violence).

Scaife, Steven (2020): "Review: Animal Crossing: New Horizons Makes You the God of the Sandbox." In: SlantMagazine.com, April 12, 2020 (https:// www.slantmagazine.com/games/review-animal-crossing-new-horizons-makes-you-the-god-of-the-sandbox/).

Zacny, Rob (2019): "Death Stranding Shines When You're Delivering Packages in a Haunted World." In: VICE.com, November 1, 2019 (https://www.vice.com/en_us/article/d3ajqv/death-stranding-review).

Zacny, Rob (2020): "The Last of Us Part II Is a Grim and Bloody Spectacle, but a Poor Sequel." In: VICE.com, June 12, 2020 (https://www.vice.com/en_us/article/wxqnxy/last-of-us-part-2-review).

Printed magazines

ACE, Advanced Computer Entertainment, February 1988, Future Publishing, UK.

ACE, Advanced Computer Entertainment, August 1990, Future Publishing, UK.

ASM, Aktueller Software Markt, June and July 1989, Tronic Verlagsgesellschaft, Germany.

Computer & Video Games, May 1984, EMAP National Publications, UK.

CRASH, August 1986, Newsfield Publication, UK.

Games

Animal Crossing: New Horizons, Nintendo EPD, Nintendo, 2020.

Death Stranding, Kojima Productions, Sony Interactive Entertainment, 2019.

The Last of Us Part II, Naughty Dog, Sony Interactive Entertainment, 2020.

Games, Politics and Society

.

"We're not murderers. We just survive."[1]

The Ideological Function of Game Mechanics in Zombie Games

Eugen Pfister

In 2019, Ubisoft lead developer Sébastien Le Prestre said in an interview with *Gamespot*: "We're creating a game here, we're not trying to make political statements in our games. We've rooted ourselves in reality, and you'll get what you get out of your playthrough – everybody will get something different out of their experience. The story might make you see different situations, but we're not trying to guide anybody or to make any sorts of statements." (Webster 2019) Contrary to such claims from the video game industry, digital games cannot be thought of as operating separately from society and its politics. Games emerge out of society and inevitably carry statements of social and political discourses within them: "The stories we tell reflect our understanding of the world and the society in which we live, even if such tales appear firmly rooted in the fantastic." (Barr 2020: 28) Games play with our hopes and fears. They reproduce – consciously and subconsciously – distinct ideas of the world and convey values whenever they construct ideas of good and evil, for example. In games, we encounter brave warriors and corrupt politicians; we fight for freedom and against oppression. In terms of historical discourse analysis, we can therefore speak of dominant ideological statements that are communicated and constructed.

How, then, can we recognize and analyze these dominant statements? Of course, the most obvious way is to spot them in the narrative running through the games: Is there a central conflict? What are the causes of this conflict? Who are the heroes? Who are the enemies? To this end we can take inspiration from media studies, or more generally from the social sciences, where phenomena such

---

1 Quote from the character Ellie in *The Last of Us*.

as political socialization and cultivation in mass media have been studied for quite some time. Studies in these fields have shown us that many narrative traditions in digital games – rhetoric methods, for instance (Schrape 2012: 12-16) – have been heavily inspired by novels, films and television series (Krzywinska 2009: 271; Kirkland 2009: 62-65; Schrape: 60). At the same time we know that a focus on the narrative level alone is not enough to reveal their dominant ideological statements, because digital games are more than just another new narrative medium, they are also an interactive experience, and, at the same time, a computer program (Schrape: 88). Thus, games not only communicate ideas through a series of meaningful events strung together in a story, but potentially allow for the emergence of many – possibly contradictory – ideas within their game rules.

Therefore the question is opportune as to whether we can investigate ideology transfers in games at all. Delimited by the framework of their code, the individual act of playing them not only creates a narrative, but within this framework lies the potential for an infinite number of different narratives. We can play games aggressively or defensively, curiously or carefully. We can try to live up to our morals in the game or, on the contrary, decide to deliberately try the opposite. What does this mean for research? Does the fact that not only is each game potentially different from every other but also every playthrough of the same game, mean that we are no longer dealing with just one narrative, but an infinite number? Does this mean that each game contains not just one set of political ideas but potentially an infinite number of contradictory ones? In the following text I would like to demonstrate, using a sample of games with zombie settings, that this is not the case.

Meaning is not only produced in games via narrative and audiovisual aesthetics, but also by game mechanics. The rules, set by the developers, raise challenges, offer opportunities for actions and evaluate the players. "To evaluate is to reward or punish, to give a positive or negative feedback" (Suter 2018: 22). Game mechanics cannot therefore be free of judgement, because they themselves judge the players. They are interwoven with the narrative and the aesthetic design (Kirkland 2009: 63). Together they form a ludonarrative (Aarseth 2012), with the result that since the vast majority of players have such similar experiences, we can speak of dominant discursive statements. Adam Chapman has used the concept of affordances to tackle a similar phenomenon where certain guidelines as to how the game should be played are embedded in the game mechanics. (Chapman 2016: 173; Schrape 2012: 76) Until now, political content in digital games has been sought – I am also referring to myself here – primarily in the story and the characters. This is due to reliance on other forms of media studies, which have, as their research topics, more traditional forms of media. The peculiarity of digital games, I would argue, requires an additional research focus on the gameplay elements, i.e. the rules and mechanics of the game. For it is also through these that ideological statements are transported in games. Therefore we can assume that all players, adhering to the game rules, encounter the same ideas. Of course, there will always be some exceptions, for example, when players deliberately play against expectation, such as in pacifist runs. But for the vast majority of players from the same cultural background, the gaming experience will be so similar that it is possible to form general assertions concerning political statements. In the following I would therefore like to show that the rules of the game (in the sense of a language) also obey discursive rules. To this end, I will examine dominant statements on the one hand, but will also search specifically for counterstatements. The latter show particularly impressively that certain elements of the game perceived as "natural" are in reality only due to discursive traditions. To demonstrate this, I will focus on some specific gameplay elements from zombie games, since these games lend themselves particularly well to such an analysis: despite their ubiquity, they all share a similar design (and narrative) and interact strongly with current political debates. (Pfister 2020b)

It is important to keep in mind that digital games – like popular culture in general – are not just an image or mirror that can be held up to society. From the understanding of historical discourse analysis, they actively construct our social reality too. (Landwehr 2009: 17; Sarasin 2003: 12) In other words: we also learn about the world we live in by playing digital games, and to an extent we are also socialized by them. (Klimmt 2009: 68) The values communicated in digital games are thus not only a product of the society that creates them, but they also actively shape that society. In our increasingly hypercomplex society, popular culture functions as a communicative space for binding common values and world views. Examples of this include public opinion on military operations abroad or questions surrounding the legitimacy of torture. If political power increases in relation to it not being questioned, then the importance of a negotiation of values through popular culture becomes apparent. The more often something (a political problem or constellation) is confirmed for us in the media, the less inclined we are to question it. Thus it seems plausible ex negativo that, for example, an increasing fear of democratic failure or the loss of trust in political figures and institutions in popular culture is not only a mirror of a "real" political development, but also contributes to it. This way of thinking becomes "naturalized". In other words: the more often we encounter incapable/corrupt/amoral politicians in film and television, the more we are inclined to also attribute this image to "real" politicians. Conversely, this would mean that a regular repetition of the "strong man" politician can also lead to a normalization of this topos (Pfister 2020a).

POLITICS IN HORROR GAMES

For my ongoing research project, I have therefore been studying the construction and communication of political ideas in popular culture, concentrating mainly on horror games. The horror genre in movies and novels traditionally helps reaffirm the outer borders of our collective identities by focusing on taboos and the abject (Santilli 2007), both aspects of which are central to the figure of the zombie. So the question to ask is whether this is also transferable to games, and if so, what role do game mechanics play? By analyzing zombie games as an additional source for a contemporary history of political ideas, we can better understand contemporary discourses on democracy, society and ethics. According to John S. Nelson, horror functions as a primer for political action: "Awaken to evils in our midst. Turn to face those shadows, revealing awful forms more human than we had imagined. Unite to track down those troubles, confronting them at home" (Nelson 2005: 382). In Nelson's logic, this call to action happens via subtext: "(S)ymbolism that creeps beneath surface meanings to assault and awaken our minds" (ibid: 382). According to Lauro (2011: 128) the figure of the zombie first and foremost serves as a narrative of crisis and threat. While this is also true for the zombie figure in games, it does not mean that all zombie games transport the same statements. In another essay I showed that in terms of their function, zombie stories can be understood in a certain way like a language. They provide a syntax and grammar, but do not fully determine the message. In the past, zombie films, novels and games therefore treated critical topics as diverse as racism, consumerism and libertarianism (Rath 2014).

We may assume that the ideological statements inherent in the figure of the zombie are also known to most game developers. In an essay about zombies and game mechanics, game designer Christopher Totten discusses the allegorical implications of the zombie figure in an entire paragraph, describing zombies as embodiment of our societal fears (Totten 2012). In his interviews held with game developers of zombie games, Matthew Barr discovered that they were well aware that their games "tap into contemporary fears" (Barr 2020: 28). This does not mean, however, that all ideological statements in games are deliberate. It lies in the nature of the discourse as a disembodied system of dominant ideas and rules of what we can say and what we can think, that the system reproduces itself in our culture, even if we are unaware of the fact (Pfister 2018). In concrete terms, this means that, in most cases, narratives and game mechanics have simply been unconsciously adopted by the developers. Even those game developers that choose zombies as a 'narrative convenience', or to disguise the poor artificial intelligence of non-player characters (Perron 2020: 198), are reproducing dominant discursive statements via the narrative, aesthetics and game mechanics.

In general, it is impossible to make a distinction between narrative, aesthetics and game mechanics in digital games, as the boundaries are fluid. The (ostensible) methodological dispute between ludologists and narratologists in the early 2000s had as its only conceivable outcome a synthesis of the two methodological approaches: "What has so far been lacking is a detailed, robust understanding of the various ways computer software have been used to combine elements from narratives and games into a number of quite different ludo-narratological constructs" (Aarseth 2012). Just as the story determines the rules of the game (War, Survival, etc.), the graphic design is an intrinsic part of the created game world just as much as the game mechanics (First-Person Shooter, Horror-Survival, etc.) determine the story. Henry Jenkins, for example, speaks of an "embedded narrative" (Kirkland 2009: 70) and thus concentrates on the level design and aesthetics of games. Ian Bogost in turn created the term "procedural rhetoric" to describe the rhetoric of games, where arguments are made "through the authorship of rules of behaviour, the construction of dynamic models." (cited in Weise 2015: 239) Since, in the past, political content in games has often been examined based on the story, I would like to concentrate here on the rules and gameplay of the game, despite the impossibility of making a clear-cut distinction, for the sole purpose of demonstrating its importance. Since it is not possible for me to list here all the game mechanical aspects of all zombie games, I will concentrate on those that I have noticed as dominant moments in my research so far.

THE CONFLICT PARADIGM

First of all, there is the paradigm of constant conflict embedded in the program. Of course, this is also connected with the fact that at the moment at least, the vast majority of all digital games are still based on conflict or competition mechanisms. No matter whether we are playing within a small team to deal with overwhelming hordes such as in *Left4Dead*, or on our own sneaking past the 'infected' in *the Last of Us*. Whether we are engaged in a First- or Third-Person Shooter, whether playing a twin-stick shooter or strategy game, as players we commonly have only one choice: kill the zombies or be killed by them (Jorgensen 2020: 133; Perron 2020: 197). At first glance, this seems to be self-evident:

236 | Eugen Pfister

If we are attacked in a zombie setting, we have to defend ourselves. Yet a brief look at other media shows that this approach is by no means self-evident. Films such as *Shaun of the Dead*, *Warm Bodies* and *The Girl with all the Gifts* and series like *iZombie* have shown that zombie films do not necessarily have to focus on combat alone. But counterexamples can also be seen in digital games. The very successful *The Walking Dead* games by Telltale are not entirely without fighting scenes. They do, however, focus much more on interpersonal relationships, which is a core element of the zombie narrative in other media. These examples show us that combat is not a natural prerequisite for all zombie settings in digital games.

On the contrary, a focus on fighting can even lead to moments of ludonarrative dissonance, which we can see in the extremely successful *The Last of Us* games. Both games rely very heavily on a well-written story and strong characters but suffer from an inherent contradiction between story and game mechanics. In the second part in particular, the extremely explicit depictions of violence between human survivors is intended to make the players think about the actions of the protagonist. But this introspection is never granted to all the NPCs killed during normal gameplay. This contradiction is a particularly challenging moment for academic research. On the one hand, we read in interviews that the game was meant as a critique of violence. At the same time, the game mechanics between the narrative cutscenes force us to repeat violent actions and – what is more important – without question. Since the routine killing of NPC goes unquestioned, but at the same time we are not usually offered alternative solutions, it is justified in the game by the rules.

This question is not trivial, quite the opposite. Interviews show that in many cases zombies were explicitly chosen as opponents for the reason of avoiding possible ethical questions. (Barr 2020: 19) At the same time, unlike aliens, demons and robots, zombies are especially frightening exactly because they are so human. So in a way, these games teach us to put aside the ethical concerns that we develop, for example, in the context of cutscenes, during gameplay. The focus on armed conflict may thus initially have been due to the limitations of the medium (Taylor 2009: 51), but is, above all, a culturally established tradition that severely restricts the ideological statements of the games in the sense of an assumed natural state of infinite conflict. (Pfister 2020b)

HUMAN NPCS

Every zombie was once human. But while other media use precisely this aspect as a narrative moment, the transformation from human to undead in games usually happens immediately and unobserved – with the exception of Telltale's *The Walking Dead*. Zombies may have been human, but now they are the others, the threat – a textbook example of "othering": "Unfortunately, video games have few instances of terror-inducing explanations for their zombies. There is rarely time to explore how someone was zombified; the outbreak has already filled the screen with zombies. Often, these monsters are either character models with no memorable features or are twisted mutations no longer resembling humans." (Totten 2012) In the games we do not even have time to ask ourselves what kind of people they might have been, be they waitresses or lawyers, grandfathers or criminals. We usually only have three forms of interaction at our disposal: fight, hide-and-seek, or flee. One could argue here that this is due to technical restrictions. Fights are easier to program than open-ended interpersonal relationships. In view of complex game worlds in series such as *Mass Effect*, *Pillars of Eternity* and *The Witcher 3*, however, this argument is increasingly losing its persuasive power. This would mean that the mechanics of the game here primarily follow discursive rules of the sayable and showable. This also raises the question of why, for example, the search for a cure almost never becomes a game objective. Even more serious than the unquestioned conflict paradigm itself is the fact that, following genre conventions, in many games it is not the zombies that are the real antagonists but people.

Particularly interesting for us are therefore those games that show that other paths can be taken in terms of game mechanics. A case in point is the *Dead Rising* game series, which is based on a constant fight against zombies, but extends it, for example, with rescue missions in which other survivors have to be protected from zombies. In *State of Decay 2*, players have the opportunity to expand their own base. In addition, they can administer remedies to victims of the so-called "Blood Plague" in their infirmary. These last two examples – as well as the two smaller game projects *Atom Zombie Smasher* and *They Are Billions* – in particular show that zombie narratives in themselves can offer more scope for diversified game mechanics than most previous zombie games would have us believe. This was demonstrated not least by Telltale's very linear narrative-heavy adaptation of *The Walking Dead*, which enjoyed more success in comparison to Overkill's classic FPS adaptations of *The Walking Dead*. The lack of possible meaningful interactions with human NPCs in most games may originally have been due to technical restrictions, but it is still not free of ideology. This is because there is a strong resonance between the narrative and audiovisual aesthetics of games, both of which also emphasize the isolation of the individual.

SINGLE-PLAYER VS. MULTIPLAYER

An examination of the differences between single- and multiplayer games is also enlightening, as interpersonal dynamics potentially cancel out the statements of narrative settings. Narrative games like *The Last of Us*, but also *Days Gone* and *Dying Light* paint a particularly gloomy picture of human nature post-zombie apocalypse. Not only have our democratic structures and social order collapsed locally or globally in the blink of an eye, there appears to be something even worse than the zombies: a battle of everyone against everyone else. (Pfister 2020b) People have been thrown back to an apparent primordial state of perpetual war for survival where, much more than the zombies, the other survivors are the enemy. The fascist military regime and its goons in *The Last of Us*, murdering psychopaths in *Dead Rising* and a gang of cultists in *Days Gone*, to name a few examples. In classic single-player campaigns, this means that the players are on their own and can only rely on their own abilities and moral decisions. The ethical choices of characters inevitably become our own. In exceptional cases they even are embedded game mechanics, as shown by the moral choices in Telltale's *The Walking Dead* (Barr 2020: 17) or *The Organ Trail*. This does not mean that we unquestionably adopt the political convictions presented here, but for the time of the play we have to identify with the character without being able to exert real influence most of the time, just as in a film. That means we have to accept the rules of the game world to find our way through it: "The most productive gameplay strategy involves correctly reading these grammatical and visual cues, completing the actions being foreshadowed [...]" (Kirkland 2009: 69). We learn from the beginning to mistrust human NPCs we meet in the game world, and we do not expect help from other survivors. Thus many zombie games communicate a worldview of a (neo-)liberal individualism: What emerges is the myth of the lone hero as the epitome of the individual, who alone is capable of making ethical decisions. This should be of no surprise to us as it simply corresponds with the current dominant political climate in line with the neoliberal paradigm, confirming my earlier statement that myths are always a contemporary phenomenon. As Zygmunt Bauman shows in his book *Liquid Modernity*, individualization is fate and not choice in the neoliberal state (Baumann 2001: 69). According to Bruno Amable, neoliberals have realized that in order for their ideology to be successful, a state's populace must internalize the belief that individuals are only to be rewarded based on their personal effort. (Amable 2011: 5)

But while single-player campaigns, both in narrative and in game mechanics, elevate the individual to the last moral authority, the opposite happens in multiplayer campaigns, not least through the cooperation of several human players. My personal first multiplayer experience in a zombie game was the Couch Co-Op mode of *Left4Dead*. Here, the personal bond with the other player(s) makes cooperation the dominant game principle. So in this instance – due to the different game situations – there are contrary ideological statements. The survivors are dependent on each other. This is true for most co-op games and naturally increases when the players know each other. However, the degree of cooperation is mainly based on existing social interactions. One feels closer to a friend or family member at home and therefore more committed than to anonymous players on the net. In multiplayer arenas like *DayZ* there are again other forms of social interaction. In these arenas, beginners – "noobs" have to beware of "trolls" and "griefers" – in a similar way to many other multiplayer arenas. At the same time, spontaneous social groups – especially clans based on close cooperation – are emerging.

A GAME OF SCARCITY

Another aspect many zombie games have in common is that they depict a world of scarcity: a lack of weapons, ammunition, and a general lack of resources (Therrien 2009: 37; Fawcett & McGreevy 2020: 86). Especially in a world of abundance this is a potent symbol. One reason for this theme is, of course, the attempt to maintain the game's balance and keep it exciting. This shortage makes the management of resources a game-determining moment. Players have to weigh up exactly when to use which weapon. In some games such as *Dead Island* and *State of Decay*, not only is the ammunition sparse, but the melee weapons themselves are exhausted over time. This mechanism teaches players to use resources sparingly, sometimes almost over-cautiously, for fear of finding themselves defenseless in major confrontations. Here, too, zombie games use the myths of nature as challenging, as well as depicting it as a simpler state of being, in the tradition of Robinson Crusoe. The focus on inventory management was introduced with *Alone of the Dark* (Barton 2020). However, it also resonates well with horror in other media in that the protagonist is introduced as a vulnerable subject. The absence of cultural resources gives the impression of a natural state of scarcity. Against the background of the "prepper" phenomenon, which is currently spreading in society, there is also a strong ideological resonance. This game mechanism also works so effectively because it serves an increasingly widespread fear of the collapse of our commodity chains.

ACHIEVEMENT HUNT

Achievements and trophies in digital games, i.e. rewards given by the program, is a topic still somewhat neglected by game studies. Basically, three different forms of rewards can be identified:

1. rewards for normal progress in the game,
2. rewards for particularly intensive and complete exploration of the game, and
3. rewards for extravagant or counterintuitive actions in the game.

These achievements and trophies "nudge" the players – which is especially true for so-called completionists, i.e. a player who feels the need to complete 100 per cent of the gameplay. In *Dead Rising*, a player receives one achievement for killing 1000, 10.000 and 53.594 zombies, called "Zombie Hunter", "Zombie Killer" and "Zombie Genocider" respectively. Incidentally, *Left4Dead* also had a "Zombie Genocider" achievement for killing 53.595 zombies in the game, in direct reference to *Dead Rising*. In *Dead Island*, 18 out of 54 achievements are centered on killing zombies or humans. "Kill 50 zombies using a vehicle" is the instruction for the achievement "Karma-Geddon". In addition to the number of enemies killed, some games also reward concrete scenarios. In *Dying Light*, for example, the achievement "BBQ" can be found. Here you have to stake a lighted zombie on a skewer.

At the same time, an increasingly visible effort is being made on the part of the developers to not only reward the killing of zombies, but also other behavior. The trophy "I want to talk about it" rewards players for engaging in all optional conversations in the game *The Last of Us*. *Days Gone* awards trophies for rescuing NPCs and gaining the trust of NPC encampments. *Left4Dead* rewards players for rescuing their co-op partners. These rewards are of special interest to us because they reveal the developers' intentions: What behavior do they want to reward players for?

POLITICAL TRANSFERS IN ZOMBIE GAMES

It was not possible for me within the scope of this article to reflect in detail on all game mechanical aspects at work in zombie games, and their ideological implications. For example, an analysis of the horde-mechanic would also have been interesting: What most zombie games have in common is that individual zombies are harmless and they build up their threat mainly through their sheer mass and by advancing in unmanageable waves. Possible ideological transfers here are apparent (Barr 2020: 19). It was not my intention to produce an exhaustive overview of all possible transfers of ideology via game mechanics, but to throw a first spotlight onto this phenomenon through some specific examples. Thus I was hopefully able to show that the majority of zombie games use game rules that convey a world of constant conflict, of scarcity, in which we can only rely on ourselves. In order to master these games we internalize these experiences and act accordingly in the game (Pinchbeck 2009: 82). However, if we want to understand the ideological statements in games in their entirety, such an analysis can only be done in conjunction with an equally intensive analysis of the narrative and audiovisual aesthetics, as I mentioned before. I am convinced that meaningful political statements – and potential ideological transfers – only emerge when these three levels interact. In that case, we combine the learned behavior in the game – i.e., for example, our reaction to a threat – with meaning, which we derive from the narrative. When we walk through the ruins of cities and government districts in games, when we learn in the story that we can no longer rely on the military, and when we are left on our own in a gameplay of constant threat and combat we learn from constant repetition in different games, but also in other media, to increasingly accept the plausibility of an overwhelmed democratic system no longer capable of guaranteeing our safety (Pfister 2020b).

The same can be said for the "othering" of groups of people who are perceived as a threat to us. In games, the others – i.e. the zombies – are dehumanized aesthetically in order to be acceptable as enemies. In a previous essay, I showed how mutual influences can be seen in a comparison of zombie games and the coverage of the so-called 'refugee crisis' in the yellow press. I do not want to insinuate that there was a direct influence of zombie narratives on the media coverage; there are, however, very strong similarities in the narration and argumentation but also in the audiovisual staging, which speaks for unconscious transfer processes. Dominant discursive statements – beware of the horde of "others", overburdened democratic systems, etc. – were used, that were already widespread. These are not only applied in a fictional framework but also in our everyday world. (Pfister 2020a)

Above all, my central concern was to show that game mechanics themselves cannot be value-free. "Computer programs, like all texts, will always be ideological constructions." (Friedman 1995). Zombie games are not only harmless fun, they are artifacts of our culture. And as such they obey the rules of discourse. When they tell us to rely only on our own judgement, this is of course due to a perceived need to strengthen the perceived agency of the players. But counterexamples of cooperative play and new narratives of cooperation show that this game mechanic is in no way a "natural" prerequisite of video games.

All of this should not lead us to a culturally pessimistic rejection of games, because games also grow and change with our society. Therefore it was important for me to present counterexamples for all dominant statements. Games that reward cooperation between players are evidence of this. Finally, the relevant question from both a historical and a day-to-day political point of view is therefore whether new dominant discursive statements will be formed from these game mechanical building blocks in the future.

REFERENCES

Literature

Aarseth, Espen (2012): "A Narrative Theory of Games." In: Foundations of Digital Games Conference Proceedings, pp. 129-133.

Amable, Bruno (2011): „Morals and politics in the ideology of neo-liberalism." In: Socio-Economic Review 9, pp. 3-30.

Barr, Matthew (2020): "Zombies Again? A Qualitative Analysis of the Zombie Antagonist's Appeal in Game Design". In: Stephen Webley/Peter Zackariasson (eds.), The Playful Undead and Video Games Critical Analyses of Zombies and Gameplay, London: Routledge, pp. 15-29.

Barton, Matthew (2020): "Resurrecting 'Obsolete' Video Game Techniques from Alone in the Dark." In: Stephen Webley/Peter Zackariasson (eds.), The Playful Undead and Video Games Critical Analyses of Zombies and Gameplay, London: Routledge, pp. 30-43.

Bauman, Zygmunt (2001): Liquid Modernity, Cambridge: Polity Press.

Chapman, Adam (2016): Digital Games as History: How Videogames Represent the Past and Offer Access to Historical Practice, London: Routledge.

Fawcett, Christina/McGreevy, Alan (2020): "Resident Evil and Infectious Fear." In: Stephen Webley/Peter Zackariasson (eds.), The Playful Undead and Video Games Critical Analyses of Zombies and Gameplay, London: Routledge, pp. 85-98.

Friedman, Ted (1995): "Making Sense of Software: Computer Games and Interactive Textuality." In: Steve Jones (ed.), Community in Cyberspace, Thousand Oaks: Sage.

Jorgensen, Kristine (2020): "Dead Rising and the Gameworld Zombie". In: Stephen Webley/Peter Zackariasson (eds.), The Playful Undead and Video Games Critical Analyses of Zombies and Gameplay, London: Routledge, pp. 126-137.

Kirkland, Ewan (2009): "Storytelling in Horror Video Games." In: Bernard Perron (ed.), Horror Video Game, Jefferson: McFarland. pp. 62-78.

Klimmt, Christoph (2009): "Empirische Medienforschung: Kommunikationswissenschaftliche Perspektiven auf Computerspiele." In: Tobias Bevc/Holger Zapf (eds.), Wie wir spielen was wir werden. Computerspiele in unserer Gesellschaft. Konstanz: UVK, pp. 65-74.

Krzywinska, Tanya (2009): "Reanimating H.P. Lovecraft: The Ludic Paradox of Cthulhu: Dark Corners of the Earth." In: Bernard Perron (ed.), Horror Video Game, Jefferson: McFarland. pp. 267-288.

Landwehr, Achim (2009): Historische Diskursanalyse, Frankfurt am Main.

Lauro, S. J. (2011): The Modern Zombie: Living Death in the Technological Age, Ph.D. Thesis, University of California.

Nelson, John S. (2005): "Horror Films Face Political Evils in Everyday Life." In: Political Communication 22/3, pp. 381-386.

Perron, Bernard (2020): "The Pace and Reach of Video Game Zombies." In: Stephen Webley/Peter Zackariasson (eds.), The Playful Undead and Video Games Critical Analyses of Zombies and Gameplay, London: Routledge, pp. 197-215.

Pfister, Eugen (2020a): „Political Communication in Digital Horror Games." In: Horror-Game-Politics (http://hgp.hypotheses.org/1062).

Pfister, Eugen (2020b): „Zombies Ate Democracy: The myth of a systemic political failure in video games." In: Stephen Webley/Peter Zackariasson (eds.), The Playful Undead and Video Games Critical Analyses of Zombies and Gameplay, London: Routledge, pp. 216-231.

Pfister, Eugen (2018): „Der Politische Mythos als diskursive Aussage im digitalen Spiel. Ein Beitrag aus der Perspektive der Politikgeschichte." In: Thorsten Junge/Claudia Schumacher (eds.), Digitale Spiele im Diskurs, Hagen: Fernuni Hagen (http://www.medien-im-diskurs.de).

Pinchbeck, Dan (2009): "Shock, Horror: First-Person Gaming, Horror and the Art of Ludic Manipulation." In: Bernard Perron (ed.), Horror Video Game, Jefferson: McFarland, pp. 79-94.

Rath, Gudrun (2014): „Zombi/e/s. Zur Einleitung." In: Gudrun Rath (ed.), Zombies, Bielefeld: Transcript, pp. 11-20.

Santilli, Paul (2007): "Culture, Evil and Horror." In: American Journal of Economics and Sociology 66/1, pp. 173-194.

Taylor, Laurie (2009): "Gothic Bloodlines in Survival Horror Gaming." In: Bernard Perron (ed.), Horror Video Game, Jefferson: McFarland, pp. 46-61.

Totten, Christopher (2012): "Building a Better Zombie." In: Gamasutra (https://www.gamasutra.com/view/feature/173144/building_a_better_zombie.php).

Sarasin, Philipp (2003): Geschichtswissenschaft und Diskursanalyse, Frankfurt am Main: Suhrkamp.

Schrape, Niklas (2012): Die Rhetorik von Computerspielen. Wie politische Spiele überzeugen, Frankfurt am Main: Campus.

Suter, Beat (2018): "Rules of Play as a Framework for the 'Magic Circle'." In: Beat Suter/Mela Kocher/René Bauer (eds.), Games and Rules. Game Mechanics for the Magic Circle, Bielefeld: Transcript, pp. 19-34.

Therrien, Carl (2009): "Games of Fear: A Multi-Faceted Historical Account of the Horror Genre in Video Games." In: Bernard Perron (ed.), Horror Video Game, Jefferson: McFarland, pp. 26-45.

Webster, Andrew (2019): "Ubisoft keeps pretending its political games don't have politics in them." In: The Verge (https://www.theverge.com/2019/5/9/18563382/ubisoft-ghost-recon-breakpoint-politics).

Games

Alone in the Dark, Infogrames, Infogrames, 1992.

Atom Zombie Smasher, Blendo Games 2011.

Days Gone, SIE Bend Studio, Sony, 2019.

DayZ, Bohemia Interactive, Bohemia Interactive, 2018.

Dead Island, Techland, Deep Silver, 2011.

Dead Rising, Capcom, Capcom, 2006.

Dying Light, Techland, Warner Bros, 2015.

Left4Dead, Valve South, Valve, 2008.

Mass Effect, BioWare, Microsoft 2007.

Overkill's The Walking Dead, Overkill Software, Starbreeze Publishing, 2018.

Pillars of Eternity, Obsidian Entertainment, Paradox Interactive, 2015.

State of Decay, Undead Labs, Microsoft Studios, 2013.

State of Decay 2, Undead Labs, Microsoft Studios, 2018.

The Last of Us, Naughty Dog, Sony, 2013.

The Last of Us: Part II, Naughty Dog, Sony, 2020.

The Organ Trail, The Men Who Wear Many Hats, The Men Who Wear Many Hats, 2015.

The Walking Dead, Telltale Games, Telltale Games, 2012-2019.

The Witcher 3: Wild Hunt, CD project Red, Bandai Namco Games, 2015.

They Are Billions, Numantian Games, Numantian Games, 2019.

QUIZ

Games for a Situationist Society

Günter Hack

SIT-REP

Science fiction, like any theory, is based on the question "what if"? This is a text about game mechanics in a science fiction novel, so let's pretend for a few minutes that Google ushered in a silent relational turn in popular epistemology. Google's early version of page rank, where the statistical weight of links determines the relevance of their unseen target, is the material realization of concepts like Jacques Derrida's *différance* and all that wonderful semantic stuff about signifiers harking back to the times of Ferdinand de Saussure. In any information theory, the time component springs from measurable differences, so if there is anything like a story, it stumbles forward along uneven cobbles like a drunkard in the streets of a medieval town.

At least since the advent of social media many users know what it means to create a link to somebody or something. A link on Facebook is a tiny fossil of human attention. Since converting attention to money via advertising still is a popular way to create wealth on the Web, semantics have now materialized as a money-making engine. If there is money to be made with links, popular understanding of relational thinking goes beyond academic circles, down to the gritty basements of search engine optimizers and Chinese click farms. The structure of the network determines the nature of its nodes.

If links are the basic elements of stories, Google and Facebook can be viewed as revenue-generating games making up their own mechanics and optimizing them to their own advantage as they go along. With reference to the Situationists, one of the most influential artist groups of the 1950s and 1960s, one could say that Google and Facebook are on their own permanent auto-*dérives*, wanderings through self-generated networks. Wherever they turn, there is ever more money to be found. The bank always wins.

After World War II, many intellectuals followed the example of the flaneur as described in Walter Benjamin's *Arcades Project* and delved into the dense fabric of everyday urban life, for example Henri Lefebvre with his *Critique de la vie quotidienne* (1947), Guy Debord (*The Naked City* 1957) or Michel de Certeau with his *L'invention du quotidien* (1980). Those thinkers came from radically different backgrounds, Lefebvre and Debord starting out as Marxists, and de Certeau being a member of the Societas Jesu, but they shared the intention to make their readers more sensitive to their everyday life and its environment, to elevate it from the depths of semi-consciousness.

Debord and de Certeau were both concerned about the relentless expansion of capitalist strategies into every nook and cranny of human existence. In his famous *Society of the Spectacle* (1967), Debord shows reification as an irresistible force subverting all human relations, turning them into services to be bought and dealt with. In the end, the "integrated spectacle" of politics and industry (commentary to *Society of the Spectacle*, 1988) will establish its total hegemony over all capitalist societies. The Society of the Spectacle represents the next generation of totalitarianism after fascism's defeat in World War II: fast, hard, clandestine, subversive, ubiquitous. The language used by Debord is echoed today in popular contemporary critiques of Internet corporations such as in Shoshana Zuboff's *The Age of Surveillance Capitalism* or Evgeny Morozov's *The Net Delusion*.

It is quite ironic that those narratives of the ever-expanding and unstoppable capitalist machinery evoke some of the aspects of "ur-fascism" as identified by Umberto Eco (Eco 1995), putting the individual in the situation of a permanent stage of siege by an overwhelmingly strong and devious enemy, to foment anger and cause some sort of revolutionary action. But those distinctly 20th-century strategies must fail, because the supposed enemies are inscrutable and deliver services most people want and need – at very low prices, if you ignore the opportunity costs. De Certeau made a famous distinction between strategy and tactics, wherein an expansive strategy is the domain of the state, the big organizations and the ruling class. In contrast, tactics are short-term lateral movements as employed by the rebels, the have-nots.

According to de Certeau, strategies can only be deployed successfully, if the driving organization owns the resources and the logistical support to do so. No wonder that contemporary super-corporations like Amazon, Google or Facebook are called "platforms". Platforms aim for total horizontal and vertical integration and are large enough to provide their own environment. They aim to rely on themselves in such a way that they don't even need the Internet communications protocol stack to run on. Google, for instance, could easily write and implement its own digital communications protocol if it should want to sideline other oligopolies. Apart from the technical aspects, Google and Facebook as corporations also modify society in order to accommodate themselves. Powerful narratives have the tendency to submit everything to their own dominant logic. At some point, they become indistinguishable from totalitarian ideologies which are game mechanics in their own right. The gamified environment provides security by a certain degree of predictability, but it also replaces life itself by channeling future options for development.

Let's pretend that Google has learned something from the Situationists. Guy Debord and his pranksters championed the *dérive*, walks around the city in order to become aware of its more or less hidden structures and power flows, in order to liberate people from the Spectacle. In 2012, the Spectacle in turn performed a *détournement* – yet another Situationist technique, the modification of popular cultural artifacts to suit one's own ends – by capturing and monetizing the *dérive*: Niantic, then a start-up within Google, launched its first version of Ingress, the first successful situation-based game for smartphones. In 2016, Niantic would launch *Pokémon Go*, which would register 800 million downloads two years later, according to the corporate website. Niantic's core system is called Real World Platform, mixing Augmented Reality with location-based services and marketing.

Debord would have to admit that the Spectacle has now used all available Situationist strategies to further consolidate its power. Corporations keep creeping into the smallest crevices of life in order to monetize the smallest movement of their subjects. It seems as if they have used an avant-garde leftist analysis like Debord's as some sort of dystopian playbook. Mobile networked computing environments have added ever more layers of reification to the physical environment. Its users can access new services, communicate with their friends and escape a cityscape becoming ever more boring with shops closing down due to overwhelming competition from Internet platforms.

The Situationists created the slogan "Ne travaillez jamais!" (Never work!) Today, work itself has become a *dérive*. Uber, the flagship of the so-called Gig Economy, sends self-employed workers with their own cars on their way through the city. The Uber app adds a software service layer to the city, a work version of platforms like Niantic's, accelerating a trend towards atypical work even in the richest countries. Even in Germany, with its still strong industrial base, the share of "atypical work" like temp work and the so-called "minijobs" in overall dependent work grew from 30,1% in 2003 to 39,6% in 2016 (Hans-Böckler-Stiftung 2019).

The more intelligent and ruthless actors of Internet capitalism have taken the best communications tools and tactics from the avant-garde of 1968 Paris and turned them against their subjects. Situationist corporations have outflanked and outperformed their more conservative counterparts. Facebook and Google sliced and diced traditional mass media business models. Like the famous butcher right out of the *Zhuangzi*, the compilation of Daoist anecdotes, they cut the most juicy – read: profitable – parts out of the slain dinosaurs with an effortlessness even the Emperor himself can only admire. In a democratic society, the Emperor is us, of course.

This, in turn, means that the shrinking traditional corporations keep losing their ground. De Certeau would state that they lose their ability to deploy strategies. Legacy media corporations, for example, are reduced to fiddling with short-term tactics. They can convince old political allies to set up improvised road blocks, around which the new-style Situationist platforms will re-route quickly and even integrate into their business strategies. For instance, German publishers can try to implement their version of an ancillary copyright at EU level via their allies in Germany's CDU-led government, but Google cannot be forced to include their articles in their indices and search results. Any new European search engine would in turn have to negotiate with the publishers and with a high degree of probability be met with demands which would be impossible to accept. Another example would be the European data protection directive GDPR. It creates a very high bureaucratic threshold for newcomers to the market for communications platforms thus protecting the existing oligopoly.

FAIL AND LET FAIL

There are many statistical parameters backing up the narrative of hyper-concentration, oligopoly-building and expansive capitalism. In 2018, for instance, the highest-earning 20% of US households brought in 52% of the country's total income (Schaeffer 2020). The Gini Index measuring income distribution, in other words, economic inequality, rose from 34.6 in 1979 to 41.5 in 2016. In Germany, the Gini Index went up from 29.2 in 1992 to 31.7 in 2015 (World Bank 2020). The share of dependent workers performing "atypical work" like temp work and so-called "minijobs" in Germany augmented from 30.1% in 2003 to 39.6% in 2016. Work has become more fragmented and is embedded in some cases into a sort of network-driven "platform economy", for example in the shape of mobility services (Uber, Lyft). In certain areas the highly concentrated Western capitalist economy begins to look like communist-era COMECON, where certain production systems are assigned more or less exclusively to select countries. Software is predominately written in Silicon Valley, cars are produced in Germany and Japan, luxury goods in France, everything else in Mainland China.

Sometimes the hegemonial structure is shaken up a bit, whether by protectionist governments throwing a fit or by natural catastrophes breaking just-in-time supply chains. Or, maybe, one of the big players misses a step like Microsoft losing out to Apple and Google in the market for mobile platforms back in the second half of the 2000s. Swiss economist Patrick Stähler already noted in the early 2000s that the Internet era would be marked by temporary oligopolies (Stähler 2002). Platform capitalism reigns supreme, but its all too human agents tend to fail at some point. It is possible to read Schumpeterian disruption stories as a series of failures. The corporations themselves permanently create the huge inconsistencies, inequalities and other differences which cause them to fall and stumble along. Ruthless dynamic progress might simply be an instance of disparate bricolage. Security and stability are always cited as paramount policy goals but looking at phenomena such as Donald Trump or Brexit, it seems that a certain breed of right-wing politician and their backers have understood that you can't make quick profits in a stable situation. Therefore every aspect of life is now to be held in permanent suspension and every aspect of society turned around quickly in a dizzying movement of spin. German sociologist Ulrich Beck captured this notion early on in the introduction to his book *Risk Society* (1986) in which he compares the state of modern society to an all-crushing juggernaut chariot. As the Coronavirus outbreak in 2019 showed, not even China's highly advanced totalitarian control systems can mitigate the kind of risk which springs from complex networked situations. On the contrary: the more control you apply the higher the impact of the fallout from a "black swan" event.

Accordingly, contemporary working and living feels like a game where the rules are constantly rewritten – mostly to the disadvantage of the weaker members of world society. Maybe sometimes one of the less adroit political or economic players stumbles and falls, but the schadenfreude never lasts too long, because there is no shortage of inept would-be leaders.

THE NORDBERG SCENARIO

So the overall modus operandi of our era is neither the modernist illusion of to-talitarian strategy nor the post-modern bricolage but rather a series of accidents. Imagine OJ Simpson in his role as Officer Nordberg in the famous slapstick sce-ne in *The Naked Gun*, where he keeps bumping into things, getting shot, touch-ing the hot oven plate ... only to continue the painful saga in real life later on.

This "Nordberg scenario" is the situation that art, in this case in the form of computer games and literature, is supposed to comment on, make sense of, give structure to, make somehow livable. For my novel *QUIZ* (2018), I invented a game which is as autopoietic as the risk-based situationism of contemporary so-ciety itself.

QUIZ' leading female protagonist Susanne is on a business trip to Kyoto where she falls out with her group of colleagues and wanders through a cluster of department stores. In one of those sophisticated shops she comes across the Quiz Machine, a device the size of a cigarette box. The networked Quiz Machine is supplied with geolocation capabilities and an array of sensors allowing it to scan and make sense of its environment and generate multiple-choice questions from it that its owner has to answer by choosing one of the four given options. No points are awarded. If a question is answered, the machine simply invents the next one, often based on the user's immediate environment.

The Quiz Machine structures reality "on the go". It follows the path of loca-tive games like René Bauer's *sniff_jazzbox* or *wardrive* (2009), wherein iPhone software picks up the names of surrounding wireless LAN networks, turning them into NPCs; or Niantic's *Ingress* (2013) and *Pokémon Go* (2016), with the distinction that it doesn't run on a smartphone. The Quiz Machine originally isn't part of a larger business model. It is sold in a store, and that's it. Perhaps that is the most unrealistic part of the story. Later on, the Quiz Machine becomes part of a live TV show linked to third-party betting applications – a development not looked upon kindly by its Japanese inventor, game developer superstar Shi-geru Moriyama.

When it comes to game mechanics, the Quiz Machine's user interface is ex-tremely simple, reduced to something barely more complicated than a roll of dice. But it can only be so simple because it uses the most modern technology available in order to reduce the world's complexity down to four options in a multiple-choice quiz. While other locative games aim to add another layer to re-ality to make it more enticing and generate profits, the Quiz Machine takes reali-ty as it is and transforms it into questions along the way. Augmented Reality sys-tems require complex hardware and software in order to add a new logic to reality, but the Quiz Machine works the other way round. Its complex logic predates the game itself: it is its precondition. Paradoxically, the Quiz Machine is powered by reality while Augmented Reality games invite us to consume a simplified version of it.

RECUPERATING SITUATIONS

The Quiz Machine is a single proprietary piece of hardware. It operates autonomously on the edge of the Internet, i.e. it is not a dumb front-end to a data center. It uses Internet communications protocol standards, at the same time eschewing any form of interpersonal communications between individual Quiz Machine owners. To Shigeru Moriyama, it wouldn't make sense to run its software on a smartphone, because it has to work independently from powerful operating system platforms like Apple's iOS or Google's Android. Moriyama aims to disembed Quiz Machine users from their usual environment, whether physical or networked.

In that sense, the Quiz Machine is a Situationist game. It simulates a drift (*dérive*) and turns objects it comes across into components of its own game mechanics (*détournement*). Every multiple-choice quiz creates a new situation. All the user has to do is to decide which button to push. It generates a "situation" which forces the user's attention to concentrate on the "here and now". Time and space are contracted into a peak decision moment. In Situationist lore, the situation was a construct, an idea, that should make people free and let them shed the shackles of the "Spectacle", the mind-numbing all-encompassing media complex installed by the capitalist elite.

Chief Situationist Guy Debord always feared that the Spectacle would co-opt and assimilate Situationism itself. In a certain sense, it acted as a phantomatic mirror-object entangled with Situationism, providing its negative. But this idea would only work if Situationism could stay independent, instigate some sort of left-wing libertarian revolution and overwhelm the corporate media complex. After the famous French riots in May 1968, Debord realized that his historical moment had passed. He amended his definition of the Spectacle twice, adapting it to the then-new conditions of mediatized capitalism.

Situationism could be perceived as a set of tactics against the distributed totalitarian powers of mediated industrialized capitalism. Guy Debord was up against intertwined large post-WWII systems in both state and industry, the dreaded military-industrial complex giving birth to the huge bureaucracies needed for planning, coordination and deployment of demanding collective technical undertakings such as nuclear weapons or Moon shots. The fitting narrative for this kind of society would be Isaac Asimov's *Foundation* cycle - or any Soviet five-year plan.

But already in 1994, the year when Debord put an end to his life, those big machines were being dismantled from within. The Soviet Union had collapsed and with it the model of an all-encompassing superstrategy. In the USA, the Clinton administration switched to an Internet-based paradigm of production with Joseph Schumpeter and Marshall McLuhan as patron saints. In the era of the Internet start-up, Debord's "situations" were superseded by "disruptive events", business plans were made for the moment and the *dérive* was repackaged as GPS-tracked digital nomadism. Shareholder value driven corporate culture punishes every CEO trying to enact some kind of long-term planning – exceptions like Steve Bezos are rare. Twenty years later, right-wing groups appropriated what was left of 1990s disruptive trolling culture in order to bring about feats like Donald Trump's presidency or Brexit. Situationism triumphed, but in the hands of corporations and oligarchs who had the means to pull it off. In his seminal text on "ubiquitous literature", German cultural scientist Holger Schulze writes: "Trolling, faking and teasing have been regarded as attributes of hacker ethics since the dawn of digital antiquity. But over the last years, the sardonic con game has mutated from harmless online prank into a violent existential threat: women, non-white and marginalized members of society are threatened with death just for fun." (Schulze 2020: 72, author's translation)

In the pivotal scene of *QUIZ*, Shigeru Moriyama apologizes publicly for having invented the Quiz Machine. It reduces, so he argues, the world's complexity down to a multiple-choice quiz, which is wrong, because "real" questions are supposed to be open. Moriyama implores his audience to think long and hard about the very nature of questions, not only from a philosophical point of view but also in terms of what it means to establish new neuronal pathways in one's own brain or the role questions might play in the context of information theory.

Those are clearly projects which ought to have an impact in the long run. Moriyama seems to be quite unsure of what will come of it, but he knows that a power structure based on Situationist techniques could not be challenged or changed by Situationist tactics. The best outcome would be a stalemate. Therefore, Moriyama does not challenge the Quiz Machine itself but its user interface and its simplistic game mechanics. He encourages his fans to ditch the pseudo-zen Quiz moments in favor of rigorous long-term thinking. At the same time, he leaves them alone and offers no credible alternative. Long-term thinking – or strategy, to paraphrase de Certeau – remains the domain of the powerful. Powerless individuals lack the resources to implement long-term thinking. But de Certeau's remedy for the powerless to fall back on tactics for defense doesn't work if a resourceful and wealthy adversary is optimized for achievement.

According to Holger Schulze, ubiquitous literature is fast, sticky and dumb (Schulze 2020). The Quiz Machine as a networked digital device, an artifact of digital poetry, would fall into this category, too. Eventually, new weak ties would coagulate in this primal soup of networked text in the mind of the reader. A new logic would emerge, which could take the form of a conspiracy theory, reproducible knowledge or even friendship. But it wouldn't be enough. Autopoiesis and algorithms are no replacement for the tedious task of building and managing an advanced society or simply organizing human interest by way of founding and maintaining a political party, a trade union or a cooperative that survives the latest fad. After 40 years of Thatcherism, the formerly powerful structures of trade unions and social democracy have fallen into disrepair in almost every country.

Given the fact that short-term focused governments and corporations are prone to fail, it is tempting to try to wait the worst of them out. Shigeru Moriyama tries to point out that tactical use of technology alone won't save humanity, not even on the level of providing basic entertainment. Moriyama's attitude is unusual for a member of the higher circle of technology innovators in so far as he admits to having made a mistake that is not totally obvious to his customers. In breaking the ranks and his story on purpose, he gives everybody the opportunity to assess the situation in a broader context. If game mechanics and narratives serve oppressive purposes, it is the creative person's duty to interrupt them. Whether by modifying the dominant game mechanics or by stopping gaming altogether.

All this is, of course, fictional material. But if both theory and science fiction are based on the question "What if ...?", it might be worth investigating Shigeru Moriyama's thoughts about the nature and form of questions. At least "What if ...?" is an open question – and will remain so forever. It is the most basic of game mechanics. So maybe it is the act of asking open questions which enables us to keep stumbling along our paths, however crooked they might be.

REFERENCES

Eco, Umberto (1995): "Eternal Fascism: Fourteen Ways of Looking at a Blackshirt", In: New York Review of Books (https://www.nybooks.com/articles/1995/06/22/ur-fascism/).

Hack, Günter (2019): QUIZ. Berlin: Frohmann Verlag, Hans-Böckler-Stiftung.

Schaeffer, Katherine (2020): "6 facts about economic inequality in the U.S.". In: Pew Research Center (ed.), Facttank (https://www.pewresearch.org/fact-tank/2020/02/07/6-facts-about-economic-inequality-in-the-u-s/).

Schulze, Holger (2020): Ubiquitäre Literatur, Berlin: Matthes & Seitz.

Stähler, Patrick (2002): Geschäftsmodelle in der digitalen Ökonomie, Köln: Josef Eul Verlag.

World Bank Gini Coefficient Data (2020), (https://fred.stlouisfed.org/series/SIPOVGINIDEU).

Ludic Meanders through Defictionalization: The Narrative Mechanics of Art

Games in the Public Spaces of Politics

Margarete Jahrmann

INTRODUCTION

In the following article we will meander. This is precisely the narrative mechanism that is used to outwit complex content. It happens mainly in public space online, in the agora of politics, and physically in the arena of the urban games in our daily lives, which has changed drastically in the times of the pandemic of 2020. Both playgrounds have political effects. The one that affects the personal is from now on hegemonically decreed, by means of rules of whom you can meet and when, whether elderly relatives may be visited or not; when we meet friends or have corona parties, punishments are executed. New magic circles of distance are imposed by the state, borders are raised, rituals of contactless greeting are established, the game of controlling the body has become *realpolitik*. Apps for the purpose of self-optimization and health care were already popular, now they are being considered whether to become legally binding or at least a condition of freedom of travel. Once the use of the body has been gamified in biometric apps, the new contact apps will not only make a possible chain of social contacts as source of infection traceable for a benevolent purpose, but also express acceptance of state social control. Probably because they appear in the guise of a mobile snowball game, for example.

Reacting to changing social conditions is a basic mechanic of art. It uses emotio-political effects for the purpose of enlightenment. Here, it is helpful to refer to a conceptual comparison of the theory of game mechanics in narrative text as a model. Art has always applied game mechanics, fed by artistic strategy and the primal logic of art as an emotionally touching experience. Understanding political contexts then becomes part of the reward and motivation system in art.

EIGEN-MECHANICS OF ART

Figure 1: Cluster Art Mechanics, "Eigen-Mechanik der Kunst", Jahrmann 2020.

Source: Margarete Jahrmann

If text comprehension is known as a traditional narrative mechanic, then art can be read as a narrative mechanic of social intervention. Sets of rules are anchored in the logic of art with its installation settings and the paradigm of becoming public. Art that is not shown does not exist (in the collective consciousness) in society. Artistic actions have moments of decision. The reaction and the behavior of the audience is always calculated in the creation of art and included in the concept. Reward and punishment mechanisms become permanently effective at the reception level of the artwork. As art viewers, just as when reading a text, we must be able to understand the content of the statement, to decode the syntax. We have to learn to read the set of rules of a performance, and as a reward we can sometimes act on our own – or at least take a content-related/political statement with us. We are punished if we cannot do anything with the coding of the work. We are dissatisfied, cannot understand why this work is exhibited. Being able to read a work in its form (artifact, installation, performance, etc.) is a challenge and a short-term motivation. We have to translate artistic rule sets into our personal state and emotional condition and let them work there. Only then does the understanding of the statement regarding a work of art begin. The personal touch connects the artistic with the playful. The long-term motivation of the art public lies in identification with the statement made by a work of art. Works without a statement would only be decoration.

In art, one can speak of game mechanisms as having political effectiveness, since art always intervenes socially – in contrast to classical game design. Composite artifacts in the cultural context of the exhibition space and public space (online and offline) become objects of political intervention. In the semiosis of already seen and experienced art and expectations regarding the statement the construct becomes art with its own corresponding mechanics.

The rules are thus given both on a paradigmatic (meaning) and syntactic (associative) level. If we assume that the narrative mechanics of art represent a special kind of motivation design, the question arises as to which narrative is associated with the communication of pandemic preparedness.

NARRATIVE GAMES

When looking at narrative games, we can observe a great variety in how these games try to evoke mental narratives. Some games rely heavily on a pre-authored storyline, taking the player through a more or less predefined narrative path (e.g. *Last of Us*). Other games leave more room for the player to explore and to direct the course of the narrative, for example through branching structures (e.g. *The Walking Dead*), or alternatively, through emergent structures (e.g. *Middle-earth: Shadow of Mordor*).

Regardless of how games try to trigger processes of narrativization, in each case, mechanics and rules play a key role. As also recognized by Salen and Zimmerman: "[…] it is the dynamic structures of games, their emergent complexity, their participatory mechanisms, their experiential rhythms and patterns, which are key to understanding how games construct narrative experiences." (2003: 382-383) Whether a game relies on a predefined narrative path, or uses branching storylines, or creates a narrative experience through emergent structures, in each case the mechanics, in tandem with other narrative devices, are responsible for the overall narrative experience.

When we look at the current game industry, some of these narrative devices have already been brought to fruition. For example, many of the existing critically acclaimed narrative-driven games have perfected the device of environmental storytelling, also known as narrative architecture (Jenkins 2004; Nitsche 2008). In games like *Firewatch*, *What Remains of Edith Finch* and *Everybody's Gone to the Rapture*, the environment is cleverly used to communicate relevant narrative information, such as backstory, conflict and character personalities.

Alternatively, popular games like *Until Dawn* or Telltale's *Game of Thrones* make extensive use of on-screen choice prompts. At specific moments during the game, the system presents the player with a limited set of predefined choices in form of prompts on the screen. These can be mundane, like choosing which road to take, or they can be more dramatic, like deciding which character perishes.

Unlike environmental storytelling and on-screen choice prompts, narrative game mechanics are still underdeveloped in the industry, and underexamined in academia. To counter this, I have conducted additional research on the topic (Dubbelman 2017), and used the outcomes to develop the aforementioned tools for aspiring game designers. One of these tools, the Narrative Design Canvas, is discussed below.

PANDEMIC MECHANICS

(My) experiences from urban games and exhibition games show how public space can be defined as narrative space. Pandemic apps as recent examples of "real-life games" contextualize the way we deal with technical toys that affect our personal freedom through the body and our social contacts. Just as the mobile phone and tablet were used for social networking, the latest "games" of political control use algorithms to track one's own actions and sensitivities, to measure and quantify one's own health-promoting contactless behavior, and to evaluate these statistically. Individual action and access to public space are thus increasingly regulated.

These prescriptions took on an extreme form at the outbreak of the Coronavirus Pandemic. Effects on the cognitive self-image of keeping one's distance are created by framing one's own behavior. I have addressed the original question of social distance keeping in a spontaneous performance with a sculptural frame, together with the sculptor Talos Kedel (A) and the cognitive researcher Stephan Glasauer (DE). Between April and June 2020, during the first total lockdown, we realized a series of game performances in Vienna and the surrounding area. The "Social Distancer" game art project is inspired by the bounding boxes and box colliders[1] that appear in common game design programs, game engines and 3D programs. Here, a grid frame is drawn around the body. The box around the figure's body defines its individual limits. Activities and radius of movement are graphically defined by these boxes. Also, actions and scripts can be triggered by touching such boundaries. In the game, this frame is normally invisible, but in the design environment it is visually present.

Figure 2: Bounding box and box collider in game design.

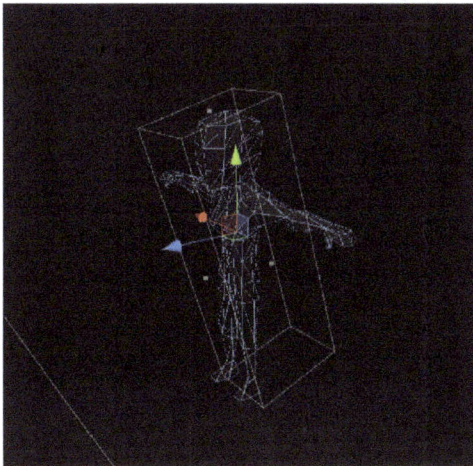

Source: screenshot (Jahrmann)

---

1   To better understand the collision outlines and object boundaries in game and 3D engines editors, so-called bounding boxes, see this extract from an online manual: "The first thing you must understand is the idea of the 3d Bounding Box. If you run through all the vertices of a mesh and record the lowest and highest x values, you have found the x *min/max*---the complete boundary for all x values within the mesh. Do this again for y and z, then make a rectangular prism out of these values, and you have a *Bounding Box*. This box could be oriented relative globally to the world or locally to the object's rotation." Blender Wiki (https://wiki.blender.jp/Doc:2.6/Manual/Game_ Engine/Physics/Collision_Bounds), accessed July 12, 2020.

In the game art piece #Sozialer Abstandhalter, we have transferred these frames into the physical space and thus started a narrative about the pandemic and its social impact. Hence, in the urban game in times of the coronavirus, the play figure takes on a new role as a political actor. The Social Distancer game with the real bounding box is categorically an *ilinx* and *mimicry* game, in the sense of Roger Caillois (1958). This categorization of game types has remained valid in today's culture which is dominated by computer games, because it proactively incorporates real-life games that are now very widespread.

Figure 3: First #Sozialer Abstandhalter/ Social Distancer tweet, March 2020.

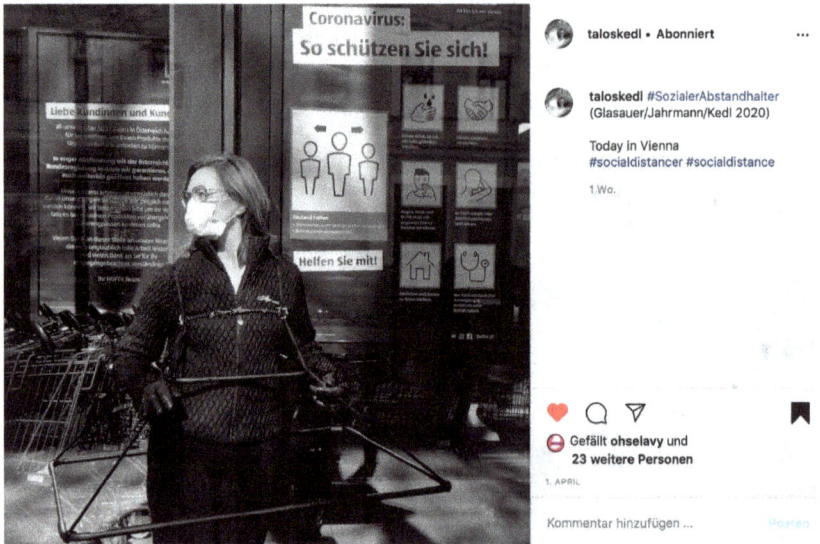

Source: Margarete Jahrmann

Ilinx because the bouncing between the aisles of the supermarket or strolling in the street during the lockdown creates a physical adrenaline rush, each step is part of an (Instagram) shooting session. *Mimicry* because the players inside the real-bounding box frame imitate virtual figures and also hint at the earlier art performances of Vienna actionism as well as today's activism — both in game art and political demonstrations, as in the work of Chris Solarski and Anonymous capitalism critique.

"The art figure wearing a distancing frame" (as I would call it) triggers actions in public urban space. The essence of this bounding box play object is that a narrative on Twitter is created from it. All actions were posted on Twitter and Instagram, spread over different accounts. The narrative emerges from the mechanics of a public art performance as a game. Players who are not familiar with the game start a discussion that reaches into real political life. It is about the question of social distance which was made necessary by the pandemic – as a restriction of personal freedom or as protection of individual life and limb, and the danger of infection in relation to hegemonic violence in the form of radical interventions into private life.

Figure 4: Bounding box performance at a supermarket, Vienna 2nd district, March 2020, Twitter feed.

Source: Margarete Jahrmann

Our Social Distancer game with the title *Sozialer Abstandhalter* was played in various contexts and places that conjure up historical references to social distance and the transgression of this distance: at the Donnerbrunnen in Vienna, the place where high-class prostitutes gathered in the 17th century and strolled with hoop skirts, thus transgressing social hierarchies; and at Wiener Graben, the site of the role-playing performance by Valie Export with Peter Weibel on a dog leash (1972).

Various random passers-by unknowingly became participants, at the moment they asked questions like "Is this art or is this for real?" or "Is this a protest?" The latter question already refers to the political potential of the game in urban space. The police, who paid attention to distancing rules and photographed our sculptural spacer (and perhaps put it on the internal police tweet?), were unsettled – did a sizeable portable metal frame constitute a punishable offence? Thus, the Social Distancer game *Sozialer Abstandhalter* can be seen as an investigation of political intervention in a narrative urban game.

Figure 5: Tweet, April 4, 2020: #SocialDistancer #SozialerAbstandhalter – homage to Malevich, (Glasauer/Jahrmann/Kedl 2020).

Source: Margarete Jahrmann

An Easter performance was "played" in April 2020: In the vineyards around Vienna, in the world-famous village Gumpoldskirchen, walkers meet, despite a travel ban. Similar to the butts of the vintners in old times, the new sculptural social spacers of the artists can be squeezed through the narrow rows of the cultivated plant. A highlight of the work results from the play mechanics – how to achieve closeness with a bounding box, overcome the forced distance or resist the desired closeness. It happens just before the pillory, an old emblem of jurisdiction in the town. In a surprising encounter with a well-known professor of the philosophy of technology and social robotics, the performer reflexively extends her hand to the expert in social techniques for a polite greeting. The professor accepts and shakes her hand. His partner, who accompanies him, cries out, immediately gets out the sanitizer and disinfects him, but without offering the performer anything.

An ethical deficit becomes visible, due to a plague danger? Everyone is only and exclusively taking care of themselves (and their partner)? The narration of the Social Distancer game with the game object turns in the social discrimination but remains in the private sphere, which becomes political. The problems of social ethics, of makeshift technologies of distance and viral prophylaxis and their deficits become clear when the performers accidentally meet their research partner from the field of ethics and artificial intelligence (cf. Coeckelbergh 2020). Designed as a participatory examination of technologies, game interventions such as the Social Distancer game can reveal current political narratives in the public space.

AFFECTIVE DEMOCRACY MECHANICS

Figure 6: Pinar Yolda (2016): Kitty AI: Artificial Intelligence for Governance.

It is year 2039. An artificial intelligence with the affective capaticies of a kitten becomes the first non-human governor. She leads a politician-free zone with a network of Artificial Intelligences. She lives in mobile devices of the citizens and can love up to 3 Million people.

a precious item on European Union's tech agenda

Source: screenshot (Jahrmann)

If we understand narrative mechanics as a special kind of motivation design, this leads to an increased motivation to intervene socially – especially in relation to surveillance, participation and political narratives. In connection with affective mechanics in art, Pinar Yolda (2016) takes this up in *Kitty AI: Artificial Intelli-*

gence for Governance[2]. In this installation with game character and game elements, he expands the theme towards affective computing and AI. Democratic politics is absurdly handed over to an AI, and we are incapacitated in the interaction, in the gameplay with the AI. In a fictional society, Kitty AI takes over the mechanics of democratic politics for us. The form of representation (the mechanics paradigm) promotes emotional attachment to technological entities in a kind of Tamagotchi[3] effect. By this I mean a reverse cultural technique – in the case of the electronic counterpart marketed as a toy in an egg shape, we take care of an artificial entity – but in a "technology of care[4]", we ourselves become the toy of the AI, to whom we willingly give up basic democratic rights. In dialogue, Kitty AI, accompanied by emoticon hearts with a Mickey Mouse-like distorted vocoder voice, tells us that she herself is an emotional being who wants to address our most intimate emotional worlds and in return takes over our civil duties and rights. The appearance of the AI in the shape of a cat is so absurd that we have to laugh when she tells us which democratic processes we have already handed over to her. This list is not fictitious but real – the reward is analogous knowledge, emotionally mediated knowledge in the art installation.

Machine learning and so-called artificial intelligence are thus essential elements of the reality of our lives and are adopted in affective narrative mechanisms in the social surveillance games of the present – therefore occurring both in reality and in games.

---

2   The piece was shown in a show curated by Inke Arns at Haus der Kulturen der Welt in the context of transmediale festival (https://www.pinaryoldas.info/WORK/The-Kitty-AI-Artificial-Intelligence-for-Governance-2016), accessed August 20, 2020.

3   Tamagotchi was a highly successful series of early artificial pets in Japan and Europe in the 1990s, aimed at the care instinct of their owners. Developers were Akihiro Yokoi (WiZ) and Aki Maita (Bandai), 1996.

4   Compare the Ludic Method/ Ludic Society soirée Vienna of November 2019 with Oliver Schürer (robotic Expert TU and h.a.u.s. Vienna) and the curator Daphne Dragona, with a game on s[c]are robots with the pepper android as main player/character by Margarete Jahrmann and Oliver Schürer, 2019.

Figure 7: Do Not Feed the Monkeys (2018).

Source: screenshot (Jahrmann)

A commercial game that also communicates this theme through a narrative mechanic of experience in a simulation similar to Bentham's[5] surveillance towers is *Do Not Feed the Monkeys*[6] (2018). In this game, the narrative of surveillance is doubled; on one's own computer screen, another computer screen is displayed as a graphical user interface which is divided into a multitude of surveillance images. Monitoring the split screens across the players' multiple live video feeds via a desktop computer in the game corresponds to an introduced visual mechanism of doubling and recognizing media systems. However, the direct micro mechanics of the game only convey that communicating with the monitored subjects is not allowed.

The essential macro mechanics of the critique of surveillance, which turns us into laboratory animals, is not communicated directly but through the visual style of characters with animal heads. Addressing the subject of surveillance, the role of laboratory animals, and the prejudices built into current technical systems, such as gender, race, and, for example, also those against animals, this work following the mechanics of artistic affective narration radicalizes the play-

---

5   Compare also the position of Michel Foucaul expressed in his book Surveiller et punir, La naissance de la prison, 1975.

6   A digital voyeurism simulator where you watch strangers through surveillance cameras. Invade their privacy and witness their most intimate moments (donotfeedthemonkeys.com).

ing subject. The discrimination against lab monkeys and apes, that are often sacrificed in the neurosciences are also a topic of the Ludic Art installation described in the following paragraph.

I Want to See Monkeys (2017) is a game art work by *Area7 Lab* (a collective of the neuroscientist Stefan Glasauer and the artist Margarete Jahrmann — the roles are frequently exchanged here). The exhibition "The Future of AI" at the Ars Electronica Festival provided the framework for this work[7]. In an installation setting with a medical examination couch, neuroscientific devices and monitors, visitors were classified with the help of a specially designed Artifical Intelligence (AI) program – at the end of a "Deep Dream Process", the AI made all humans appear as monkeys in a cognitive science experiment. The installation *I Want to See Monkeys* was touching because it triggered a discourse about the game with the machine system. In the setting described above, one was seduced by a supposedly entertaining game to be filmed and categorized when dealing with a machine learning system.

Figure 8: Area7 Lab (2020): I Want to See Happy Monkeys.

Source: photo by Jahrmann/Glasauer

---

7   Parts of the following paragraph appear in the reader of the Danube Festival 2020, see Jahrmann, M. (2020): "PLAN A for I/motions. The art of playing with emotions and new forms of cognition." In: Thomas Edlinger (ed.), Machines Like Us. Reader Danube Festival, Vienna: Falterverlag, pp. 95-103.

2020 saw the creation of a "passive gaming" work, *I Want to See Happy Monkeys*, which was considerably expanded in terms of the narrative. It was supplemented by a narrative mechanics in the form of a game goal. The visitors have the goal of being classified as happy and are rewarded with a percentage classification score in the graphical display. Their face is then entered into the database and serves as the basis for the distorted memory of the system, which classifies the visitor according to the prejudices trained into that system.

This will create a new narrative concerning the political dimension of machine learning and how these systems deal with our emotions. The game installation piece *I Want to See Happy Monkeys* is a playful arrangement: participants lie on an examination couch wrapped in a fabric pattern with Alexa Fluor Green tinted images Margarete Jahrmann from an experiment on eye movements of the tadpoles of African clawed frogs. The green colour on the hand printed fabric by Jahrmann is the same which is used to stain Margarete Jahrmann's isolated neurons in examined tissue — and it is reminiscent of the green colour of a radar monitor. The test subjects in the game art piece also look at three monitors with frequently green displays, equipped with tracking cameras which measure them and their emotional state like a radar of emotional states, evaluating their faces supposed attributed emotions.

The narrative in this installation game revolves around the uncanny dimension of emotion as a classification factor in an artificial neural network. How emotionally cognitive can an artificial system actually be, which structurally draws conclusions in a multi-level process, builds on each one and exponentiates them? In the AI system used, images are captured, analyzed and assigned to a certain predefined category, which they seem to resemble most. The way in which correspondences are found, however, differs substantially from the human way of recognition – even though the functioning of the program levels is modeled on a biological neural network. The problem with this type of artificial intelligence is more the question of making sense in connection with facial recognition and emotions than that of correct allocation and classification (rules of narrative social mechanic).

BIAS MECHANICS

The well-known freely available artificial neural network AlexNet[8], which is used in many artificial intelligence applications, is classified according to certain paradigms, following a kind of prejudice that was trained into this network. Categories or events that were not learned during training cannot be recognized by the network – likewise, incorrect assignments are not corrected but adopted. This shows how sensitive and delicate the use of such systems is, if we assign users in everyday life to these artificial neuronal networks in an anthropomorphizing way. Such meaning is inherent in the word intelligence in our humanoid understanding. Due to this misallocation on our part, we grant artificial intelligence systems decision-making power over democratic processes, hand over competence assessments in recruitment procedures and assessment processes of large companies to artificial assistance systems and allow so-called AIs to validate creditworthiness in the credit checks of banking institutions. All these application areas illustrate the enormous effectiveness of the narrative mechanics surrounding these AI systems. They affect decisions that are essential for the lives of individuals and for many in society as a whole. The question of whether these machines really like us, as the ambiguous title of the very amusing book on this subject by Ian McEwan *Machines Like Me* (2019) playfully implies, is still unanswered. At least we, the other side, face the artificial entities, if not with emotion, at least with affects.

Affective computing and affective AI is an area in which we – and not the machines – transfer ascriptions of sympathy and empathy from our behavior into the machine systems in order to be better able to deal with them. The artistic play in and with the AI here couples technology-critical narratives with political questions that are of importance to society as a whole — this is applied Ludic method!

---

8   AlexNet is an artificial neural network for image classification. It has been trained with over 1.2 million pre-classified images from 1000 image categories, including various objects and animals, but not human faces (which consequently cannot be recognized). Cf. Krizhevsky, Alex/Sutskever, Ilya/Hinton, Geoffrey (2012): "ImageNet Classification with Deep Convolutional Neural Networks". In: NIPS'12: Proceedings of the 25th International Conference on Neural Information Processing Systems, December 2012, pp. 1097-1105.

LUDIC AGITPROP MECHANICS

Structural coupling is a method of second-order cybernetics[9], also known as an artistic strategy of game art, which is politically effective. It is a game mechanic of Ludic-artistic research, encountered in the Dadaist original meter, the "Urmeter"[10], and in the socio-politically inclined *Game of War*[11] by Alice Becker-Ho and Guy Debord (1967).

Figure 9: Alice Becker-Ho and Guy Debord (1977): Le Jeu de la Guerre (board game).

Source: screenshot from http://www.classwargames.net (Jahrmann)

Following Guy Debord, war games, or rather strategic Clausewitz simulators, are a continuation of politics by other means. Debord and his partner Alice Becker-Ho dedicated themselves to the development of the board game over two dec-

---

9   Coupling and autopoiesis are described by the neurobiologists Humberto Maturana and Francisco Varela as generative creative concepts of systems theory. Cf. Maturana, Humberto R./Varela, Francisco J. (1986): The Tree of Knowledge: The Biological Roots of Human Cognition, Frankfurt: Suhrkamp.

10 Rational sciences are addressed through an artistic experiment. "Trois Stoppages Étalon", 1913-14. In: Anne d'Harnoncourt/Kynaston McShine (eds.) (1973), Marcel Duchamp, exhibition catalogue, Philadelphia: Philadelphia Museum of Art.

11 Becker-Ho, Alice/Debord, Guy (1987): Le Jeu de la Guerre ("A Game of War"), republished 2006 by Éditions Gallimard, Paris.

ades. Both saw in this game a possibility to become effective on a social level. The idea was that the game could provide real orientation in life and supply the narrative of a social resistance against capitalist conditions. Debord formulated the narrative mechanics of coupling in political art as a theoretical work of art. He grotesquely combined incompatible content and visuals as well as media in his 1973 film *La Société du Spectacle*, which was based on the book of the same name: when he provided news images with a new narration, he successively edited Fidel Castro with Kungfu movies and subtitled these images with well-known sociological text.

Based on Debord's concept of the society of the spectacle, contemporary art and game designers also understand Debord's approach in the *Game of War* as a guide to acting in a mode of "war" on the cultural terrain of a still existing class struggle.

The British initiative Class War Games[12] solves political and social conflicts using tabletop applications and simulations of social intelligence in a new form of clever gamification of political decision-making, as described by Richard Barbrook (2014). A Labour activist, Barbrook founded the Class War Games initiative. The English working class theoretician, lecturer at Westminster University and game designer, describes how ludic subversion can overcome what he calls "spectacular capitalism". He deliberately uses the term "ludic", which brings to mind activities around the initiative Ludic Society (2006-2016).

Compared to the game mechanics that have become narratives in many games, Class War Games finds ways to socially overcome the competition of other narrative mechanics and their spectacles. In the re-released version of *Game of War*[13] (2007) by Class War Games, a highly elegant game reminiscent of chess is presented in prominent public exhibition spaces. In this version of the game, what Alice Becker Ho and Guy Debord had developed is now transferred to the public area of the exhibition space – and thus becomes more effective than the private version of the war game of Ho and Debord. The narrative mechanics of making things public in art has a political effect.

12 Barbrook, Richard (2014). Class Wargames: Ludic Subversion Against Spectacular Capitalism (paperback ed.), London: Minor Compositions.

13 This version of *Game of War* deals with strategic theory (cf. http://www.classwar games.net/?p=1636).

Figure 10: Corbyn Run (2019).

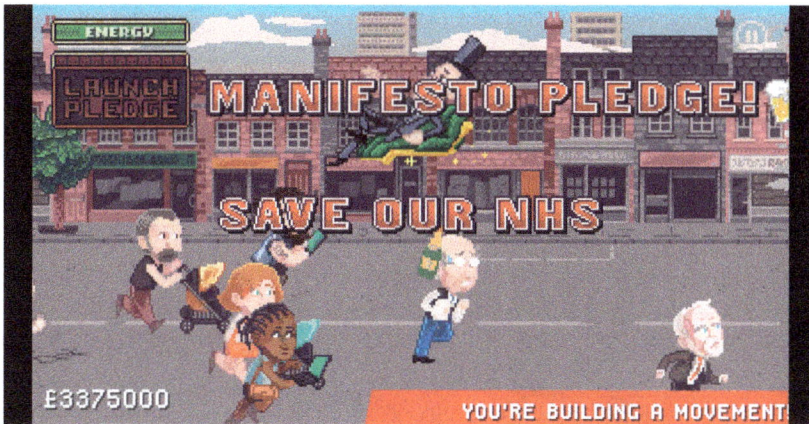

Source: screenshot (Jahrmann)

As a small excursion, a reference may be allowed here to the amusing platform election campaign game *Corbyn Run*[14] (2019), which Barbrook helped to develop. Unfortunately, the game could not influence the outcome of the election away from Conservative populism. Nevertheless it contains some nice agitprop narratives. Designed as a casual game, it conveys political messages and slogans in short sequences and calls for support for a movement. This is more likely to be accepted in an amused rather than annoyed way after experiencing this feeling of social movement in the incessant running of the characters in jump 'n' run mode. Parents pushing baby carriages and grannies carrying empty shopping bags run for coins, their capitalist opponents throw moneybags and champagne bottles out of helicopters at them. The highlight of the game is a "manifesto pledge" that promotes the effectiveness of the old form of the manifesto as a political text.

With the game only moderately effective politically, Barbrook was, however, successful in the "Ludic cadre training" of leftist politicians in parliament. In April 2019 and at the party conference of the UK Labour Party in September 2019, active female politicians played a board game he had developed based on

---

14 *Corbyn Run* (2019), app on Google Play. The game contains a manifesto pledge. PR text excerpt: "Real change is coming. Join Labour Leader Jeremy Corbyn to build a movement and chase out the Tories! People in Britain need hope and prosperity." (https://play.google.com/store/apps/details?id=com.digitalliberties.corbynrun&hl=en_ US), accessed July 20, 2020.

The Landlord's Game (1904) on urban development[15]. The model was patented by Elizabeth Magie, as a board game whose content constituted a criticism of the landlord system and in general of the evil of increasing money at the expense of others. Although Lizzy Magie was with this game design literally the inventor of *Monopoly*, albeit with a different narrative mechanics, she was not appreciated for it. Behind it all is a patent dispute, and above all, it is also clear that a narrative game mechanic can be turned into reality – and is of the greatest political importance.

Figure 11: Patent drawing for Lizzie Magie's board game, January 5, 1904.

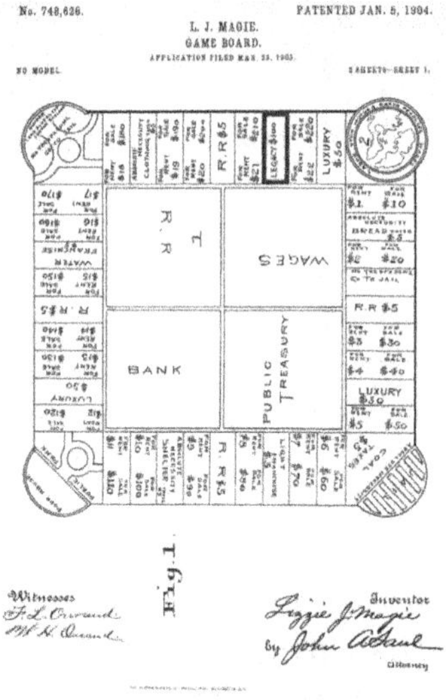

Source: Lizzie Magie

Unfortunately, there was no reference to the creator of the original *Landlord's Game* either. Nevertheless, the narrative game mechanics in this version of the game were again oriented toward a critique of capitalism. The multiplayer strategy game *Taste of Power: The Great Municipal Socialism Game*[16] (2019), de-

---

15 Stephens, Ric (2016): "Urban Planning Games and Simulations: From Board Games to Artificial Environments." In: Simulation and Gaming in Network Society, p. 253.

16 The designers of the game are also politically conscious as a company. Political narration plays an essential role in their corporate communication under the name Digital Liberties. You work in a socially committed cooperative which tries to create pockets of local activism as a company. "In this mass-participatory role-playing game, a re-

veloped especially for the party conference, was intended to give a feeling of how to act as a political radical within a government. The game was supposed to be an aid to strategic action in municipal councils and in parliament, i.e. to increase motivation in real political life. In the role play, oppositional political positions are taken, and the consequences of the development of individual city districts are made visible in a simulation. The narrative mechanics implemented here, which are applied in such political persuasion games, are no longer simple linear tree branches but real political "storytelling machines" that subsequently create reality.

In the fall of 2019 at the Kunsthalle Wien at Karlsplatz, I was able to participate in a "Prediction Game Workshop" in the form of a game situation concerning strategies and practices of socio-political intervention, led by Richard Barbrook – and after having been allowed to act as a radical anarchist within the municipal council, I am personally convinced of the effectiveness of performing political action socially in games like this!

DEFICTIONALIZED POLITICAL MECHANICS

"Donald Trump must fear the Lincoln Project"[17] reads the headline of the news magazine Der Spiegel on August 15, 2020. Republican election strategists launched an initiative to prevent the re-election of a candidate from their own camp, namely that of Donald Trump. What is special about this is not only this fact, but also that a media narrative is being used which incorporates the very mechanics Trump himself used: emotion, in addition to defamation, false facts, and an aggressive tone.

Nevertheless, this peculiar new form of political life is above all about affective moments, the triggering of emotions through narratives in social media. Using a contemporary interpretation of the Kuleshov effect[18], the initiative's online video clips show images of corpses and people wearing masks, and talk about

---

cently elected radical local council must battle with the legacy of their neoliberal predecessors and halt a disastrous redevelopment scheme." (https://www.digital-liberties.coop/digital-liberties-privacy-notice), accessed July 20, 2020.

17 Neukirch, Ralf: "Republikaner gegen Donald Trump. Angriff aus den eigenen Reihen." In: Der Spiegel online, August 15, 2020.

18 The Kuleshov effect says that people often misinterpret images because the brain creates connections where there are none. (https://en.wikipedia.org/wiki/Kuleshov_effect), accessed July 12, 2020.

how America has become poorer and weaker. Reactions by Trump follow his usual mechanics of political communication, not through official channels but on Twitter, calling the originators "losers" according to a capitalist rhetoric of success. And as a result, he spends a lot of time in public appearances denying or justifying what was claimed in the Lincoln Project. It is precisely the fictional approach that is obviously most effective in a system of fictional facts in politics, as opposed to realistic arguments.

Particularly in American politics in recent years, it has become clear how much fictional narrative mechanics are reinforced by rewards and punishments in their own ranks – just as in games. But now there is a twist in the direction that I would like to call "defictionalized political mechanics". Similar to Jorge Luis Borges' (1940) story "TLÖN, UQBAR, ORBIS TERTIUS", the narratives of such a mechanic displace "realities". Essential to Borges' fictional dialogue with his writer colleague Casares is that, over the course of the narrative, more and more artifacts from a fictional world appear in reality – until the world itself turns into the fictional land Borges intended to discover. Francesco Franchi (2011) has created a beautiful graphic design for this.

Figure 12: Francesco Franchi (2011): "Bi-dimensional versions of classic literature."

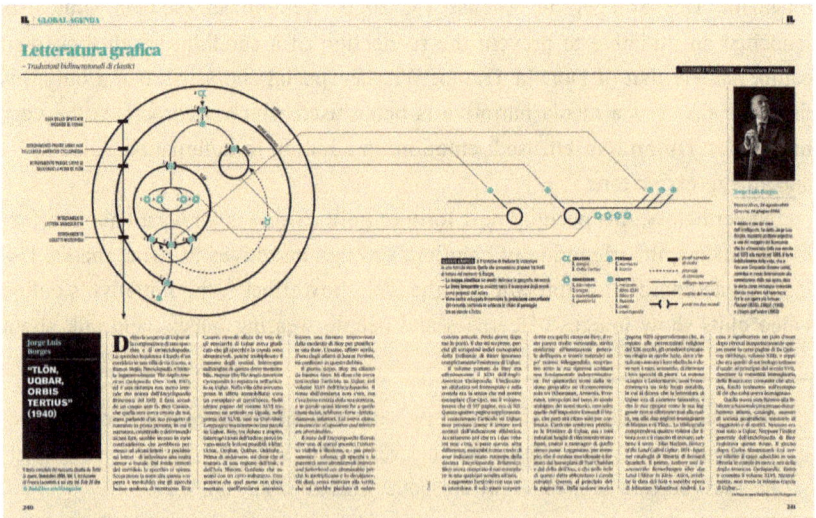

Source: Malofiej18 Annual Publication, Index Books, Spain, p. 50

In the appendix to his story, Borges also introduces a literary fictional authentication strategy as a narrative means. This double strategy, the false format of a scientific report and false references, is readily accepted in current political argumentation, which generates a strong immersive force regarding media communication – in the capitalist spectacle in the Barbrook sense. In the Fox News war room of the impeachment procedure 2019 it became clear that narrative mechanics had already become the sole rewarding extension of world perception and the basis for journalistic action. The corresponding political message defictionalizes the narrative mechanics as an analogous reward in the suspension of the intended impeachment proceedings. As the motivational mechanism of society, narrative is elevated above all the facts, as in "TLÖN".

So in the end we come back to the pandemic situation. This has definitely gotten out of hand in the USA. In biopolitics, fictionalization is being countered with Permadeath. The price for this is irresponsibly high.

CONCLUSION: NANO MECHANICS

The conclusion to be drawn from this narrative fictional defictionalization, which can increasingly be found in politics and journalism, is that a new phenomenon is emerging, namely that individual statements can suddenly acquire wider significance ("Never Trumpers"). A new "nano mechanics" in which individual words, individual events acquire mega-meaning and create realities has become apparent within a very short time in 2020. The pandemic has shown us how political narratives can turn, how absurd rules of the game may take effect in physical space and how the limits of our own physicality can be exceeded.

Subsequently, the importance of the affect and the emotion become clear – especially in dealing with the technological systems of everyday surveillance, which has been intensified by the pandemic. The semiosis between expectation and construct becomes particularly pronounced when we look at artistic game mechanisms in public space.

The question of how art inherently applies narrative game mechanics is wonderfully illustrated by the activist games of computational face recognition and emotion classification. Further to this, we can clearly see from the evidence in the activist political games cited here how we can create a new classification out of the mechanics that are presented as political narrative in the real politics of defictionalization. It can only be hoped that it does not stop there and that the pandemic of "faketionalization" will be overcome soon. The turn of reality in the outcome of the presidential election 2020 gives hope!

REFERENCES

Literature

Barbrook, Richard (2014): Class Wargames: Ludic Subversion Against Spectacular Capitalism, Westminster: Minor Compositions.

Borges, Jorge Luis (1940): TLÖN UQBAR ORBIS TERTIUS, Argentinia.

Caillois, Roger (1958): Les Jeux et les Hommes: Le Masque et le Vertige, Paris: Gallimard.

Coeckelbergh, Mark (2020): AI Ethics, Boston: MIT Press Essential Knowledge series.

Debord, Guy (1967): La Société du spectacle, Paris: Buchet/Chastel.

Franchi, Francesco (2011): "Bi-dimensional versions of classic literature." In: Malofiej18 Annual Publication, Index Books, Spain, p. 50.

McEwan, Ian (2019): Machines like me, London: Penguin Random House Children's UK.

Games

Do Not Feed the Monkeys, Fictiorama Studios, Alawar Premium. 2018.

Game of War, Class War Games, 2007.

I want to see Monkeys, Area7 Lab, Margarete Jahrmann/Stefan Glasauer, 2017.

Kitty AI: Artificial Intelligence for Governance, Pinar Yolda, 2016.

Le Jeu de la Guerre (Board game), Alice Becker-Ho/Guy Debord, 1977.

The Landlord's Game, Lizzy Magie, 1904.

If You Play It, Do You Believe It?

Making Game Stories Become Real with Embedded Design

Mary Flanagan

I will start with a simple question: If you play something, does that mean that somewhere, somehow, you suppose it is happening? Believe in it? Does a game change you? Over the last decade, scholars have conducted research on the use of games in education, healthcare and other areas where an engaging "gamified" approach might be "useful". But what about deeper things, such as our beliefs? Is it possible for a game to affect our personal values or behaviors? Are players of games swayed, enticed or brought into new states of understanding with games?

As all games express and embody human values (Flanagan/Nissenbaum 2014), they express "big ideas" like democracy, justice, equity, honesty and co-operation. They also express other ideas, including violence, winner-takes-all mentalities, exploitation and greed. These values emerge in games whether designers intend them or not, so it is important that designers understand their impact. So, when we consider whether and how game stories can "become real", that is, have impact on our lives, shift our actions, beliefs or behaviors, we need to ask several questions. One, what actions, beliefs, or behaviors do we mean? Two, what about the game story, in the larger sense, facilitated this shift? Three, how does one go about measuring shifts? And finally, what are the unintended consequences of game stories impacting on everyday life?

This essay details a game design approach called embedded design, developed in my game design research laboratory, Tiltfactor, that was founded to study and create pro-social, pro-people games that strive to have a positive impact in the world. Concerning social challenges like public health crises, sexual assault, mental health challenges and more, games in fact can play a role in tackling them. From *Depression Quest* (2013) to *That Dragon Cancer* (2016), games increasingly are used to empathize, educate and transform.

The core idea behind embedded design is that using a collection of narrative mechanics, games can be effective at shifting beliefs and biases when these are carefully designed employing subtle techniques (Flanagan/Kaufman 2016; Kaufman/Flanagan 2015; Kaufman/Flanagan/Seidman 2015). Transformative moments can be designed and studied utilizing psychological approaches from social cognition, bias and persuasion fields. These intentionally transformative methods inspire new ways of thinking through the narrative mechanics that designers initiate in games. A game can mix in or even hide an overt message, activate fantasy, position a mindset and introduce "aha" moments, all of which have the potential to shift player' attitudes and beliefs, and thus change not only the game story, but the real world.

In this chapter, I will articulate three key aspects of how an embedded design approach can help game stories have real-world impact. By stories, I mean not only narratives in the stereotypical sense, i.e. a linear story with a narrative arc (one might initially think of a game story as constituted by the plot, the script, with authentic characters whose motivations we invest in). However, games also tell stories through genre, style, images and animation, and music. The most important sites for storytelling in a game lie in a given game's game goals, player actions and the model of the universe this framework represents. From narratives in the most abstract games (Go, Chess) to the character positioning in PC games like *Papers, Please* (2012), the spatial storytelling in games like *Gone Home* (2013) and the social experience in board games like *Monarch* (2015), games tell their stories in many different ways: by their very mechanics-based nature, by their context, by their rules and patterns, and ultimately by us, the players. What is and is not possible in the rule system communicates what is valued and what is important; stories can be generated by rewards, player interaction and play aesthetics, depending on platform, advertising and target audience. Games create meaning through the models they express, and the logic of the game universe. Thus, game stories are the result of a constellation of intersecting points from all of these ingredients at play, realized ultimately in the player's own mind – right alongside the unquantifiable experiences and beliefs and situations that are preloaded, instilled or built up by the cultures and customs which form the respective context for each and every player.

Such transformational games use specific techniques ranging from the embedded design approach to attitude and behavior change. These techniques are not at first obvious, but are based on years of research into games concerning impact and bring to light notions that game stories are themselves kinds of mechanics, just as game mechanics lend themselves to certain kinds of game stories.

OBFUSCATION

Games can tackle very difficult topics, but the one thing they can't do is tell a player what to do and how to think. That is inherently anti-play and cannot work in a game structure in which players voluntarily enter into the space. Take as an example a game design project from my research lab that was specifically aimed at promoting "bystander intervention" in situations of potential sexual assault at college. The US has grave statistics about sexual assault on college campuses, with one in five college women and one in sixteen college men reporting assaults. With such a crisis, it is critical to shift mindsets so that students find tools and strategies to keep themselves and their friends safe. Our research partners turned to games as a way to engage the attention of students in order to introduce them to ideas about bystander intervention, an effective set of counter-measures to sexual assault.

A key challenge is that students have typically been lectured on the dangers of sexual assault in earlier schooling and by families, and "tune out" college workshops on the topic. Many students therefore display *psychological reactance* to such ideas: where certain types of messages or topics meet resistance. Dillard and Shen (2005) found that public health programs promoting teeth flossing or limiting student drinking produced *reactance*, resulting from a combination of negative cognition and anger, perhaps because such messages undermined feelings of personal freedom or the participants' concept of self and identity. Challenging topics or training programs (such as multicultural training, as studied by Mio and Awakuni (2000)) actually lead to resistance among students. Some programs in fact cause students to hold on to their original beliefs much more strongly. This phenomenon is consistent with the original research in psychological reactance theory (Brehm 1966; Brehm/Brehm 1981). Studies on some sexual assault prevention programs even suggest a boomerang effect, in which the training produced the opposite result and led to poor attitudes towards women (Spikes/Sternadori 2018). Malamuth et al. (2018) note that boomerang effects are produced by an individual counterarguing against the message and even displaying hostility, which shows that among high risk males, sexual assault training interventions may actually do more harm than good. Thus, overt approaches can and do backfire, and require instead a method that aims to de-emphasize the overt message. One of the core principles of embedded design is obfuscation, that is, designing for psychologically powerful player choices that do not at the time appear to be as "on topic" as they truly are. Obfuscation changes the frame or the narrative to decrease psychological reactance to challenging materials.

Our design team decided that in order to subvert psychological reactance, we had to obfuscate any overt message and study this approach to see if it could still be effective given such a highly-charged and important topic. We decided to try two very different game approaches and wanted the games to look nothing like one another so that the messages about bystander intervention, developed across two games, could be tested against each other and possibly work in tandem. The first game we developed, *Ship Happens*, is a single-player interactive comic that tackles bystander intervention through a ridiculous narrative involving a future college student "spring break" holiday trip on alien planets. Our space traveling spring breakers encounter a few strange situations in which they have the option to intervene. The choices offered to players ultimately embolden them to try out bystander intervention in the game. Though it is a point-and-click comic involving funny characters and outlandish space travel, the choices strengthen the idea that the player has agency, and that taking action can have a positive effect, narratively speaking.

Figure 1: A player playing Ship Happens (2017).

Source: Mary Flanagan

The second game developed, *Mindflock*, is a same-room, multi-device mobile trivia game. What this means, is that players play with a team of friends in the same room, but each player is using their own phone. Players answer trivia questions, and each correct answer is a point for the team. At the start of each round, each player gets a bunch of trivia question categories, such as "College Football" "Harry Potter" or "Contemporary Art". Teams shout back and forth amongst themselves to figure out who is going to be the best person to answer each question. If a teammate knows a lot about college football, players drag that question to that person's name, and it will send the question to their phone. Then, after the questions have been moved around, everyone has a very short time to answer the ones they ended up with, so teams have to hope that they sent the right questions to the right people. The teams are competing over the internet, so whichever team has more points at the end wins. Here, the trivia game obfuscates its intent (it is pitched as a team-building exercise), and it also uses "intermixed" content. More on this theme will follow.

Figure 2: A group of players engaged with Mindflock (2016).

Source: Mary Flanagan

Thus *Mindflock* appears to be nothing more than a team-based trivia game, but it is working to encourage eventual bystander intervention. Our longitudinal study on these two games aimed at first-year male college students took place over month. The research team was happy to find evidence that through time the games continued to shift thinking towards bystander intervention, even though it was not obvious to the players that the games were doing so (Potter et al. 2018).

Longitudinal studies are notoriously difficult to fund and run in any subfield, and attrition in these types of studies is a very real challenge across the social sciences. Yet the effort was incredibly valuable, for our findings show that well-designed yet not obvious messages embedded into each of the games, in very different ways, have the power to shift beliefs and attitudes. In this case, the game story may lead to real-world intervention, as first-year male college students reported that they are more likely to intervene in instances of potential sexual assault after playing the game.

Therefore, a game designer taking a responsible role in designing for a game's impact needs to take into account that their approach could cause unexpected reactions, or even harm. In fact, a word of caution: while it is true that messages are a part of a game's story, messages that a designer thinks are in the game may actually not be there, or may not be read/experienced as intended. This is why research is an important component of understanding how game mechanics gel into narratives themselves. Framing the game narrative or choices away from the game's true purpose can reduce unintended consequences and counterintuitively increase its impact.

INTERMIXING

The principle of intermixing involves using both relevant and irrelevant content in the game so that the blend of content does not reveal the intentions of the game (Flanagan/Kaufman, 2016; Kaufman & Flanagan, 2015). Intermixing is close in its approach to creating a research survey that contains distractor questions, or "cover stories", so that participants in the research are not led to answering in a certain way, are less aware of the study's purpose and do not become biased. Examples of intermixing includes trivia questions that are on- and off-topic, choices that mix "just for fun" with more related choices, and other ways that a message can be present but "mixed in" to feel "natural". Part of the reason intermixing is effective is that the over-representation of on-topic content can trigger reactance or have unintended consequences.

Mindflock, mentioned above, addresses this problem by containing trivia questions that increase players' likelihood to intervene in cases of sexual assault. We used particular strategies to develop the content of this game that could have the potential to change players' likelihood of intervening. As we wrote questions, we looked at setting positive norms, teaching intervention methods, increasing risk of not intervening, fostering anti-rape culture role models, minimizing perceived embarrassment and humanizing bystanders. Taken together, these various approaches were mixed together with random trivia questions. In fact, these "just for fun" questions constituted less than half of all of the questions and therefore did not cause reactance.

To take another example, in a study we conducted about role models and representation, we found that "overdoing it" with counter-stereotypical role models can backfire. We tested the representation of characters in a science game, where we created one version that featured six female and two male scientists, while the second version was balanced, including equal numbers of male and female scientists. We tested the game on girls to see if more role models would be more effective in encouraging them to pursue science careers. Even though girls were exposed to more female role models in the imbalanced condition, these role models had virtually no effect on girls' inclination to see themselves pursuing computer science as a career. Perhaps counterintuitively, the female-dominated version was harder for female players to identify with. Reasons could be that an overabundance of female scientists was simply unbelievable and could have reduced perceptions of attainability of career goals. This condition could also have made players see the gap between role models and the self (i.e. "I'm not like them"). Ultimately, being less subtle was also less effective than a balanced representation of male and female scientists.

ACTIVATING FANTASY

Imagine two different scenarios: You are watching a documentary film about a mountain community across the world from where you live. The film shows stunning, unfamiliar scenery but you quickly learn of political turmoil in the area. You become very wrapped up in the emotional plight of one particular family as they struggle. You see the circumstances of unfairness that led to this family losing their farm. Now they have no food. The mother of three has resorted to begging on the street. There is a small girl in particular who needs warmer clothes and could really use help. From deep in your heart you want to reach out ... Now imagine you are watching a program after coming home from work. This show is about a homeless family who live in your city. You hear how they lost their house due to job loss in the economic downturn. Now they can't afford food. The youngest daughter needs better clothes to go to school. The mother of three small children spends her days asking people for money as they pass, going off to their jobs. In fact, now that you look at the image of the mother and where she sits, you realize that you walk near that spot every day on your way to work.

Which story pulls the heartstrings more? These two scenarios invoke ideas of *psychological distance*. This is a phenomenon where places, ideas and people that aren't present in our direct experience of reality are interpreted differently to things that are present in our daily environment. In short, something "far away" engages the imagination and makes us less likely to judge. Things can be distant through time ("once upon a time"), space (on a planet far far away or across the world) or by relation (strangers). Researchers have found that because we simply know less about the distant past and distant future, and because we know less about more remote places that might be difficult to imagine, this lack of knowledge means that our minds must represent these phenomena more abstractly and fill in the blanks. Distant entities in time, space or familiarity are just more abstract to us. This abstraction can be useful: employing psychological distance, for example, can help improve decision-making. Distance, after all, helps us to see "the big picture". Liberman, Trope and Stephan (2007) have shown that temporal distance (thinking about the future, thinking about the past), spatial distance (remote locations), social distance (working from someone else's perspective) and hypothetical distance (counterfactual claims and alternative endings) are all ways of traversing psychological distance. Psychological distance encourages us to use the strategic mind, the part of the mind that slows down, thinks hard and chugs through details as we reflect.

The notion of psychological distance is useful in embedded design to actually help players connect with difficult topics. It may seem counterintuitive, but shifting into a fantasy setting in order to address a real-world problem can allow players to feel more open to the message or the "moral of the story". In order to address bias in scientific fields and in academic programs, for example, we thought repositioning women's struggles in science would possibly be more engaging and cause players to invest if the scenario were psychologically distanced.

In one of my laboratory's research projects, we sought to understand whether or not a game could increase self-confidence in women scientists. In our digital point-and-click adventure puzzle game entitled The Enchanter, our team employed our embedded design strategies to help female scientists reposition the biases they faced and restructure the lingering sense of self-doubt they reported feeling. To play the game, players take on the role of Gertie who has been named the head alchemist, but on her way to the research lab, she encounters bias and discrimination. For example, an authority figure will not let her enter the lab because he is expecting the head alchemist to be a man – not a woman. The (unreliable) narrator undermines Gertie by casting doubt on her abilities. To make progress in the game, players must learn to fight back against these doubting voices on Gertie's behalf and not give in to negative self-talk (e.g. "maybe they are right and I'm not smart enough).

In our study, we looked longitudinally at the effectiveness of *The Enchanter* on women's attitudes, and in particular, on women's self-doubt as it relates to academic achievement and science. Women college students studying science were involved in a two-week study wherein participants came into the lab to play the game at the beginning of the research period, in the middle and at the end of the study, answering questions along the way. The research results showed that playing just one session of *The Enchanter* game decreased self-doubt immediately and that players maintained this feeling for at least a week after playing the game. Thus, the game became the framework through which the young women scientists could silence negative thoughts and focus on overcoming obstacles by externalizing "negative self-talk". *The Enchanter* offered provocative results: they suggest that people who are the victims of bias, such as women in science, can be able to overcome real-world effects of biases (like self-doubt) by fighting against negative self-talk, something that can be practiced in a computer game.

SUMMARY

The three approaches to the embedded design concept presented in this essay show how, from a psychological standpoint, narrative mechanics can operate around difficult topics. Obfuscating, that is changing the frame or the narrative to lower psychological reactance to challenging materials; intermixing, or using relevant and non-relevant content in a game; and psychological distancing, using some kind of distance, including employing the power of fiction, to increase engagement in the game. These techniques can increase what is effective and possible with narrative mechanics.

In closing, I wanted to contextualize the attention to psychology in this essay. By discussing these science-backed approaches, I am not arguing that everything humans produce needs to be quantified and measured. But designers don't always understand the role our games can play out in the world. The Gamez and Rulez conference was filled with astute talks and inspiring projects, and I am honored to be among people who are really digging into what "story" means in games, and how game mechanics, informed by psychology, not only determine what the player can and cannot do within the environment, but what it means and how they feel about it from a psychological perspective. The psychological impact of narrative mechanics, goals and player choice, more than anything else, determines what kind of stories the player will experience.

I have offered some ideas about embedded design approaches and discussed experiments that reveal that games can work to engineer social change. While games are no panacea to the world's problems, game designers can create "microsolutions" to some of these challenges. I have shown that one can use techniques from embedded design to hopefully boost measurable impact as narrative mechanics increasingly become concrete in the analog world. I hope this essay inspires you to push the connections among traditionally disparate disciplines – philosophy, social science, design, play and more – as you seek to understand and craft games that change the story and make sure the best game stories become real.

HOW CAN GAME DESIGNERS BETTER UTILIZE NARRATIVE MECHANICS?

Some practical tips

Do: Know that messages in games don't have to be directly on-topic to be effective.
Don't: Be heavy-handed with your message.
Do: Use the ideas in embedded design: obfuscating, intermixing and psychological distance to name a few, to your advantage, just like artistic techniques such as metaphors and symbols.
Don't: Avoid the responsibility of understanding what your game is doing.
Do: Use fiction to your advantage. Fiction can be powerful.
Don't: Think games have to "tell the truth" about a social issue, acting like a documentary film.
Do: Get players hooked before you delve into difficult subjects, delay the reveal of any particular perspective or "agenda". Remember that all games have messages and carry cultural values, whether the designer intends them or not.
Don't: Think fun and serious issues can't go together.
Do: Work with researchers to run experiments if you really want to know in what ways your game is changing the story.
Don't: Think researchers or game players won't be interested. They will be!

REFERENCES

Literature

Brehm, J. W. (1966): A theory of psychological reactance, New York, New York: Academic Press.

Brehm, S. S./Brehm, J. W. (1981): Psychological reactance: A theory of freedom and control, Orlando: Academic Press.

Dillard, James Price/Shen, Lijiang (2005): "On the nature of reactance and its role in persuasive health communication." In: Communication Monographs 72/2, pp. 144-168.

Flanagan, Mary (2009): Critical Play, Cambridge, Massachusetts: The MIT Press.

Flanagan, Mary/Nissenbaum, Helen (2014): Values at play in digital games, Cambridge: The MIT Press.

Flanagan, Mary/Kaufman, Geoff (2016): "Shifting implicit biases with games using psychology: The embedded design approach." In: Yasmin Kafai/ Gabriella Coleman/Brendesha Tynes (eds.), Diversifying Barbie and Mortal Kombat: Intersectional Perspectives and Inclusive Designs in Gaming, Pittsburgh: CMU/ETC Press.

Freedman, Gili/Seidman, Max/Flanagan, Mary/Kaufman, Geoff/Green, Melanie C. (2018): "The impact of an 'aha' moment on gender biases: Limited evidence for the efficacy of a game intervention that challenges gender assumptions." In: Journal of Experimental Social Psychology 78, pp. 162-167 (https://doi.org/10.1016/j.jesp.2018.03.014).

Kaufman, Geoff/Flanagan, Mary (2015): "A psychologically 'embedded' approach to designing games for prosocial causes." Cyberpsychology: Journal of Psychosocial Research on Cyberspace 9/3 (http://doi.org/10.5817/CP 2015-3-5).

Kaufman, Geoff/Flanagan, Mary/Seidman, Max (2015): "Creating stealth game interventions for attitude and behavior change: An 'embedded design' model." In: Proceedings of DiGRA 2015.

Kaufman, Geoff/Flanagan, Mary (2016): "Playing the system: Comparing the efficacy and impact of digital and non-digital versions of a collaborative strategy game." In: Proceedings of the First International Joint Conference of DiGRA and FDG 1/13.

Liberman, Nira/Trope, Yacov/Stephan, Elena (2007): "Psychological distance." In: Arie W. Kruglanski/E. Tory Higgins (eds.), Social psychology: Handbook of basic principles 2, New York: Guilford Press, pp. 353-383.

Malamuth, Neil M./Huppin, Mark/Linz, Daniel (2018): "Sexual assault interventions may be doing more harm than good with high-risk males." In: Aggression and Violent Behavior 41, pp. 20-24 (https://doi.org/10.1016/j.avb.2018.05.010).

Mio, Jeffery Scott/Awakuni, Gene I. (2000): Resistance to multiculturalism: Issues and interventions, Philadelphia: Brunner/Mazel.

Potter, Sharyn J./Flanagan, Mary/Seidman, Max/Hodges, Hannah/Stapleton, Jane (2019): "Developing and Piloting Video Games to Increase College and University Students' Awareness and Efficacy of the Bystander Role in Incidents of Sexual Violence." In: Games for Health Journal (doi: 10.1089/g4h.2017.0172).

Spikes, Caitlin/Sternadori, Miglena (2018): "Boomerang Effects of Sexual-Violence Prevention Messages on College Men's Attitudes." In: Building Healthy Academic Communities Journal 2/2.

Trope, Yacov/Liberman, Nira (2010): "Construal-level theory of psychological distance." In: Psychological Review 117/2, pp. 440-463 (http://doi.org/10.1037/a0018963).

Ball Games and Language Games

On Wittgenstein, Football Fan Culture and Pop Culture

Martin Lindner

> Doesn't the analogy between language and games throw light here? We can easily imagine people amusing themselves in a field by playing with a ball so as to start various existing games, but playing many without finishing them and in between throwing the ball aimlessly into the air, chasing one another with the ball and bombarding one another for a joke and so on. And now someone says: The whole time they are playing a ball-game and following definite rules at every throw.
>
> And is there not also the case where we play and—make up the rules as we go along? And there is even one where we alter them—as we go along.
>
> (Wittgenstein, *Philosophical Investigations* 1958, No. 83)

It is probably no coincidence that it was in Great Britain in the late 1920s that Wittgenstein found his model of the "language game" – according to an occasional legend, inspired by a 'wild' football game in a park.[1]

---

1 This is almost certainly just an anecdote. What is certain is that the metaphor "game" appears for the first time in a very abstract form, when Wittgenstein moves from a view of language as a mechanical "calculus" (metaphor chess) to a view of language

Wittgenstein used his metaphor to refer to the rules by which people played on the grass: how exact or blurred they were, how children learn such games, namely by doing and imitating rather than studying the set of rules, and to what extent such rules become apparent to the observer while they watch the seemingly chaotic processes. The parallel game played by the fans in the stands, which has become increasingly dense and complex (in its semiotics) over the course of now more than hundred years of football, can be viewed in much the same way.

The wider game, which is not limited to the 22 players, consists of at least four levels: the clear demarcation lines (sections of the pitch, hand play, clear foul play), the blurred demarcation lines (offside, unclear fouls), the patterns effective in the game (the characteristic play of individual teams and players), the patterns projected from outside (e.g. fight and discipline as "German virtues", self-sacrificing British "kick and rush", Brazilian "samba", etc.) ... and finally the semiotic games of the fans in the stands, which are necessarily related to the football game as a reference, but largely develop their own internal logic and dynamics.

This fan culture is no atavism, even if it is reminiscent of old village rivalries. Evidently, there is some kind of border that divides a homogeneous space into two parts and subsequently is charged with meaning. This usually happens not because there is a particular conflict, but because of a basic drive in people or the socio-cultural system to create meaning where there was none before.[2] In

---

as a "game" with fuzzy rules (metaphor ball game; cf. *The Big Typescript*, section 47, published in 1933). For this purpose, "ball games" are then actually used in the philosophical investigations and compared with the game of chess (paragraphs 66 and 83). There is a – of course British – Wittgenstein sweatshirt, which adapts the famous text of paragraph 83 specifically to the world of football: "Imagine people playing football, kicking the ball in the air, chasing, fouling each other ... "

2   The rival clubs West Ham United and Tottenham Hotspur are based in two close quarters in traditionally proletarian North-East and East London. The Munich clubs FC Bayern München and 1860 München share one of the most semiotically fertile 'enmities', and they even originate from the same neighborhood: Giesing was a so-called "shattered glass quarter" [a socially deprived area] of Munich. In this sense, according to a favorite saying by Franz Beckenbauer, "Obergiesing vs. Untergiesing" was actually played here. In the process, an opposition was formed between the proletarian 1860 ("Untergiesing", so to speak), and the rising FC Bayern (quasi "Obergiesing") personified by the 'football Kaiser' Beckenbauer himself, who came from the most modest of Giesing backgrounds. Interesting from a semiotic perspective, by the way, is that 'proletarian' 1860 seems to have been far more susceptible to National Social-

20th century Europe, this old game of demarcation is particularly associated with football, the new game of the working class and urban mass culture. The elaborate fan culture itself, with its associated semiotic games, probably did not emerge until after Wittgenstein's death: parallel to the triumphant advance of the new medium of television over the course of the 1960s.

The semiotic games that now proliferate around the game of football have a thoroughly contradictory relationship to media. In a certain sense, they are the exact opposite, because they insist on the almost caricature-like 'tangible' reference, something that is more and more lost in the age of media: it is all about a round ball, a game that lasts 90 minutes, and the tangible, sweaty bodies of the players, who have to deliver "honest work". Even if the true fans are not primarily concerned about winning, as the motto of *www.topspurs.com*, the fansite of Tottenham Hotspur F.C., states[3], competition still remains a necessary condition for the semiotic games of the fans. The fans present themselves in opposite ends of the stadium as a uniformly dressed "block", singing and waving flags. In the peculiar, self-contained space of the football stadium, their actions function as unmediated physical acts in a way that is otherwise hardly possible in contemporary culture. No one actually needs radio or television on site. Their place is taken by the stadium, as it were, the "medium" of urban "mass" culture. (This has changed with the technical innovation of the digital scoreboard that shows slow motion and, not least, the audience itself.)

Nevertheless, the semiotic games of the football fans are no longer comparable to medieval spectacles such as the *Paglio* in Siena, where participants wear the colors of their respective neighborhoods. Especially in football, the game of the modern urban "masses", they are determined to a considerable extent by the media. And not only because the fans perceive and reflect their own chants and visual patterns on the radio and television as a work of art. The new British fan culture did not emerge until the new media culture brought about the disintegration of the old social milieus and with them the neighborhood cultures which, up to that point, had provided quasi "organic" semiotic material. Thus, the need for new boundaries arose. And at the same time, the free-floating semiotic game ma-

ism and anti-Semitism than FC Bayern, which has always been considered 'snotty'. (cf. Fischer/Lindner/Marschik 2000)

3 The TOPSPURS philosophy: "The great fallacy is that the game is first and last about winning. It's nothing of the kind. The game is about glory. It's about doing things in style, with a flourish, about going out and beating the other lot, not waiting for them to die of boredom." Danny Blanchflower (TopSpurs Website, 2003/2020).

terial that was available to fans hungry for signs and meaning grew exponentially through the media.

Football fan culture developed parallel to pop culture, which is also a media-affiliated disintegration product of the old urban milieus. Nick Hornby in his popular novel *Fever Pitch* (1992) was not the first to draw attention to the striking closeness that connects the two subcultures. Both are expressions of an uninhibited semiotic game that serves to generate new vital energies out of nothing, semanticizing and involving the body, the traditional bearer of the most primary reference, in a complex way.

Indeed, the pop-oriented youth subcultures, which in turn emerged for the first time in Great Britain in the 1950s, knew not only the tension between performers and audiences, but also that between competing groups with their own sign systems: around 1964, the legendary street battles between "Mods" (soulfans in suits) and "Rockers" (rock'n'roll fans) took place, which were later repeated by Teds vs. Punks and then Punks vs. Skinheads. Also in the mid-1960s, new British TV comedy was born. Without inhibitions, respect or good taste, it ripped every sign out of its context and subjected it to grotesque games. [4] At the very beginning, there was the now legendary series *Till Death Us Do Part* with Warren Mitchell as the fascistically inclined East-End tory "Alf Garnett". It was first aired between 1966 and 1969 to great success, and also played an important role in connection with the "Yids" from Tottenham[5].

At the end of the 1960s, Great Britain was the experimental semiotic laboratory of European media culture, where the game of language and signs intensified considerably. It included traditional "heavy signs" (Baudrillard): On the one hand, the violent subculture of skinheads emerged, which, against the media trend of devaluing all signs, brought the "proletarian" body into play as a pseudo-primary reference and thus an anti-sign. While that group incorporated the British Union Jack into its newly constructed pop-chauvinism, the heavy signs of National Socialism appeared elsewhere in strange contexts: The British glam-

---

4   These include the "German/Nazi" jokes of Harry Enfield and ex-Monty Python John Cleese (*Fawlty Towers*) or, more recently, the politically extremely incorrect jokes of Sacha Baron Cohen (alias "Ali G.").

5   The word "yid" and its related term "yiddo" refer to the supporters and players of Tottenham Hotspur. Originally, they were used in a derogatory manner by rival fans, but the Tottenham fans started using them as a self-designation in a non-pejorative sense.

rock proles[6] of The Sweet, who had numerous singles in the charts between 1971 and 1977, combined camp make-up and high heels with swastika bandages. One of the alter egos of David Bowie (besides Ziggy Stardust and many others) was the "Blond Fuehrer" around the same time. And the demonstratively 'degenerate' and 'sick' Sex Pistols, who also integrated the swastika into their deliberately chaotic mix of signs, recorded a punk song in 1976 entitled "Belsen Was A Gas" – a song that referenced the Nazi concentration camp Bergen-Belsen but refused to convey any particular message.[7] For the glam rockers and punks, the reference to Nazis and anti-Semitism worked as a provocative game with seemingly empty signs. Nevertheless, it was and is dependent on the remnants of the old heavy connotations and references that still stick to it. It is only because there were bodies, millions of dead bodies, that these extreme signs still work in a totally mediatized media culture in which there can no longer exist a foreign body.

Since the end of the punk cultural revolution, i.e. since 1978 at the latest, the postmodern findings of Bowie and Baudrillard have become everyday experience. The semiotic game that commercial pop stars such as Madonna continue, has become the domain of advertising. The profusely circulating signs no longer refer to anything 'real', but through them alone, no taboo can be broken or bourgeois parents shocked. There is no longer any policy that is not media policy, and there is now in Europe, too, no clear social order that is impressed upon the individual. Since then, young TV generations have been zapping from sign to sign. Their members are basically able to deal with signs just as freely and ironically/cynically as advertising is now doing more and more radically – something that was previously the prerogative of the artistic avant-gardes (Dada, Surrealists, Situationists).

One could interpret this as meaning that we are now finally freed from the shackles of reference to enter a more humane, postmodern age under the sign of

---

6 Characteristic of the British delight in playing with signs, strange conversions were apparently possible without any problems. Slade, another very popular teenybopper-glam-rock band, around 1970 had still appeared as first-generation skinheads. On the cover of their first record, re-released in 1976 under the title „Whatever Happened To Slade", they pose in full-on glam outfits and smile at photos in the background showing them as skinheads.

7 "Belsen was a gas I heard the other day
In the open graves where the jews all lay
Life is fun and I wish you were here
They wrote on postcards to those held dear
oh dear oh dear oh dear." (Sex Pistols 1976)

play. This is what the German buzzword of "Spaßkultur" ("the culture of fun") ultimately meant: an eternal children's birthday party that dissolves the boundaries between entertainment, advertising, consumption and 'real life'. But in contrast to Baudrillard's use of words, there are no "empty signs". Postmodern media culture does not escape the basic law that every sign must have two sides so that semiotic and social energy can flow between these poles. Not only does the empty body always seek out new signs and meanings – the apparently empty signs of media culture also soak up physical-material reality time and time again.

In media culture especially, the specter of reference cannot be banished, as pop theorist Diedrich Diederichsen states using the example of the disintegrating punk subculture, which was finally dragged down by the burden of the originally anarchically empty signs that "became increasingly laden with meaning and interpretation" over the course of their use. The end result was the undead caricature of "punk", the sincere and rebellious beer punk with the leather jacket and the spiky hair, who shows "the system" their middle finger (Diederichsen 1983: 174). It was the very experience of the semiotic catastrophe brought about by the media and marked by punk in 1976/77 that led to a reactionary return to the body, to the "roots", to authenticity. But these primary experiences, in turn, had to be conjured up through secondary games of signs and symbols. Consequently, people from punk circles revived the proletarian cult style of the skinhead, which had been extinct since about 1974: "Just like the exis [Existentialist youth movement in 1950s Hamburg], the skins need the heavy signs: The fascistic [...] is almost only a coincidence of this discourse [...]. The skin is the hard nut, and it does not matter with what content he fills the sign." (Diederichsen 1983: 173) A casual remark by Dick Hebdige fits in very well here: he reminds us that the skinheads of the first generation already imitated the tone of "Alf Garnett", the contemporary TV caricature of the narrow-minded working class chauvinist from the East End (Hebdige 1983: 93).

This text was originally published in the German language as part of the essay "Sem und Antisem. Sekundärer Antisemitismus als Zeichen- und Sprachspiel in der Neuen Medien-Kultur." in: Frank, Gustav und Wolfgang Lukas (hgg.) (2004): Norm + Grenze + Abweichung. Kultursemiotische Studien zu Literatur, Medien und Wirtschaft. Michael Titzmann zum 60. Geburtstag. Passau: Verlag Karl Stutz, pp. 321-356.

REFERENCES

Literature

Diederichsen, Diedrich (1983): "Die Auflösung der Welt – Vom Ende und An-
fang." In: Diedrichsen, Diedrich/Dick Hebdige/Olaph-Dante Marx (eds.),
Schocker. Stile und Moden der Subkultur, Reinbek bei Hamburg, pp. 166–
188.

Fischer, Gerhard/Lindner, Ulrich/Marschik, Matthias (2000): "Stürmer für Hit-
ler. Vom Zusammenspiel zwischen Fußball und Nationalsozialismus." In:
German Journal of Exercise and Sport Research 30, München, pp. 228–231.

Hebdige, Dick (1983): "Die Bedeutung von Stil". In: Diedrichsen, Diedrich/Dick
Hebdige/Olaph-Dante Marx (eds.), Schocker. Stile und Moden der Subkultur, Reinbek bei Hamburg, pp. 87–96.

Hornby, Nick (1992): Fever Pitch, London: Gollancz.

Sex Pistols (1979 [1976]): "Belsen Was a Gas." In: The Great Rock'n'Roll
Swindle, Soundtrack Album, London: Virgin Records, track 10 and 11.

Wittgenstein, Ludwig (1958 [1953]): Philosophical Investigations. Translated by G.E.M. Anscombe, Oxford: Basil Blackwell.

Wittgenstein, Ludwig (2005 [1933]): The Big Typescript. TS 213. Malden Massachusetts, Oxford, Carlton: Blackwell Publishing.

Case Studies

Florence

A Playful Narrative Experience That Lingers in Your Heart and Mind

Mela Kocher

About a year ago, I played *Florence* for the first time, and it deeply impressed me – not only because of its delicate sound design, the effectively reduced, carefully colored visuals (stills and very few animations), or the humble, almost sober story. First and foremost, *Florence* impressed me by the unique way in which game mechanics are applied for storytelling purposes: its game mechanics are, in every detail, narrative mechanics, serving the purpose of the story.

Florence is not a game as such, even though you still play it in some way. Game-wise, the player is, throughout the 20 chapters, confronted with a set of mini-games, many of which consist of visual puzzles or click-based actions. But those mini-games are not fun to play, in other words, you would not play them for entertainment purposes.

Florence is, in a certain sense, an interactive story. Yet, it is not one of those interactive stories or cybertexts that let the player choose between different paths and experience the same story from different perspectives. There is just one story – the life of a young woman named Florence and her first love relationship with Krish, a young musician. The reader cannot alter or influence the story, nor can they choose the perspective. Functionally and aesthetically, *Florence* resembles a comic in which the reader scrolls down or right, depending on the chapter. Sometimes one can interact within the frames, sometimes it is only possible to observe. But seeing *Florence* as partly storytelling, partly mini-games, does not explain its fascination.

FEEL – NOT TELL, SHOW OR PLAY

Florence is, as a story-*telling* piece, situated somewhere in the matrix of "show & play". "Show, don't tell" being a rule for drama writing, to make the plot more lively by showing/acting, not narrating it. Applying this strategy to the designing of stories for games, the new guideline proposes "Play, don't show", as a way to play around with narrative scenarios, to interact and to influence the plot (Fine 2011).

It skillfully *shows*, in six acts, a piece of Florence's life centered around the love story. It allows the player to *play* some parts of that life, lets them assist Florence eating sushi, drawing a painting, communicating with her mom, meeting Krish. None of them are extraordinary things per se. It is the specific framing inside the narrative setting which expands the "tell – show – play" line into the *feel* range. The player is not just told or shown the story, nor can they really play it. Instead, they are allowed to *feel* it: feel the essence of the story, feel empathy with the characters, the lightness and anxiety of falling in love, the sadness and anger when falling out of love, and, at last, to feel the sweet, distant memory of the first love, while life goes on with new perspectives, when Florence finally realizes her dreams on her own.

INTERTWINED GAME AND STORY

In its way of using game mechanics as narrative mechanics, *Florence* is as unique as the well-known *The Secret of Monkey Island* (1990) – which conveyed, in a humorous manner, the mechanics of sword fighting as a sparring match with words. Close to it comes *Heavy Rain*, an action-adventure game with a certain micro mechanic. In some narratively meaningful sequences, for example when trying to help a drowning child, the player rapidly has to push certain controller buttons displayed on the screen. This challenging game task results in a stressful feeling, especially since the player will often not succeed, which has consequences for the subsequent story. Therefore, the stressful feeling the player gets from playing – from engaging with the game mechanics – matches the narrative feeling the story wants to convey. This works well in *Heavy Rain*, even though the represented actions (pressing matching symbols on the screen with the game controller) that the players need to execute, have no connection to the content of the story.

The mechanics of pushing depicted buttons in a certain sequence has been used in other games, of course, such as *Fahrenheit*. Mostly it is not embedded cleverly in the narrative scenes. In *Fahrenheit*, you have to push buttons to help a character climb a wall – there, the stressful player activity does not match the narrative, thus leaving the player strung out; this effect is heightened as this mini-game appears too often and is hard to master.

This narrative functionality of game mechanics is brought to a whole new level in *Florence*, where everything the player does in *play* has a meaning in terms of what is being *told* and *shown*.

NARRATIVE MECHANICS OFFER DIFFERENT ROLES

Since this is an interactive and playful piece, the reader/player does not just scroll and look, but participate, sometimes even against their will. This playful narrative experience comes with a variety of roles – that of spectator (even voyeur), observant participant, conspirator, helper, destructor. These roles change during the progression of the story.

Florence is divided into six acts (and 20 chapters), which mostly relate to the Shakespearian five-act structure (*exposition, rising action, climax, falling action, resolution*) (cf. King 2004), with Acts 3 and 4 falling in the *climax* category. According to these six acts, the mini-games proceed and the game mechanics change or assume new narrative meanings. They all work, with a few exceptions, with one button or, respectively, one touch (being an iOS and Android game). At the beginning, the player starts with Act 1, Chapter 1. After having read and played it through, the next chapter unfolds for the player, and so on. In the following section, the main mechanics and their narrative function will be explained.

"SIMULATION" OF THE ORDINARY MECHANIC

The exposition of the first act focuses on the everyday life of Florence. The player has to carry out a set of ordinary activities to get to the next chapter: Put sushi in Florence's mouth. Wiggle her toothbrush back and forth. Choose Florence's evasive answers in awkward phone conversations with her mother. Like the social media posts of her friends. The gaming activities all seem quite dull, simulating Florence's everyday, uninspired life, and the monochrome colors (white, gray/black) and sound design support that message. The first time that color (in the visual, and also the narrative sense) pops up, is in the second chapter "Memories", when Florence remembers how she loved to draw in as a child, and the player gets to color a butterfly painting.

A few chapters later (in "Dreams"), Florence finds that very drawing in an old memory box in her storage closet, and her wish to apply her artistic skills returns – a key element in her personal development. It is brought about through a small detail, but makes the story coherent, and emphasizes the agency of the player: her or his actions matter.

PUZZLE MECHANIC

Figure 1: To begin with, it takes a while to get the conversation going for Florence (left). Later, during their argument, the puzzle pieces become angular and fast-paced (right).

Source: screenshots (Kocher)

In the second act, after Florence has met Krish – drawn to him by his spherical cello playing on the street – the player becomes Florence's collaborator in helping her get closer to him through conversation (Chapter 5, "First Dates"). This is cleverly done through a very simple gameplay: In comic-style animation, Krish's speech bubbles appear fast. Florence's bubbles have to be put together first. At the beginning, her conversation bubble consists of eight puzzle pieces which the player needs to drag and drop into the speech bubble. Therefore, it takes a while until Florence can respond to Krish. Soon, the puzzle pieces become fewer, and their conversation flows more smoothly. Florence and Kish move closer to each other, and when there is only one piece to put into her speech bubble, they kiss.

In Act 4, Chapter 9 ("Groceries"), the couple fight for the first time. The puzzle pieces change shape now. The connecting shapes are still round at first, but become angular as the conversation turns into an argument. The conflict is also visible in the screen design: Krish and Florence do not fit on the same screen anymore, but the player has to scroll a little sideways, to get from one to the other. The dynamic of the conversation also changes: it is not really turn-based anymore as Krish's bubbles become faster. He does not wait for (or listen to) what Florence says, and leans forward, while she leans back at every bubble emerging from him. The player cannot help Florence fast enough with her conversation anymore.

In Act 5, Chapter 14 ("Fight"), the couple fights again, this time in a much fiercer manner. This is visible at the level of the game mechanics: there seems no end to the angular puzzle pieces the player has to put together. While the color of the puzzle pieces – during the couple's first argument – used to be bright turquoise and pink, they are all red now. And, to bring the puzzle mechanic to a new level, the following chapter presents a picture of the couple sleeping in bed at night, facing away from each other, both disassembled into puzzle pieces. The player can only put each person together as a whole, but there are no connecting pieces that match. The couple cannot be made whole again.

And in the last act, after their breakup, in Chapter 17 ("Fragments"), Krish has to literally be removed from the picture, puzzle piece by piece. At the end, just Florence is left in the picture, looking at an empty spot next to her.

RUB MECHANIC

Rubbing a spot on the screen is used several times during the game, in order to literally and figuratively bring something to the surface. For example, the player has to rub a gray picture, and the underlying dream of Krish becoming a famous musician, or of Florence becoming a joyous artist, are then visible in full color. Alternately, in other mini-games, the player rubbing on the screen represents the waving of polaroid photos. Waving makes the photos become colorful and sharp; in doing so, the player discovers the activities the young couple has been enjoying, such as skating, hiking or going to art galleries.

The rubbing goes both ways, from reality to dreams, and back to reality: In Act 5, Chapter 13 ("Erosion"), the player has to rub on a picture of Krish proudly playing the cello, where everything glows in bright yellow. Gradually, reality's surface is exposed, toned in gray as Krish plays with hanging shoulders.

TURN THE WHEEL OF TIME MECHANIC

In the "Erosion" chapter, the player has to turn the minute hand of a clock to fast-forward through the relationship of Florence and Krish. This makes it possible to observe how each of them will behave in the next months: from hugging each other and standing close, to her looking at her smartphone and him eating a sandwich, closing his eyes. By turning the wheel of time with the focus on Florence's desk, the player discovers that the watercolors which Krish gave to Florence as a gift are now buried under a pile of papers.

IDLE MECHANIC

Probably the most difficult interactive game task in *Florence* is presented in the last act, Chapter 18 ("Let Go"). Florence and Krish are walking. He then lags behind more and more, his silhouette slowly fading out. When the player taps Krish, Florence stops until Krish is catches up, his outline being black and clear again. The two of them keep walking, and again, Krish is falling back. The chapter does not close until the player remains idle and lets Krish fall back forever, out of Florence's life. This mechanic shows how difficult it can be to let go, and how tempting – yet futile – it sometimes is to hold on. Also, it forces the agency of the player – now taking an active part in their breakup.

CONCLUSION

The game mechanics of *Florence* do not create an exciting gameplay at all. On the contrary, they are repetitive, do not challenge the player, and are simple and short. Nevertheless, the way they work as a narrative driver is unique: the literal actions that the player has to carry out match exactly what they figuratively represent in the unfolding narrative. Sometimes the same game mechanics, especially in the puzzle mini-games, convey different messages depending on their coloring and sound design, their pace and narrative meaning. In this way, the mechanics also define the changing roles of the player, from helping the couple get closer to playing an active role in ending their relationship. The result is a compelling, close, unforgettable emotional experience that indeed, as the developer's website states, "lingers in hearts and minds" (Mountains 2018).

REFERENCES

Literature

Fine, Richard (2011): "Opinion: Play, don't show." In: Gamasutra. April 11, 2011 (https://www.gamasutra.com/view/news/124172/Opinion_Play_Dont_Show.php).
Mountains (2018): Craft Games Melbourne (http://mountains.studio/).
King, John (2004). "Shakespeare's Five Act Structure." In: No Sweat Shakespeare (https://www.nosweatshakespeare.com/plays/ five-act-structure/).

Games

Fahrenheit, Quantic Dream, Atari, 2005.
Florence, Mountains, Annapurna Interactive, 2018.
Heavy Rain, Quantic Dream, Sony Computer Entertainment, 2010.
The Secret of Monkey Island, Lucasfilm Games, 1990.

The Last Guardian

Narrating through Mechanics and Empathy

Beat Suter

> In my dream I was flying.
> Flying through the darkness …
> I awoke to find myself in a strange cave.
> I noticed with a start that I was not alone.
> Beside me lay a great man-eating beast.
> (*The Last Guardian* 2016)

Thus an older man begins with a deep voice from offstage and tells in retrospect his story, which he experienced as a boy. The poetic beginning is quickly replaced by the presence of the boy and the beast that have to get familiar with each other and find their way in a foreign environment. Together they learn the mechanics of interaction and progress.

The narrative mechanics of the game *The Last Guardian* couldn't be easier at first. A boy and an animal find themselves in a chasm, which looks like a dungeon. The large beast is chained and injured. The boy wakes up from unconsciousness and does not know where he is. It quickly becomes clear that the boy and the animal are in mutual dependence to each other. One cannot move forward without the other.

EMPATHY AND SMALL NARRATIVE INTERPERSONAL INTERACTIONS

It takes time for them to get to know each other and develop mutual support and cooperation. It is a slow approach. The boy tries to win the trust of the animal, which is much more powerful than him. This is the only way he can free the animal from the chain and pull the spears from its wounds. And the boy can get the animal to help him reach the openings in the rocky ruins that hold both creatures captive. But the beast does not always do what the boy wants. It is an idiosyncratic and independent creature. The boy has to listen to it, watch its behavior and be patient. Certain interactions change the beast's behavior, and often the beast indicates where to go. The narrative mechanics of the small interactions between man and beast are the core of the game. This empathetic beginning is formative because the boy embodies the avatar role of the player and every approach and setback is experienced directly by the player.

The critic Mark Brown calls this "design by subtraction" (Brown 2015) – reduced design. This applies not only to the mechanics and the environment, but also to the narrative. The story begins, with as little baggage as possible, in a closed area: a prison. This is what game designer Fumito Ueda had in mind when he did his first sketch for the game with the beast behind prison bars (Ueda 2018). The two characters have to feel their way through this environment and get to know each other and bond. And the player has to learn the mechanics with which the two characters can advance through caves and ruins. The boy brings the animal food in the form of glowing barrels. The animal lets the boy climb on its back and ride, and lifts him up to ledges, which highlights the unusual vertical orientation of the game.

Due to the slow build-up of empathy, the player in the role of the boy is later able to trust and always count on the big beast, Trico. The player knows they can rely on Trico to catch them at the right moment after a jump into the void or to come to the rescue in time when the guards attack and threaten to kill them.

SPATIAL PROGRESS STORY

This empathetic, interactive relationship of mutual dependency, which seems so simple at the beginning, is embedded in a more complex framework of a spatial progress story as well as a very complex backstory that is hinted at by the narrator's persona from offstage, but is only slowly revealed as the game progresses.

The game world and its sequences of rooms are constructed in such a way that closed claustrophobic rooms are replaced by taller ones, until finally an outdoor area is reached that allows you to breathe and marvel. You start in the Cave, a very small-enclosed area that feels like a prison. Then you go forward through the mountain, across slightly larger rooms towards a first small outdoor area. From there you can already see the big tower for the first time, which is the setting for the final events of the game. Next, the game world reverts back into the mountain, across the fallen-statue bridge, through partly cathedral-like rooms in the mountain and out into the second outdoor area, from where you can see up into the sky, but also encounter some fog that limits your view. The journey continues in a spiral movement through the strange world of ruins and rocks called the Nest, which leads upward, becoming higher and higher. The further up you are, the greater the outdoor distances become between the levels you have to cover. And during this part, you will temporarily lose height by falling down or rescuing Trico.

The locomotion takes place as a spiral from bottom to top, through a labyrinthine world with strange ancient equipment. One room after another must be mastered. The boy must climb beneath a high ceiling, balance himself over wooden beams, climb up on ropes and chains, squeeze himself through ledges, and call out to the big animal, Trico. Trico usually finds another way and can jump up onto unreachable walls. Sometimes the boy has to climb on the animal's back or head and hold on while it jumps over spiky rocks or runs over rickety wooden scaffolding to reach the next play area.

As the world is gradually explored, the game gains speed and becomes faster and faster, so that in the end the player is under permanent pressure and therefore has to act a lot quicker.

FLASHBACKS AND BACKSTORY

The backstory is hinted at in the third cutscene, "The First Antenna", with some pictures that remain mysterious for the time being. Seven or more hours of playing will pass before it is explained in the longer cutscene, "Capturing the Boy". Up to this point the player is left in the dark. Only after the boy has fainted again and lies in a delirium in the next antenna room, is his story revealed. But until then. it is the relationship between the two characters and the carefully increasing gameplay that enables immersion and a narrative path. After that the backstory becomes important for the further progression of the game.

Almost at the top of the tower, the player begins to realize that they are in a funnel of ruins or a crater which serves as a nest for big animals. You realize how the crater world (The Valley) is laid out, structured and limited – and that there is probably a world outside. And finally, in the fourth cutscene, it is revealed how the boy and Trico ended up in the cave prison ruin in the first place!

The game has classic, but inconspicuous and cleverly embedded cutscenes – seven in total (Glaser 2017: 254ff.). Two short cutscenes at the beginning (Setting the Scene, Awakening), a disordered delirium cutscene (The First Antenna), and the story of the encounter of the boy and the beast in the Memory Dream (Capturing the Boy). The fifth and longest cutscene in three parts is the live fight scene in the tower (Atop the Tower). In the following sixth cutscene (Saving the Boy) the boy has destroyed the master core of the tower, which now explodes live, whereupon he is rescued by Trico and brought to his village unconscious. The backstory is hinted at in the first and third cutscenes and told in the fourth cutscene. The second, fifth and sixth cutscenes are embedded in the live gameplay. And the seventh and last cutscene (Many Years Later) brings the story to a conclusion with the boy as the grown-up older man – the one that tells the story.

MYSTICAL AND MECHANICAL PREMISES

The backstory is the tribal history of the boy, as well as the story of the enslaved animals, of which Trico is one. Thus, an extraordinary or even alien power or energy is fought in the last third of the game. The two types of creatures became enemies through the action of a technical apparatus or unit located in the tower. This could already be perceived from far below as something apart and clearly different in its technological construction from the rest of the ruins of buildings in this crater world.

CHANGE OF PERSPECTIVE

Anyone who has played the game will inevitably ask the question: which is the main character, the boy or the animal Trico? The answer takes some getting used to: the player only plays the sidekick as the avatar of the boy. The main character is played by an amazing AI – Trico! This change of perspective is deliberately employed by Fumito Ueda, the designer of the game. The boy may partly lead the beast Trico, but at many moments it is Trico who leads and drives the game. Trico probably means "the third Ico" (Brown 2017). The first two were played in Ueda's games, *Ico* and *The Shadow of the Colossus*. So the boy takes the role of the companion, which in the first game, *Ico* (2001), was played by the girl Jorda who was not able to carry out any actions herself. The boy is able to act and give orders but cannot progress alone and does not show signs of character change. By contrast, Trico undergoes a character development, overcomes the fear of the colored glass eyes and in the end is able to fly again. Finally, he saves the boy and brings him back to his village. Trico then takes off alone and flies away into a liberated world. Years later, the children of the village find the light shield again. The boy, now grown into an older man, begins to tell his experiences retrospectively. And the narrative circle is completed – formally and fictively – with Trico who has established his home in the Cave.

The Last Guardian is one of the best examples of a game in which the narrative is told through mechanics. The story is conveyed through gameplay and gradual (spatial) progress in the game. The most important prerequisite, however, is the empathetic relationship between the boy and the beast Trico, including the noticeable character development of the beast into a very reliable companion and friend.

REFERENCES

Literature

Glaser, Frank/Kraut, Jörg (eds.) (2017): The Last Guardian. An Extraordinary Story, Hamburg: Future Press.

Ueda, Fumito/Tanaka, Masanobu/Masami Tanji (2018): Special Symposium with the staff of The Last Guardian Part 1, 13.06.2018 (http://gendesign. co.jp/qa_01/interview01en.html).

Games

Ico. SIE Japan Studio, Team Ico, Sony Interactive Entertainment, 2001

Shadow of the Colossus, SIE Japan Studio, Team Ico, Sony Interactive Entertainment, 2006

The Last Guardian, SIE Japan Studio, Team Ico, Sony Interactive Entertainment, 2016.

Videos

Brown, Mark (2015): Ico, and Design by Subtraction | Game Maker's Toolkit. In: YouTube, 05.10.2015 (https://www.youtube.com/watch?v=AmSBIyT0 ih0).

Brown, Mark (2017): The Last Guardian and the Language of Games | Game Maker's Toolkit. In: YouTube, 09.01.2017 (https://www.youtube.com/ watch?v=Qot5_rMB8Jc).

Murder at the Museum

Narrative Audio Games for Museums

Stefan Schmidlin

Murder at the Museum (*MaM*) is an experimental audio game featuring a multi-linear crime story that turns the museum's exhibits into witnesses and suspects. Players take on the role of a grumpy detective and help him solve a murder case: they decide which suspects they want to question by choosing a path through the museum and, ultimately, which one they want to accuse as the prime suspect.

With *MaM* we tried to overcome a common issue of many museum games which tend to shift the visitor's attention to the game app and away from the museum itself. Therefore, we developed the game as an audio-only experience that barely requires any screen interactions.

In this case study we will discuss the design process with a special focus on the narrative design and game experience. In particular, we will show how the use of open-world games helped us deal with the unpredictable movement of players in the museum.

MAIN CONTENT

Game experience

Two variations of *Murder at the Museum* (*MaM*) have been created and play-tested, one at *Stadtmuseum Aarau* and the other at *Ortsmuseum Küsnacht*, two local history museums near Zurich, Switzerland. Typically, museum games are location-specific and cannot be transferred to other museums easily. Each version of *MaM* features its own location-specific detective story, but they both share the same game system and design tools as well as the same player-avatars, Detective Bissig and sidekick Isabel Minischock.

The game experience revolves around the idea of an interactive audio book in which museum exhibits come to life by turning them into life-like characters: a fancy-looking swan-shaped sled is turned into a chatty older lady; a small toy figurine in a display cabinet into a sweet but sad gentleman who is frustrated at being locked in and unable to visit his wife. The interaction between the player and the characters adds emotions and liveliness to the museum visit. It is a multi-linear story, similar to those children's books which allow readers to decide how to continue the story by choosing one of the page numbers. In *MaM*, by contrast, decisions are location-based: walking to the "swan lady" instead of the "toy gentleman" will make the story progress differently.

Figure 1: Basic game loop.

Hear a Choice

Go to next Location

Listen to Outcome

Source: Stefan Schmidlin

We used Bluetooth beacons to track players' locations in the museum. Beacons function as proximity sensors and automatically trigger the next section of the story as soon as the player arrives at their destination.

Thus, the basic game loop (Figure 1) resembles a tabletop role-playing game with story prompts, player actions and the narration of the outcome following in turn. During the 20-30 minutes it takes to complete one session, players gather clues and are then able to accuse suspects of the crime. At the end of the game, players receive a star rating depending on their choices in the game.

Development process

Despite the simple game mechanics, the experience was not initially self-explanatory. A lot of effort was spent on the on-boarding process and the polishing of the game experience.

We adopted an iterative design process as is common in game development. In the first version of the game, players did not have an avatar. Suspects spoke short monologues and a narrator then offered options as to where the player could go, referring to a color-coded map of the museum. Players reported that they had struggled to follow the instructions (which they could hear but not see) and read the map. Holding both the map and the navigation device in each hand was cumbersome, too. In addition, players found the monologues to be lacking interactivity.

Figure 2: Player with iPad and headphones looking at one of the exhibits that appears as a character in the game.

Source: Stefan Schmidlin

We replaced the map with color markers which we positioned next to the path. This allowed us to use instructions like "follow the blue markers". Players could follow these more easily because they were actionable. To address the issue of interactivity, we invented the role of Detective Bissig who acted as the player's avatar and led the conversations with the suspects. With the help of the avatar, we were able to turn the monologues into conversations, which made the interactions feel more natural and helped immersion. During this same step, we also replaced the narrator with the in-game character Isabel Minischock who acted by Bissig's smart sidekick and cheeky assistant. Isabel became the tutorial voice, narrated the players' choices and also occasionally teased Bissig about his clumsiness with technology and inability to navigate.

As the next important step in development, we introduced a neck pouch to enable hands-free play and let players almost forget that they were wearing the device. In combination, these measures demonstrably made the game feel more immersive.

Young players especially were not yet satisfied by this level of interactivity through dialogue, and wished for more game-like interactivity. Hence, the version of the game used in Küsnacht featured a puzzle which had players combine several objects to reveal a code that provided an important clue.

Story and narrative design

Murder at the Museum is a detective story, revolving around a murder or the disappearance of an exhibit at the museum. The genre was determined early on because it lends itself well to a narrative game in a museum: the crime inherently establishes the task that players have to solve and primes them to take an investigative mindset. Additionally, the classic detective story has a long tradition in the German-speaking world and has remained appealing for older and younger players alike.

The character-led nature of the story involved selecting exhibits that we could turn into interesting characters and then shaping them, and was the key driver of the writing process. We let ourselves be guided by intuition, visiting the two museums' permanent collections many times, looking at exhibits, assigning character traits, voices and personalities based on the historical facts, their appearance or position in the exhibition. We then wrote sample dialogues in which the characters would interact with Detective Bissig to assess if the characters worked well in the setting. A few characters dropped out at this stage because they were simply not interesting enough.

When testing the early prototypes, it became obvious that players would often stray off-path, either because they got lost or because they just found something intriguing to look at that had nothing to do with the game. Museum visits should of course reward such exploration and discovery, but our prototype did not support that mode of play. It assumed that players would choose one of the proposed options and walk there immediately. Yet this model, which was based on a multilinear storybook offering limited choice, proved to be wrong! Physical space affords a degree of choice that is nearly unlimited. We had to factor unpredictability into our design, so we made it a paradigm that every previously discovered character would always have something to say. They would either help players to get back on track, or open up secret paths or a shortcut. This open-world approach was more complex, because instead of just two or three options, players could now choose to visit every character in the game world at any time. We modelled this concept using a world state as shown in Figure 3. If players discover a crucial piece of information, the world state then changes (represented by the vertical lines), and characters adapt their dialogues to offer meaningful help relating to this new state (represented by the little numbers next to the letters each of which stands for a character). Characters that are not so important in a given state do not necessarily say anything new, but still give useful hints (represented in gray). If players are inactive for too long, Isabel will give them hints, too.

Figure 3: Using world state to drive the story enables players to always interact with any of the known characters and obtain pertinent information.

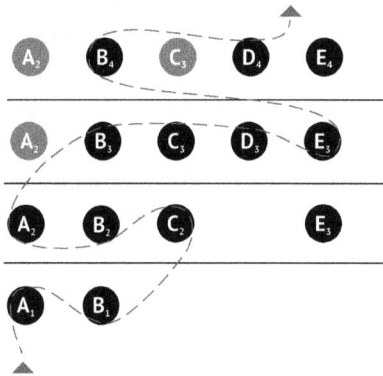

Source: Stefan Schmidlin

The physical layout of the museum's exhibition had a strong influence on story progression. There were two important factors to take into account: the players' perceived *cost* of taking a decision and the *design limitations* associated with the use of Bluetooth beacons and the open-world approach.

Figure 4: Avoiding unintended interactions by selecting characters at locations that prevent unintentional visits.

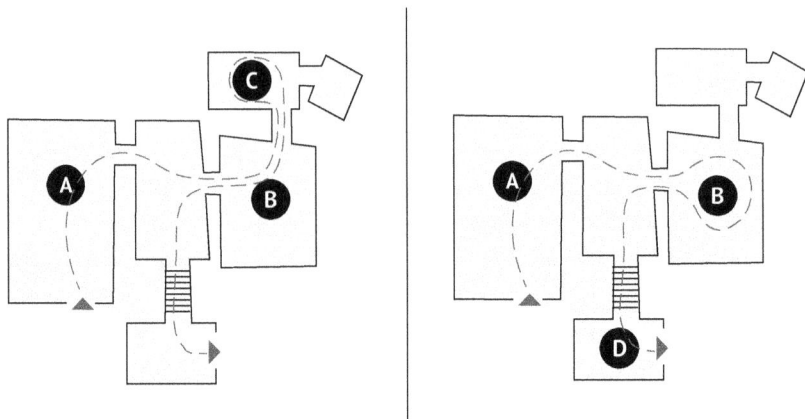

Version 1: When returning from C, players must pass B and trigger unintended interactions

Version 2: Avoids unintential interactions with B.

That *cost* was a factor became apparent in the earliest prototypes: players did not make decisions based on the rationale presented in the game, but rather based on a ratio of *cost* versus the promise of fun. For example, players would rather visit a new character than one they had already met (backtracking), and prefer to stay on the same floor rather than climb stairs (physical cost). In Aarau, the exhibition is located in a historic tower spanning seven floors, so the *cost* is obvious. Play testers mentioned that they thought backtracking was boring, even more so if it meant climbing down stairs they had ascended before. For us, this meant that we modelled the story to progress as players climbed to higher floors, which allowed visitors to discover new areas of the museum with each decision and thus conveyed a sense of exploration. But we also exploited this in order to reward players who engaged in more exploration. Secret routes, shortcuts and side quests often meant having to backtrack.

The *technical limitations* stem from our decision to create a hands-free open-world experience. The use of beacons meant that they would trigger whenever a player walks up to a character, and the open-world design dictated that the character would always say something when the player approached them. For comparison, in a normal open-world adventure, game designers are free to remove a NPC when they have nothing to say. In a museum, said NPC being a physical exhibit, it cannot just disappear. We opted to remove characters that would provoke unwanted interactions due to their geographical location, instead of inventing idle dialogue. This is visualized in Figure 4. At B, the player has to decide whether to backtrack to A or visit C. Most players would want to choose C because it is the explorative choice. In Version 1, players visiting C would invariably come into the proximity of beacon B on the way back, and trigger a reaction from the character. If players had not planned to talk to B, they interpreted this as a mistake. In Version 2, we dropped C in favor of D. After D, the player could choose to go back to B or A without unwittingly visiting any characters. This felt more natural.

The short duration of a game session lent itself well to a simple three-act structure. The adventure hook and in-story familiarization with the game system are followed by a phase of free exploration where players can widen the field of suspects, until they finally discover a decisive clue that allows them to identify the murderer. What makes the game experience stand out is the juxtaposition of fictionalized characters and the reality of the exhibition. This allowed many visitors to form an emotional connection with the exhibits and left them interested in learning more.

OUTCOME AND CONCLUSION

We conducted studies at both museums. Our goal was to evaluate players' experiences and assess the game's ability to enhance the museum visit and make it more memorable.

Overall, the game was very well received at both locations. Three out of four respondents awarded it at least four out of five stars. More than half of the players responded that they would visit a museum just to play this game, and would like to play more episodes. Among the negative points the most frequently mentioned were low interactivity and slow pacing, a feedback that mostly came from young adults who were used to playing video games. The inclusion of a puzzle in the second version of the game received a lot of positive feedback, and we estimate that including more puzzles could further improve the game experience.

Using beacon technology and neck pouches to allow for hands-free play proved to be crucial in keeping players focused on the museum's exhibition and the story, rather than being glued to the game app.

REFERENCES

Game

Murder at the Museum, Stefan Schmidlin, Game Design, Zurich University of
the Arts, in Collaboration with Engagement Migros and Stadtmuseum Aarau,
2019.

Even *Missile Command* Tells a Story

Beat Suter

Many games without stories still manage to tell good stories. *Missile Command* (1980) is one of them and may serve as a good example for two kinds of narrative mechanics: gameplay mechanics that are used as narrative elements, and a political context that is embedded in such a way that players can experience an ethical dilemma about the consequences of their actions while under threat. In fact, a simple game like *Missile Command* confronts you with a surprising amount of ethical choices and moral depth (cf. Extra Credits 2012).

It is the year 1980, at the height of the Cold War. Politics and the older generation practice nuclear deterrence and generate an atmosphere of fear and anxiety. So much so that the younger generation declares a new ice age, starts a rebellion in the streets and adopts ironically absurd slogans. The possibility of nuclear war hangs over everybody. Any day could be the last one. Any day could be the "day after". It is all forgotten now, but it was tangible and concrete then. These days, the nuclear threat is not so concrete, even though many missiles are still ready in their silos, and the leaders in control are as unpredictable as ever.

PROTECT YOUR ENVIRONMENT

Missile Command is a game that lets you feel these things in an intensely immersive way. In this arcade game, you are under threat and use a trackball and a crosshair to fire missiles from three missile defense platforms, targeting and then shooting at incoming projectiles. You have to protect six cities from an unending rain of these intercontinental ballistic missiles (ICBMs). The graphics of course don't seem too impressive. After all, it is 1980. Incoming missiles are single-pixel glowing dots, cities are bichromatic skyscraper silhouettes, and the sound of explosions has that great old Atari rumble (Extra Credits 2012). The noise and the darkness of a 1980s arcade makes you feel like you are sitting in a bunker and the missiles are raining down on you. You are trapped and will most likely die in this arcade-bunker.

Believe it or not, if you look at it from the player's perspective, the game is non-violent. The player never launches a nuclear missile. You never fire at an enemy. The enemy, in fact, is unknown, and the game is entirely about trying desperately to save lives. The player, rather than assuming a dominant position as is often the case in games, is in a weak position here, with merely reactive and very limited options. There is not enough time to revel in nuclear explosions or heroically shoot down enemy planes, ward off spaceships or go after the enemies themselves. The player is simply at the receiving end of a nuclear strike, something that could have happened any day in 1980. In this way, the experience of playing the game is very human and down-to-earth.

A DECISION GAME

The player takes the role of a local missile commander who controls three bases of missiles and has to defend six cities close-by. This is something easy to identify with. Unfortunately, the missile bases have limited resources, yet there is a seemingly unlimited onslaught of incoming ICBMs. The player soon realizes that they cannot defend all six cities and have to make decisions about which ones and how many to defend. And they also have to keep the missile platforms alive in order to protect as many cities as possible. It is a tough dilemma: Do you sacrifice cities with civilians just to keep a military installation with your soldiers functioning? How many can you keep alive? Do you sacrifice two cities containing presumably millions of people, so that the other cities with their own civilians may survive? There is no time to think about this. The tension builds up. You have to make the decisions instantly. Maybe you can manage to keep one city alive?

"I always ended up sacrificing cities to save others, ran out of missiles, lost bases... no matter how hard I tried, I always, ALWAYS lost in the end. Now I know why." (Mind Fracture 2017 in: Extra Credits 2012)

You can't win the game of *Missile Command*. There comes the time when your last city burns and explodes. You can't win a nuclear war. The message is clear.

"To paraphrase Joshua from War Games, 'Nuclear war is a strange game. The only winning move is not to play.'" (Mind Fracture 2017 in: Extra Credits 2012)

Figure 1: Front of manual for the Atari 400 and 800 versions of Missile Command (left), defending against incoming missiles and blasting them out of the sky in the arcade version (1980).

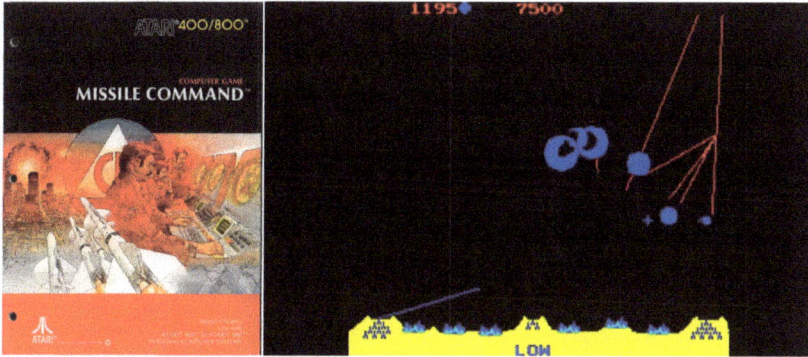

Source: Mobygames, screenshots (Suter)

Basically, in Missile Command, as in many arcade games of the 1970s and 1980s, the simple background story serves as a narrative framework for a crucial gameplay that totally immerses the player in an action and reaction scheme. But Missile Command works in a much more direct way. The narrative framework is fictional, yet at the same time it reflects realistic political and mass psychological conditions and forces the player into a quasi-real role. The fiction is so closely interwoven with reality, and especially with people's real fears, that players experience emotional tensions themselves. This was definitely the intention of the developers of Missile Command.

MISSILE COMMANDER IN BUNKER WITH TRACKBALL AND RADAR

The screen interface remains very technical and simple, as in many other simulation games Atari produced at that time. And if you look closer, you realize that the arcade machine interface seems to be designed in order to familiarize the player with operating a radar screen. An important component is the trackball that makes sure there is free and quick movement for the cursor. Developer Dave Theurer refers to military history when he states in an early memo that the screen would mimic a real radar display: "The color monitor will display a radar scan view of the coast and the offensive and defensive missile action. [Missiles] will appear as a blip on the monitor as the radar beam scans over them. A cursor will be displayed on the screen and guided by the trackball." (Temple 2016) This brings the player even closer to a realistic situation of defending their environment from a bunker and making difficult decisions. In this respect, it is an early ethical decision-game, maybe even a serious game.

Game designer David Theurer recalls having had nightmares – first as the inspiration for the game, but also during its development. "Missile Command embodied the Cold War nightmare the world lived in. [...] I had nightmares about nuclear attacks", Theurer said in an interview with game critic Alex Rubens in 2013. "During that time, I lived near Moffett Field, where the Air Force would randomly launch spy planes, which made a tremendous roar when taking off. I'd wake up, and while half asleep, hear the launch sounds and for a moment wonder if it was an atomic blast." (Rubens 2013)

REAL NIGHTMARES

Theurer's nightmares were recurring events during the development of the game for Atari. This was a very sobering experience for the game designer. "I would dream that I was hiking in the mountains above the Bay Area, with the fabulous views of the San Francisco Bay. In the dream, I'd see the missile streaks coming in and know that the blast would hit me while hiking there on the mountain." (Rubens 2013). This internalization of the events in the game naturally also had to do with the obsessive way Theurer went about his work, creating numerous scenarios and reprogramming them again and again. And finally, they also helped him to focus on the essential events and elements the game needed. Various additional elements were then deleted in order not to dilute and endanger the immediate experience.

ADAPTIVE NARRATIVE FOR A "SERIOUS GAME"

And finally, the closing point of the game stems from those nightmares. In line with the real political references, there was no sneering "game over" screen at the end, but a simple "THE END". Symbolically, Theurer thus created a nuclear explosion with the appearance of the words "THE END" as the conclusion of the game. "Missile Command was a social commentary ahead of its time." (Rubens

2013) A reminder that you will never be able to win a nuclear war. And a reminder that a real-world context may very well be able to generate direct emotional immersion in a video game as well as awareness for that context, while playfully simulating the immediate consequences and scenarios of precarious social and political situations.

The narrative mechanics of *Missile Command* are nothing less than the direct transfer of a real political situation into a scenario: the defense of one's own environment against an attack from outside. The player is given a decisive role in which he or she is faced with an immediate ethical dilemma. Dave Theurer had first planned a concrete geography in which six named Californian cities had to be defended. In that version, it was also clear that the enemy leading the attacks was called the Soviet Union. Just as he discarded parts of a more complex GUI with flashing scores, he also deleted the geographical references so that *everyone* could feel directly addressed. Thus, in the published version, the player is allowed to interpret their own geography and their own enemy.

REFERENCES

Literature

Temple, Tony (2016): "The Secret History of the Arcade Trackball." In: Arcade Blogger, July 29 (https://arcadeblogger.com/2016/07/29/the-secret-history-of-the-arcade-trackball/).

Rubens, Alex (2013): "The creation of Missile Command and the haunting of its creator, Dave Theurer." In: Polygon, August 15, 2013 (https://www.polygon.com/features/2013/8/15/4528228/missile-command-dave-theurer).

Game

Missile Command, Atari, Atari, 1980.

Video

Extra Credits (2012): Narrative Mechanics – How Missile Command Tells a Story. In: YouTube (https://www.youtube.com/watch?v=JQJA5YjvHDU&t=323s&ab_channel=ExtraCredits).

Shave

Playing with Conventions in Society and Game Design

Sonja Böckler

SHAVE (Böckler 2018) is an art game which explores the social conventions surrounding shaving and hair within a game system. The main mechanic of the
game comprises the task of completely removing the hair from a variety of hairy
objects. The player can interact with the objects directly via touch input on a
mobile device. During the game the combinations of hair and object become
more and more bizarre, and players begin to question the sense of their actions.
Diverse sensations and associations emerge, which point beyond the actual
game.

THE BACKGROUND

SHAVE was developed in the context of a master's project at Zurich University
of the Arts. Based on the premise that we have many implicit expectations and
fixed concepts relating to the games medium, art games were examined as a tool
for expanding the limits of conventional game design. These are mostly short
games, produced in small teams and with little focus on commercial success, and
therefore offer game designers the necessary creative freedom in order to develop strong and extraordinary experiences.

THE THEME – A GAME ABOUT SHAVING?

In the field of Triple-A computer games, certain topics are repeatedly dealt with,
including war, territorial power struggles or rebellion. Their narratives are

formed from archetypes, cultural-historical clichés and stereotypical themes that can be easily read and understood by the player. Content in which we can predict what kind of experience will await us is appealing, and many Triple-A computer games operate according to this lowest common denominator. For comparison, imagine a visit to a fast food restaurant which promises us a predictable and consistent experience. By contrast, an experimental food choice, such as molecular cuisine, offers new flavors and taste combinations – with the high risk that it may not be for everyone. And you probably won't order the same food twice. The motivation for visiting an experimental kitchen is not pure pleasure, but entertainment, which also contains an element of surprise and curiosity for the new and unexpected.

Figure 1: Shaving a tea cup in the game as homage to Meret Oppenheim (1936).

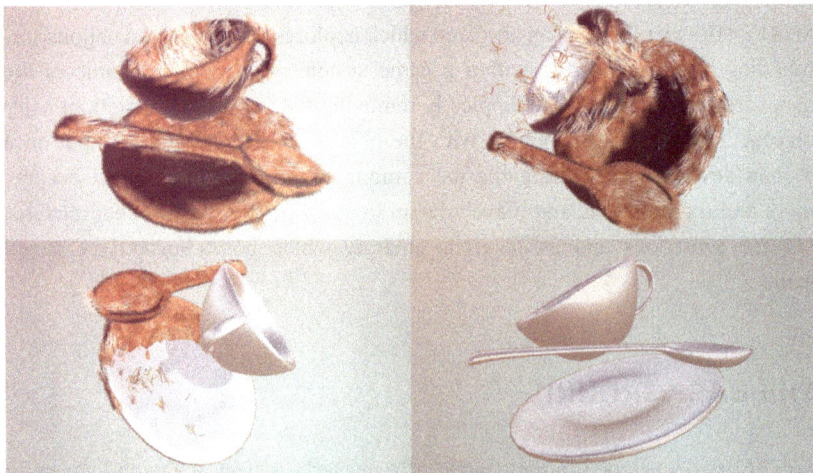

Source: Sonja Böckler

THE AMBIVALENCE OF HAIR AND PLAYING WITH UNPLEASANTNESS

There is no conventional story in *SHAVE* to guide the player through the game. Instead, the game engages the player by means of a topic from everyday life that almost everybody can relate to: body hair and our weird conventions around it. In our society this topic contains a great ambivalence of meaning, and it illustrates how our interpretation of one and the same thing vastly depends on the context. Full thick hair on the head is considered beautiful, representing health and youthfulness. But as soon as the hair is no longer anchored to the head and eventually ends up in the drain or in the soup, we feel disgusted. Hair on women's legs or under the armpits is unattractive, but a hairy male chest can stand for masculinity.

These ambivalent views about hair are the essence of the intended gaming experience. The player is confronted with abstract fur-covered objects and the simple task of shaving them. In this basic set-up, different meanings, stories and interpretations arise. It is useful that people tend to recognize meaning and context in everything they encounter, but, to keep the disgust in the player's imagination, the style of the game is very clean. Soft-looking objects float in a clean white room, reminiscent of a clinical facility or futuristic laboratory. The simplicity and reduction to the essentials also supports this imaginary space. Only the strong contrast between hair and skin invites the player to intervene.

Some players are already disgusted as soon as they touch the virtual hairy objects. They get goose bumps from the noise or cannot watch how the hair falls down while shaving. Others feel great joy when they remove the inappropriate hairs from this otherwise clean world. A field of tension opens up between sensual pleasure and disgust. The experience can even take on a symbolic or metaphorical character, and so a rather untypical gaming experience is created.

At some point the player is introduced to a popsicle which is completely devoid of hair. When the popsicle is touched, hair starts growing on it. The shaving mechanic is reversed and the goal in this level is to cover the whole popsicle with hair. Players often reacted with disgust, because they could not avoid associating the sensual delight of licking a popsicle with their feelings of disgust at having a hair in the mouth at the same time.

Figure 2: Popsicle with hair growth.

Source: Sonja Böckler

ACTIONS CREATE MEANING

Big game titles often rely on tried and tested mechanics, for instance, a first-person shooter or a strategy-building game. Just like the similarities in the themes chosen, games are based on the same game design ingredients that have worked so many times before. Therefore, the mechanics are often not perfectly tuned to the narrative and the interactions the player performs. In *SHAVE*, the mechanic and the setting both contribute to a certain curated experience. Based on the idea "Do It, Don't View It" (Mechner 2008), the experience is created through the player's interaction with the game, with a special emphasis on the sensations encountered. To challenge our common sense of purpose and target-orientation, every level in *SHAVE* ends with a pleasant sound and burst of hairy confetti raining over the screen, highlighting the absurdity of the goal that the player is aiming for.

SURREALISTIC REFERENCES

In this game, various motifs from surrealism are employed and thus further scope for interpretation is invited into the game experience. The shapes, animations or colors of the objects deviate slightly from reality: through a nuanced shifting in the representation they appear subtly different and slightly disturbing.

A fur-lined teacup, for example, is inspired by Meret Oppenheim's *Object* (1936). The delicate porcelain is hidden under the wild hair, and the players usually very much enjoy freeing the cup from the hair. As a further homage, reference is made to René Magritte's *The Treachery of Images* (1929). The original painting features the famous text "C'est ne pas une pipe", which plays with our perception of reality and representation. In the 'hairy' context of the game, this pipe raises questions such as: Does it make a difference to my sensation whether I shave real or virtual hair? And is my emotional response as artificially generated (perhaps through social conditioning) as the pipe I am shaving?

PLAYING WITH EXPECTATIONS

Most objects and shapes in *SHAVE* seem to be easily readable, and players can tell which object is hidden under the hair by its silhouette. Others toy with the expectations of the player. For example, a hairy triangular object is presented. At this point the player has already learned that they can 'shave' the objects with one finger and turn them with two fingers. But now, when they start to rotate the object, it is no longer stiff, as they learned to expect from the tea cup, pipe or egg they shaved in the previous levels. Instead, this object wobbles vividly as if it were made of soft flesh. While turning and watching the movement of the object, the player still cannot see what is under the hair. Only after shaving is a disembodied fleshy nose revealed.

In another level the player is presented with a dog, on which only the bright eyes are not covered by thick brown fur. The form underneath is not clearly discernible due to its long hair. From the stiff pose, one might think of a stuffed animal. But as soon as the player starts to 'shave' the dog, a bright pink plastic skin appears under the hair. The sound of rubbing a balloon is heard and the part of it that is being shaved dents a little, as if the material is yielding. The whole interaction here is only slightly different from the previous levels, but the player now thinks of the sharp razor blade one generally uses to shave. Unlike before, they now fear that the balloon dog will burst if they touch it.

Figure 3: Will the hairy balloon dog burst if the player is not careful enough?

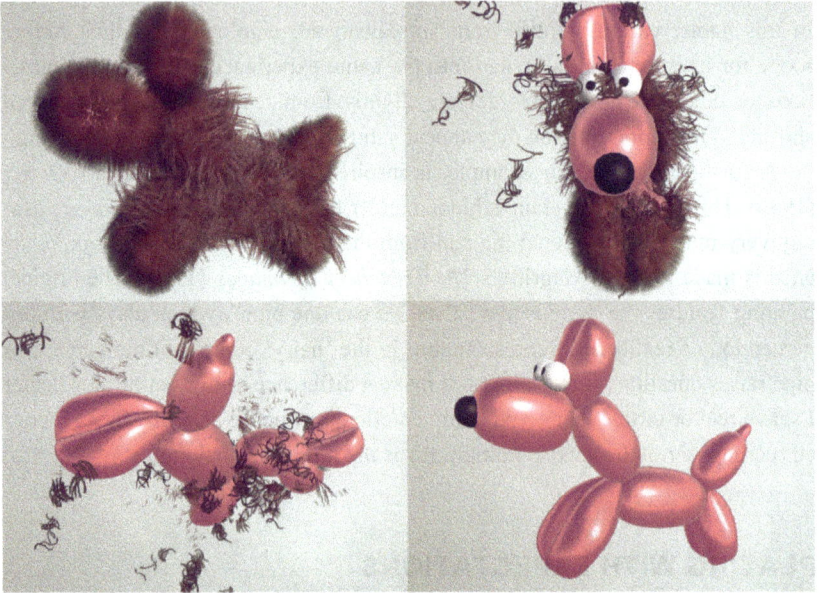

Source: Sonja Böckler

FINDINGS

SHAVE is not just a game that is enjoyable and entertaining, but it also invites the player to reflect on their own attitudes towards hair and how rarely we fundamentally question whether our conventions make sense at all. If we understand conventions as rules of our society, then the transfer of these rules into a game can make the essence of a convention visible. In this way, simply shaving objects is contributing to a larger discussion. Keeping it symbolic and not too concrete allows the player to find their own meaning in their actions within the game. Consequently, players did not feel instructed by the game, but rather invited to reflect on the justifications behind the real-life conventions concerning hair.

Deliberately limiting the entire game to one particular experience, with a strong focus on a specific interaction throughout its duration, has highlighted the need to adjust common game design approaches and develop custom solutions instead. Furthermore it can be very inspiring introducing a somewhat unusual topic into the medium of computer games and shaping one's own expressive voice to suit the game.

Not relying on proven game and motivation design patterns made it difficult to predict the outcome of certain game design decisions. That in turn made the development probably more extensive than an out-of-the-box approach would have done. Sometimes I consciously broke with common game design patterns. Because many people have a certain expectation of how games work, there is a risk that gamers become so irritated that they stop playing, which also reveals our narrow expectations of games. However, games that invite new themes and new storytelling approaches in game design are an important element in the evolution of computer games.

REFERENCES

Literature

Mechner, Jordan (2008): The Sands of Time: Crafting a Video Game (jordanmechner.com/articles).

Art/Games

Böckler, Sonja (2018): Shave, Zurich: Zurich University of the Arts.
Magritte, René (1929): La trahison des images [oil on canvas], Los Angeles: County Museum of Art.
Oppenheim, Méret (1936): Object (Le Déjeuner en fourrure) [Assemblage sculpture], New York City: Museum of Modern Art.

The *Twitter* Game

Game Mechanics of *Twitter*

René Bauer

Many people use social media as a kind of game, but the individual *Twitter* (2006) player doesn't even notice that they are playing. The reasons for this are that the setting (framed by the *Twitter* bird) and the surface don't look like a game and many 'play' so seriously that "this certainly can't be a game".

However, the motivational mechanisms of using *Twitter* are all too often similar to games, ranging from simple single-player games with links, retweets and tweets to epic multiplayer games with long epic battles of insults, arguing in endless threads – and all this every day! It is a kind of social media '*EVE Online* game' (*EVE Online* 2003). It uses all kinds of narrative mechanics: from simple text, images, animations, links, interactive surveys to clever rhetorical tricks but also simple insults and plain provocations. Keeping up appearances is paramount. Facework as a skill of constantly maintaining the face (Goffman 1967) becomes a dominant strategy for the individual *Twitter* users. Their aim is to receive the respect they think they deserve. Establishing and sustaining a preferred social identity during interactions is so important that its techniques underlying this process become completely lost in the magic circle of social media games – something that is very common in games.

Of course, *Twitter* users pursue different goals and directions. Is it ultimately just about the fun of getting attention from other people? Or is there more? From a more playful point of view we might draw an analogy from the taxonomy of player types developed in the Bartle Test (Bartle 1996). In MultiUserDungeons (MUDS) there are four different types of players: socializers, explorers, achievers and killers. The group of socializers is mainly interested in meeting, getting to know each other, doing something together. The explorers are looking for new information, new ideas, new territory. The achievers want to solve all kinds of challenges. And the killers take up rivalry, want to win, want to be the best and crave maximum attention. These four different player types emerge on *Twitter* when narratives and assertion-driven statements come into play.

'TWITTERGAME'

Twitter is a game and therefore has a game mechanic that motivates and drives the *Twitter* player. But how is this game mechanic built and designed? Most games use simple motivational mechanisms such as challenges, options, selections and rewards or punishments via the system. Whoever gets involved in this system is pulled deeper and deeper into the game and, in the best case, ends up in the flow of this social media game. The challenges are designed so that they are neither too easy nor too difficult. To ensure this, games usually have simple rating systems, so that the players can be easily rated and the reward or punishment can be easily operationalized.

CHARACTER DEVELOPMENT

The first focal point of narrative activity – often real-world references are used here – can begin with the profile picture and the accompanying text. The character profile itself offers more than most games: Avatar or real name? Avatar or real image? Personally chosen background image? Text about yourself with possible references, perhaps a web address and location? And if necessary, you can also attach a post as pars pro toto. Additionally, there is automatically generated information like followers (trophies) and a view of the timeline. Thus, there is a wide choice of optional narrative mechanics just in the profile area. This means you create a fictitious character even if you use your real name. Others will only know of you what you tell them. This gives you the opportunity to carefully construct an image of yourself that focuses on a special activity of your life, on an opinion, an economic or political view or, for example, your preferred cultural interests. You create a public image for yourself that amplifies certain traits and activities but also reduces your character to something that is tailored for the social media streams and mostly targets a specific audience. It is no wonder the *Twitter* profile is advertised as "your personal landing page" and as being most important for "your personal brand". A *Twitter* profile may indeed work like a personal brand. When you follow someone, they have to make the decision on whether to follow you back in a few seconds.

Figure 1: Three examples from Swiss Twitter users.

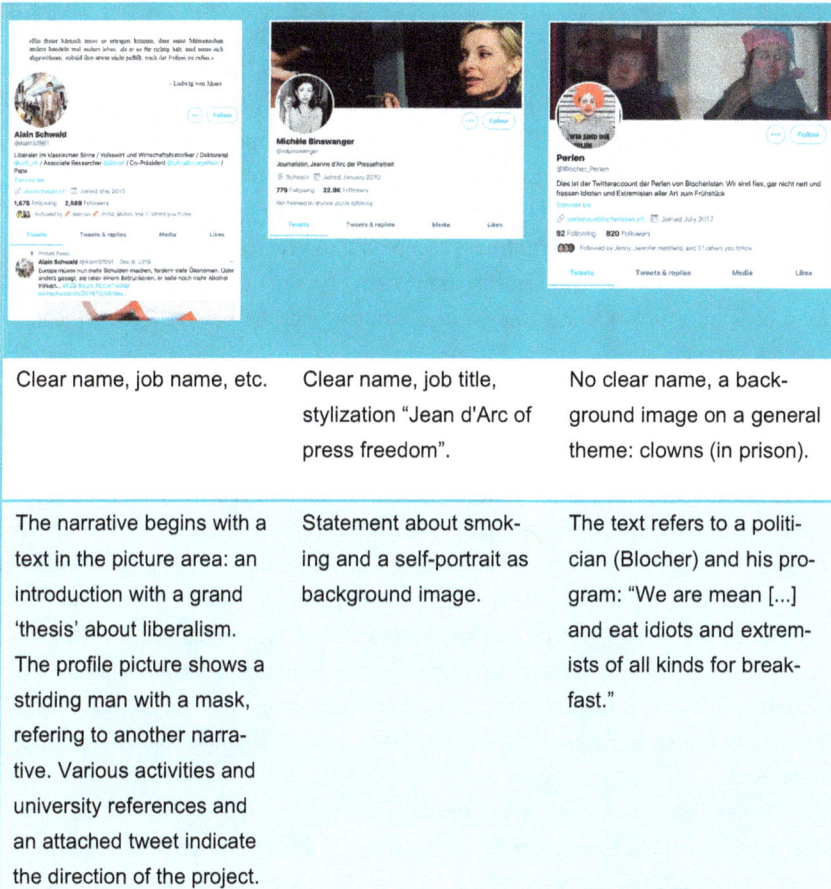

Clear name, job name, etc.	Clear name, job title, stylization "Jean d'Arc of press freedom".	No clear name, a background image on a general theme: clowns (in prison).
The narrative begins with a text in the picture area: an introduction with a grand 'thesis' about liberalism. The profile picture shows a striding man with a mask, refering to another narrative. Various activities and university references and an attached tweet indicate the direction of the project.	Statement about smoking and a self-portrait as background image.	The text refers to a politician (Blocher) and his program: "We are mean [...] and eat idiots and extremists of all kinds for breakfast."

Source: *Twitter*, screenshots August 8th, 2020 (Bauer)

Of course, there are many other profiles and completely different ways to use the profile picture. But what mechanics does the 'Twittergame' use?

NARRATIVE AND ASSERTION-DRIVEN MECHANICS

The mechanics most frequently used in social media are assertion-driven mechanics. They occur in a composite form, especially in narratives paraphrased as "The right-wing scene has the solution for all things", "The market solves all problems", "Together we are strong", "Nature is good", "America the great",

"Freedom is the most important thing", etc. It is an endless list of pretentious assertions.

It seems at first that assertion-driven mechanics might come from a scientific context. In the subsystem of science (cf. Luhmann 1997), these assertions take the shape of hypotheses which are then evaluated, or in other words, corroborated or falsified by the scientific community. For this purpose, there are different formats – from Master to PhD theses, from papers to books, and from lectures to conferences on specific topics. Scientific hypotheses are always discussed on the basis of the difference "true/untrue", accepted into science or rejected (and even suppressed for years). The resulting knowledge is then stored in books for the long term and further disseminated in education. The formats range from short articles to books.

The picture is very different for narrative and assertion-driven mechanics in social media battles on platforms like *Twitter*: Here, everything is renegotiated almost every day. Nothing is older than yesterday's tweet, nothing falls apart faster. What is not in the timeline, is no longer reproduced in the system. Furthermore, there is no verification of the various assertions. In fact, they are mostly just 'verified' by individual communities in their own narrative or assertion-driven thinking. This makes them perfectly suitable for social media. They can only be answered with yes/no and are therefore ideal for evaluations. For the follower of a narrative, it is then also clear whether or not an assertion supports the narrative. Thus, it is not surprising that many conspiracy theories are actual narrative mechanics and contain many assertions that are adaptive and adaptable to a situation.

Twitter favors assertion-driven mechanics and narratives with only 280 characters of basic text. Consequently, every tweet is already an assertion and functions as a micro mechanic based on its content, what it refers to and whatever comments it provokes.

What we have here is a community that uses narratives, develops its own logics, partly also its own concepts and its own language. "Freedom", for example, has a different connotation for a liberal than for a democrat. The word "liberal" alone is used differently by various communities: as comprehensively liberal, as economically liberal, as socially liberal. It is interesting to note that all these increasingly radical "liberal" narratives were once part of a narrative of the "liberal" that was supported by left and right. This collapsed when it became clear that our planet does not have enough resources for everyone. Consequently, the Paris Climate Convention was revoked and a better future for all buried (cf. Latour 2018).

JOURNALISM OF ASSERTION – ESCALATION AS MECHANICS

An entire branch of journalism shows how well assertion-driven mechanics and their complex forms, the narratives, function. Here, assertion-driven mechanics are used to fill news portals or newspapers. Nothing is easier to write than an assertion: just gather the pro-arguments and leave out all counter arguments or trade-offs. Moreover, this is easy to monetize: an assertion-driven text not only invites the supporters of the assertion-driven narrative to read it ("What are the reasons given?"), but also the opponents of the assertion ("What is their point? What are their reasons?").

In the following example, the title suggests that Montessori schools create geniuses, an assertion that literally went around the world.

IN THE SCHOOL OF GENIUSES

Figure 2: Article in Swiss paper states that Montessori is the "school of geniuses" since people like Bill Gates, Jeff Bezos and Mark Zuckerberg attended it.

Abo

In der Schule der Genies

Bill Gates, Jeff Bezos und Mark Zuckerberg waren in der Montessori-Schule. Müssen wir unsere Kinder auch hinschicken?

Source: Tagesanzeiger, screenshot (Bauer)

The mechanics of assertion-driven journalism is thus the opposite of weighing up and including all points of view in order to allow the reader to form their own opinion. Clickbait can be easily instigated with pro and con texts – preferably spread over days. Logically, the clicks, likes and comments also give rise to increasingly radical opinions. Whether an assertion or hypothesis is true or false is not important, because every assertion can gradually get more support, so it may become plausible one day. They are only "pending judgments" or "floating narratives". But unlike in news portals or forums, the discussion does not end in one location as a single commentary but can be shared exponentially via the channels of social media platforms and spread further via timelines and notifications.

NARRATIVE AND IDENTITY

The mechanics mentioned above can also be found in social media – especially since some of the articles reappear as tweets. But social media games go a step further, because the assertion-driven narrative is linked to the personality of the user. Just like in journalism (with the exception of political reporting), the most important factors are the sale of news, advertising, subscriptions or user data – the topic, however, is rather a means to an end. And so even marginal topics can be skillfully dealt with and brought into the mainstream.

One can even go as far as to ask the question: Do the followers of a narrative in social media create a social field in the sense of Bourdieu's (1987) Field Theory? Or a system in the sense of systems theory where certain narratives even explicitly exclude others? Is the 'Twittergame' – at least in its political variant – a field and system game? The individual players want to keep their own system alive at all costs, but it permanently falls apart through new tweets and news. Therefore, it is also their own identity that is up for negotiation. Because more than any other players, those engaged in *Twitter* understand that only constant reproduction can keep their system alive and weaken others.

MOTIVATIONAL MECHANICS – CHALLENGES

The challenge in the social media game follows a certain logic: maintaining one's own narrative (or assertions) against all odds in order to maintain one's own identity or job. And unlike in the scientific system, where a scientific community wants to find the truth (and is paid to do so) and truth is the transcendental signifier (cf. Luhmann 1997), in social media everyone fights against everyone else for followers, supporters, arguments, counter arguments, or simply for power. These are systemic struggles or struggles for narratives and their subordinate assertions.

Of course, every assertion and every narrative are constantly threatened, no matter how good it is and how many supporters it has. And the threat in social media consists of ever newer messages and facts spreading like wildfire, whether they are tweeted journalistic texts, new facts, new assertions, new narratives or new comments, new links and connections.

The constant supply of new challenges is therefore ensured. If this is not enough, then everyone can of course write their own comments to stave off the disappearance of the topics, the assertions or their own narrative. Luhmann might say: it is the fight against the disappearance of their own system, or presumably even more aptly with Bourdieu here, people fight for their own field or the field that provides them with monetary, symbolic or social capital.

Figure 3: A tweet can confirm your own narrative/assertion and be included (+), neutralized or left as a correct point (-).

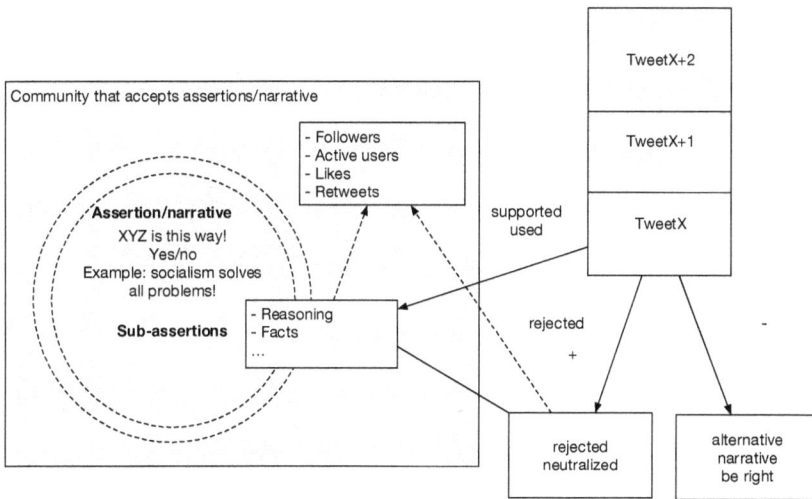

Source: René Bauer

To draw a comparison with the game universe: Like in *Tetris* (1989), it is raining information, and tweets and assertions have to be accommodated and classified for the player's own community as well as for or against the 'enemy narratives'. In *Twitter* as in *Tetris*, things have to be cleaned up and put in line.

PROTECT THE TREASURE: THE NARRATIVE AND ITS ASSERTIONS

At first glance things look very simple: widen your field, find new users, convince others, reject all hostile tweets. All this earns you points in your own community, strengthens the narrative, respectively your field.

But most narratives today are already much more complex. They have long since mirrored their competitors' narratives within themselves and built entire constructs to neutralize them. The counter-assertions with all the trimmings are embedded and tell you why they are void and that only one's own assertion is the right one. And in every argument, the reasoning grows and with it the possibilities how this narrative can react to others.

This means that the multiplayer game that is *Twitter* only appears clear and simple to the individual in their own narrative. The multiplayer aspect makes the game rather complex. In the following example, two self-contained systems fight each other: radical market advocates turn against social market economy advocates.

Figure 4: The respective view of the other narrative. The counter-assertion narrative is already included each narrative.

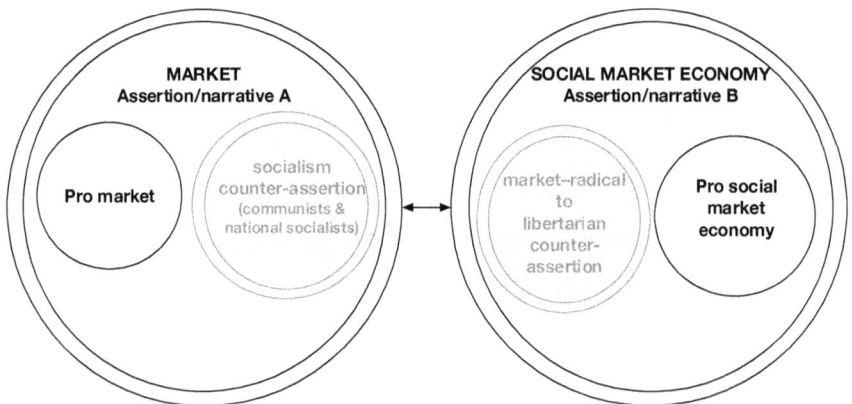

Source: René Bauer

The next figure (5) is an example of how such narratives shape and adapt a specific perception of the world. The Nazis become Socialists via a quote and a picture of the economist Friedrich A. Hayek.

In the eyes of radical market proponents, Hayek's ideas form a perfect open and closed core for a narrative. The free market is everything and ultimately 'decides' (about truth as well). Through an unregulated market anyone gets the chance to be successful (regardless of differing possibilities and capital). This often results in a closed pseudo-Darwinian reasoning which assumes that 'economic selection' will lead to the best product, company or society (economization). A free-market economy appears as a 'natural' continuation of evolution and has supposedly always been around. Objections and responses from newer economic findings are thus disregarded. This increasing closedness becomes all-encompassing when anything else but the market is labeled as non-market and therefore as 'socialist'.

Figure 5: A quote built into a tweet and authenticated by a picture of the author.

Source: Twitter, screenshot (Bauer)

Of course, such narratives can also be completely closed and therefore applied to every context. The logic of a narrative then overlays the world with its complexities and offers simple assertions for highly complex contexts. In this way, the world itself becomes a narrative – from the narrative of "the West", for example, to the views of an American president, and fully fledged, absurd conspiracy theories.

GAMEPLAY OF THE *TWITTER* GAMES

What concrete possibilities do *Twitter* players have in the battle for their narratives? How do they fight? Or in other words, how and where do the players make decisions?

The first thing that stands out is the possibility to generate content directly, for example as a new tweet or a reply. In their tweets, however, players often make use of everything that *Twitter* provides in order to generate intertext: from inserting external articles, images and references to adding hashtags or addressing the other party directly.

Table 1: A Twitter player has the following options for action with tweets.

Action types	Direct impact	Indirect impact
Tweet		
compose tweet	Tweet with content appears. A plus for an assertion or a narrative.	All followers see the tweet and have a chance to react.
reply to tweet	Tweet with content appears for everyone below the tweet. A plus or a minus. The Tweet also appears in the timeline/notifications and is a direct invitation to act.	The whole narrative community is involved and informed via the timeline. Exponential distribution is possible.
Integrate tweets into your own tweets	Cross-references and integration of a thread. Can also be used to ridicule others.	The original tweeter and their community are also included. Often used for counter-narratives.
address specific individuals in your tweet @	Direct link. Appears in the notifications.	The individual must react more or less (to notifications). Often used in hostile narratives.
assign a tweet to a specific trend via hashtags #	Tweet becomes visible in a larger environment (trends) and reaches completely different communities.	Tweet is put into a certain context and classified. For example: #capitalism. Sometimes also used as a provocation. Exponential distribution possible.
embed screenshots in your tweets	Feedback in the *Twitter* universe is prevented. Only your own community will know about it.	Made visible only to your own community. Disables general exponential distribution.

Since players have to expose themselves when writing tweets, there are many other possible actions at their disposal that need far less justification than a tweet. They can use 'private' likes to show support, they can just do retweets to reiterate an idea or they control their own feed of information with actions relating to those of other users.

Table 2: And these are a Twitter player's additional options for action.

Action types	Direct impact	Indirect impact
Likes		
liking	Saves the tweet, supports the tweeter, makes the tweet available to your own followers.	Can be used as pinpricks for comments on tweets, because it is also shown to the original tweeter (notifications). Exponential distribution possible.
Retweet		
retweets/retweets with comments	Support of the tweeter, the tweet and its community/narrative. Distribution in your own *Twitter* network. With comment: concretization.	Exponential distribution possible.
User actions		
follow user	User support, visible in notifications, tweets appear in the timeline.	Accumulation and increasing potential distribution. But also a problem of complexity and confusion.
mute user	Tweets no longer appear. But the muted user does not notice anything.	Less exponential distribution.
block user	Tweets no longer appear, therefore the worst punishment for another user. Also visible in threads.	Suppression. Encourages narrative communities with little contact to the outside world.

MULTIPLAYER: ENDLESS STREAMS OF PROVOCATION

Whoever dives into this game has to swim all the time and therefore must be constantly motivated. *Twitter* does not provide a protected environment with habitats in which you can create your narratives in an undisturbed atmosphere. It is a tool that fights for its existence and its daily survival – and the community does the same. Every minute, every hour, every day, every week and every month is about existence and survival, about not becoming the dreaded boring platform it might turn out to be without all the silly, idiotic and radical provocations.

Likes, retweets and followers are the easiest and most objective reward and punishment systems in the 'Twittergame'. However, this is only half the truth. The ways in which to be rewarded are manifold and sometimes much more individual. For the socializers, it is important to maintain the community. The achievers win on points when new arguments supporting their narrative emerge. Killers, on the other hand, enjoy nothing more than beating their 'opponents' with a news item. Every individual and every group have their own resources and capital which they don't need to share with other narratives and their communities.

Social media games are especially explosive through the embedded 'social' distribution mechanisms such as the timeline and notifications. These simple sorting and messaging functions spread narrative mechanics exponentially into other (opposing) narratives. This is where cybernetics turned into software unfolds its true explosive potential: it creates an infinite number of provocations and contradictions in 'opposing' narrative communities. And the conflict grows and is radicalized simultaneously in all narrative communities.

Thus, sets of multiplayer game mechanic waves of provocation and escalation endlessly roll to the shores and fulfill themselves anew every day: they grow larger, more radical and become faster and faster.

SOCIALIZE TECHNICAL POSSIBILITIES!

The constant modifications of the medium *Twitter* show how much and how fast the 'Twittergame' changes – at least in its designed mechanics. For example, the maximum number of characters was altered from 140 to 280 to enable more detailed information and longer opinions. And the possibility for a user to restrict replies was introduced in order to help stop abuse.

It is never quite clear whether the intended effects will be achieved or whether the community will use the technical possibilities differently. A longer tweet also allows for a longer rant. A targeted restriction of replies may be used to silence critics. This is what social media games are all about – users tend to 'socialize' them for their own needs. The 'Twittergame' is purposefully used and abused when it is adapted to suit its users' narratives.

REFERENCES

Literature

Bartle, Richard (1996): "Hearts, Clubs, Diamonds, Spades: Players Who suit MUDs." In: mud.co.uk, Colchester, Essex: MUSE Ltd. (https://mud.co.uk/richard/hcds.htm).

Bourdieu, Pierre (1987): Die feinen Unterschiede – Kritik der gesellschaftlichen Urteilskraft, Frankfurt am Main: Suhrkamp.

Goffman, Erving (1967): Interaction ritual: essays on face-to-face interaction, Chicago: Aldine.

Latour, Bruno (2018): Down to Earth: Politics in the New Climatic Regime, Cambridge: Polity Press.

Lumann, Niklas (1997): Die Gesellschaft der Gesellschaft, Frankfurt am Main: Suhrkamp.

Schöpfer, Linus (2018): "In der Schule der Genies." In: Tagesanzeiger, 10.02.2018 (https://www.tagesanzeiger.ch/leben/bildung/schule-der-genies/story/17608447).

Games

EVE Online, CCP Games, CCP Games, 2003.
Tetris, Nintendo, NIntendo, 1989 [1984].
Twitter, Twitter Inc., Twitter Inc., 2006.

Tweet

Hartmann, Martin (2019): In: Twittter, @hardmanpolitics, October 5 (https://twitter.com/hardmanpolitics/status/1180481883760726017).

Commander Kurz

A Short Essay on Videoludic Heroes and Political Strongmen[1]

Eugen Pfister

What does Sebastian Kurz have in common with Commander Shepard from the *Mass Effect* computer game series? One is currently the democratically legitimated chancellor of the Austrian Republic, the other commander of a spaceship in a fictional future. What purpose is there in comparing two such different characters? The Austrian politician, who, after a hiatus, returned to form his 2nd government in 2020, is often said to have a great talent for staging himself as a political victim and savior. But what if all he is doing is in fact only adopting a narrative already successfully established in pop culture?

"Das Parlament hat bestimmt. Das Volk wird entscheiden!" ("The parliament has determined. The people will decide!"), commented Sebastian Kurz at the end of May 2019 on his resignation as chancellor of Austria (Krieghofer 2019), in consequence of a vote of no confidence, which had been passed by MPs for the first time in the Second Republic's history. Some journalists and politicians were irritated by Kurz's statement (Wolf 2019). After all, the parliament is charged by the sovereign people to represent their will. What is parliament, if not the representation of the people? Surveys however showed that Sebastian Kurz had successfully managed to present himself and his party, the ÖVP, to the public as victims of an "undemocratic" party-political intrigue (Seidl 2019). But how is it possible that a large part of the Austrian population put more trust and hope in a toppled chancellor than in the National Council they had previously elected to

---

1   The following text is a revision and translation by the author of an essay originally published in the online edition of *Der Standard*, July 1st, 2019 (https://www.der standard.at/story/2000105478011/commander-kurz-was-der-altbundeskanzler-mit-einer-videospielfigur-gemein-hat).

represent them? I deliberately chose a comparatively moderate case as an example for my thoughts: the Austrian Federal Chancellor, who challenged basic democratic principles when faced with a vote of no confidence. There are, in fact, many more extreme examples of powerful men in politics worldwide today who are undermining basic democratic principles in a much more vehement way, such as Viktor Orban, Donald Trump, Recep Erdogan, to name but a few.

The number of convinced democrats seems to be: "[R]egulative constitutional institutions, such as the judiciary and law enforcement, enjoy considerably more trust than representative institutions." (Bertelsmann Stiftung 2019: 10f.) The idea that one single man (women rarely choose this role) can solve all the problems of a nation and clean up the corruption and sclerosis of inefficient political systems sells a dangerously tempting solution to all possible problems to disenchanted voters (Triffitt 2018). It is literally too good to be true. However, this political idea did not come out of nowhere. Part of the explanation for its success can be found in our popular culture, where we have been learning to rely on these solitary heroes for decades. Because of this, an analysis of the history of ideas of the motif "lonely political hero vs. corrupt system" can help us to better understand this phenomenon.

Allow me, therefore, to conduct a thought experiment. If we analyze the best-selling video games of recent years, the sentence "The Parliament has determined. The people will decide!" (this was the shortened advertising slogan that the ÖVP put on banners) suddenly no longer seems like a contradiction in terms. In digital games we normally do not come across an elected parliament. Instead, we encounter political action almost without exception in the guise of the morally acting individual – usually the protagonist, a figure which, incidentally, also often crops up in most Netflix series and movies. Here, of course, the logic of digital games (meaning maximum agency for the players) and the tradition of the hero in our culture in general, also play a defining role.

Political compromises and consensus apparently have no place in the fast-paced and often dystopian world of digital games. They are "unsexy" in pop-cultural terms. Instead, in games we expect individual characters to save the world: Joel in *The Last of Us*, Gordon Freeman in *Half-Life*, the Inquisitor in *Dragon Age: Inquisition*, Iron Man, Batman, etc. We are also used to the fact that established political structures in these games are usually either no help to our protagonist or even obstruct the character's attempt to do the "right thing": the Council in *Mass Effect*, the Environmental Protection Commissioner (!) Walter Peck in *Ghostbusters*, Senator Stern in *Iron Man*.

Even more important than the (occasional) discrediting of democratic institutions is, in my opinion, the extreme valorization of the individual in these games.

We have faith in our digital heroes because they never choose their own fate. They were chosen by it, or were simply in the right (or wrong) place at the right time. They dare to speak "uncomfortable truths". They have to make decisions for the good of society – even if it means personal sacrifice and isolation – because no other character is prepared to take action. Unlike the democratic institutions portrayed, they can react immediately and "rightly" when necessary. When the player's game world is threatened by zombie dragons, mass-murdering machines, evil characters such as Bowser from the Nintendo *Super Mario* franchise or other digital alien lifeforms, the game simply allows no time for political compromise and complex decision-making.

Of course, one must never overestimate the "influence" or even the "impact" of mass media on individuals. Players are not blank slates that simply adopt the political ideas presented to them. At the same time, however, we are exposed through our popular culture to new role models every day, who offer us another possible worldview. Here we learn the limits of the "sayable" and the "thinkable": a world in which moral heroes act quickly and correctly.

In doing so, we like to forget how unrealistic it is to expect a single person to be able to solve the world's problems in the real world. Even a brief glance at human history reveals the limits and dangers of political savior figures. And yet it is terribly comforting to believe that we only have to wait for the "right" person to save us. Especially today, many popular autocrats like Trump, Orban and their ilk are happy to adopt the narrative of the "lonely hero". On the other hand, if a party lacks such a charismatic leader, we automatically see it in crisis. And this crisis narrative is often even adopted by the parties themselves. The search for a savior is, then, paramount.

Digital games are not the "cause" of the public's apparent skepticism towards democracy, as illustrated by the Kurz case. They simply reproduce narratives found in popular culture and make use of dominant discursive statements. Or, in other words: successful narratives will be further consolidated. Popular culture also functions here as an amplifier of processes that have potentially originated in political environments, as long as there are no real counternarratives.

But what does all this have to do with the Sebastian Kurz?
1) Kurz has successfully transferred the culturally learned narrative of the lonely hero – the only one who knows what is "right" – to his own person.
2) He can be confident that a large part of the population will understand if he has to stand up against democratic institutions in an emergency because it is "right" at that time.

And, as absurd as the comparison with the game series *Mass Effect* may have sounded at first glance, in the end, Commander Kurz remains at the helm of the Normandy. He was deposed by the Council but came back nevertheless to save the world from a dark threat.

REFERENCES

Literature

Bertelsmann Stiftung (2019): Schwindendes Vertrauen in Politik und Parteien Eine Gefahr für den gesellschaftlichen Zusammenhalt? Gütersloh.
Krieghofer, Gerald (2019): "'Das Parlament hat bestimmt. Das Volk wird entscheiden!' Sebastian Kurz." In: https://falschzitate.blogspot.com/ (https://falschzitate.blogspot.com/2019/05/das-parlament-hat-bestimmt-das-volk_28.html).
Seidl, Conrad (2019): „Mehrheit der Bevölkerung würde an Regierung Kurz festhalten." In: derstandard.at, 25.05.2019 (https://www.derstandard.at/story/2000103772847/mehrheit-der-bevoelkerung-wuerde-an-regierung-kurz-festhalten).
Triffitt, Mark (2018): "A growing mistrust in democracy is causing extremism and strongman politics to flourish." In: theconversation.com, 09.07.2018 (https://theconversation.com/a-growing-mistrust-in-democracy-is-causing-extremism-and-strongman-politics-to-flourish-98621).
Wolf, Armin (2019): Tweet, 28.05.2019 (https://twitter.com/ArminWolf/status/1133278108512075776?s=20).

Games

Dragon Age: Inquisition, Bioware, Electronic Arts, 2014.
Mass Effect, BioWare, Microsoft, 2007-2009.
The Last of Us, Naughty Dog, Sony, 2013.

Authors

Tarn Adams is the co-founder of Bay 12 Games with his brother Zach, where they work on their fantasy simulation, *Dwarf Fortress*, one of the first video games acquired by the Museum of Modern Art in New York. He has been writing procedural interactive narrative projects for over 20 years.

René Bauer has an M.A. degree in German philology and literary studies, biology and computer linguistics from the University of Zurich. Presently, he works at the Zurich University of the Arts (ZHdK) as a lecturer, researcher and head of Master's education in the subject area of Game Design. His interests encompass coding, game mechanics, game studies, art in/with games (www.and-or.ch) and social media/knowledge systems (www.ixistenz.ch).

Sonja Böckler studied design at the University of Applied Sciences Nuremberg before finishing her Bachelor's (2016) and Master's (2018) degrees in Product Design with a specialization in Game Design at Zurich University of the Arts (ZHdK). Since July 2018 she has been working as a research associate at ZHdK developing serious and applied games for various purposes. Sonja Böckler's main areas of research concern arthouse games and new fields of game design: exploring the potential of translating human experiences into playable systems in order to reveal the underlying structure of our perceived world. In her M.A. project, she analyzed the mechanics and narrations of uncommon video games, which express human experiences of various kinds. Her game prototype *SHAVE* showcases the established patterns of the culture around shaving body hair. In her B.A. project in 2016, in collaboration with Michael Müller, she developed a new concept of interaction in virtual reality. The resulting game *Meantime* was exhibited at several festivals in Europe.

Teun Dubbelman currently holds a position at Avans University of Applied Sciences. He is considered an expert in interactive narrative design and storytelling in the new media landscape. He was vice-director at HKU University of the Arts

Utrecht, where he started the professorship of Interactive Narrative Design and created the world's first minor pathway on the topic. Dubbelman received his PhD at Utrecht University, with a thesis on narrative game design. He was a Fulbright Scholar at the Massachusetts Institute of Technology (MIT), working in the Singapore-MIT GAMBIT Game Lab. His recent research focuses on the topics of design pedagogy, narrative game mechanics and design for change.

Florian Faller is a Zurich-based game designer, playful media artist, lecturer and researcher. The co-founder of the Swiss studio Bits & Beasts teaches at Zurich University of the Arts in the Department of Design's subject area of Game Design, with a focus on visual arts, animation, game feel and game culture. His projects revolve around artificial liveliness, animacy, playfulness and emergence. Their vivid, physics-based worlds are brought to life by untamed AI-driven creatures, organic visual styles and dynamic and emergent gameplay. Faller's work ranges from independent games and experimental projects to commercial titles and serious and applied games. Before starting his career as a game designer, he studied German philology and literature at the University of Basel and lived in Berlin for several years, where he produced electronic music and worked with various audiovisual media.

Mary Flanagan is an artist, author and game designer with works exhibited at museums and galleries around the world such as the Whitney Museum, the Guggenheim, Tate Britain, and institutions in Spain, New Zealand, South Korea, Germany, China and Australia. In 2018, Flanagan won the Award of Distinction at Prix Ars Electronica in the Interactive art+. Flanagan was awarded an honorary PhD in Design by Illinois Tech, has held numerous honorary fellowships, and holds a distinguished professorship at Dartmouth College, USA. Flanagan is also author and co-editor of numerous books, such as *Critical Play* and *Reload: Rethinking Women in Cyberculture*. Her research laboratory in Hanover, New Hampshire, is www.tiltfactor.org.
www.maryflanagan.com

Robert Glashüttner holds a Master's degree in communication sciences and a Bachelor's in recording arts. He is a senior editor at Radio FM4, part of the Austrian Broadcasting Corporation ORF, where he is in charge of the game culture department. For about 20 years, he has been reporting and researching on digital games mostly as a journalist and sometimes as an academic. Special research interests are video game journalism and pinball culture. Glashüttner is a presenter, consultant and writer for different initiatives and media outlets like Die Presse,

SUBOTRON or WASD Magazine. Also, he is still the reigning runner-up world champion of Pac-Man.

Ulrich Götz is professor at Zurich University of the Arts (ZHdK), where he has headed the ZHdK subject area of Game Design since 2004. He was trained as an architect at Berlin University of the Arts and the Escola Tècnica Superior D'Arquitectura in Barcelona. He lectures and publishes on the comparative analysis of spatial design in architecture and game spaces. He has built up extensive experience in research and development of serious and applied games over years of cooperation with numerous partners from medical, therapeutical, educational and economic contexts. His university teaching focuses on the analysis and design of game mechanics, game concepts, motivation design, and spatial design in virtual environments.

Günter Hack holds a doctorate in communication sciences. He has worked as a lecturer at the University of Erfurt, Germany, and at the University of St. Gallen, Switzerland, and as a journalist for various publications including the Frankfurter Allgemeine Zeitung, Zeit Online and Spiegel Online. He currently works as a project manager for the Austrian public broadcasting service ORF, Vienna. He is the author of two novels: *ZRH* (2009) and *QUIZ* (2018).

Margarete Jahrmann is an artist, researcher and activist game designer, as well as founder of Area7lab and Ludic Society, a magazine series on experimental game art and ludic interventions. In 2020 she was awarded the media arts price of the City of Vienna, in 2019 a fellowship at the Center of Advanced Studies LMU Munich. She was artist fellow at the Leibniz-Zentrum für Literatur- und Kulturforschung Berlin in 2017. In 2010 she researched at the MIT gamebit Lab for her PhD, which she finished at the University of Plymouth with her work *Ludics for a Ludic Society. The art and Politics of Play*, introducing a specific Ludic method (ludic-society.net). She and the artist Max Moswitzer received the software arts award transmediale Berlin and the prix ars electronica with distinction in interactive arts for the game the anti-war-shooter *Nybble-Engine*. Jahrmann is professor of Game Design at Zurich University of the Arts (gamedesign. zhdk.ch/personen/team/margarete-jahrmann/) with a focus on persuasive games, political play and experimental game design, Univ.-Prof. Artistic Research PhD program University of Applied Arts Vienna (zentrumfokusforschung.uni-ak.ac. at/index.php/profile/team/). Since 2020 she leads the Austrian Science Fund FWF research project Neuromatic Game Art: Critical Play with Neurointerfaces. www.margaretejahrmann.net

Hiloko Kato studied German, art history and philosophy at the University of Zurich. In 2015 she received her doctorate on the topic "At the Edges of Texts". She collaborated in the project "Textualisation Cues" for the Swiss National Science Foundation (SNF). She works as a postdoc at the Chair of German Linguistics of the University of Zurich. In recent years, her research interests have shifted significantly towards game studies and human-nonhuman interaction, with pragmatic linguistics remaining the main methodological approach. In her current scientific projects, she takes an ethnomethodological and conversation analytic approach to playing and designing video games and to human-animal interaction both in real and virtual worlds.

Mela Kocher studied German literature, computer science and history, and wrote her dissertation on the topic of aesthetics and narratology in video games ("Follow the Pixel Rabbit!" 2007). Her post-doctoral research included studies at the University of San Diego, California, and the Mobile Life Institute in Stockholm, Sweden. There she followed up on her research on pervasive games and participatory transmedia storytelling. Since 2009 she has been with Zurich University of the Arts (ZHdK) as a senior researcher, teaching in the Master's program of the Game Design specialization and working on R&D projects, mainly in the area of serious and applied (urban) games. Since 2019 she has also been working with the e-learning team of the ZHdK. Besides that, she enjoys studying local cultural life and is a freelance writer for a small-town newspaper.

David Krummenacher is a game designer with a background in IT and film making. In 2018 he received a Master of Arts in Game Design from Zurich University of the Arts. His master's thesis "Storytelling in Pinball Machines" examined pinball machines in terms of their narrative elements and structures and applied the insights gained in a practical project called "Bosch – The Pinball Machine". He currently works as a senior game and experience designer at Zurich-based FitTech startup Sphery Ltd.

Martin Lindner is a consultant and author. He received his doctorate at Ludwig Maximilian University Munich and is a certified "Author of Interactive Learning Media" (Macromedia Academy, Munich). He has been working with digital learning and knowledge media for many years in the areas of research and development (microlearning, micromedia), e-learning and MOOCs (conception, implementation), new hybrid formats for learning and collaborative knowledge work (beyond the online/offline gap). Lindner is also an expert in the development and implementation of projects in e-learning, web learning and knowledge management in organizations, large corporations and medium-sized companies.

Eugen Pfister is project lead of the SNF-Ambizione research project "Horror-Game-Politics" at Bern University of Arts (hgp.hypotheses.org), in which he examines ideological transfer processes in digital horror games. He studied history and political sciences at the University of Vienna and at the Université Paris IV – Sorbonne. He wrote his dissertation in co-tutelle at the Johann Wolfgang Goethe University Frankfurt and at the Universita degli studi di Trento in the field of history of political communication. He researches and teaches the history of ideas in digital games, and is also a founding member of the "Arbeitskreis Geschichtswissenschaft und Digitale Spiele".

Chris Polus studied Business Informatics at FFHS and worked as IT consultant for major Swiss companies. In 2011 he switched to creating sound for games and movies and helped found and grow stillalive studios in Innsbruck, Austria, which now employs 37 people. Polus teaches sound design for game design students at Zurich University of the Arts (ZHdK). In his early days, he helped develop a multimedia software whose core is still used to run light and video walls at events like Eurovision Song Contest, and Cirque du Soleil shows in Las Vegas.

Stefan Schmidlin studied computer science and computational linguistics at EPFL (École polytechnique fédérale de Lausanne) and McGill University and holds an M.A. in Game Design from Zurich University of the Arts (ZHdK). He wrote his thesis on the topic of dominant games, investigating the manipulative and controlling properties of games. Currently, he works on games and interactive installations at the Insert Coin collective and as a researcher on serious and applied games at ZHdK. Recent projects he was involved in include Foodscape, a learning game about sustainability, BrainDriver, a racing game using brain signals as game input and Shock Fighter, an experimental game delivering electric shocks as a reward. As a board member of the IGDA Switzerland he promotes inclusivity and LGBTQ representation in the games industry.

Beat Suter is senior lecturer for Game Design at Zurich University of the Arts (ZHdK), Switzerland, specializing in concepts, storytelling, mechanics and the history of games – and he manages the GameLab (gamelab.zhdk.ch). He holds a doctorate in literature from the University of Zurich, with a focus on digital literature. For some years Suter has worked as lecturer for the Merz Academy Stuttgart, as project manager for a communications agency and as publisher of books and electronic literature (edition cyberfiction and netzliteratur.net). He also works as an independent scholar and curator, and as editor and author. Suter co-organizes the annual conference GameZ&RuleZ (gamezandrulez.ch). He is a founding member of the art group AND-OR that specializes in gameart and net-tart (www.and-or.ch). Recently, he co-authored a series of creative tools for game designers: two card sets, *IdeasForGames* and *StoriesForGames*, and a *Prototyping Box* (www.ideasforgames.org).

www.cybersuter.ch

Cultural Studies

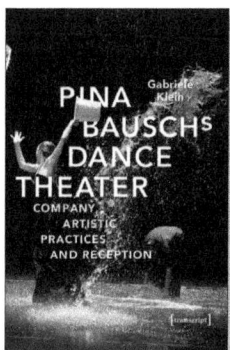

Gabriele Klein
Pina Bausch's Dance Theater
Company, Artistic Practices and Reception

May 2020, 440 p., pb., col. ill.
29,99 € (DE), 978-3-8376-5055-6
E-Book:
PDF: 29,99 € (DE), ISBN 978-3-8394-5055-0

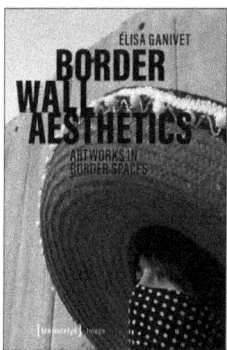

Elisa Ganivet
Border Wall Aesthetics
Artworks in Border Spaces

2019, 250 p., hardcover, ill.
79,99 € (DE), 978-3-8376-4777-8
E-Book:
PDF: 79,99 € (DE), ISBN 978-3-8394-4777-2

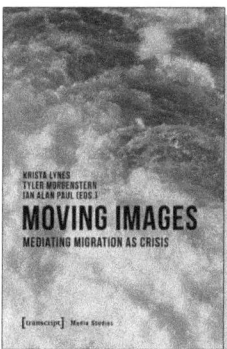

Krista Lynes, Tyler Morgenstern, Ian Alan Paul (eds.)
Moving Images
Mediating Migration as Crisis

May 2020, 320 p., pb., col. ill.
40,00 € (DE), 978-3-8376-4827-0
E-Book: available as free open access publication
PDF: ISBN 978-3-8394-4827-4

**All print, e-book and open access versions of the titles in our list
are available in our online shop www.transcript-publishing.com**

Cultural Studies

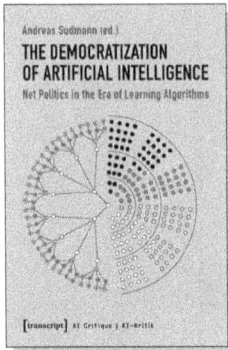

Andreas Sudmann (ed.)
The Democratization of Artificial Intelligence
Net Politics in the Era of Learning Algorithms

2019, 334 p., pb., col. ill.
49,99 € (DE), 978-3-8376-4719-8
E-Book: available as free open access publication
PDF: ISBN 978-3-8394-4719-2

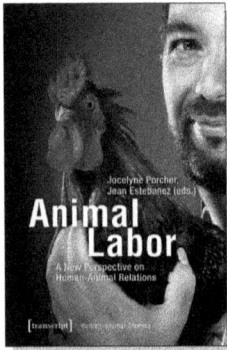

Jocelyne Porcher, Jean Estebanez (eds.)
Animal Labor
A New Perspective on Human-Animal Relations

2019, 182 p., hardcover
99,99 € (DE), 978-3-8376-4364-0
E-Book:
PDF: 99,99 € (DE), ISBN 978-3-8394-4364-4

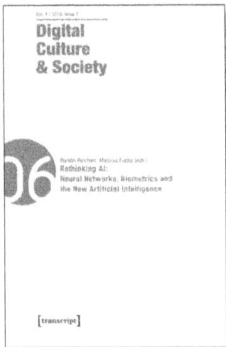

Ramón Reichert, Mathias Fuchs,
Pablo Abend, Annika Richterich, Karin Wenz (eds.)
Digital Culture & Society (DCS)
Vol. 4, Issue 1/2018 – Rethinking AI: Neural Networks,
Biometrics and the New Artificial Intelligence

2018, 244 p., pb., ill.
29,99 € (DE), 978-3-8376-4266-7
E-Book:
PDF: 29,99 € (DE), ISBN 978-3-8394-4266-1

GPSR Authorized Representative: Easy Access System Europe, Mustamäe tee 50, 10621 Tallinn, Estonia, gpsr.requests@easproject.com

www.ingramcontent.com/pod-product-compliance
Lightning Source LLC
Chambersburg PA
CBHW070053030426
42335CB00016B/1870